WRITING GREEK LAW

The use of writing in the development of Greek law was unique. In this comparative study Professor Gagarin shows the reader how Greek law developed and explains why it became so different from the legal systems with which most legal historians are familiar. While other early communities wrote codes of law for academic or propaganda purposes, the Greeks used writing extensively to make their laws available to a relatively large segment of the community. On the other hand, the Greeks made little use of writing in litigation whereas other cultures used it extensively in this area, often putting written documents at the heart of the judicial process. Greek law thereby avoided becoming excessively technical and never saw the development of a specialized legal profession. This book will be of interest to specialists in the history of law, as well as ancient historians.

MICHAEL GAGARIN is James R. Dougherty, Jr. Centennial Professor of Classics at the University of Texas, and has published widely on Greek law. Recent publications include *Antiphon the Athenian: Oratory, Law and Justice in the Age of the Sophists* (2002) and *The Cambridge Companion to Ancient Greek Law* (co-edited with David Cohen; 2005).

WRITING GREEK LAW

MICHAEL GAGARIN

University of Texas

CAMBRIDGE
UNIVERSITY PRESS

CAMBRIDGE UNIVERSITY PRESS
Cambridge, New York, Melbourne, Madrid, Cape Town,
Singapore, São Paulo, Delhi, Tokyo, Mexico City

Cambridge University Press
The Edinburgh Building, Cambridge CB2 8RU, UK

Published in the United States of America by Cambridge University Press, New York

www.cambridge.org
Information on this title: www.cambridge.org/9780521297288

First published 2008
First paperback edition 2011

A catalogue record for this publication is available from the British Library

ISBN 978-0-521-88661-1 Hardback
ISBN 978-0-521-29728-8 Paperback

For Donna, Daniel, and Alexandra

Contents

Illustrations

Preface and Acknowledgments

The ideas in this book have been developing in my mind for more than a decade, but they first began to take shape as a comprehensive view of Greek law when Joseph Mélèze-Modrzejewski invited me to give a set of lectures at the Sorbonne in 2001. (See "Ecriture et oralité en droit grec," *Revue historique de droit français et étranger* 79 (2001) 447–62.) I had earlier presented ideas about writing and law in lectures to audiences at the Centre Gernet in Paris, and in Copenhagen, Milan, Houston, and Columbia, MO; but during this month-long stay in Paris I first worked out a comprehensive thesis about the role of writing in Greek law and its very different role in other comparable societies. I am grateful to Jo for this opportunity, for his hospitality, and for the stimulating sessions of his seminar at the Ecole Pratique des Hautes Etudes, to Pauline Schmidt for arranging for me to address a session of her Greek History seminar, and to Jean-Marie Bertrand for helping in so many ways make my time in Paris both fruitful and enjoyable. Since that visit I have presented different parts of my ideas to audiences in Glasgow, Chicago, Philadelphia, Knoxville, San Diego, Austin, Athens, Graz, Lexington KY, Caen, Marshall CA, Marburg, Manchester, Charlottesville VA, Salerno, Nicosia, Montreal, and Auckland; I am grateful for the criticisms and suggestions I have received on all these occasions. Several of these lectures have been published in various conference proceedings (see Bibliography), but in writing this book I have rethought all these earlier presentations, and in some cases I have changed my mind significantly in the process. Faraguna (2007), which covers some of the same ground as I do but takes issue with some of the positions I have expressed, reached me only when this book was in press. A shorter version of his paper together with my response to it will be published in *Symposion 2007*.

Research leave for this project was provided by a Guggenheim Fellowship in 2002–3, and by several semester-long leaves from the University of Texas. I am most grateful to both organizations for support.

I also thank Paula Perlman, Lene Rubinstein, and Josh Sosin for reading earlier drafts of chapters, correcting errors, and making many helpful suggestions (not all of which I followed). Harvey Yunis and one other anonymous reader for Cambridge University Press gave me very useful criticism. My editor Michael Sharp provided encouragement and useful advice throughout, and copy-editor Linda Woodward improved the manuscript in many ways. Deena Berg of Georgetown, Texas prepared the illustrations.

Although the material in this book will (I hope) be of interest to scholars and students of Greek law, I have throughout tried also to make it accessible and of interest to those in other fields, including readers who know little or no Greek. I have relegated almost all the Greek to footnotes and have put the longer Greek texts in Appendices at the end of the book. Chapters Two, Five, Six, and Seven include texts from early non-Athenian inscriptions, which even those who know classical Greek may not find easy to read. I have tried to provide enough information about these to allow classicists to work with the original Greek texts if they wish, without creating a burden for other readers. Those who would prefer more scholarly presentations of these texts can consult specialized publications. In addition, Paula Perlman and I are currently preparing a full edition (texts, translations, commentaries, and essays) of the laws of ancient Crete, which will provide more detailed support for some of the views about Cretan laws that I express here.

Finally, I would like to dedicate this book to my family, who have provided me love and support for more than thirty years. I have dedicated previous books to each of them individually, but together they are more than the sum of three individuals.

Austin, March 2007

Abbreviations

CH	= The Law Code of Hammurabi.
GC	= The Gortyn Code.
ICret	= Guarducci 1935–50 (*ICret* 4 contains all the inscriptions from Gortyn).
IGT	= Koerner 1993 (references are to the inscription number).
IJG	= Dareste *et al.* 1891–1904 (references are to volume and page number).
ML	= Meiggs and Lewis 1969 (references are to the inscription number).
Nomima	= van Effenterre and Ruzé 1994–5 (references are to the volume and inscription number).
IPArk	= Thür and Taeuber 1994 (references are to the inscription number).
SEG	= *Supplementum Epigraphicum Graecum* (references are to volume and inscription number).
SB	= Preisigke and Rupprecht 1913– (*Sammelbuch*).

For editions of papyri, I follow the abbreviations in Wolff 2002: 213–48.

Introduction: Writing Greek Law

This book examines the history and significance of writing in Greek law. I start from the assumption that although writing in general, and writing law in particular, share certain common features in almost any culture, there are also culturally specific aspects to writing and writing law. I shall argue, in fact, that writing, and specifically writing law, played a significantly different role in Greek law than in other comparable "premodern" societies.[1] Moreover, both by its presence and just as importantly by its absence, writing was a key factor in shaping the special, even unique, nature of Greek law. Thus, a study of the history of writing and Greek law from the beginning through the classical period and (briefly) into the Hellenistic Age will help us understand what Greek law is, how it developed in the special way that it did, and why it became so different from the legal systems with which most legal historians are familiar. The results of this study have important implications for resolving the long debated question of "the unity of Greek law" – that is, in what sense, if any, it is useful to speak about "Greek law" as a coherent institution – and for understanding the special nature of Greek law.

My thesis, in brief, is that from the beginning, the Greeks used writing extensively for legislation with the intent of making their laws available to a relatively large segment of the community, whereas other cultures wrote extensive sets (or codes) of laws for academic purposes or propaganda but these were not intended to be accessible to most members of the community and had relatively little effect on the actual operation of the legal system.

---

[1] I leave the term "premodern" intentionally vague, but in general I use it to designate a society that has some sort of state, as opposed to tribal, organization, that makes use of writing, and has established judicial procedures. For this study I will draw my comparisons primarily from the premodern legal systems of the ancient Near East, particularly the code of Hammurabi, from early English common law, and from early Roman law. Several other premodern legal systems I have examined, such those of medieval Europe and China during the Qing dynasty, seem to be consistent with my thesis, but to keep this study manageable, I confine my comparisons to the three areas mentioned above.

On the other hand, the Greeks made very little use of writing in their legal procedure and allowed only a minimal use of writing during the trial itself; other cultures made far more use of writing in this area, often putting written documents at the heart of the trial process. These features of writing in Greece worked to keep the law from becoming overly technical and to prevent the development of the sorts of legal professions found in most other legal cultures.

The three words in my title, "Writing Greek Law," may seem fairly straightforward, but they raise important issues that need to be discussed at the outset. I begin with writing, a complex phenomenon that developed at different times, in different ways, and for different purposes in societies all over the world. No single theory explains the invention or the effect of writing, and so I will confine myself to writing in post-Bronze-Age Greece. Our earliest evidence for the Greek alphabetic script, the ancestor of later Roman and Cyrillic scripts, comes from inscriptions dated to around 750 or a bit earlier.[2] Whether this script was first invented in the half century or so before this time, as most classicists think, or perhaps two or three centuries earlier, as many Near-Eastern scholars and a few classicists think, is of no relevance for this study, since in the absence of earlier texts, we can only guess what writing was like before the time of these inscriptions. Greek script is clearly based on Near-Eastern consonantal scripts in use in the ninth or tenth centuries, and most probably on the Phoenician version of these scripts. The most important Greek innovation was to take several signs for consonants not used in Greek and use them for Greek vowels, thus producing the first fully alphabetic script, as distinct from the consonantal scripts that preceded it. This development made it easier for a reader to pronounce unfamiliar words phonetically, and this enabled more people to gain the ability to read and write. This was probably one reason why, as we shall see, rates of literacy in Greece, though low by standards of modern developed countries, were certainly higher than those of the ancient Near East or the Greek Bronze Age.

As for the term "Greek," the decipherment of Linear B has shown that Greek-speaking people entered the area we now call Greece during the Bronze Age, perhaps around 2000. This civilization came to an end around 1150 and with it knowledge of the Linear B syllabic script, used to write Greek, also ended. Whether Greeks in the Bronze Age had law in

---

[2] All dates in this book are BCE unless the contrary is either noted or obvious. For further discussion and references, see below, Chapter 2.

any sense is a subject of speculation,[3] but if they did, we can do nothing more than guess what it was like; thus, in this study I will ignore this period; for our purpose, Greek civilization begins in the prehistoric period following the fall of the Bronze Age, the period often called the Dark Ages, which lasted until around 750.[4] Greek civilization continued through the archaic and classical periods (ca. 750–500 and 500–323 respectively), and then into the Hellenistic period, which began after the death of Alexander the Great in 323. With the Roman conquest of Greece from about 150 to 30 BCE (later in parts of the Near East) Greek culture usually coexisted with Roman culture (and with Roman law). This study will focus largely on the archaic and classical periods, with some brief remarks on the Hellenistic period (down to the first century BCE) at the end.

The meaning of the term "law" has been discussed extensively. In *Early Greek Law* I accepted the systematic and logical, though fairly narrow, positivist view of H. L. A. Hart, that law required a relatively formal procedure for settling disputes together with a set of rules that were in some way recognized as special and as having a special authority, and could thus be called laws (Gagarin 1986: 1–9). I also argued that before the Greeks wrote laws, they had no true laws, because they had no other means besides writing to "recognize" (in Hart's sense) a law – that is, to differentiate a law from other kinds of rules. In preliterate Greece rules that we might call laws existed, but, as we see in a work like Hesiod's *Works and Days*, these rules were preserved and transmitted side by side with religious rules, rules of etiquette, practical rules of agriculture, and many others. I concluded, therefore, that in early Greece, legal procedures came into existence before substantive laws were "recognized" by being put in writing.

I continue to find Hart's positivist framework useful for the study of law, and in particular for understanding the effects of writing, but we need to be more flexible in thinking about law, particularly law in a preliterate society. Anthropologists have long studied law as dispute-settlement – that is, law settles disputes and resolves conflicts that threaten the social order, thereby maintaining order and benefiting society. The Greeks themselves arguably took this view of law, which is implicit in Hesiod's portrayal of the iron age, in which law is absent, in the story of Deioces (below Chapter One), and

---

[3] See van Effenterre 1989 and C. Thomas 1984 for two different approaches to this question. Both scholars assume a moderate degree of continuity between the Bronze Age and later Greek civilization, but it seems that in most respects the break was nearly complete (Raaflaub 1997a: 625–6 summarizes the argument).

[4] Some would dispute the term "dark" age, and of course as archaeology unearths more material, this period becomes steadily less dark.

elsewhere. But this is not the only way that law can be understood, and stimulated by recent work in anthropology, scholars are beginning to understand Athenian law in terms of "regulating [not resolving] conflict" (Osborne 1985: 52) and even as promoting conflict in some cases by providing a forum for (male, aristocratic) conflict to play out. In this view, litigation is not only a means of punishing violations and restoring order, but is also an important ritual process working to construct and validate the community's norms and values.[5] From this perspective, law (*dikē*) resembles other forms of competition (*agōn*) in Homer, such as athletic contests: just as games negotiate and validate athletic status (X is the fastest runner, Y the best wrestler, etc.), so too, *dikē* negotiates and validates an individual's general standing in the community.

Even if we understand law in this way, however, we should not deny its value in settling disputes. Just as the games at the funeral of Patroclus, with their host of minor conflicts all peaceably resolved in different ways, stand in sharp contrast both to the conflict between Achilles and Agamemnon (which could not be resolved by the community itself but was finally brought to an end by external events) and to the war that has been suspended, but only temporarily, so too, the "trial" that takes place on Achilles' shield (Chapter One) is a prominent feature of the city at peace because it prevents disputes like this from becoming destructive. Thus law may be a forum for regulating and even promoting conflict, and for negotiating community values, but at the same time, it prevents conflict from becoming open warfare.

In what follows, I will thus treat law both as conflict resolution and conflict regulation, resolution being more often the explicit message of a law, with regulation often observable in the background. In addition, the positivist view of law as a set of certain kinds of rules will also be useful, especially in thinking about the significance of the introduction of written laws.

Whatever the problems raised individually by the words "writing Greek law," combinations of these words are even more problematic. To begin with "writing Greek," in addition to the dispute about the date when the Greek alphabetic script was invented, there is considerable disagreement about issues such as why the Greek alphabetic script was invented, and who could (and who did) read and write this new script. The reasons why the Greeks first wrote are not directly relevant to this study, since as far as we know, laws were not written for at least a century after writing was first

---

[5] Among those sharing this approach are Cohen 1995; Foxhall 1996: 133–40; and Johnstone 1999.

used. Unlike other cultures, it does not appear that the Greeks invented writing for commercial purposes, since during this period there is scarcely any evidence of writing for commerce or of laws written to meet commercial needs. Commercial accounts may have been kept on perishable materials, as they were in the Bronze Age (where the accident of fire led to their preservation), but it is nonetheless striking that among the hundreds of surviving archaic inscriptions, none (to my knowledge) is a commercial document *per se*, and very few early legal texts are relevant to commerce. As we shall see, the experience of writing was not the same for the Greeks as for other cultures, and it seems highly unlikely that they invented writing for commercial purposes.[6]

A more important question for us about writing Greek is whether the creation of a more fully alphabetic script, including vowels, than the Near-Eastern script from which it was derived made the experience of reading and writing Greek something different from what it was in other cultures. Here, we need not follow Havelock in maintaining that (to oversimplify) the creation of a true alphabet led the Greeks to think rationally;[7] but it does seem likely that from the beginning Greek would have been easier to read and write than other early scripts, and in particular that it was easier to read unfamiliar texts in Greek. A notable feature of early Greek writing is the variety of texts we have and the spontaneity many of them suggest (see B. Powell 1989). This is particularly striking in contrast to the uses of writing in the Greek Bronze Age, which was mostly for keeping records within the large palace administrations, or even the ancient Near East, where writing is confined mostly to traditional works of literature, official historical records, commercial and legal documents, and a few other purposes. It is also generally accepted that whereas in these other cultures writing was primarily in the hands of professional scribes, a far greater diversity of people could write and read in Greece.

As for "writing law," I have already alluded to Hart's analysis of laws as rules. He distinguishes "primary rules" (rules of conduct) from "secondary rules." These latter are of three types, rules of recognition, rules of change, and rules of adjudication, which specify (respectively) how we know that a rule is a law, how existing laws are changed or new laws are enacted, and how disputes are settled concerning the meaning or application of a law or

---

[6] This is not to say that B. Powell (1991, 2002) is correct that the Greeks invented the alphabet in order to write down the Homeric poems. But the Greek alphabet does appear to have been designed to record the sound of speech, not to record objects, as commercially inspired scripts often do.

[7] See Havelock 1963, 1982, and other works. Herrenschmidt 2000 takes the idea that reading Greek creates a special mentality even further (below, Chapter 2, n. 3).

set of laws.[8] Particularly useful is Hart's notion of rules of recognition. These may take many forms, from the widely accepted understanding that a specific list of rules is authoritative, to more complex rules specifying, for example, enactment by a certain body or pronouncement by a certain magistrate. But a major limitation of Hart's analysis for our purposes, is that (as noted above) it sheds little or no light on the situation in early Greece, where a legal process existed without "recognized" legal rules.

Although in Hart's analysis writing usually plays a crucial role in recognition of law, he does not claim that recognition necessarily requires writing. A set of rules that are preserved and transmitted orally from one authoritative poet or speaker to another and are widely understood to be authoritative would satisfy Hart's rule of recognition. But actual historical examples of this are rare. The best known may be medieval Icelandic society as portrayed in the sagas, particularly in *Njal's Saga*, which I discuss in detail below (Chapter One). But even if a few other such examples of recognized oral laws could be cited, there is no evidence for oral or unwritten laws with this kind of authority in ancient Greece.

The Greeks did sometimes speak of unwritten, or oral, or sung laws, and in Chapter One I will consider the evidence for and implications of these concepts. I shall argue there that although "law" can be a useful metaphor for a diverse assortment of rules, and the concept of oral law is helpful in, for example, characterizing the period before writing in Greece, the writing down of laws gave these texts a qualitatively different status than that of oral or unwritten laws as they are usually understood. In Greece, at least, as we shall see in Chapter Three, writing law did not mean taking a preexisting oral text and committing it to writing, but creating a new text to be written down. This written text might be based on earlier oral rules, but the written law was qualitatively different from the oral rules that preceded it. In this sense, writing could be said to have created law for the Greeks – law, that is, in the sense of statutes. But writing down these statutes also started the process of establishing the institution of Law – always however in the plural for the Greeks: *hoi nomoi* ("the laws").[9] And not only was writing a crucial tool in the creation of law, but in some archaic cities the word "writing" served all by itself to designate a law or laws.

---

[8] Hart 1994, esp. 91–9.
[9] The Greeks never had a word corresponding to our word Law in the sense of a single institution encompassing both rules and procedures. The singular *ho nomos* ("the law") can designate a single statute or a broad concept, but the closest expression to, say, "Athenian law" would be the plural, "the laws (*hoi nomoi*) of the Athenians."

The third combination of words in my title, "Greek Law," is equally problematic, though it may not appear so to readers new to the field. The issue here is whether, or in what sense, we can legitimately or usefully speak of Greek Law as in some sense a single institution or system when, as is well known, throughout the archaic and classical periods, and to some extent even after the conquests of Alexander, Greece was divided politically into scores of independent poleis ("city-states") and other territories. Each polis had its own legal system, and though some of these could be more or less similar to one another, and some poleis copied or borrowed rules from others, in cases where we have sufficient evidence to judge, notably Athens and Gortyn, significant differences between the laws of the two cities are evident.

Although the question of "the Unity of Greek Law" had been addressed by many earlier scholars, it was Moses Finley, some fifty years ago, who drew attention to its importance, first in a book review and then in a more comprehensive paper entitled "The Problem of the Unity of Greek Law."[10] Using the example of marriage, Finley asserts (140):

> If we take as nodal points the Homeric poems, Gortyn, Athens and the earliest Greek papyri from Ptolemaic Egypt, I am unable to discover a single common 'basic conception' or 'principle' except for the notion, familiar from societies of the most diverse kinds all over the world, that marriage is an arrangement involving families past, present and future, and the transmission of property.

For Finley, in other words, to the extent that we can speak of general features of "Greek Law," these are so general as to make the concept useless, whereas at any useful degree of specificity, the evidence (which, to be sure, is limited) contradicts the theory of a unified entity.

With some exceptions, Finley's challenge has been accepted by Anglo-American scholars[11] but rejected by continental scholars, who have continued to speak of such things as an abstract spiritual unity (*geistige Gemeinsamkeit*) formed around certain basic concepts (*Grundvorstellungen*) of the sort that Finley dismissed as useless.[12] I have elsewhere defended Finley's view with regard to the substantive provisions of the law, but these may not represent the whole story (Gagarin 2005), and it should not surprise us if the common

---

[10] Finley 1951 (reviewing Pringsheim 1950), Finley 1966 (which I quote from the 1986 reprint).
[11] E.g., Todd 1993: 15–16 (more fully in Todd and Millett 1990: 7–11). Sealey (1990, 1994) is the main exception.
[12] The quotes are from Wolff 1975: 20–2; see also Biscardi 1982, whose very title (*Diritto greco antico*) is assertive.

cultural heritage of Greece manifested itself in some way in the legal systems of the different poleis.

My own view is that a useful concept of unity can be found in judicial procedure in a broad sense, including not just the process of litigation but also such matters as the organization of justice (legislation, courts, judges/jurors, magistrates), structural features of legislation, and particularly the use of writing (Gagarin 2001). Among the broad similarities in this area are that laws in Greece reveal a large concern with procedural matters, that automatic procedures involving oaths or witnesses are relatively rare as opposed to open forensic debate on the part of the litigants and free and rational decision making by a judge or judges, and that writing is extensively used for legislation but is relatively little used during the legal process. In all these respects, most other premodern legal systems differ from Greek law.

This study will begin (Chapter One) with what we know of law before writing was introduced to Greece some time before 750. Evidence for law in this preliterate period necessarily comes to us indirectly from literary sources, especially the poems of Homer and Hesiod, and we will examine passages from both poets for information about rules governing conduct and procedures for dispute settlement at this time. The poems portray a well-developed public process for resolving disputes peacefully, which seems to have enjoyed widespread support in the communities portrayed. I will describe the main features of this process and examine performative and ritual elements in it. I will refer to this process as "oral law" in the sense of a legal process conducted without writing. This does not mean that the Greeks had oral laws – that is laws preserved and transmitted orally. None of the evidence commonly cited for oral laws in this sense (unwritten laws, sung laws, or remembered laws) in fact supports this view. This is especially clear by contrast with early Icelandic society, which has the best claim to have had oral laws. Since there are no signs of anything similar in Greece, I prefer to designate the norms and standards we find in the poems that look like laws as "oral rules."

In Chapter Two I turn to the earliest inscriptions, which in the first century (ca. 750–650) are all private. The range and variety of these suggests that writing rapidly became popular among many people, not just the elite, in many parts of the Greek world. After a brief survey of these early private inscriptions, I examine some of the earliest legal inscriptions, which begin to appear about 650. These come from all over Greece, though the greatest concentration is on the island of Crete and especially the city of Gortyn. Another Cretan city, Dreros, is also of special interest as the site of the earliest surviving Greek law. I will pay particular attention in this chapter to the physical features of these early inscriptions, which are often ignored, since these provide evidence that from the beginning laws were inscribed and displayed publicly in order to be read. This is not to deny the important role of some of these legal texts as visual monuments, but the legislators' primary intent was to make the texts available for reading by the community.

Building on this conclusion, in Chapter Three I ask why the Greeks first began to write laws. There is not a single answer to this question, but certain general motives are apparent, namely the desire accurately to fix and preserve detailed regulations that can not easily be preserved orally and the community's desire to affirm its own authority. Moreover, all this legislation was written within the larger context of the growth of communities during the archaic period, when many cities were exerting control over larger territories and larger and more diverse populations and were experiencing steady economic growth. Such growth would have increased the occasions for disagreement and dispute and the likelihood of conflict among members of the community, as well as increasing the potential for disagreement or uncertainty about traditional rules. It was the need for greater public authority and clearer and more detailed rules, I will argue, that ultimately produced the need for written legislation.

Chapter Four will continue this discussion of the reasons for writing laws by closely examining one single law, Draco's homicide law, which was first written in Athens in 621. We do not have the original inscription, but a late-fifth-century copy will provide the basis for this discussion. I will challenge the common explanation scholars have given, that this law was written in response to a crisis in Athens. I will instead argue that with Athens undergoing the same kind of growth as other Greek cities, Draco was motivated by the same concern as lay behind some of the early inscriptions, in particular the need to add a large amount of new detail to traditional rules and to preserve and communicate these details accurately. In addition I will show that Draco conceived of his homicide law as a comprehensive law, and that he consciously strived to organize its provisions clearly and logically in order that those who might need to use the law could do so more easily.

Chapters Three and Four together argue that the purpose of early legislation in Greece was not to resolve specific crises or to strengthen elite control over the majority of citizens, but rather to establish precise and detailed rules that could be used with relative ease by members of the community. The ultimate cause of this legislation was not so much conflict, between rich and poor or between competing aristocratic families, as the pressures of population growth, economic expansion, and increasing diversity. Taken together these trends rendered the traditional oral rules and customs no longer adequate for settling the increasing number and different kinds of disputes that arose. Written laws, with their fixed, detailed rules and procedures served the needs of these diverse populations and in so doing also helped strengthen their sense of being a unified political community. In strengthening the people's sense of community, written laws in early Greece have a similar effect as written laws in other early legal systems, but in other respects, such as their attention to detail and concern with procedure, Greek laws are different. We will explore this and other such differences at greater length in later chapters.

Chapter Five will examine the little evidence we have for writing in other areas of law besides legislation in archaic Greece. Only one such use is well attested – writing was an essential part of the new procedure of *graphē* ("writing") instituted by Solon, but was only used for the initial charge or indictment. Otherwise, I will note the highly questionable evidence for the writing down of rules (*thesmia*) by the Thesmothetae in early Athens. No other use of writing is attested in archaic legal procedure, and the essential orality of procedure is confirmed by the duties of the *mammon* ("rememberer"), which we will examine. One of these rememberers, Spensithios, is employed both to write and to remember, but his duties are not inconsistent with the basic duality of written laws and an oral legal process in archaic Greece.

Because of the disproportionately large number of fifth-century inscriptions from Gortyn, the next two chapters (Six and Seven) will be devoted to these. In the first, we will consider all the inscriptions except for the Great Code, which we will take up in Chapter Seven. First, I examine a sample of texts that show some of the same features as earlier inscriptions but a greater degree of organization in the physical layout of the text, as well as the syntactical and structural organization of its provisions. These inscriptions, which range in length from one to seven columns, are particularly important in providing a fuller context for the Great Code. They show that Gortynian legislators in the fifth century were inscribing larger, more complex collections of laws in one continuous text, and were developing techniques of organizing these provisions clearly and coherently. These developments prepare the way for the even larger and more sophisticated organization we will find in the Code.

Chapter Seven is devoted to the Gortyn Code, both in itself and in comparison with the equally grand inscription of Hammurabi's laws, which is similar in length and breadth of coverage but very different in other important respects. I first consider the references to writing and written texts in each code; at Gortyn these always refer to laws, but in Hammurabi's laws they always designate other sorts of documents.

Moreover, written documents have a role in Babylonian litigation but are unknown at Gortyn. Then, after some discussion of the nature and purpose of Hammurabi's laws, which differ from those of the Gortyn laws, I will focus particularly on the organization of provisions at Gortyn, trying to show how the legislator has created a logical and hierarchical ordering of provisions on different subjects that differs significantly from the more linear structure of provisions in Hammurabi's code. The topic of adoption, which is treated at similar length in both codes, reveals the difference especially clearly. I end the chapter with more general observations about the use of writing for legislation and in litigation in Greece and in the ancient Near East. In both its use of writing for legislation and the absence of writing in litigation, Greek practice was almost the reverse of Near-Eastern practice, and this difference sheds interesting light on the nature of Greek law and Greek culture.

In Chapter Eight I turn to classical Athens, for which we have the extensive evidence of about a hundred forensic speeches. I begin with legislation, showing first that a broad range of Athenian litigants are portrayed as reading laws; litigants evidently take it for granted that laws were intended to be read and used in litigation. This is confirmed by the legal reforms at the end of the fifth century, which resulted in a new collection of inscribed texts of all valid Athenian laws, and new legislation at this time prohibited litigants from using any law not included in this collection. In addition to laws, other sorts of written documents became increasingly common in classical Athens, and litigants made increasing use of these written documents in litigation. During the trial, however, all this documentary evidence, which Aristotle categorizes as "non-artistic proofs" (i.e., not a product of the speaker's rhetorical art), was presented orally to the court by a clerk. Thus, in trials everything was communicated to the jury orally, and the heart of Athenian procedure, the trial, remained an entirely oral process. Classical Athens thus reveals the same duality as earlier Greek law – widespread use of writing for legislation but restricted use in litigation. The forensic orators express this duality in contradictory assessments of written legal texts: on the one hand, speakers value written texts (in contrast to oral speech) as objective and authoritative, but on the other hand, they also argue that written texts are false and deceptive, whereas oral discourse can clarify facts and reveal the truth. In most cases, speakers can express either of these attitudes depending on the needs of their case, but written laws have a special status and are never discredited.

In Chapter Nine, I assess the overall place of writing in Athenian law. I argue that both the abundant use of writing for legislation, which was generally written in clear, ordinary, and non-technical language, and the general absence of writing in the legal process played a crucial role in making Athenian law accessible to ordinary citizens so that they could use it without needing the assistance of legal professionals. I will further argue that in this respect, law in other Greek cities was similar to classical Athenian law, though these cities are not as well documented. These similarities underscore the fact that these features of law are characteristically Greek, not specifically Athenian or democratic, as is often thought. Finally, the significance of using writing in legislation but not in litigation becomes even more apparent by comparison with the effects of writing law in early Roman law and early English common law. In both societies, writing infiltrated the legal system at an early period, and as a result, both systems became virtually inaccessible to non-specialists (as are the legal systems of all modern societies). The contrast with these other societies illuminates the unique non-professional nature of Athenian and indeed all Greek law.

As an epilogue to this study, in Chapter Ten I look briefly at how writing was used in law during the Hellenistic period. In the older Greek cities that became part of Alexander's empire we find considerable continuity from the classical to the Hellenistic period, both in law in general and specifically in the use of writing in legal matters: legislation continued to be written and publicly displayed, whereas written documents, although increasing in number, remained peripheral to the process of litigation. In the areas conquered by Alexander that were not previously Greek, on the other hand, of which only Ptolemaic Egypt provides enough evidence to allow conclusions to be drawn, the situation was just the reverse. In Egypt, as in early English law, little legislation was written but large numbers of legal documents of all sorts were written by scribes and notaries for use in all phases of the legal process, including the trial. The resulting professionalization of Ptolemaic law resembles the same developments in early common law.

Chapter Eleven concludes this history of writing in Greek law with some reflections on the significance of our conclusions. The study of writing not only sheds light on such features of Greek law as its open texture, its non-technical nature, its absence of professionalism, and its accessibility, but shows us a way to understand the unity of Greek law as a broad, procedural unity within which there was considerable substantive diversity. Furthermore, comparison with the use of writing in other premodern legal systems allows us to appreciate the uniqueness of Greek law and the cultural and political context in which it developed. Finally I add a few remarks on the significance of Greek law for the study of law today.

CHAPTER I

Law before Writing

The earliest period of Greek law for which we have evidence, albeit indirect, is the era portrayed in the poems of Homer and Hesiod, which we may loosely refer to as the period of "Homeric society." Although the events in Homer take place at the end of the Bronze Age (ca. 1200–1150), the institutions portrayed almost certainly represent those of a later period, most likely the eighth century, shortly before these poems were put in writing, probably around 700.[1] Moreover, the works of both Homer and Hesiod contain episodes and allusions pertaining to judicial matters on the basis of which we can sketch a picture of a more or less formal process for judging or settling disputes between members of the community. Certain details of this process may vary, but there is enough consistency among the different episodes to conclude that early Greek legal procedure was a recognizable institution with well-established parameters within which there was room for variation in detail. Like the rest of the Homeric/ Hesiodic world, the legal process shows no knowledge of writing, even though writing was probably introduced to the Greek world a century or so before these poems were written down. Thus, we are justified in assuming that legal procedures such as those portrayed in the poems existed in Greece in the eighth or ninth centuries and probably continued with little change (and without the use of writing) until the mid seventh century, when laws first began to be written.

The best known and most discussed passage pertaining to law in Homer is the trial scene on Achilles' shield. In making a new shield for Achilles, the god Hephaestus creates a panorama of the universe, in which are located three separate places where human activity occurs – a city at peace, a city at war, and a rural scene. In the city at peace the god represents just two

---

[1] There is continuing discussion and debate about the nature of "Homeric society" and whether it corresponds to any historical time and place, but most would accept that it has affinities with Greece in the eighth century. See, e.g., Finley 1978; I. Morris 1986; Raaflaub 1997a; Hall 2007: 25–6.

events, a wedding and a trial, and in the latter he portrays two disputants
seeking a resolution to their dispute from a group of elders in a rather
formal setting (*Iliad* 18.497–508):

> Meanwhile a crowd gathered in the agora, where a dispute
> had arisen: two men contended over the blood-price
> for a man who had died. One swore he would pay everything,
> demonstrating this to the people. The other refused to accept
> anything.   500
>   Both were eager to find a conclusion at the hands of an umpire
> (*istōr*).
>   People were shouting out on both sides, supporting both litigants;
> but the heralds restrained them. And the old men
> took seats on polished stones in a sacred circle;
> they held in their hands the scepters of loud-voiced heralds.   505
>   Then the two men came quickly before them, and one after the
> other they gave their judgments (*dikazein*).
>   In the middle lay two talents of gold,
> to be given to the one among them who would speak the straightest
> judgment (*dikē*).[2]

Although the scene conveys much information, Homer is not a court
reporter and many details are understandably left vague, allowing scholars
to engage in nearly endless disputes over issues on which we will probably
never achieve consensus. Among the more commonly debated questions
are: Is the dispute about the amount of the blood-price, whether or not it
has been paid, or whether the victim's relative is required to accept it? Is the
umpire (*istōr*) one of the elders or a separate official, and if the latter, what
does he do? What sort of judgment or settlement does each elder give, and
does it have to take a prescribed form such as a directive that one or the

---

[2]   λαοὶ δ' εἰν ἀγορῇ ἔσαν ἀθρόοι· ἔνθα δὲ νεῖκος
ὠρώρει, δύο δ' ἄνδρες ἐνείκεον εἵνεκα ποινῆς
ἀνδρὸς ἀποφθιμένου· ὃ μὲν εὔχετο πάντ' ἀποδοῦναι
δήμῳ πιφαύσκων, ὃ δ' ἀναίνετο μηδὲν ἑλέσθαι·
ἄμφω δ' ἱέσθην ἐπὶ ἴστορι πεῖραρ ἑλέσθαι.   500
λαοὶ δ' ἀμφοτέροισιν ἐπήπυον ἀμφὶς ἀρωγοί·
κήρυκες δ' ἄρα λαὸν ἐρήτυον· οἳ δὲ γέροντες
εἵατ' ἐπὶ ξεστοῖσι λίθοις ἱερῷ ἐνὶ κύκλῳ,
σκῆπτρα δὲ κηρύκων ἐν χέρσ' ἔχον ἠεροφώνων·   505
τοῖσιν ἔπειτ' ἤϊσσον, ἀμοιβηδὶς δὲ δίκαζον.
κεῖτο δ' ἄρ' ἐν μέσσοισι δύω χρυσοῖο τάλαντα,
τῷ δόμεν ὃς μετὰ τοῖσι δίκην ἰθύντατα εἴποι.

other litigant swear an oath?[3] And who receives the two talents of gold, and if it goes to an elder (as most scholars think), how is the recipient determined? I will not rehearse these issues once again, since most of them do not affect the overall picture of early procedure I wish to draw.[4]

The scene portrays two disputants, one of whom has killed a man; the other, who is seeking satisfaction for the death, is most likely a relative of the victim. The process is evidently initiated by the disputants themselves, who have voluntarily come before a circle of elders in order to find an end to their dispute (501). Wolff (1946: esp. 36–49) disputes the voluntary nature of the process; he recognizes that line 501 ("Both were eager to find a conclusion at the hands of an umpire") "speaks strongly in favor of the theory that the parties submitted their case to the *istōr* voluntarily and by mutual consent," but he argues, nonetheless, that since the killer speaks first, he must have brought the case; and therefore, he must be seeking the community's protection against a relative of the victim, who is seeking vengeance for his relative's murder by the traditional method of self-help. According to Wolff, if this vengeance-seeking relative refuses to join with the killer in asking for a trial, the community will protect the killer. Thus, the victim's supporters are, in essence, required to use the legal process if they want to see the killer punished.

Wolff's view has found many followers, but there are serious objections to it. First, the poet actually says that "both [litigants] were eager" (ἄμφω δ' ἱέσθην) for a resolution, not that one party wanted it and the other came reluctantly.[5] Second, several other examples in early Greek literature illustrate the voluntary nature of this procedure in early Greece; these include the story of Deioces (see below), the dispute between Hermes and Apollo in the *Hymn to Hermes*, and the case of Orestes and the Furies in Aeschylus' *Eumenides*, where (*pace* Wolff 1946: 47) both disputants ask Athena for a trial (see lines 431–5, 467–9). Of course, by "voluntarily" I do not mean to exclude the considerable pressure in support of a peaceful resolution that could be brought to bear on disputants by friends and family. In the relatively small communities of early Greece, communal pressure would have played a considerable part in inducing disputants both to bring their

---

[3] A closely related question is what is the meaning of *dikazein* in line 506?

[4] Among the many previous discussions, interested readers will find a sample of different approaches in Wolff 1946; Gagarin 1986: 26–33; Thür 1996 (cf. Thür 1970); and Cantarella 2002, 2005a.

[5] Even if the killer does speak first and is therefore the "plaintiff" (in some sense), this does not mean that the case he is bringing will involve his being the defendant in a homicide trial. There are many sorts of complaints he might be bringing as plaintiff, such as that the relative reneged on an agreement about the blood-money.

dispute to others and to accept a settlement that was deemed reasonable by the community. Wickham's description of a similar situation in medieval Europe is worth quoting (Davies and Fouracre 1986: 235).

> No one in Europe lived only among kin; one needed support from neighbours, dependants, lords, and this was available above all in the public arena . . . Going to court was the only way that much of one's reserve of support could be brought into play at all. The importance of the court was sufficiently great that a party could seldom refuse to take his case there in the end if his opponent demanded it, or, if he did, might well lose even the support of his kin. Courts were only part of disputing, but they were that part that was most likely to bring a party the backing he needed to construct victory, or at least advantageous compromise.

Similarly, in early Greece the small size of communities would to a large extent have blurred the distinction between "voluntary" and "compulsory" procedure.

In the scene on Achilles' shield, each of the litigants comes with a crowd of supporters, who loudly make their views known (502). The setting (a circle of polished stones, 504) suggests that the procedure has ritual elements. After each litigant speaks, each elder in turn proposes a judgment or settlement, and eventually one of these is accepted as best ("straightest"). The most likely method for determining whose settlement is best, in my view, is by general consensus of the audience, as representative of the whole community.[6] The two talents of gold mentioned at the end (507–8) is not a large enough amount to be the blood-price, and so like most scholars, I take it to be a prize for the elder whose settlement is accepted as best.

The oral and performative nature of the process being depicted is clear. All the participants are described as expressing themselves orally: the disputants affirm or deny something (*eucheto, anaineto*), the people shout out their support (*epēpyon*), the heralds who keep order are "loud-voiced" (*ēerophōnoi*), each elder delivers his judgment or settlement (*dikazon*), and at the end the prize will go to the elder who speaks the straightest settlement (*dikēn ithyntata eipoi*). All the Greek words cited indicate speech acts, including (I would argue) *dikazon*, which is usually translated "judge" or "decide." The specific meaning of this verb has been much disputed,[7] but Benveniste makes a good case that *dikē* is related to Latin *dico* and thus *dikazein* – "to perform a *dikē*" – designates from the beginning a verbal

---

[6] Larsen 1947 presents other evidence indicating that in Homer decisions were regularly reached by consensus.

[7] The best treatment of its meaning in Homer remains Talamanca 1979.

process or speech act.[8] In every passage in the epics, the context either requires or suggests or allows that *dikazein* be an act of speaking, and the final line in this passage, "the elder who speaks the straightest settlement," confirms that *dikazein* is used to designate a speech act. In addition, like many other Greek institutions, the legal process is structured as a competition, here not just between two litigants but also among the judges. Other features mark the scene as an oral ritual performance, including that the participants form a circle, that one litigant supports his plea with a display (*piphauskōn*), and that each judge, and perhaps each litigant holds a scepter when he speaks as a sign of authority.

In Homeric procedure, then, as portrayed in this vignette, two members of the community with a dispute can bring it for a hearing to the agora, the gathering place for assemblies and other public business. They are seeking an umpire from among the respected, elder members of the community. Each brings supporters (presumably friends and relatives), and other members of the community are probably also present, especially for a dispute relating to homicide, which would be a concern to all even if the identity of the killer is apparently not in question. After hearing the two pleas, the elders rise in turn and propose settlements; the order in which they speak was probably determined by age or some other measure of authority. The crowd, who are being restrained by the heralds, probably indicate their response to the proposals vocally by shouts of approval or disapproval,[9] thereby providing feedback to the elders and helping them find an acceptable settlement. Settlements are thus reached by a process of negotiation and compromise, and when an elder eventually proposes a settlement that meets with the general approval of the crowd, both litigants will have to accept it, since it would be impossible for them to survive in the sort of small community we find in Homer without the support of friends and family. The only alternative to accepting the proposed settlement would be to leave the community and go into exile. For this reason, neither this scene nor any of the other scenes we will examine below says anything about enforcement of the settlement, because it goes without saying that

[8] Benveniste 1973: 385–8 (originally 1969: vol. II, 107–10). Although I agree that *dikazein* designates a speech act, I am convinced Benveniste is wrong to understand *dikazein* as the recitation of a "formula" of law (*dikē*) that had been handed down to the judge orally. Connecting *dikazein* with *dico* does not mean it cannot also be connected with *deiknumi* ("show"), as was argued by Palmer 1950. Palmer takes the sense to be "pointing out" and sees *dikē* as designating a "mark," such as a boundary mark. In that case, the sense of *dikazein* as "show verbally" (Benveniste 1973: 386) would mean that a *dikē* is a verbally confirmed or performed mark and *dikazein* is the performative speech act of designating or showing that is embodied in the pronouncement of a judgment.

[9] Compare the later *thorubos* ("uproar") often mentioned in Attic forensic oratory (Bers 1985).

once the community has found a settlement to be acceptable, the disputants will have to abide by it (or at least appear to do so). Specific enforcement is not needed, though the same or a related dispute may erupt again at
any time.

   This kind of procedure has parallels in other preliterate societies.
Especially interesting is the process for settling disputes among the Tiv, a
people of northern Nigeria, who have been described by Bohannan (1957)
on the basis of his observations in the early 1950s. The Tiv set aside many
days during the year for *jir*, which (like *dikē*) can designate both a case
that someone brings and the process for settling that case. The *jir* that
Bohannan observed were presided over by a man named Chenge, the chief
or leader of the Tiv subgroup Bohannan was observing. People would
gather in Chenge's compound, where he and various other officials,
collectively known as *mbatarev*, "sat in a sort of semi-circle outside under
the trees" (17). A large crowd of ordinary citizens sit in front of them, filling
out the circle.[10] Anyone with a complaint can request a *jir*, which costs two
shillings, but he or she generally consults informally with *mbatarev* beforehand, and they may suggest that it would be best to resolve the matter
without a *jir*, for the Tiv are not sympathetic to trivial or frivolous
complaints.

   Once the *jir* begins, the complainant speaks first. *Mbatarev* try to
understand all the facts and may interrupt, ask questions, or make suggestions. Then the accused speaks; he also can be questioned or interrupted.
Then witnesses are called if necessary. This sometimes requires adjourn-
ment of the *jir* for a few hours or a few days until a witness can be located. If
necessary, the *mbatarev* will ask more questions. Also anyone in the crowd
may comment or ask a question. Then, finally, the *mbatarev* consult
among themselves and issue a decision.

Usually the decision involves pointing out a mode of action that will be satisfac-
tory, or least unsatisfactory, to both parties; action to which both will agree, and
which will resolve the dispute. Both should concur in the decision, and each must
agree to carry out his part of it. If such concurrence and agreement are not
obtained, the case will probably be said to have been settled arbitrarily. No chief
or official who develops a reputation for such arbitrary rulings can long retain his
prestige or his influence. (Bohannan 1957: 19)

Concurrence of the litigants never occurs without concurrence of the entire
community: no one is ready to make concessions while any portion of public

---

[10] "Many private citizens attend sessions of the *jir*, for Tiv are a litigious people and enjoy listening to
   and participating in *jir*" (Bohannan 1957: 13). The Greeks seem to have shared this trait.

opinion still supports him. It is the opinion of the community which forces concurrence. Judging, like all other activities of Tiv leaders, consists largely in the timely suggestion of what the majority thinks is right or desirable. (*Ibid.* 65)

Several interesting similarities are evident between the Tiv *jir* and the Greek procedure portrayed on Achilles' shield. The litigants come together in a space that is circular and open to all; there is a separation between the leading men and the rest of the community, but the community plays an active role in responding to the proceedings, and their response in turn conditions the course of the discussion and the eventual resolution. Any such resolution must have the support of the community, and in fact, one might define a successful settlement as one that wins the approval of the community, which in the scene on Achilles' shield probably decides collectively which of the proposed settlements is the most acceptable and thus which elder will receive the two talents of gold for "speaking the straightest settlement." Finally, the community's approval will play a crucial role in bringing the litigants to accept the final settlement.

Other scenes and briefer allusions in Homer and Hesiod also illustrate this judicial process and indicate that it was a common activity. For instance, when Odysseus, after his second confrontation with Charybdis, is hanging from a fig tree waiting for the whirlpool to regurgitate the remnants of his makeshift raft, the pieces finally appear "late, at the time when a man stands up from the agora [to return home] for dinner after deciding many quarrels of young men seeking settlements" (*Od.* 12.439–40).[11] And when Glaucus tells the Lycians that their lord Sarpedon is dead, he describes him as "he who protected Lycia with his dispute-settlements and his strength" (*Il.* 16.542).[12] These passages suggest that a man could commonly spend a full day in the agora hearing disputes, and that settling disputes and fighting battles are the primary benefits a king gives his people. Remarks like these help us understand why, when Homer includes just two scenes in the city at peace on Achilles' new shield, one of them is a trial. Judicial procedure, Homer implies, like weddings (the other scene in the city at peace), is fundamental to the survival and prosperity of a community.

Homer's contemporary, the poet Hesiod, is also much concerned with law and justice. He focuses his attention particularly on the role of the

---

[11] ὄψ'· ἦμος δ' ἐπὶ δόρπον ἀνὴρ ἀγορῆθεν ἀνέστη
κρίνων νείκεα πολλὰ δικαζομένων αἰζηῶν.

[12] ὃς Λυκίην εἴρυτο δίκῃσί τε καὶ σθένεϊ ᾧ.

"kings" (*basileis*),[13] who judge disputes singly or collectively, and who apparently want to judge a dispute Hesiod has with his brother over their inheritance. In the proem to his *Theogony* Hesiod observes that like a poet, a king benefits from the gift of the Muses (80–92):

> For she [the Muse Calliope] accompanies honored kings.   80
> And whichever of the divinely nourished kings
> the daughters of great Zeus [the Muses] honor
> and look upon at birth, on his tongue they pour sweet honey
> and soothing words flow from his mouth. And the people
> all behold him, distinguishing the rules (*themistes*)[14]   85
> with straight settlements (*dikai*). And he, speaking surely,
> quickly and skillfully puts a stop to even a large dispute.
> This is why there are intelligent kings, so that for people
> who have been disadvantaged they may restore matters in the agora,
> easily, persuading them with soft words.   90
> And as he comes to the gathering, they honor him as a god
> with gentle reverence, and he is conspicuous among those

assembled.[15]

This is followed immediately by a similar tribute to the poet (93–103):

> Such is the holy gift the Muses bestow on people;
> for from the Muses and far-shooting Apollo
> come men on earth who play the lyre and sing,   95
> but from Zeus come kings. And he prospers whom the Muses

---

[13] Since there were apparently several kings even in the small communities in Hesiod's Boeotia, these must be thought of as lords or nobles, not kings in the usual sense. I retain the traditional English translation for convenience.

[14] *Themistes* (sing. *themis*) are the traditional rules and customs of a community; they are often said to have come from Zeus.

[15]
> ἡ γὰρ καὶ βασιλεῦσιν ἅμ' αἰδοίοισιν ὀπηδεῖ.   80
> ὅντινα τιμήσουσι Διὸς κοῦραι μεγάλοιο
> γεινόμενόν τε ἴδωσι διοτρεφέων βασιλήων,
> τῷ μὲν ἐπὶ γλώσσῃ γλυκερὴν χείουσιν ἐέρσην,
> τοῦ δ' ἔπε' ἐκ στόματος ῥεῖ μείλιχα· οἱ δέ νυ λαοὶ
> πάντες ἐς αὐτὸν ὁρῶσι διακρίνοντα θέμιστας   85
> ἰθείῃσι δίκῃσιν· ὁ δ' ἀσφαλέως ἀγορεύων
> αἶψά τι καὶ μέγα νεῖκος ἐπισταμένως κατέπαυσε·
> τούνεκα γὰρ βασιλῆες ἐχέφρονες, οὕνεκα λαοῖς
> βλαπτομένοις ἀγορῆφι μετάτροπα ἔργα τελεῦσι
> ῥηιδίως, μαλακοῖσι παραιφάμενοι ἐπέεσσιν·   90
> ἐρχόμενον δ' ἀν' ἀγῶνα θεὸν ὡς ἱλάσκονται
> αἰδοῖ μειλιχίῃ, μετὰ δὲ πρέπει ἀγρομένοισι.

cherish; a sweet voice flows from his mouth.
Even if someone has grief in his recently troubled spirit
and is withered with the pain in his heart, even so the singer,
servant of the Muses, will sing of the glorious deeds of men long
ago,   100
and of the blessed gods who live on Olympus,
and he will quickly forget his cares, and his troubles
he will not remember. Quickly the gifts of the goddesses change
him.[16]

The association of Muses with kings has puzzled many scholars.[17] It has
been suggested (C. P. Roth 1976) that with the Muses' help a king could
memorize and recite orally transmitted laws in much the same way a poet
recited orally transmitted verses. But Hesiod does not say anything about
speaking or reciting rules, and "soothing words" would be an odd way to
describe the recital of a law or set of laws. Moreover, a king cannot be
reciting the text of a law when he "persuades them with gentle words." No,
Hesiod is saying that a king's success, like a poet's, depends in large part on
his eloquence. To be sure, the king must be honest and intelligent, as a poet
must be truthful (in some sense) and insightful, but he must also be able to
speak with eloquence so as to frame a proposed settlement in such a way
that litigants and others present will consider it fair and will agree to accept
it. It is not necessary that every one of his decisions be accepted as fair by
everyone, but over time most of his decisions must be seen by most people
to be fair and acceptable. If they are, his authority will grow, people will
continue to bring their disputes to him for settlement, and litigants who are
not completely satisfied with a settlement will nonetheless be under strong
pressure to accept it. This king is honored "like a god with gentle rever-
ence." But if over time a king's settlements are not perceived as fair, his
authority will diminish, people will lose confidence in his judgment, and

---

[16]   τοίη Μουσάων ἱερὴ δόσις ἀνθρώποισιν.
ἐκ γάρ τοι Μουσέων καὶ ἑκηβόλου Ἀπόλλωνος
ἄνδρες ἀοιδοὶ ἔασιν ἐπὶ χθόνα καὶ κιθαρισταί,   95
ἐκ δὲ Διὸς βασιλῆες· ὁ δ' ὄλβιος, ὅντινα Μοῦσαι
φίλωνται· γλυκερή οἱ ἀπὸ στόματος ῥέει αὐδή.
εἰ γάρ τις καὶ πένθος ἔχων νεοκηδέι θυμῷ
ἄζηται κραδίην ἀκαχήμενος, αὐτὰρ ἀοιδὸς
Μουσάων θεράπων κλεῖα προτέρων ἀνθρώπων   100
ὑμνήσει μάκαράς τε θεοὺς οἳ Ὄλυμπον ἔχουσιν,
αἶψ' ὅ γε δυσφροσυνέων ἐπιλήθεται οὐδέ τι κηδέων
μέμνηται· ταχέως δὲ παρέτραπε δῶρα θεάων.
[17]   See however West 1966: 185 (on line 90); Gagarin 1992.

they will take their disputes to someone else. This is why the Muses' gift – the ability to speak eloquently and persuasively – is so valuable.

Before examining this scene further, we might pause to note that we have a fine example of the sort of king Hesiod describes here in the person of Deioces, the first king of the Medes, whose (largely fictional) story is told by the fifth-century historian, Herodotus (1.96–100). In early times, Herodotus reports, the Medes lived scattered in small villages, in one of which Deioces judged disputes brought to him by the villagers. Being ambitious for power, he devised a plan: he became so good at judging disputes that he gained a wide reputation for justice, and soon everyone from the whole region would bring their disputes only to him. In this way he gained a monopoly over dispute-settlement. We will return to the story of Deioces at the end of this chapter and will see how things changed with his ascension to power, but I simply note here that the early history of Deioces illustrates how Hesiod's good king is so honored by the people that they no longer patronize the other judges, who presumably do not have his qualities.

Returning to Hesiod, his king, like the poet, is also a performer playing to an audience that is affected by his eloquence. It is well recognized that the audience is a crucial participant in any performance: every performer performs for an audience and his performance is always conditioned by his audience and its response (Bauman 1986). As we saw, the audience (here the community) participate actively in the scene on Achilles' shield, and audience participation is particularly emphasized in Hesiod's description of the king's performance. All the people (*laoi*) observe him in action (84–5), and they revere him like a god, as they crowd around him in the agora (91–2). As Hesiod describes them, both king and poet confront a troubled audience, and both must use the sweet voice flowing from their mouth (*ek* or *apo stomatos rheei*, 84, 97) to accomplish their task quickly and easily (*aipsa*, 87, 102; *rhēidiōs*, 90; *tacheōs*, 103). The word *glykerē* is used in both descriptions (83, 97): in the first the Muses pour sweet dew on the king's mouth; in the second it is the poet's voice that is sweet. From the king's mouth flow words, *epea* (84), from the poet's flows an *audē* (97), which seems to be a voice of special narrative authority. I do not want to overplay the similarities between the two, for there are differences too. The king's audience, as we noted, includes the community (*laoi*), whereas the poet is described here as having only a single listener, though we are surely meant to assume that in most cases the poet's audience is larger than this. But by presenting both descriptions together, Hesiod is stressing the importance of the resemblances, showing that the king must be a performer whose eloquence wins over the litigants and the community and alleviates their troubles, and who in return is praised and admired by them.

Several other passages from Homer and Hesiod give a similar picture of this oral judicial process, which can vary in its formality.[18] The most important of these comes in *Iliad* 23 during the funeral games in honor of Patroclus. Several of these contests give rise to disputes of different kinds, all of which Achilles settles quite easily in scenes that have none of the formal trappings of the two scenes we examined earlier. These contests are apparently held not in the agora, the formal meeting place, but near the beach, where Achilles sits the people down "in a large gathering" (*agōn*, 23.258) and disputes are settled right there, as they arise.

The contest that draws the most attention is the chariot race, during which Nestor's son Antilochus, in a risky maneuver, passes Menelaus on the turn and finishes in second place, just ahead of Menelaus. But when Antilochus comes forward to receive the second-place prize (a mare), a dispute arises that is described at some length (*Iliad* 23.566–613):

> But Menelaus, bitter in his heart, stood up among them
> implacably angry at Antilochus, and the herald
> put the scepter in his hand and gave the order for silence
> among the Argives. And then the god-like man addressed them:
> "Antilochus, you who once had good sense, what have you done? 570
> You have cast shame on my valor (*aretē*) and have harmed my horses
> by cutting yours in front of them, though yours were much slower.
> Come then, leaders and counselors of the Argives,
> settle this matter (*dikassate*) for both of us impartially and without favor,
> so that none of the bronze-clad Achaeans will ever say: 575
> 'By lying and using force against Antilochus, Menelaus
> went off with the mare; for even though he had much slower
> horses, he was greater in valor and power.'
> But come, I myself will propose a settlement (*dikasō*), and no one else, I tell you,
> among the Danaans will find fault with me, since it will be straight." 580

Menelaus does not address his complaint solely to Achilles or seek to convene a formal tribunal, but instead he asks his colleagues ("leaders and

---

[18] For other evidence from Homer, Hesiod, and other early poets not discussed here, see Gagarin 1986: 19–50.

counselors of the Argives") to settle his dispute. Although many of these would have been considered kings and some were undoubtedly elders, as a group they are a less formal body than the judges in the two scenes we examined earlier.

Menelaus first asks them to propose a settlement that will not only be fair but will have the appearance of fairness and will not make it appear that he is just asserting his own greater authority. Before the others have a chance to say anything, however, Menelaus rather abruptly says he will settle the dispute himself, and he makes a proposal to Antilochus that he is confident everyone will approve of, "since it will be straight." He then proposes that Antilochus swear a solemn oath by Poseidon:[19]

> "Come here, Antilochus, cherished by Zeus. As is right,
> stand in front of your horses and chariot, and take the pliant whip
> in your hands, the one with which you were driving earlier.
> Put your hands on the horses and by the earth-embracing, earth-shaker
> swear you did not intentionally impede my chariot by trickery." 585

Antilochus does not directly accept or reject Menelaus' proposal but instead responds with a deferential offer to give Menelaus as a gift the prize that (he says) he won, and to give him anything else he might want too.

> Then sensible Antilochus answered him in turn.
> "Hold on, now, for I am much younger
> than you, lord Menelaus, and you are superior and more valiant.
> You know the sort of offenses a young man commits,
> since his mind is hasty and his intelligence is slender.   590
> So let your heart be patient, and I myself will give you
> the mare that I won. And if there is something in my house
> in addition that you should desire, I would prefer to give it to you quickly,
> right now, than to fall from your favor for all time,
> you who are cherished by Zeus, and offend against the gods." 595
> Then the great-hearted son of Nestor led forth the mare

---

[19] Menelaus' proposal of an oath should not be confused with the procedure, well known in many cultures and found occasionally in Greece (e.g., at Gortyn) whereby a judge imposes a decisive oath on one of the litigants who can then swear it and automatically win the case (see Gagarin 1997, *contra* Thür 1996). As one of the parties to the dispute, Menelaus cannot impose an oath on his opponent, but can only propose an oath and hope the opponent accepts it. Such oath-proposals are common in classical Athenian litigation (see Gagarin 2007a).

and put it in Menelaus' hands, and his spirit
was warmed; as when the dew on the ears of corn
of the crop growing in the bristling field,
even so, Menelaus, the spirit in your heart was warmed.   600

With this speech Antilochus in fact affirms his own right to the mare, which he claims he has won (592), but his deference to the older man has its desired effect, and Menelaus in turn responds with an equally eloquent and flattering speech, in which he praises Antilochus and agrees to give him the mare, all the while insisting that the prize is rightfully his ("even though she is mine").

And he spoke addressing him with winged words:
"Antilochus, I for my part now yield to you,
despite my anger, since you were by no means deranged or foolish
before this, only now your youth overcame your intelligence.
Just avoid trying to deceive your superiors again,   605
for no other man of the Achaeans would quickly dissuade me;
but you have endured much suffering and difficulty,
and so have your good father and brother, for my sake.
Therefore, I am persuaded by your entreaty and will give you
the mare, even though she is mine, so that these men also
will   610
know that my spirit is never reckless or unyielding."
So he spoke and to Antilochus' companion Noemon, he gave
the mare to take away. And then he took the gleaming cauldron
[the prize for third-place].

I have quoted this scene at some length because it is the fullest example we have of a process of negotiation that achieves a resolution to a dispute that is acceptable to both parties and (it goes without saying) to the rest of the community that is present. The process is unusual in that Menelaus first uses the language of more formal dispute-settlement, treating the group of other Greek leaders as a quasi-judicial body with himself in the role of a disputant seeking a settlement. But he then switches, putting himself in the role of the judge, and proposes a settlement himself. Menelaus' proposed settlement involves an oath, but Antilochus ignores this and the whole question of his allegedly unfair maneuver, and instead addresses the underlying issues of status and honor by making a highly respectful offer to give Menelaus his prize. In this way, the final settlement will confirm Menelaus' superior status (his *aretē*), satisfy his honor, and appease his anger, while leaving Antilochus in possession of the mare. This is a good example of how eloquent words on both sides can lead to a settlement that is "straight" in the sense of acceptable to all. Whether it is "just" by some higher standard (i.e., did Antilochus in fact play by the rules? Does he deserve the mare?) remains unanswered, but in the end, this question seems beside the point. Homeric disputants generally seek acceptable resolutions, which often involve many other factors besides the question of strict, rule-bound justice.

Of course, not all attempts to resolve disputes succeed, and before we conclude this examination of oral procedure in Homer and Hesiod, it will be instructive to examine one dispute that is not resolved. Formal or informal procedures tend to succeed when the litigants themselves seek a resolution, as in the examples considered thus far. But intervention by a third party may not work when the litigants are not ready to seek a settlement, especially if they are of high standing in the community. This is the case in the dispute that sets off the *Iliad*, the quarrel between Agamemnon and Achilles at the beginning of Book One. This dispute rapidly escalates until the two nearly come to blows, but at one point, after Achilles has poured out a string of invectives against Agamemnon, Nestor rises, uninvited, to intervene (*Iliad* 1.247–9).

> Before them Nestor
> of Pylos arose, the clear speaker of sweet words.
> From his honeyed tongue his voice flowed sweetly.

The description Homer gives us of Nestor before he speaks emphasizes his age and his ability as a public speaker; and the resemblance to Hesiod's description of a king settling disputes indicates that Homer is here presenting Nestor as a judge who would settle this dispute with his eloquence.[20] And not only does he set forth his proposal in eloquent and ceremonious words, but the settlement he proposes is fair and reasonable, and it would serve the best interests of both to accept it. Moreover, Nestor understands that the issue here, as in the dispute between Menelaus and Antilochus, is not so much the material prize (in this case, the girl Briseis), but status and respect, and his settlement tries to address these. But despite all this, and despite Agamemnon's explicit praise of the proposal,[21] the anger of both heroes has reached the point where they do not even consider

---

[20] Note especially 249 ("From his honeyed tongue his voice flowed sweetly" – τοῦ καὶ ἀπὸ γλώσσης μέλιτος γλυκίων ῥέεν αὐδή) and compare Hesiod, *Theogony* 83–4 ("on his tongue [the Muses] pour sweet honey and soothing words flow from his mouth" – τῷ μὲν ἐπὶ γλώσσῃ γλυκερὴν χείουσιν ἐέρσην, | τοῦ δ' ἔπε' ἐκ στόματος ῥεῖ μείλιχα).

[21] *Iliad* 1.286: "you spoke all that fittingly" (*panta ... kata moiran eeipes*).

a settlement. Moreover, their high status makes them less susceptible to any pressure to accept a compromise, even one that may have the tacit support of all the other Achaeans. But although Nestor's attempt at settlement fails, the scene illustrates the same basic procedure we find elsewhere in Homer and Hesiod.

All these scenes allow us to understand that before the invention of alphabetic writing in Greece an oral procedure for peaceful dispute-settlement had developed as an alternative to violence and self-help. In Homer, most people who suffer harm act on their own, or with relatives and friends, to take revenge on or exact retribution from the offender. In cases of homicide, of course, it is the victim's relatives who seek revenge, as we see from about two dozen examples in Homer.[22] The most common response by far to homicide, even if it is accidental, is for the victim's family to ensure that the killer goes into exile, with the threat of death if he does not. This provision is affirmed by Odysseus right after he and Telemachus kill the suitors (*Odyssey* 23.118–20 – see below).[23] But there is also evidence of a different custom, that blood-money should be accepted after a homicide. This rule is cited by Ajax (*Iliad* 9.632–6 – see below), but is not evident elsewhere in Homer except in the trial depicted on Achilles' shield, where the dispute concerns blood-money, not the homicide itself. Thus, the practice of accepting blood-money and the practice of pursuing the killer into exile exist side by side in Homer, though the latter is far more common. We can surmise, however, that as it became more common for the killer and the victim's relatives to seek a peaceful resolution rather than pursue violent revenge, then the communal pressure to reach a settlement would grow stronger and the procedures whereby the rest of the community and its leaders helped the parties reach a settlement would gradually become more formal and would convey more authority.

A dual system of self-help and public procedures for resolving disputes is also evident in some other early societies. Of particular interest in this regard is medieval Iceland as portrayed in the Icelandic sagas (roughly 930–1030 CE). Since this culture raises the issue of oral law and may shed light on the question of oral law in Greece, it is worth pausing for a moment to examine it. Like the world of Homer, medieval Iceland is known primarily through literary sources. In the sagas, when someone is killed, a relative's first reaction is almost always to seek revenge by killing in

---

[22] There is a complete list in Gagarin 1981a: 6–10.
[23] There is also an allusion to this rule in *Odyssey* 3.196–7: "It is a good thing for a man who is killed to leave behind a son, since he can punish his father's killer."

return; in this he usually has the support of his family or other friends. In some cases, however, he is inclined, or is persuaded by others, to accept compensation instead, and in this event, a relatively formal procedure for reaching a settlement is evident. Disputants who want to settle their differences peacefully normally wait until the summer meeting of the Althing, the annual assembly where local chiefs and other important men from all over Iceland gather, often accompanied by many friends and followers, to discuss matters of concern to all. At a certain point during this meeting disputes are heard. The disputing parties will have consulted beforehand with other leading men in the country, seeking their advice and support. If both parties are willing to accept a peaceful settlement, this is normally arranged after a period of negotiation. The process bears some similarity to what is pictured on the shield of Achilles, but there are also important differences between the procedures in these two societies, in particular the apparent existence in Iceland of specific, detailed rules of procedure that are not evident anywhere in Greece.

These are most clearly seen in *Njal's Saga*,[24] which portrays a society with a number of "lawmen," individuals with high standing in the society who possess legal expertise that they learned from their predecessors. One of these lawmen with the greatest expertise is elected lawspeaker for a three-year term, and reelection is common. His duty is to recite one-third of the laws every year at the meeting of the Althing; the cycle is repeated every three years. He also decides cases where there are uncertainties about the law or disagreements among the lesser lawmen. In the culminating scene of *Njal's Saga*, one group brings charges of homicide against another group and the complex legal maneuverings on both sides are described in some detail (Chapters 141–4). First, several challenges to jurors' qualifications are rebutted and then it is argued that the case was brought in the wrong court. Further charges of bribery and introducing irrelevant material are filed and a conviction is obtained but is then overturned when the number of judges is challenged. Several of these disagreements are referred to the lawspeaker. In the end, no verdict is reached and a battle ensues, which is finally settled informally among the disputants themselves (Chapter 145).

Although the legal process does not in the end succeed in resolving this dispute, the episode sheds interesting light on the use of oral rules in the process. It portrays a society that apparently relies only on oral processes for

---

[24] I have used the Penguin translation by Magnusson and Pálsson (1960). A good brief account of Scandinavian law is Jones 1984: 345–8. For a fuller account see Byock 2001: 170–84.

the preservation and transmittal of detailed rules of procedure (which comprise most of the rules cited by the lawmen or the lawspeaker in *Njal's Saga*). A premium is put on a lawman's ability to remember the most rules, and in particular to remember obscure rules that others may not know or may have forgotten. Thus, medieval Iceland appears to be one of the clearest examples of what many scholars mean by oral law – a fixed set of specific rules preserved and transmitted orally – and Iceland is sometimes looked to by those arguing for a similar sort of oral law in early Greece. Of course, the existence of such a system in Iceland does not mean that a similar system existed in Homeric times, and even in Iceland the matter is not so simple as it first appears.

Like Homer and Hesiod, the sagas give no evidence of writing being used in the legal process. But writing had been introduced into both cultures before the poems were put in their final form, and we know that in Iceland (though not in Greece) written laws existed long before *Njal's Saga* was set in its present form around 1280.[25] Serious doubts have been raised, moreover, about the reliability of the sagas as historical sources, and some scholars now dispute the historicity of the picture we have from *Njal's Saga* of the oral preservation of laws, their annual recital at the Althing, and their use in resolving disputes.[26] Studies of the preservation and transmission of oral texts have shown that verbatim transmission can be achieved only very rarely (if ever), and only in works composed according to very rigid metrical and syntactical constraints that are preserved in a culture (often religious) that puts a premium on completely accurate memorization.[27] Thus, we cannot know for certain whether the medieval Icelanders in fact transmitted sets of rules from

---

[25] A formal written codification took place in 1117–18 and the process of writing laws probably began in the late eleventh century (Byock 2001: 309–10).

[26] Miller 1990: 43–76 argues that the sagas can validly be used, though with caution, for historical information, but he considers the great legal scenes in *Njal's Saga* particularly unreliable, and others agree that the scene described above may well represent thirteenth-century law, aided by writing, rather than conditions at the time of the saga (Jones 1984: 346). In addition, *Njal's Saga* in particular shows Christian influence, which would be opposed to the traditional system of feud and settlement of the earlier period, and this may have led to further distortion; see Lönnroth 1976: 143–9. On the other hand, Sigurdsson has recently argued (2004, esp. Chapter 1, 50–92: "From Lawspeaker to Lawbook") that not only did lawspeakers rely on oral traditions before writing but many continued to do so for a century or more after the introduction of writing ("the tradition of oral learning remained strong at least into the 13th century and was held to be of considerable importance in the world of politics *vis-a-vis* the new technique of writing that had been gaining ground since early in the 12th").

[27] Questions about the accurate oral transmission of data will be discussed further below, Chapter Four.

lawspeaker to lawspeaker without any use of written texts,[28] but if they did, the transmitted rules would almost certainly have varied over time.[29]

If for the moment, however, we ignore these questions about the possible role of writing and look only at the way law works in the sagas, where procedures for settling disputes are portrayed as entirely oral, we see that disputants and lawmen may appeal to and cite rules and customs of the community at all stages of the process – in pleading cases, proposing settlements, or simply voicing opinions. In *Njal's Saga* these rules, which almost all pertain to procedure, can be quite detailed, as for example, when a litigant asserts, "The law says that any man has the right to be on a jury if he owns three hundreds of land or more, even though he owns no milch animals. The law also says that any man has the right to be on a jury if he owns milch animals, even though he owns no land" (Chapter 142, p. 306). The speaker's opponents do not know this obscure rule and so they ask the lawspeaker, who confirms that it is correct, though very few know it.

Rules such as this may be what some people (e.g., C. P. Roth 1976) have in mind when they suggest that in prehistoric Greece a judge's expertise lay in his superior knowledge of orally preserved and transmitted rules, which he would then recite in order to settle a dispute. But the rules found in Homer and Hesiod are quite different. Kings are often said to know *themistes* (general "rules" or "ordinances"), which are said to come from Zeus or from the gods more generally. These are probably the traditional rules and customs of the community, and every judge (and most other people too) would be familiar with them. But none of these rules in Homer contains the same degree of detail as the rule in *Njal's Saga* cited above. Rather, the Homeric rules are phrased in general terms and scattered throughout various episodes, and many more such rules undoubtedly existed in other contexts that no longer survive.

One likely candidate for the sort of general rule of conduct that would count as one of the *themistes* is the advice Ajax gives Achilles when he is

---

[28] Foote 1977 reviews stylistic features of Scandinavian laws that may indicate oral preservation and transmission. There are very few such features in the earliest Icelandic laws as compared with Swedish and Norse laws. Foote leaves open the question whether or not this means that written texts of laws were in use at an early period in Iceland, but he makes clear that, at the very least, assessment of the orality of early Icelandic law is a very complex matter.

[29] Another example sometimes cited of "oral laws" is the Albanian *Kanun* ("Code"), a loose collection of communal norms and standards, going back (it is said) to Lekë Dukagjinit in the fifteenth century (though thought to be much older), that was assembled in the form of a code in the early twentieth century (Fox 1989). But many questions surround the exact status and the nature of these rules before they were codified in writing.

trying to persuade him to put aside his anger and resolve his differences with Agamemnon (*Iliad* 9.632–6):

> A person accepts from the killer of his brother
> or his dead son the blood-price (*poinē*),
> and when he has paid a large compensation, the killer remains in his land,
> and the person's heart and manly anger are curbed,
> when he has received the blood-money.

This rule could certainly be cited in the trial portrayed on Achilles' shield, but as a rule of (oral) law it has two major shortcomings. First, it describes a practice in rather general terms leaving crucial questions unanswered: Must a person accept the *poinē*? Can another relative accept it if there is no brother or father? How much compensation qualifies as "large"?

Even more problematic is the rule's authority. There is no person in Homer who can formally authorize a rule, and so a rule's authority can only come from the consensus of the community, which it derives in part from being recited repeatedly by bards like Homer. But this tradition-based authority is tenuous, and can be called into question if, for example, someone cites a different rule that is equally sanctioned by tradition. Take, for example, Odysseus' words to Telemachus after they have killed the suitors (*Odyssey* 23.118–20).

> A man who kills another man in his community
> even one who leaves only a few avengers behind
> that man flees into exile, leaving behind family and fatherland.

This rule directly contradicts the rule cited by Ajax. Both cannot be authoritative at the same time, nor can both be treated as (oral) laws. And it would be purely arbitrary to declare one a law and not the other. Although conflicting messages are a common feature of traditional popular rules such as maxims,[30] a legal system cannot tolerate such obvious contradictions in its laws.

These are among the problems that arise if one speaks of "oral laws" in Homer. The root of the problem is the absence of any specific designation of certain rules as laws as opposed to other rules that are not so designated – in Hart's terms, there is no rule of recognition by which someone could know which rules are laws and which are not. This is clear if we consider the

---

[30] E.g., "Haste makes waste" vs. "He who hesitates is lost." Or, "There's no such thing as a free lunch" vs. "Don't look a gift horse in the mouth."

advice Phoenix gives Achilles, shortly before Ajax's advice. Phoenix evokes
the allegorical spirits of Prayer (*Iliad* 9.508–12):

> If a man respects these daughters of Zeus when they approach,
> to him they give great benefits, and they listen to his requests;
> but if a man spurns them and harshly rejects their plea,
> then they go to Zeus, son of Cronos, and entreat him
> to bring ruin on the man so that he is led astray and punished.

We would not call this rule that one should respect prayer a law, but
nothing here indicates that it differs in kind from the rule about accepting
compensation that Ajax refers to a few lines later.[31] That we might call
Ajax's advice a law (oral law) but not Phoenix's stems from our own
assumptions about which kinds of issues are the provenance of law and
which are not, and we would be using modern criteria to make a distinction
the Greeks at this time did not make.

In short, we cannot simply designate as an oral law any rule that looks
like a law to us, or that the Greeks might have considered one of their
themistes. In order to designate a rule as a law, we need some means of
"recognizing" it – of marking it and certain other rules as having a special
status or authority. Writing is the normal way of doing this, though other
means are possible, such as the authoritative word of a lawspeaker. But no
such figure or comparable institution existed in early Greece.

Furthermore, rules as such do not seem to have much of a role in early
Greek dispute-settlement. Judges in Homer and Hesiod do not excel by
their knowledge of obscure rules, like the lawspeaker in *Njal's Saga*, but by
their ability to devise an acceptable resolution to a dispute. Of course,
general rules, often unspoken, form the background for these settlements:
killing a member of your community is wrong; so is stealing another's
property, and so forth. But the disputes that arise are not settled, as far as
we can see, by applying rules such as these but, as we saw in the dispute
between Menelaus and Archilochus, by negotiated *ad hoc* solutions that are
acceptable to both sides.[32] Similarly, Nestor's proposed settlement of the
dispute between Agamemnon and Achilles is ultimately grounded on the

---

[31] Similarly, we might consider many of the rules in Hesiod's *Works and Days* laws, but not others:
compare "wealth is not to be seized; god-given wealth is much better" (320) with "be friends with one
who is friendly and visit the one who visits you" (353). We might classify the former as a law, but
surely not the latter. See further below n. 36.

[32] Cf. D. Roebuck 2001: 67, who remarks with regard to all the disputes in Patroclus' funeral games,
that "rules do not play a predominant part in decision-making." He mentions fairness, rank, and
"political reality" as other factors that influence settlements.

very general rule that both superior warriors and commanders-in-chief deserve respect and the booty that goes with it, but his proposal that they put aside their anger and respect one another is not based on any specific rule but is tailored to the emotional course the proceedings have taken up to this point. Homeric Greeks put great emphasis on resolving disputes peacefully, but processes, not rules, were their means of doing this. In terms of the distinction made by Comaroff and Roberts (1981: 4, etc.) between "rule-centered" and "processual" paradigms, the Homeric Greeks are much closer to the processual end of the scale.

For all these reasons, I will not speak of oral laws (or an oral law) in preliterate Greece, although I find the expression "oral law" useful to designate the totality of procedures and rules (including customs, norms, and traditions) that regulated disputes among preliterate Greeks (see further R. Thomas 2005). And in fact those who maintain that early Greece had oral laws generally draw on post-Homeric evidence (Piccirilli 1981, R. Thomas 1996). In arguing for oral laws, they cite three related phenomena, unwritten laws, sung laws, and officials who remembered laws.

The first category, unwritten laws (*agraphoi nomoi*), includes among other things the famous appeal of Sophocles' Antigone to "the unwritten and unfailing *nomima* ("rules")[33] of the gods" (*Antigone* 454–5), and Pericles' praise for those *nomoi* ("laws") "which, being unwritten, are agreed to bring shame [on those who violate them]" (Thucydides 2.37.3). These and other passages have been studied by Ostwald, who concludes (1973: 101), "All that *agraphoi nomoi* ["unwritten laws"], *agrapha dikaia* ["unwritten justice"], and related expressions have in common is that they are envisaged as different from those rules and regulations which form the valid and published written code of laws of the state." In other words, phrases such as these express the sense that there are valid rules or principles of conduct other than the written *nomoi* of the state, but "as they constitute norms that are only negatively defined, their conceptual content is as varied as anything opposed to the written statutes can be" (*ibid.* 103). Thus, these references to unwritten laws give us no reason to think that the Greeks ever developed a concept of a recognized and authoritative body of unwritten or oral laws.

One factor complicating this discussion is that the common word for a law or statute in the classical period, *nomos* (pl. *nomoi*), was not used for written laws in the archaic period. In early Greece *nomos* designated any traditional custom, practice, or rule of conduct, and *nomos* retained these

[33] *Nomima*, a diminutive form of *nomos*, is often translated "laws" here, but the term makes it clear that these are general moral rules, not laws in the strict sense.

meanings even after it began to be used for written statutes, around 500 (Ostwald 1969). When the Greeks first started writing down laws in the seventh century they did not use the term *nomos* for them but instead used terms like *thesmos* ("ordinance"), *graphos* ("writing"), and *rhētra* ("pronouncement"), or variations of these terms. In the classical period, it may be evident from the context in some cases that *nomos* designates a written law or statute; in other cases it clearly designates a general rule or custom; and sometimes the sense is unclear or both senses are present. But in archaic poetry, *nomos* only designates custom, rule, or traditional practice, never a written law. And later, when *nomos* acquired the additional meaning of a written law, it was this extension of its use that stimulated the Greeks to begin speaking of unwritten laws.

The line between law and custom may be a fine one, but in most cases we distinguish them without much difficulty, and the Greeks did too. In the archaic period they used *nomos* for the latter and created new terms for the former, but even when *nomos* could be used of both written laws and unwritten customs, the Greeks knew the difference between them. This is clear from a passage in Plato's *Laws* (793a–c), where the discussion turns to the education of the young, who are first taught general habits of good behavior. The Athenian Stranger remarks that all these rules are commonly called "unwritten laws" (*agrapha nomima* – the same term used by Antigone) and are also called "ancestral customs" (*patrioi nomoi*), which are the same thing, but they have agreed that these should not be called "laws" (*nomoi*). But neither should they be neglected because in a constitution they act as bonds between the laws, both those that have already been enacted in writing and those that are yet to be written.[34] In this passage Plato uses *nomos* for both "custom" and "law," but the two meanings are clearly kept separate.

In the case of sung laws, the problem of terminology is even more serious, since *nomos* can also mean a "tune" or "song," as well as a law. The main evidence for sung laws is Athenaeus' report (619b) that "at Athens even the laws of Charondas were sung at wine-parties." R. Thomas (1996: 14–16) also cites later evidence for sung laws, including a passage from Strabo (12.2.9) that the Mazakenoi in Cappadocia used Charondas' laws and had an official called a "lawsinger" (*nomōidos*) who explained the laws to them, and another from Aelian (*VH* 2.39) that the Cretans required free children to learn the laws with music in order to remember them better. The main obstacle to treating these sung *nomoi* as oral laws is

---

[34] For further discussion of this passage, see Bertrand 1999: 60–2.

that in all cases, what is being sung are either actual laws that were previously written, or a poetic version of these laws, presumably greatly simplified from their written form, whose legal authority would still be their written version. This is a far cry from orally composed, preserved, and transmitted laws.

Moreover, the Athenians certainly, and the Mazakenoi probably, did not treat the laws of Charondas as their own laws, since he was lawgiver for the city of Catana in Sicily. The Athenians had their own laws, and it is unlikely that the Mazakenoi, who are far removed in time and place from Catana, simply adopted Charondas' laws. If they did, and if they had an official called a "lawsinger," it is not impossible that he resembled in some ways the Icelandic lawspeaker, but even so, the laws he would be singing would have been written laws or simplified oral versions of these. As for the Athenians, it seems highly unlikely that they sang actual laws at their drinking parties. We know a fair amount about behavior at Greek symposia, but the recital of a set of laws is otherwise unattested and seems extremely improbable. Even the idea of setting Greek laws as we have them to music is problematic, for the legal texts we know from inscriptions or literary preservation are prosaic in the extreme. It is nearly impossible to imagine someone putting, say, the Gortyn laws or Draco's homicide law to music. It is not impossible that music was used by children in Crete or elsewhere to help them memorize laws, but if so, the rules they learned were probably simplified oral versions of written laws.[35]

The most likely explanation for these reports of sung *nomoi* is that they refer not to laws in the strict sense but either to *nomoi* in the musical sense ("melodies") or (more likely) to general rules, such as those in Hesiod's *Works and Days*, put to music, probably for teaching purposes. As we saw, this work contains a mixture of rules that might be considered legal and others that are religious, moral, or practical (esp. agricultural).[36] A collection of *nomoi* like these could be taken up and chanted by Greeks anywhere, and since Charondas was a legendary lawgiver, his name might have become attached to a report about singing *nomoi*.[37] As I have said, we may, if we wish, select some of the rules in *Works and Days* and treat these as

---

[35] A parallel is often seen in Cicero's report (*De legibus* 2.59) that as a boy he learned the Twelve Tables as a *carmen necessarium* ("required text," not necessarily sung). But whether sung or recited, the Twelve Tables were still written law.

[36] Some examples from *Works and Days* are "as much as you can, sacrifice to the immortal gods" (336), "call your friend to a feast but let your enemy be" (342), and "when the Pleiades, daughters of Atlas, are rising, begin your plowing" (383–4).

[37] Ruzé 2001 also rejects the idea that actual laws were sung; she suggests Solon's elegies as a possible example of what were later called sung *nomoi*.

(oral) laws, but these rules still differ significantly from written laws. And as we will see (Chapter Four), putting a rule in writing changes the nature and function of the rule in important ways. Thus, before writing we can speak of oral law – viz. judicial procedures without writing – but not oral laws.

The third type of evidence sometimes cited in support of the concept of oral law in Greece is that inscriptions from Gortyn and other Dorian cities sometimes mention an official connected with legal activity called a *mnamōn* (*mnēmōn*, pl. *mnamones*, *mnēmones*) or "rememberer." There is some evidence that this official also existed in the sixth century, notably the agreement with Spensithios, which we will examine in detail in Chapter Five. Spensithios' title is *poinikastas* or "writer," not *mnamōn*, but the agreement requires that he and his descendants should "write and remember (*mnamoneuein*) public business, both divine and human." Since the duties of the *mnamōn* that are specified in the Gortyn Code involve remembering but not writing, the agreement with Spensithios most likely requires him to remember what happened at trials and other public events and perhaps to write down legislation. But nothing in the agreement with Spensithios or elsewhere indicates that a *mnamōn* remembered a set of (oral) laws. Thus, he seems to have been a living rememberer of judicial proceedings, but not a singer of laws.

In sum, although preliterate Greece as portrayed in the poems of Homer and Hesiod can be described as a period of oral law, no specific set or body of rules existed at the time that could be identified as oral laws. Like many other oral cultures, the Greeks at this time had relatively well-developed procedures for resolving disputes and regulating conflict. They also had orally preserved customs and traditions, norms of behavior, and other rules of all sorts that guided their behavior and influenced the course of these procedures. But within this "large body of assumptions and traditions" (R. Thomas 2005: 53–4) no subset of rules was marked in any way that would allow us to designate them as oral or unwritten laws. Using the expression "oral laws" may usefully convey the point that there is a relation-ship between these oral customs and traditions and later written laws, but at the same time it obscures the important changes that occur when certain rules are written. Thus, I find it more useful to avoid the expression "oral laws" and speak instead of oral law as existing in the context of orally preserved and transmitted rules.

That the Greeks themselves were aware of the radical changes that writing could bring about is suggested by the story of Deioces, the first king of the Medes, the beginning of which I related earlier (Herodotus 1.96–100). Recall that Deioces began his career in a system of oral law in which he heard disputes brought to him voluntarily by the people. In this fully public system he earned a high reputation by the superiority of his judgments. But one day he abruptly stopped hearing disputes. As a result, violence and lawlessness broke out everywhere, and in desperation the Medes decided they needed a king. Naturally they chose Deioces, who promptly restored law and order by creating a very different kind of legal system. Like an oriental despot, he removed himself completely from public view, so that all access to him was controlled by his advisers. As for settling disputes, "people put their cases in writing and had them sent in to him. And he decided the cases brought in to him and sent them back" (Herodotus 1.100.1). There is no historical truth to this as an account of the unification of the Medes,[38] but it indicates that Herodotus and his contemporaries considered a judicial process dependent on writing as characteristic of a monarchy or tyranny. As we shall see, the Greeks themselves managed to use writing while maintaining the traditional oral and public nature of the judicial process, but their attitude toward writing was often ambivalent (Steiner 1994): they understood its potential both as a means for bringing law to the people and as a tool for antidemocratic repression. The story of Greek law is in large part the story of the unique way in which they used this double-edged technology for the benefit of the community.

The story of Deioces ends with a system of written judicial decisions, but it begins, as we have seen, with the regular oral procedure in early Greece by which all members of the community can seek resolution of their disputes. The procedure is public, it takes place in a public space, often the agora, and it is regularly attended by many other members of the community. It is also fully oral, a series of speech acts, with everyone, disputants, judges, and the community, contributing their views. None of these speech acts is constrained to take a specific form, and there is no sign of the formalism found in Roman and many other legal systems. Even when someone proposes a formal procedure such as an oath, as Menelaus does in *Iliad* 23, he apparently has full control over the wording of his proposal, although he, like all Homeric speakers, will likely include in it some traditional formulaic language.

The most common word for the act of settling or judging a dispute, *dikazein*, essentially means "speak so as to resolve a dispute" (so Allen 2000: 317). Judgment may be rendered by a single judge or by several, and they may be kings or elders or other respected members of the community, but

---

[38] Although the story is set in Mesopotamia and Deioces was probably a historical person, he was probably not a king or a Mede or a unifier; see Helm 1981.

they are apparently not professional judges, for in Homer, at least, they have many other duties. But the Greeks (like the Tiv) appear to have been a fairly contentious people, and judging appears to have been one of the main tasks of kings in peacetime. Even the legendary Minos in the underworld is portrayed as settling disputes for the dead souls who crowd around him; and in Hesiod, it seems as if almost all that kings do is settle disputes.

Settling disputes is a well-established and important communal institution, to which leaders devote a significant amount of time. In this quasi-formal process the customs and traditions of the community and the general rules of conduct they embody play an informal role, and in the poetic tradition some of these customary rules may be formulated as rules of conduct in the same general form as written laws have later. But no body of "oral laws" ever became an authoritative text of rules that could be considered the laws of the community. Not until the invention of writing and its subsequent use in the process of writing legislation did the Greeks create laws for their community that were distinct from their customs and traditions.

CHAPTER 2

Writing and Written Laws

Although writing makes no appearance in the poems of Homer and Hesiod, when these poems assumed their final form ca. 700, writing was already widespread in the Greek world. Our earliest examples of writing, scratched or painted on pottery, come from around 750 or a little earlier. Whether this means that writing was introduced not long before this date, or two or three centuries earlier is a matter of debate.[1] For our purposes, the exact date is of little importance. We can only use the material we have, and since none of the inscriptions from the first century of our evidence is legal in nature, we can be fairly confident that whatever the date of the invention of the alphabet, the Greeks did not begin writing laws before ca. 650.

As we noted earlier (Introduction) after the collapse of Bronze-Age civilization in the twelfth century, a new kind of writing emerged, an alphabetic script that developed from a Phoenician alphabetic script, with the important innovation that the Greeks added signs for vowels, which were lacking in the Near-Eastern alphabets of the time. This innovation made the Greek script easier to read than the consonant alphabets of the Near East (see most recently B. Powell 2002). As far as we know, all other scripts at the time, including Linear B, cuneiform, and Egyptian hieroglyphics, were written and read by a small number of professional scribes, who would have been familiar with the subjects written about and could thus fairly easily supply the correct vowels (for

---

[1] Most classical scholars accept an eighth- or late ninth-century date for the introduction of writing to Greece; see Jeffery 1982: 823, and more strongly Johnston 1990: 426–7. Some Near-Eastern scholars, on the other hand, point to the shapes of the earliest Greek letters, which seem closest to a Phoenician script of the ninth or tenth centuries, and conclude that the Greeks must have invented writing earlier than the eighth century, even if no examples of earlier writing have yet been found; see Naveh 1991, and for a different theory Isserlin 1991. Surveys of the issues can be found in Murray 1993: 92–101; Whitley 2001: 128–33; Hall 2007: 56–9.

consonant scripts).[2] When the vowel sounds are made explicit, as in the Greek alphabet, a text could then be read even by someone who was not familiar with the subject or the words of the text, since without prior knowledge they would be able to pronounce a word phonetically purely on the basis of the letters they saw. Writing with a full alphabet is thus easier to read, especially for inexperienced readers, and the invention of this alphabet in Greece would have opened up the possibility of a higher degree of literacy than existed in the contemporary Near East or in the earlier age of Linear B.[3]

The reasons for inventing a full alphabetic script have been much debated. The traditional view is that Greek writing was the work of merchants who used it for commercial purposes (Lombardo 1988; W. Harris 1996: 60–1). This is the generally accepted reason for the invention of writing in many other cultures, but if that were the reason in Greece, it seems odd that no early Greek text is commercial (B. Powell 1989: 347), and in fact very little commercial writing survives from before the fourth century. Even if most commercial texts were written on papyrus, references to commerce ought to appear in other texts if this were the main reason for writing. Also unlikely is the recent theory of B. Powell (1989, 1991), that the alphabet was invented to record the Homeric poems. Although some of the earliest inscriptions are in hexameter verse, most are not and most have nothing to do with epic matters. Moreover, the lack of the long vowels *eta* and *omega*, which are absent from early inscriptions, would have significantly hindered the accurate transcription of Homer. But Powell is right to emphasize the closeness of the Greek alphabet to speech (B. Powell 2002: 112–24), and so I would accept the conclusion that the alphabet was invented in order to record speech, but not necessarily poetic speech.

As we noted, there are no laws among these early Greek texts, but a brief survey of the first century of writing in Greece may help provide a context

---

[2] Most scholars accept that Near-Eastern scripts were more difficult to read and writing was restricted to a relatively small group of scribes. M. Powell 1981 argues that "cuneiform was not as difficult as usually assumed," and "the superiority of the alphabet over cuneiform has been exaggerated," but he is speaking of later Semitic (consonant) alphabets, not Greek. Palaima 1987 argues that it was not difficult to write Linear B, and that the restriction of writing to administrative matters and the absence of personal texts was thus the result of societal attitudes not technological considerations.

[3] These implications of the Greek invention of the alphabet were first proposed by Havelock 1976, 1982, etc. Herrenschmidt 2000 argues that in consonant alphabets, reading requires simultaneous interpretation (96: "understanding became blended with reading"), but "with the complete [i.e. Greek] alphabet, reading is not identical to understanding" (101). Thus, in theory, "with the Greek alphabet, one could read everything without understanding anything." So far so good, but when she adds that "the complete alphabet introduced a body-mind dualism," I fail to follow her.

for the earliest legal writing. Several recent surveys of early Greek inscriptions[4] show that the earliest (750–650) were written by many different people. Powell (1989) lists more than fifty shorter inscriptions, most of them with fewer than six words. These include many that give personal names, often the name of the writer, and are scratched or painted on pottery ("Kalikleas made me," "I am the cup of Korakos"), on tombstones ("This is the tomb of Deinias, whom the shameless sea destroyed"), or on votive figures that were intended as gifts to the gods ("Isodikos dedicated me as a votive to [Apollo] Pythios"). Some are erotic, such as "Eumelos is best in the dance." Other early inscriptions are typical of travelers even today, as when Greek mercenary soldiers in Egypt carved their names (in Doric dialect) on a statue at Abu-Simbel, Egypt in 591 (Jeffery 1990: 358, no. 48). Moreover, various short phrases were written on flat rocks in the Attic countryside, some of them apparently by shepherds with time on their hands.[5] And about 15 percent of the shorter inscriptions Powell surveys are abecedaria, presumably written by people who are learning to write, who would practice their new skill on pieces of broken pottery or other materials. Finally, Powell examines five longer inscriptions, several in verse, either on pottery, which was probably intended for use in symposia, or on dedicatory statues.

These remains – and they presumably represent only a small fraction of what was actually written in this period – show the widespread diffusion of alphabetic writing in Greece during the first century after its discovery. There does not appear to be any duplication of handwriting, and the rather crude nature of much of Greek early writing, together with the prominence of abecedaria, makes it clear that these were written not by scribes who specialized in writing, but by individuals from a full range of social classes, who learned to write themselves.[6] Writing was clearly a social activity, in the sense that the texts were almost always intended to be read by others, and one senses an exuberance in these early texts, as if

---

[4] A convenient account is B. Powell 1989; see also Jeffery 1982: 831–2. Recent finds have added to the total number of inscriptions but have not changed the overall picture (see Jeffery 1990: 58–63, 430; Whitley 1997; Langdon 2005).

[5] In some of these inscriptions the author identifies himself as a shepherd (Merle Langdon, personal communication; see also the notice in *SEG* 49.2).

[6] Much of our evidence may come from an aristocratic, largely sympotic, context, but there is an inherent bias in the evidence toward such a context. As Snodgrass argues with regard to Attic vase inscriptions, "if the application of painted inscriptions to the *symposion* is so self-evident, then the remarkable fact is not that so many, but that *only* some two-thirds of the inscriptions are on vessels which lend themselves to this context" (2000: 28). See further below n. 9.

people were rushing to learn this new art so that they could show off their skill to their friends and associates. One also senses that people were experiencing the power of writing to give the writer and his message greater authority (Várhelyi 1996).

Equally interesting is the absence of certain kinds of inscriptions that are common in other early Mediterranean cultures. There is no evidence in Greece at this time of the kind of record keeping or information storage connected with economic or political administration that dominates the earliest writing in the Near East as well as the Linear B texts, or of historical accounts, often celebrating the deeds of a monarch, which are common in Egypt and the Near East.[7] This is not surprising. Monarchy was a peripheral phenomenon in archaic Greece, and Greek monarchs from Homer on must work with an assembly or smaller group that has a significant degree of authority.[8] Neither in these areas nor in cities ruled by tyrants do we find the large, centralized administrative structures that are the rule in the non-Greek or Bronze-Age societies. The Greeks must have been motivated to write by something other than the need to administer large territories or to facilitate commercial activity. And whatever their motivation, the writing they invented was not limited to a small group closely associated with the ruling elite, but was practiced by a wide range of members of the community.[9]

The other characteristic of these earliest written texts that is important for our purposes is that they include no public documents:[10]

---

[7] "Eighty-five percent of the tablets from the early levels at Uruk are economic" (C. B. F. Walker 1987: 11). The first non-economic texts (such as dedications) were written 200 to 300 years later than the earliest inscriptions. For details see Nissen 1993. The Linear B documents record almost nothing but commercial and other activity associated with the palace administrations. Not a single personal graffito survives written in Linear B (see Palaima 1987).

[8] For monarchies in Epirus and Macedonia, see Davies 2000; Carlier 2000.

[9] Hölkeskamp 2000: 84 stresses the difference in this regard between Greece and the Near East. Stoddart and Whitley 1988 contrast Attica and Etruria, noting that in the former the introduction of an alphabetic script led to "generalised social literacy," whereas in Etruria "literacy was mainly the preserve of an élite ... tied ... to the élite's need for ideological legitimation and interpersonal exchange" (771). But Cornell 1991 examines the evidence for literacy in Etruria and Latium and concludes that "the surviving epigraphic evidence is unrepresentative, biased and misleading" (33), and that literacy was far more widespread (cf. Snodgrass 2000 for Attica, cited above, n. 6). For writing in Crete, see below, Chapter 3.

[10] By "public documents" I mean texts inscribed and displayed by a public authority, either individual or collective, concerning matters of public interest, as distinct from texts inscribed and displayed by private individuals to serve their own interests. This distinction is not rigid – many private inscriptions (e.g., epitaphs) were also intended for public viewing – but it is clear enough for our purposes.

not a single public inscription – decree, treaty, or remembrance of common martial exploit – not one dedication to a god on behalf of a public body; no inventories, catalogues, records of treasure, or building specifications; not one word connected with the doings of one state or collective body with another. (B. Powell 1989: 346)

And, I should add, not a single law or legal document, public or private. For whatever reason, at this time writing was still the province of private individuals, and the community had not yet begun to use writing to assert itself as a public or political entity.

About a century after the earliest inscriptions, however, in addition to the dedications, epitaphs, and other private graffiti that turn up earlier, public inscriptions begin to appear. The vast majority of these are legal in nature,[11] and virtually all of these are texts of laws.[12] There are no legal documents such as contracts, wills, or receipts, no indictments or verdicts, no judicial opinions, indeed, no legal texts whatsoever except for laws and related texts like treaties.[13] All references to written legal texts in archaic inscriptions, moreover, are to laws.

Legal inscriptions are found in many parts of the archaic Greek world, but for some reason a high proportion come from Crete.[14] Since we probably have only a small fraction of the texts originally inscribed on stone from this period, and nothing written on more perishable materials such as wood or papyrus, we cannot necessarily conclude that the Cretans wrote more laws than other Greeks; they may simply have inscribed more of them on stone, or (less likely) archaeologists may just have found more legal inscriptions on Crete than elsewhere. We are told, for instance, that Solon's many laws were written on wooden *axones*; had all such inscriptions been written on stone, our picture of archaic legislation would look different.

---

[11] See Jeffery 1990: 58–63. The non-legal public inscriptions are mostly lists of names of office holders or contest winners, and other public records.

[12] I include decrees in the general category of laws, and treaties can also be so classified to the extent that they have legal force. The study of these inscriptions is aided by two very useful recent collections of archaic legal inscriptions, Koerner 1993 (= *IGT*) and van Effenterre and Ruzé 1994–5 (= *Nomima*). Also helpful for the archaic period are the concordance in Fell 1997, and the detailed studies of many of these texts in Hölkeskamp 1999. The old collection of Dareste *et al.* 1891–1904 (*IJG*), which is not limited to the archaic period, is also occasionally useful. Paula Perlman and I are preparing a complete edition with translation and commentary of the archaic and classical laws from Crete, in which we will treat in more detail many of the texts discussed here.

[13] Some early curse tablets may have been intended to affect the outcome of a trial but for our purposes, at least, these are not legal texts.

[14] A slight majority (53 percent) of the entries in *IGT* are Cretan laws; the figure for *Nomima* is about 40 percent.

Thus, the accident of survival may distort our understanding of the nature and distribution of early legal texts. But it still appears that the Cretans were especially fond of writing laws.

In addition to the inscriptions, we have evidence of another sort for early legislation in the stories the Greeks later told about "the first lawgivers," who in the seventh and sixth centuries wrote laws for different cities. These stories vary in their reliability, and some scholars dismiss almost all of them as essentially worthless.[15] But several of these lawgivers are well known from other sources, particularly the Athenians Draco and Solon, and it seems unlikely to be mere coincidence that these stories place the activity of the earliest lawgivers in the seventh and sixth centuries, at roughly the same time as the inscriptional evidence indicates that laws were first being written. This suggests that at least some of these figures did live at about this time and did write laws, though the later stories may be misleading about the nature and scope of their legislation.

One point, repeatedly stressed by Hölkeskamp (1992, 1995, and most fully 1999), is that reports of large-scale archaic legislation tend to come from unreliable sources such as Diodorus and Plutarch, whereas more reliable authors report only that Zaleucus, Charondas, and the others "wrote laws," or attribute only one or two specific laws to a lawgiver. Hölkeskamp concludes that modern scholars are wrong to speak of early legislation on a large scale, and especially codification. The inscriptional evidence, he argues, suggests rather that early laws consisted of "single enactments, independent, complete and self-contained statutes" motivated by specific problems or crises (Hölkeskamp 1992: 91).

Hölkeskamp's observations are important but should not be taken too far: there is strong evidence that Solon, at least, enacted legislation on a large scale. Plutarch, though not the most reliable of authors, cites several of Solon's laws by *axōn* number and even reports seeing parts of Solon's original *axones*. And Solon himself (fr. 36 West) speaks of writing *thesmoi*, "laws" (in the plural). To be sure, in the fourth century many laws were attributed to Solon that were certainly enacted at a later time, but this does not mean that he did not also enact many laws himself. Ruschenbusch 1966 tries to sort out all the laws attributed to Solon according to the likely degree of authenticity; one may disagree with many of his decisions, but he nonetheless presents a strong case that Solon's original legislation contained a large number of provisions and addressed a wide range of different

---

[15] The strongest doubt has been registered by Hölkeskamp (see below). See also Szegedy-Maszak 1978; Gagarin 1986: 51–80.

matters (see further Chapter Three). Later authors who write about archaic legislation are highly selective and probably biased in favor of unusual or idiosyncratic laws; they are not seeking a balanced or comprehensive view of the lawgivers' activity but are looking for provisions that will exemplify a specific point. Thus, they are likely to cite only one or two laws from what may originally have been a much larger collection.

Another consideration is that most early inscriptions are fragmentary; sometimes only a few words survive from texts that must have been longer and in some cases may have been much longer. And as Osborne 1997 observes, many of the inscriptions which appear to preserve single enactments presuppose much other legislation from the same city. If we are willing to "connect the dots," we find that the inscriptional evidence actually testifies to some degree of large-scale legislation in early Greece. Finally, the early inscribed laws we will examine below do seem to show that in some cases groups of laws on the same subject were inscribed together. Thus, the absence of large groups of inscribed laws from the seventh and sixth centuries, though worth noting, does not prove that legislation on a large scale was not written at the time. More important, Hölkeskamp's sweeping rejection of early large-scale legislation overlooks the demonstrable steps the Greeks were taking during the archaic period to organize increasingly large amounts of legislation on their inscriptions. The Gortyn Code, as we shall see, was not created *ex nihilo*.

In order to understand the reasons for writing laws during this period, and the purpose and effect of these laws, we must first review the legislation that survives from seventh- and sixth-century Greece in the form of legal inscriptions. Since it would require more than one book to present all the surviving texts, I will be selective, confining myself to the more substantial texts from archaic Dreros and Gortyn (both in Crete) together with a selection from other cities. In this chapter I will look primarily at texts down to about 500, concentrating on physical characteristics and certain features of style and organization, which show clearly that the writers of these texts were making an effort to assist potential readers of the law. In Chapter Three, I will say more about the substance of early legislation when we take up the question of why Greeks first wrote laws and what effect the writing and public display of legislation had on law. Chapter Four will then be devoted primarily to one particularly interesting archaic text, Draco's homicide law.

I begin with the laws from Dreros, one of which is generally agreed to be our earliest surviving Greek law. In 1936 French excavators discovered the remains of eight archaic laws, most of them fragmentary, in a cistern just east of the eighth-century temple of Apollo Delphinios in the hilltop town of Dreros.[16] They concluded that each of these laws was originally inscribed on one or more blocks from the temple's east wall, which formed one edge of the main public gathering place at Dreros.[17] Thus, these texts would have been prominently displayed at the heart of the community.

The largest (1.74 meters long and 0.25 meters tall) and best known of these inscriptions (*Nomima* 1.81, *IGT* 90, ML 2, see Appendix 1.1 for the Greek) contains four lines of text and a group of letters between lines 1 and 2 that reads *thiosoloion* (*thios oloion?*) and is apparently a reference to a god, though the precise sense of the words is in doubt.[18]

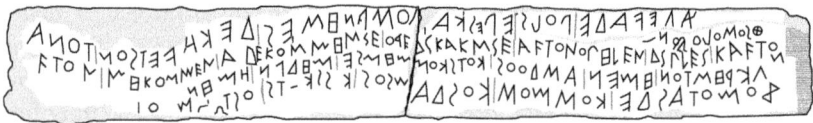

Dreros 1

The polis has decided: when someone has been *kosmos*,[19] within ten years the same person is not to be *kosmos* again. But if he does become *kosmos*, whenever he gives judgment, he himself is to owe a fine of twice the amount, and he is to be without rights (to office?) as long as he lives, and whatever he does as *kosmos* shall be void.

And oath-swearers (are) the *kosmos* and the *damioi* and the twenty of the polis.

This extraordinary text has been the subject of much discussion since its discovery; its location and physical features, however, have drawn little attention. Displaying the text on the wall of the temple of Apollo would have implicitly added a sense of divine authority to the civic authority asserted in the law's first words, especially if the marginal text means something like "may the god be kind" (so ML). And the fact that this temple wall formed

---

[16] Demargne and van Effenterre 1937a. For the date of the temple and further information about the site, see Prent 2005: 284–9.

[17] See Mazarakis Ainian 1997: 216–18 (with Figures 454–60) for a full description of the site, and Perlman 2004: 191–5 for a catalogue and full description of the eight inscriptions. Hölkeskamp 1992: 102 (followed by W. Harris 1996: 69–70) wrongly claims that written laws at Dreros and elsewhere "were deliberately kept at a distance" from public space.

[18] I do not translate these letters, but print them as the first line of the Greek text, which together with the other inscriptions treated below will be found at the end of the book. The letters are usually considered a later insertion, but they may actually have been written first.

[19] The *kosmos* was the highest official in most Cretan cities. Some cities apparently had a single *kosmos*, others a group of them ruling together.

one side of the community's central gathering place, which was situated in a saddle between the two hilltops that comprised the community, meant that the law had a prominent place in the public life of the polis.

The text itself is written on one large block of stone (now broken). A border is marked on the right edge of the stone; the left edge is more irregular. The moderately large letters (2–5 cm.) are irregular, and the lines are not nearly straight, in part because of irregularities in the stone face, which the mason needed to work around. Later masons would use smoother surfaces, but whoever wrote this text was apparently, like most early Greek masons, relatively unskilled. And yet he generally kept his letters large, and took pains to stay within the upper and lower confines of the stone. Moreover, there are signs that he was concerned to help readers read and understand the text.

The first three lines (ignoring the inserted letters) comprise the basic provision of the law and the punishment for its violation (the first paragraph in the translation given above). Like many archaic laws, they are written as a continuous text "boustrophedon" style, or "as the ox turns": the first line runs from the right border to nearly the edge on the left side, the second returns from the left to the right edge, and the third then runs back to the left. This style is common in early Greek inscriptions, the idea presumably being that when the reader reaches the end of the line, he (or she) can continue reading without having to return to the other side of the inscription to begin the next line. It also allows the mason to conserve space, since he can write letters up to the end of his space and then begin going back the other way immediately below, even if this means breaking a word in the middle, as happens, for example, between lines 1 and 2.

The third line ends before it reaches the left-hand border, and the text that follows in line 4 (the last sentence in the English translation) was evidently felt to be a separate, additional provision because it begins again on a new line, running from right to left as in line 3, and preceded by a special sign (𐤙) to mark the division. Writing the first line of a new topic from right to left is common in archaic Cretan laws, and is somewhat akin to modern paragraphing. This suggests that the last line is both related to but in some way separate from the preceding text. Most likely, the first provisions provide a reference point for the last one, allowing us to understand that the officials named swear oaths concerning some matter addressed in the preceding lines; perhaps they swore to comply with the law or to punish violations of it, or both.[20] We cannot know whether this

---

[20] It is curious that the noun *omotai* ("swearers") is a nominative, leaving the reader to supply the verb "are" in the present indicative. Present indicatives are very rare in early legislation, which relies on

last provision was enacted at the same time as the rest of the law or later, but it was probably inscribed at the same time or soon after, since the amount of space left on the stone after the first three lines is just enough to allow line 4 to be written below, suggesting that the initial mason left room for this provision.

The reader is also assisted by the two other devices. First and most evident, the mason used vertical lines (|) to mark divisions between single words or small groups of words (there is no word division in most Greek inscriptions). The approximate effect in English would be as follows:

> the polis | has decided | when someone has been *kosmos* | within ten years | the same person | is not to be *kosmos* again | but if he does become *kosmos* | whenever he gives judgment | he himself is to owe | a fine of twice the amount | and he is to be | without rights | as long as he lives | and whatever he does as *kosmos* | is to be | void and oath-swearers are | the *kosmos* | and the *damioi* | and the twenty | of the polis

Some of these division lines mark off clauses in much the same way as a modern comma or semi-colon; others mark expressions that are not full syntactical units. But they all mark a division between words, and even though their placement does not follow strict rules, they surely would have made it easier for readers to understand the text.

Similar division lines are common in early Cretan legislation, though they disappear around 500. In some inscriptions dots are used as dividers rather than continuous lines. But such dividers are less often found in early private inscriptions.[21] This suggests that those who inscribed early laws were concerned to make these texts as easy to read as possible for an audience that would have included some whose reading skills were rudimentary. Dividing lines would be less necessary if these archaic inscriptions were intended solely for display or were meant to be read by only a small group of elite members of the community.

The other kind of assistance we find in archaic laws is the syntactical device of asyndeton, or the absence of a connecting particle between independent clauses, though the effect of this is not always so clear or easy

---

imperatives and infinitives, both with the force of imperatives. If the list of oath-swearers has the same function as a list of witnesses commonly found at the end of an agreement in later periods, then these people may swear at the time of enactment of the law, perhaps to confirm the enactment.

[21] Of the more than sixty texts discussed by B. Powell (1989), only two have these division marks: no. 20, a list of names with marks separating each name from the next, and no. 55, the famous "Nestor's cup" inscription, with irregular division markers.

to determine.[22] The next sentence after the enactment clause ("The polis has decided") begins "when someone has been *kosmos*" without any connecting particle. Here the asyndeton marks a distinction between the enactment clause and the provision that was enacted.[23] The next sentence, however, begins normally with a particle: "but if he does become *kosmos*" (*ai de kosmēsei*), indicating a more continuous line of thought from the preceding sentence. The effect of asyndeton in legal inscriptions varies,[24] but it can be helpful in several ways. Here it indicates a significant shift in focus, in this case from the enactment clause to the substance of the law.

Finally, it is commonly noted that Greek laws are often casuistic; that is, they have the form of a conditional sentence stating the violation and its punishment or other consequences.[25] But in this law from Dreros we find a more complex, though still rudimentary form of organization, in which first a regulation prescribes or prohibits a certain action (no one can be *kosmos* more than once in ten years), and the next provision, linked by the particle *de* ("and/but"), spells out the consequences of non-compliance: "but if he does become *kosmos*, etc." The condition of non-compliance is often stated in the negative, particularly when the law prescribes a penalty and then continues, "but if he does not" pay the prescribed penalty. This structure – rule followed by the consequences of non-compliance – represents one of the earliest and most elementary form of organization in Greek law,[26] and as we shall see, it will be the basis for some of the more sophisticated forms of organization we find in later texts from fifth-century Gortyn.

The seven other inscriptions from the cistern at Dreros, some of them fragmentary, can be treated more briefly.[27] The first six show some of the same physical characteristics as the first law, though they are shorter, except for 8, which has two lines of Eteocretan (a local dialect) and three lines of Greek. As far as we can tell, all are inscribed within the top and bottom

---

[22] A Greek sentence normally includes a small particle at or near the beginning that marks its relationship to the preceding sentence (e.g., "and," "but," "therefore," "indeed"). These are often omitted in an English translation. Asyndeton, or the absence of any connecting particle, is thus significant and commonly marks a sharper than normal break between sentences.

[23] *ICret* 4.78, discussed in Chapter 6, has a similar feature.

[24] See Gagarin 1982 on the use of asyndeton in the Gortyn Law Code.

[25] Casuistic laws are sometimes thought to characterize primarily Greek and ancient Near-Eastern (including biblical) law; see Hagerdorn 2001: 228. But they are also found elsewhere, for example at the beginning of the Twelve Tables.

[26] It is also found in *ICret* 4.1 and 4.14 from Gortyn and the laws from Eretria and Tiryns discussed below.

[27] These were published in van Effenterre 1946a and 1946b. He numbered them 1–7, but this leaves the main Dreros law (discussed above) without a number. I will refer to the main law as Dreros 1 and will number the other seven 2–8. Five of this latter group are included in *Nomima*: 2 = I.66, 3 = I.64, 4 = I.68 and II.89 (see below, n. 30), 5 = I.27, 6 = II.10; three are in *IGT*: 3 = 91, 4 = 92, 5 = 94.

edges of one stone, and most are written boustrophedon[28] and use the same
vertical dividing lines as the main law (Perlman 2004: 194–5).

In four of these seven inscriptions the beginning of the text is preserved,
and in each case the law begins, like the first law, with an enactment phrase
(using the same verb *ewade*).[29] To the extent that we can determine the
subjects of these seven laws, they vary considerably: 3 provides immunity for
someone, 4 either specifies the date (the 20th of Hyperboios) for the *agelai*
or youth age-groups to begin or sets a date for the end of hunting season,[30]
and 6 mentions oaths and purification; the subjects of the others cannot be
determined. It appears, then, that laws concerning a wide range of subjects
were prominently displayed on the temple wall bordering the main gathering place at Dreros, where they would have been seen and read by many.
And if van Effenterre (1946b: 136–8) is correct that 8 is a bilingual text, then
the Drerians even made an effort to ensure that this text could be read by
those whose primary language was not Greek.

Many of these same features are common in the earliest laws from
Gortyn.[31] All these texts were inscribed on the walls of the temple of
Apollo Pythion, which at the time was probably visited frequently.[32] As
at Dreros, this temple was apparently felt to be the appropriate place for
laws to be displayed, because the site would reinforce the idea that the
god supported and would watch over the laws. Laws displayed here would
also have been easily visible and accessible to anyone who wished to read
them. The texts were written in large letters (4–25 cm.; see Perlman 2002:
214–16, Col. v), and were painted with red ocher: "These inscriptions were
intended to attract an audience" (Perlman 2004: 182).

The temple was probably constructed before anyone envisioned inscribing
texts on it, and it had a limited number of surfaces adequate for inscription.
Laws were thus inscribed either on long narrow horizontal blocks

---

[28] On 5 all three lines begin from the right; it is possible that these are three separate provisions.
Remarkably the second line of 4 is written (boustrophedon) above the first. On 8 the two Eteocretan
lines are written right to left but the three Greek lines that follow are written boustrophedon.

[29] In 3, the polis enacted the law; in 4 and 5 other groups are mentioned whose identity is not certain; in
8 *ewade* occurs near the beginning but we cannot read who approved the law.

[30] Van Effenterre 1946a: 597–600 proposes one text (followed in *Nomima* 1.68) and van Effenterre
1961: 549–52 proposes a different text and interpretation (followed in *Nomima* 11.89).

[31] *ICret* 4.1–40, dated by Jeffery (1990: 315) to 600–525? *ICret* 4 contains only inscriptions from Gortyn,
and so I will refer to these by the simplified notation 4.1, 4.3, etc.

[32] Perlman 2000: 72–4 suggests that placement on the walls of the temple, as in other Cretan cities in
the archaic period, was a higher priority than placement in the agora, some 500 meters away. But
(*ibid.* 88: n. 114), the agora may not have been laid out until the end of the archaic period, after these
laws were inscribed. Seventh- and sixth-century dates have been proposed for the temple, but this
remains uncertain (Prent 2005: 274–5).

extending for many meters over several blocks in a row with one (4.8–12), or two (4.13–17) lines of writing, or on taller but narrower blocks with several lines of text extending horizontally across several blocks, but apparently not for so great a distance. In either case, the texts normally followed a "one-course rule" (Perlman 2004: 186; cf. 182), that is they were confined to a single row of stones and did not stray above or below their own course.

The best known of these early Gortyn texts is 4.14, a long inscription with two lines of text (*Nomima* I.82, *IGT* 121, see Appendix I. 2). Each line was originally at least fifteen meters long and perhaps much longer, but less than half survives today as a continuous text (stones *g–p*).

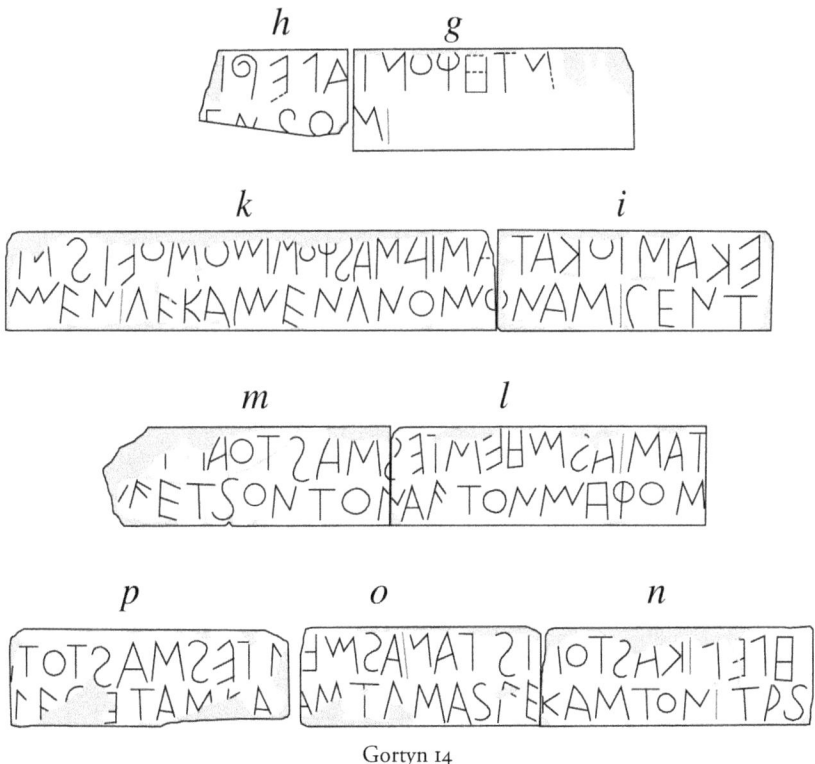

Gortyn 14

Line 1 . . . he is to pay fifty cauldrons in each case. The *kosmos* in
      charge, if he does not exact full payment, shall owe it
      himself, and the *titas*, if he does not exact full payment,
      [shall pay double?] . . .

> Line 2 . . . each is to pay . . . cauldrons. The same person is not
> to be *kosmos* again for three years; for the *gnōmones*
> ten years and for the foreigners' (*kosmos*?), five years.
> *vacat*

It is clear that the two lines are related: they are inscribed as a continuous
text boustrophedon, and each contains regulations pertaining to officials.
In line 1 the official must either collect the fine or pay it himself; line 2 may
also impose fines on officials and prohibits certain ones from holding the
same office for a number of years.[33] The similarity between this and the first
law at Dreros is often noted, but the Gortyn law provides more extensive
regulation than the Dreros law, which only applies to the *kosmos*. The
inscription at Gortyn regulates the iteration of three offices and the failure
to enforce verdicts, and the missing parts of the inscription may have
regulated other activities too.

The most striking physical feature of 4.14 is its length.[34] Someone
wishing to read the inscription would have to walk along one side of
the temple and perhaps even turn a corner before reaching the end of
the first line, though the boustrophedon writing would at least allow
him to read the second line while returning from that point rather than
having to start over from the beginning. The Gortynians may have been led
to inscribe such a long text by the limited number of available surfaces for
writing, but they seem to have realized the inconvenience this posed, for
they inscribed only a few early texts in this manner. The text also suggests
that the mason did not plan well, for line 2 ends about half way back; careful
planning could have produced two shorter lines of more equal length. In
other respects, the text has some of the same features as the first Dreros law,
including the use of vertical dividing marks and asyndeton. Line 1 also has a
provision about paying a certain amount followed by one that fines officials
for not exacting payment, a form of organization similar to what we noted
at Dreros. Here, however, the two provisions are linked by asyndeton,
which is a looser connection than connection by the particle *de* at Dreros.

None of the other long inscriptions provides enough continuous text
to allow comment, though we should note that the best preserved of these
(after 4.14), 4.13, speaks of "the whole polis" in line 2 – the only sixth-
century instance of this word at Gortyn – and also mentions the agora,

---

[33] For further discussion of the non-iteration provision in 4.14 in the light of 4.72.5.5–6 ("when the
Aithalian *startos*, Kyllos and his colleagues, formed the *kosmos*"), see Perlman 2002: 207–11; Link 2003.

[34] 4.14 is not the longest preserved text. Forty-four separate blocks survive from 4.10, so that the
original text of this law must have extended at least 30–40 meters.

apparently as the place where someone obtains a civic trial (*wastian dikan*), whatever that is. But several of the early texts inscribed on taller blocks are of interest, even though they are quite fragmentary, and I shall look briefly at 4.1, 4.3, and 4.21, in which parts of five, ten, and eight lines of text respectively are preserved.

4.1 (*Nomima* II.22; *IGT* 116, see Appendix 1.3) must originally have run across at least ten blocks, though only six survive. Each of the five lines runs from right to left, so we have here five separate provisions:[35]

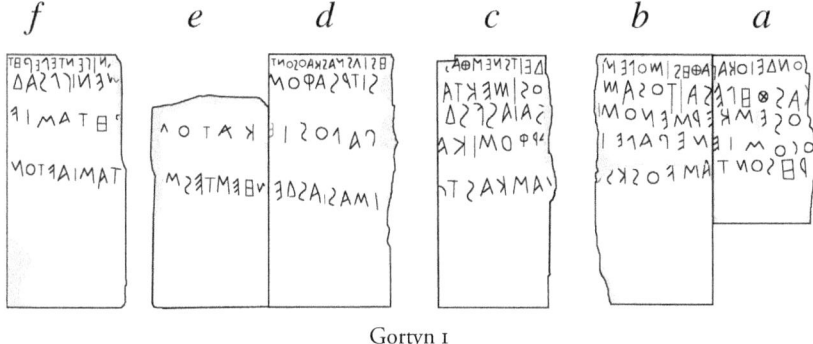

Gortyn 1

1. . . . of these (?) whatever harm is done to him, let him plead (in court) . . . pay a fine . . . a woman, of sheep . . . five cauldrons . . .
2. . . . female, to the lamb (?) . . . thirty [cauldrons?] . . . pay (?) but (not) more . . .
3. . . . the sheep and from a male . . . if personally (?)
4. . . . person (?) has attacked . . . the magistrate (?) . . . attacks, 100 cauldrons each
5. . . . debts (?) . . . of the female inhabitant (?) . . . is to pay (?), but if he does not pay the fines, he himself

Although these are separate provisions, there are apparent links among at least 1–2 and 3–4. Each mentions fines, with the first three prescribing a specific number of cauldrons in ascending order – five, thirty, a hundred; 1–3 also mention sheep; 1 talks of a woman, 2 of a female, 3 of a male and 5 (probably) of a female inhabitant. This does not necessarily mean that all five provisions, or even the first four,

---

[35] When the six stones comprising this law are seen in alignment, as in Figure 3 above, it is clear that the bottom two lines on stones *d–f* are a continuation of lines 4 and 5, not lines 3 and 4 as traditionally thought. Therefore, the following translation and the corresponding Greek text in the Appendix differ from the text printed in *ICret* 4.1 and elsewhere.

"belong to a single, coherent law" (Perlman 2002: 192), but it does seem likely that the five provisions were intentionally placed together because they address aspects or stages of the same general subject, perhaps "fights among shepherds or injuries caused to their herds" (*Nomima*, II.88).

At first glance, the five lines appear to have been written in different hands, since several letters are quite obviously written in different forms in different lines. This would suggest that the provisions were separately inscribed and quite probably separately enacted (so Gagarin 1982: 136), though they still could have been placed together because of their similarity of content. But Perlman (2002: 193–4) notes that on this inscription and others from this period there are also clear variations among letter forms within the same line (e.g., *nu* in both line 1 and line 2), so that we cannot rule out the possibility that one person wrote the entire text himself. This would make it more likely that the provisions were enacted at the same time and inscribed together because they all treat the same subject. In addition, they may have been arranged in order of ascending penalties. On the other hand, they were still considered separate provisions and so were not inscribed boustrophedon.

Only the first four lines of 4.3 preserve enough text to allow for comment (see Appendix 1.4). As in 4.1, each line runs from right to left, indicating four separate provisions.

1. (These) sacred rites have been performed . . . in the month Welkanios . . . on the fifth day . . .
2. . . . a grown (bull?) and a goat on (the ? day?), a ewe to Apollo . . . a bull . . .
3. . . . to Hera a ewe, to Demeter a pregnant ewe . . .
4. . . . the two females but the two males and a goat . . .

The four lines apparently contain a list of sacrifices of common animals, male and female, to at least three different gods, on different days of the month. As in 4.1, the lines may appear to be in different hands, but here too it is possible that one person inscribed the whole text (Perlman 2002: 193–4).[36] It seems quite certain, in any case, that the provisions were inscribed together as a list of sacrifices.

---

[36] The first letters of line 1 ("sacred rites have been performed") are slightly larger and more deeply incised than in the other lines, and this opening expression may have served as a kind of title for the subject matter it treated (Comparetti 1893: 21). But the letters later in this line (stone *d*) are also slightly larger, so the mason may simply have started with larger letters and reduced the size after the first line.

4.21 (*Nomima* ii.38, *IGT* 123, see Appendix 1.5) may be one of the earliest of these texts, since "it occupies the most prominent position (to the right of the door) on the first course of the temple wall."[37] The eight lines form five separate provisions, with the first three provisions occupying a single line each, and the fourth and fifth two and three lines respectively, written boustrophedon. The beginning of each line is preserved.

1. The pleader . . .
2. Whoever enters into arbitration (?) . . .
3. The family should not proceed (?) against an adopted son . . .
4–5. A woman with the same mother and the same father . . . if one person contends that the property is paternal and another claims otherwise.
6–8.[38] If witnesses testify for both sides . . . (if?) he chooses to decide himself, he shall pay five cauldrons; but if he contends . . .

It is possible that all these provisions concern disputes about inheritance when an adopted son is involved. The basic rules for adoption are presented at some length on the Great Code (4.72.10.33–11.23, see Chapter Seven), but the provisions here do not appear to overlap with these. Rather they address the procedure to be followed in certain disputes that might arise when an adopted son becomes an heir. Whatever the precise content, all the provisions address procedural aspects of litigation and presumably were all inscribed together for this reason.

Some, or perhaps all, of the four inscriptions from Gortyn we have examined thus far seem to contain provisions on the same subject, and were presumably inscribed together for this reason. The more fragmentary inscriptions generally do not show such coherence, though some of them might if more text survived. 4.4 (*Nomima* ii.61, *IGT* 117), for example, has four lines, all written retrograde indicating separate provisions. The few words we can decipher concern (1) not buying or exchanging, (2) four pigs and a sheep, (3) the oath-swearer and not to be opposed, and (4) a men's club and (perhaps) drinking. We cannot rule out a connection among these four lines but no connection is evident in these scanty remains. On the other hand, the four lines of 4.20 (*Nomima* ii.37, *IGT* 122) are written boustrophedon, indicating that they were considered a single law. The preserved text seems to concern inheritance, perhaps by an adopted son: (1) ". . . a garden; but if . . . equal, (2) parts . . . those who are legitimate . . ., (3) the male will inherit . . . female, (4) . . . and the maternal property . . ."

---

[37] Perlman 2002: 191; see generally 190–2, 217.

[38] I treat line 6 as the beginning of a new provision because of the asyndeton, but since line 5 ends right at the right edge of the stone, 6 may have been intended to continue the text of 5. In that case, 4–8 form a single provision concerned with pleading in court, witnesses, and judgment.

In most cases, then, early inscriptions at Gortyn contain provisions that are related to one another and were presumably placed together for this reason. It is reasonable to think, moreover, that when the provisions appear especially coherent, as in 4.3, they were enacted at the same time. And as at Dreros, all these texts were prominently displayed on the wall of a temple so as to be accessible to all members of the community, and some effort was made to assist those who wished to read them.[39]

Turning now to other parts of Greece, let us review a few inscriptions that either provide a large amount of readable text or are of special interest for some other reason. First, a law from the island of Chios, inscribed ca. 575 (ML 8, *Nomima* 1.62, *IGT* 61, see Appendix 1.6),[40] establishes, among other things, some basic constitutional rules, including such matters as the duties of a people's council.[41]

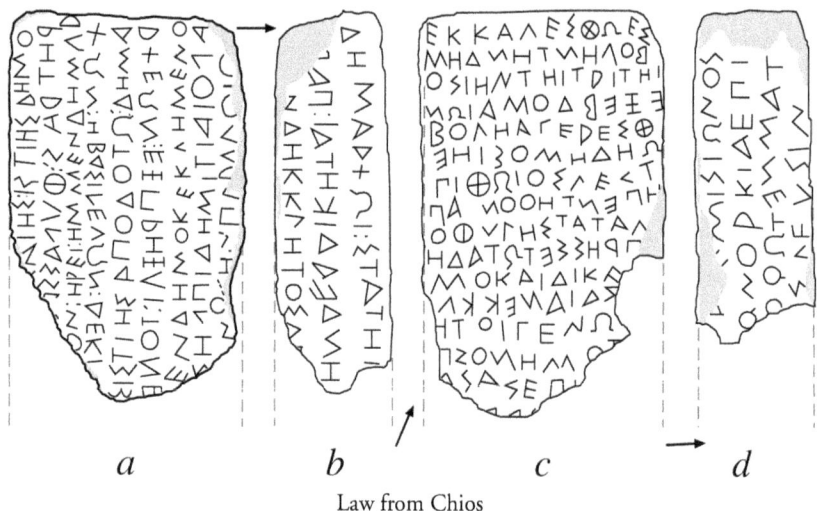

a   *b*   *c*   *d*

Law from Chios

A. … of Hestia, protecting the ordinances (*rhētrai*) of the people (*dēmos*) …
   If, while he holds the office of demarch or basileus, ten (?) … let him

---

[39] All forty of the earliest texts from Gortyn have vertical dividing lines as at Dreros, except for those where only a few letters are preserved (and even some of these have dividing lines).

[40] All recent editors start from the text of Jeffery 1956, whose study is fundamental. See also Robinson 1997: 90–101, who accepts a date in the 570s; Hölkeskamp 1999: 80–6.

[41] My translation is based on the rather conservative text of van Effenterre and Ruzé, except that instead of beginning with face D and continuing with A, B, and C, I retain the order of faces proposed by Jeffery (ABCD).

pay back ... of Hestia, while he is demarch. The ? is to exact ... when the people have been assembled, the sanctions are a double penalty ... as much as ? ...

B. ... being summoned, a trial ... if he is wronged, before the demarch [a certain number of?] staters ...

C. let him summon (him) to the people's council (*boulē dēmosiē*). Let[42] the people's council be convened on the third day after the Hebdomaia[43] with the power to inflict penalties, fifty selected from each tribe. Let it conduct the other business of the people, and in particular, all the lawsuits that have been summoned during the month ...

D. ... the month of Artemision. [*gap?*] ... let him take a solemn oath and swear ... for the kings (*basileis*) [*gap*].

The physical features of this inscription are striking. The text, which appears to be continuous, is inscribed on all four sides of a freestanding stele, beginning at the bottom left of the broad face A and running vertically boustrophedon up and down, ending at the top right corner of A. From there it continues on the right at the top left corner of the narrow face B, running down from the top along the edge that B shares with A, then up and down to the bottom right corner. It then resumes, probably continuously, at the top left of C, this time running horizontally boustrophedon down to (perhaps) the bottom right corner, whence it continues at the bottom left of the narrow face D, running vertically up to the top, where there may be a small gap at the end. The text then begins again from the bottom, running boustrophedon for its last three lines (up, down, up) and ending with a gap at the top right corner. Vertical writing[44] is not uncommon on pots or other irregular surfaces, and is also found on several other archaic inscriptions. It is least surprising on the narrow sides (B and D), where the continuous vertical text would probably be easier to read than horizontal lines of only three or four letters. But on side A we may see an example of the mason trying an experiment that he abandoned on side C, perhaps realizing that horizontal writing was easier to read.

The vertical writing here has many of the same features as the horizontal texts we have examined thus far. The same effect of paragraphing is

---

[42] There is asyndeton in this and the next sentence, indicating separate but still related provisions.

[43] A monthly festival in honor of Apollo.

[44] As is clear from the illustration above, "vertical writing" means that the letters are all rotated 90°, so that the reader would have to tilt his head to the side in order to read (and the mason probably turned the whole stone on its side in order to write).

achieved, for example, by starting a new line in the same direction (from the bottom) on side D. The letters are moderately large (2.5 to 4 cm.) and, though a bit crude, are not difficult to read. And the text on each side is completed before the next side is begun, allowing the reader to read one side at a time as he or she moves around the stone. The reader also would be assisted by the occasional use of dividing markers, in this case two or three dots in a row.

Since an unknown amount at the bottom of the stele is missing, only side C, running horizontally, yields continuous sense. A mentions public ordinances (*rhētrai*) and may impose a fine on one or more officials; B may indicate the procedure to be followed in that case; and D gives a date and specifies an oath to be sworn. On C the mention of a people's council has occasioned much discussion of early democracy in Chios. This council of fifty per tribe[45] meets once a month to conduct public business and to hear court cases, perhaps appeals, and has the power to punish. In conducting public business it presumably enacts the public ordinances which, according to side A, are to be protected. This may mean that an official is to safeguard the written texts of these ordinances, or that he is to enforce their provisions, or perhaps both. In any case, this is a fundamental constitutional law, resembling in this respect laws at Dreros and Gortyn as well as the Spartan *rhētra* (Chapter Four, n. 2).

A slightly later inscription from Eretria (*IG* XII 9, 1273/1274, *Nomima* 1.91, *IGT* 72–3, see Appendix 1.7),[46] probably from the third quarter of the sixth century, also has writing on the front (texts 1–3), running horizontally, and on one side (text 4), running vertically, all of it boustrophedon.

1. (1–4) He shall judge after he has taken an oath. He [the convicted defendant] shall pay on the third day in goods which are acceptable and sound.[47] If he does not pay, he [the plaintiff] *shall seize him.*[48]

---

[45] We do not know the number of tribes in Chios at the time, but judging from other Ionian states, "there would have been at least three and perhaps as many as six" (C. Roebuck 1986: 87).

[46] For the text, Vanderpool and Wallace 1964 is fundamental, though I generally accept the further suggestions of Cairns 1991 and my translation is adapted from his. See also K. Walker 2004: 192–7. I omit lines 14–16, from which no significant sense can be obtained.

[47] Accepting Cairns' restoration of *hygia* instead of the more common reading *phygia* ("exile"). *Phygia* would be taken with the next sentence to indicate the penalty for non-payment, and would make it a little easier to understand the dividing marker after *ian* ("if"), but it poses many other difficulties; see Cairns 1984: 152.

[48] The italicized words are Cairns' proposed translation of *hērai* (1991: 304–5), which has been neatly chiseled out of the stone so only traces remain (the standard way of erasing epigraphic texts). This may indicate that some part of the punishment was later repealed. Cairns suggests that lines 5–9 were inscribed only after this erasure, with lines 6–9 recording new fines and line 5 specifying the date that the new penalty took effect.

2. (5) When Golos was archon in the city . . .
3. (6–9) [If he does not pay, ?] he shall owe on the next day two [staters, on the third day?] ten staters. If he (still) does not pay, the officials are to act in accordance with the ordinances (? *rhēta*).[49] Whoever does not do so shall himself owe.
4. (10–12) Those who sail should receive wages if they go beyond Petalai or Kenaion. All should contribute toward this payment. Those who are in the country . . .

The four texts appear to be in separate hands, though this is not certain. There is little agreement about how the first three are related; the fourth, on the side of the stone, appears unrelated to the others and also seems to be slightly later. The letters are generally clear and moderately large – mostly 2.5–3 cm., but as large as 5 cm. in text 1 and as small as 1 cm. in text 4, where the rougher surface of the stone and the awkwardness of inscribing on the side of a stone *in situ* probably caused the mason to write in smaller letters and less neatly than he might otherwise. But he (or they) still took the trouble to add a good number of dividing markers (vertical rows of two or three dots) to help the reader. Even so, this is one of the least reader-friendly among the early legal inscriptions.

The inscription was found in the area of the harbor, and it is generally assumed to concern fines or taxes on shipping and trade. It begins with what seems to be a general procedural regulation, perhaps applying to matters involving shipping and trade, that any payment specified in a court judgment must be paid within three days in goods that are acceptable and sound. If not, the debtor may be seized and presumably enslaved. The provision implies a time before coinage, which probably came to Eretria near the end of the sixth century. Later (perhaps), enslavement as a penalty was repealed and replaced by a series of fines that increased over time (text 3). One cannot help thinking of Solon's repeal of debt-bondage near the beginning of the century, and many have thought that this later regulation indicated the beginning of democracy in Eretria. The fourth text too, though unconnected, may also have been a democratic step if it provides payment by the city for those serving in the fleet. These are rather tenuous hints at political reform, however, and I would hesitate to draw significant conclusions from them.[50]

---

[49] Cairns and others take *rhēta* as a variant of *rhētra*, "ordinance"; van Effenterre and Ruzé (*Nomima* 1.91) and others take it as "things spoken" and understand it as referring to "what was said (in the case)," which they take to mean "the facts of the case," but in my view this stretches the possible sense of *rhēta* too far.
[50] Robinson 1997 does not include Eretria among archaic democracies.

Also (most likely) from the last quarter of the sixth century is a well-preserved bronze plaque with land regulations for a Locrian colony, perhaps Naupactus (ML 13, *Nomima* I.44, *IGT* 47, see Appendix I.8).[51]

> (Side I) This law (*tethmos*) concerning the land shall be in force for the partition of the plain of Hyla and Liskara, both the separate lots and the public land. The right of pasturage shall belong to parents and to a son; if there is no son, to a daughter; if there is no daughter, to a brother; if there is no brother, let the closest relative pasture according to what is right (*ka to dikaion*); if not, to the one who pastures . . . (?) Whatever a man plants, he shall be immune [from its seizure].
>
> (Line 7) Unless under the pressure of war a majority of 101 men chosen from the best citizens decide to bring in at least 200 fighting men as additional settlers, whoever proposes a division or puts it to a vote in the council of elders or in the city (*polis*), or in the elected body, or makes civil strife about the division of land, he himself and his family shall be accursed for all time, his property shall be confiscated and his house demolished just as under the law (*tethmos*) about homicide. This law (*tethmos*) shall be sacred to Pythian Apollo and the gods who dwell with him; may there be destruction on the person who transgresses it, on him and his family and his possessions, but may (the god) be kindly to him who observes it. Half the land (Side II) shall belong to the previous settlers, half to the new settlers. Let them distribute the valley portions. Exchange shall be valid, but the exchange shall take place before the magistrate.

The text is inscribed boustrophedon in small but clear letters (0.5–1.3 cm.) on a long narrow bronze plaque, about 33 × 14 cm. The plaque has holes in the upper corners so that it could be hung on a wall and turned over if someone wanted to read the other side. There is only one dividing marker (line 20). There is also one instance of asyndeton (line 7), which clearly marks the beginning of a new topic; in the translation I have indicated this with a new paragraph.

---

[51] My translation is adapted from ML, who understand the perplexing word *epinomia* to mean "right of pasturage." The text is traditionally divided into three "sides" (A, B, C), despite being written on just two sides of the plaque. I will thus refer simply to Side I and Side II. I do not translate line 17 (the first line on Side II), which may be the end of a law inscribed elsewhere, and I omit the last four lines (22–5), which were inscribed, probably later, by a different hand upside down from the bottom up.

The text explicitly calls itself a law (*tethmos* = *thesmos*, "enactment") and also refers to "the homicide law" (*kat ton androphonikon tethmon*, 13–14), which must have been inscribed separately. It clearly belongs to a period after the colony is well established: several governing bodies are already functioning, at least one other law, on homicide, has already been enacted, and the land has already been divided among the first settlers. Thus the law addresses concerns that might arise several years after the colony's founding as the original settlers grow old and begin to die, such as conflicts concerning the inheritance of land or the desirability of bringing in new settlers. Punishment primarily takes the form of a religious curse, which probably meant automatic exile, with the city confiscating the person's property and destroying his house. Divine punishment as the ultimate sanction is not uncommon in archaic legislation, because most archaic communities lacked effective means of punishing wrongdoers (Parker 2005). It is unclear whether the colony has functioning courts, although it does appear to have a council, an "elected body" and a *polis* (assembly?).

This text contains the first instance of cross-referencing (lines 13–14) we have encountered. Cross-referencing is significant because it indicates a sense of coherence among a city's laws, and also confirms the public nature of law (since the homicide law referred to here must also have been publicly displayed). It occurs often in the fifth-century laws from Gortyn, and we will consider its implications at greater length in Chapter Six. We should also note that at the beginning of Side I, the regulation that a son has the right of pasturage is followed by a conditional statement giving the consequences if there is no son; this is similar to the pattern we noted earlier where a regulation is followed by a conditional statement of the consequences of non-compliance.

Another bronze plaque from about the same time (end of the sixth century) comes from Elis, which controlled the sanctuary at Olympia.[52] It is long and narrow (52 × 8 cm.), and has five lines of continuous writing, often divided into three texts (*A, B, C*, see Appendix I.9), but since there is no physical or syntactic demarcation between them, they were all evidently seen as related.

> (*A*) . . . he were a *theoros*.[53] If he has intercourse in the sanctuary, let him dedicate a bull and undergo full purification, and similarly for the *theoros*. (*B*) And if anyone judges contrary to the writing (*par to*

---

[52] *IvO* 7, *Nomima* I.109, *IGT* 41–3. See also Robinson 1997: 108–11; Hölkeskamp 1999: 104–6.

[53] In general, a *theoros* is an official envoy to a festival or other religious occasion. Here, as in some other cites, he is an official, probably with religious duties.

graphos, i.e. "against the law"), the judgment will be void; but the pronouncement of the people (*ha rhatra ha damosia*) giving judgment shall be valid. (*C*) And in the writings (*graphea*), wherever it seems better before the god, let him change it, deleting or inserting without difficulty (but only) with the council of five hundred and the people (*damos*) in full assembly; and if something is to be inserted or deleted, let it be changed three times.

There are two physical differences between this text and others we have considered so far. First, the lines of writing all run from left to right, the direction of writing that later becomes standard in classical Greek. And there are no marks indicating word division, which are a standard feature of most archaic inscriptions but are rarely used after about 500. Both features thus suggest that this inscription is later than the others we have examined and it may, in fact, date from the early fifth rather than late sixth century.

A is a religious law applying to the sanctuary (of Zeus at Olympia). According to *B*, court judgments must adhere to written laws, but a pronouncement or decree of the people giving judgment – i.e. acting as a court – can override a law. *C* is closely related to *B*: the council of five hundred and the people's assembly together can emend or supplement any law, though changes only take effect if they are approved three times. Provisions *B* and *C*, even if written specifically in the context of *A* (and anything that might precede the surviving text), almost certainly apply more broadly to litigation and legislation in general, for such major constitutional rules could not have been developed solely to regulate one small religious matter. But it is extraordinary to find, already at the end of the archaic period, clear rules for emending legislation written down and posted at an entrance to the sanctuary. Moreover, the use of *graphos* ("writing") in both singular and plural to designate a law or laws suggests a close relationship between writing and law. We will examine the significance of this and similar terms in connection with fifth-century laws at Gortyn, where they are common (Chapters Six and Seven).[54]

The last three archaic inscriptions we will consider in this chapter are more fragmentary, but each has a special interest with respect to writing. The first, from the Heraion (temple of Hera) at Argos, is dated to the

---

[54] *IvO* 3 (*Nomima* 1.108; *IGT* 38) from about the same time, was also found in the sanctuary of Zeus. It appears to present a similar pattern of a provision governing the sanctuary followed by a more general provision about the law itself (*graphos*).

second quarter of the sixth century.[55] It is the central portion of a bronze strip 13.5 cm. tall and about 15 cm. wide. We appear to have the original top and bottom of the inscription, but since an unknown amount is missing on either side, no continuous sense is recoverable, and the remains are subject to quite different interpretations.

> (If someone) ignores these writings (*ta grathmata tade*) ... or alters them, let the curses ... (he is banished?) from the land of Argos and his property (is confiscated?) ... (if someone causes) death or some other crime ... plots or lies in ambush ... the *progrophos*,[56] let him sell ... if there is no *demiourgos*,[57] for the ... of Argos and the ... the Hylleis will give back ... the land of Argos ... without compensation with respect to Hera.

The text is inscribed in traditional archaic style, continuously boustrophedon with frequent word dividers. It seems to contain several separate provisions, though the lost parts may have provided a connection among these, and all the provisions may apply to the city as a whole not just to the sanctuary. For our purposes, the law's most interesting features are its use of the word "writings" (*grathmata*) to designate laws, which becomes common in fifth-century Gortyn, and the prohibition on altering the law. As in the Locrian law discussed above, the punishment is a curse, which effectively means exile and (probably) confiscation of property. The text also apparently contained provisions concerning homicide (line 4) and other crimes.

Next, we have a sacred law from Cleonae from before 550.[58]

> (*a*) ... the purifying waters ... if someone (kills someone?) while doing something praiseworthy ... he shall not be polluted. (*b*) If someone draws blood (?) while killing a man who has done nothing, he shall be polluted. But if (he kills) a cursed man, it will be nothing (*c*) against the law (*para nomon*) if ... a person who is polluted. And there is to be purification (*katharsis*), just as when someone dies and is purified according to the law (*kata nomon*) ... a sacrifice at public expense.

[55] *IG* IV 506, *Nomima* I.100, *IGT* 29, see Appendix I.10; see also Hölkeskamp 1999: 69–70.
[56] This is apparently an official connected with writing, but the word is otherwise unknown.
[57] The *demiourgoi* were officials with religious and judicial duties.
[58] *IG* IV 1607, *Nomima* II.79, *IGT* 32, see Appendix I.11. See also Sokolowski 1969: no. 56; Hölkeskamp 1999: 149.

This is another text that was inscribed vertically, boustrophedon, on three sides of a stone block, perhaps the base of a pillar. Side *a* is rather poorly preserved and the first line seems to be missing. Whether the inscription originally began there or on the now lost side *d*, it is fairly certain that the text is continuous from *a* to *b* to *c*. The letters are large (ca. 4 cm.) and very clear on the two better preserved sides; there are occasional word dividers and incised guidelines to mark the tops and bottoms of the vertical rows.

The main interest of this inscription for us lies in the expressions *para nomon* ("against the law," perhaps one word) and *kata nomon* ("according to the law").[59] Does *nomos* here retain its traditional archaic meaning, "custom, norm, traditional rule, etc." or have its fifth-century sense of (written) "law, statute"? Perhaps both senses are present. Since the procedures for purification were unlikely to have been written down at this time, *kata nomon* may more likely mean "according to custom"; but since this law itself punishes certain forms of homicide, it would be reasonable to understand *para nomon* as "against the [i.e. this] law." It thus appears that this is an early instance of *nomos* being applied to written law, which otherwise is extremely rare before the fifth century, but that *nomos* also still retains its traditional sense of (orally transmitted) custom or tradition.

Finally, I conclude this survey of archaic laws with a strange group of texts discovered at Tiryns (*SEG* 30.380, *Nomima* 1.78, *IGT* 31, see Appendix 1.12). They were displayed on the walls of a covered passage that in Mycenean times had been used to convey water into the acropolis; it is not clear what the passage was used for in the archaic period. The group includes some nineteen fragmentary texts from the late seventh or early sixth century inscribed in a "serpentine" fashion. I present only the two texts that yield some continuous sense.

> (Blocks 1–4) ... of the years ... the drinking leaders ... shall impose fines on the drinkers in each case. If they do not punish them, they shall owe to Zeus and Athena thirty *medimnoi* [of grain?] ... double. When the drinking leaders leave office (?) ... is to give back to the *hieromnamōn* ... and the *hieromnamōn* is to [distribute? manage?] public property however the people (*damos*) decide. An assembly [will be held?] ... theater (?) ...

---

[59] Although the restoration of two letters in *kata nom[on]* is fairly certain, more than half of *p[arano]mon* has been restored; but the restoration gains support from the proximity of *kata nomon*.

(Block 7,2) ... the drinking leaders are to provide the fine consisting of (?) public funds. If they do not provide it completely (?) from their own resources, the *epignōmōn* will drive the crowd [against them?].

It is hard to know what to make of this peculiar inscription, which seems to concern a group or association of drinkers. References to Zeus and Athena, to a *hieromnamōn* ("sacred rememberer"), and in another fragment to a sacred table have led some to classify it as a "sacred law,"[60] though ultimate control is apparently in secular hands (the people, the assembly). Most puzzling is the fact that the texts were inscribed on the walls of a covered passage, where they would have been difficult to see, let alone read, in the dim light, and they were written in a curiously disorganized form. These features may suggest a cult practice rather than the sort of public law we have found elsewhere at this time. We do not know what this passage was used for – in fact we have no other evidence that Tiryns was inhabited at this time – but it is possible that it was a cult site of some sort.[61] Further study may clarify some of these matters, but for now these texts remain *sui generis* and perplexing. They are presented here primarily because of the unusual nature of their writing and location, but their content is also of interest. In particular, the law contains two provisions that are similar to other archaic legislation: that officials who do not do their duty (in this case, punish drinkers) are themselves fined and that in doing something with public property the *hieromnamōn* must follow the decision of the people (*damos*), perhaps reached in an assembly. The *hieromnamōn* will also figure into our discussion of the *mnamōn* in Chapter Five.

This concludes our survey of archaic legislation. I have been emphasizing the physical features of these texts, from the lettering and placement of texts on the stone to the display of these stones in the community. Despite the ravages of time, we can see that in most cases texts are written in clear, often large letters that would have been quite readable, that devices like word division and (less often) asyndeton are commonly used to help clarify the sense, and that texts are usually displayed in a public place, often on or near a temple, where they would be seen by many. All this suggests that the earliest laws were inscribed in order to be read. In Chapter Three, we will focus on why these laws were written, which will lead us to ask, who read

---

[60] Lupu 2005: 190 n. 1 expresses uncertainty about the classification.
[61] Van Effenterre has suggested that a group of slaves revolted after the slaughter of their masters in Sparta and took refuge in Tiryns (*Nomima* ad loc.).

them. In this connection we will examine more closely the subject matter of these laws, which ranges widely, from private matters such as inheritance, to public matters ranging from basic constitutional provisions to restrictions on officials to prohibitions on altering the texts of laws, and finally to "sacred" laws regulating sacrifice and temple conduct. We will also explore the historical context for this early legislation, which comes primarily from archaeological evidence. In Chapter Four, we will add evidence from Athens, which I treat separately since we only have the texts of early Athenian laws, not the original seventh- and sixth-century inscriptions.

CHAPTER 3

Why the Greeks Wrote Laws

To understand why the Greeks wrote these early laws we must ask several questions: Who wrote the laws? Who read them? What kinds of laws were written? What effect does putting a rule into written form have on that rule? The physical features of the inscriptions examined in Chapter Two suggest answers to some of these questions; for others we will have to look more closely at the content of laws and their social and historical context.

I begin with the vexing question, who could read these early texts? As we saw (Chapter Two), during the first century (ca. 750–650), when writing was used only for private inscriptions, these inscriptions were written, and presumably read, by a range of people including some who were not members of the elite. We also noted that, beginning around 650, archaic laws were displayed in easily accessible public spaces, were often written in large clear letters suitable for reading, and almost always contained features like word-division markers that would make the text easier to read and understand. These physical features strongly suggest that the laws were intended to be read, but this does not tell us by whom. It is tempting to conclude that the readers of archaic laws included the same broad range of people as the writers of the earliest private inscriptions, but there are at least two potential obstacles to this conclusion. First, the widespread popularity of writing during its first century may not have continued in subsequent years. Second, some of the places where the earliest legal inscriptions have been found, particularly Crete, may have had substantially lower levels of literacy than places like Attica. Thus, we cannot be certain that people who enjoyed reading and writing early private inscriptions had a similar interest in reading laws when these began to be written.

In recent years many scholars have disputed the view that early laws were meant to be read by ordinary members of the community, arguing instead that since only the elite were able to read at this time, these texts were inscribed and displayed primarily in order to make a visual impression. One influential critic, Marcel Detienne, has been quoted as saying that these texts were "une écriture destinée à être vue plutôt que lue."[1] Similar views are expressed by Hölkeskamp ("More important than the readability of a statute was evidently its visibility in the concrete sense, as a symbol and guarantee of its unchanging and lasting validity")[2] and, specifically of Cretan laws, by Whitley ("The purpose of such inscriptions is as much symbolic as practical").[3] On this view, the content of these laws was less important than their visual impact, which would have conveyed a sense of the power and authority of the elite ruling class to its mostly illiterate citizens.

Some of these legal inscriptions would undoubtedly have made a strong visual impression on members of the community, and it is reasonable to suppose that this was one reason for the large size of some of the early inscriptions and their location in public places. But this does not exclude the possibility that they were also displayed in order to be read.[4] Many of these laws were written on the sides of buildings, moreover, where they would have had less visual impact than a freestanding inscription, and many of the earliest laws were relatively short. And later texts that were added to those already inscribed on a wall would surely not have had the same visual impact as the first inscription. But if the Greeks did not add one more text to a wall just in order to make a visual impression, they must have had other reasons, and the physical features we noted indicate that these laws were inscribed to be read and used. But who were these readers?

Private inscriptions show that in Attica, at least, a broad range of people could write and presumably also read, but in Crete, where the greatest concentration of archaic legal inscriptions has been found, there is less evidence for private writing. Whitley has compiled figures purporting to show that the amount of private writing in Crete actually declined between the eighth and the sixth century,[5] and he argues that as written laws became

---

[1] "Writing destined to be seen not read." These words are a slight misquotation by Camassa 1988: 151 from Detienne 1981: 69, who actually writes, "l'écriture doit être plus visible que lue." Detienne continues (English trans. p. 32), writing "is shown to everybody, evidence of the required publication of information, without ever being called upon to relay speech as a means of communication within the social interconnections of the first democracies."

[2] Hölkeskamp 2000: 88 ("Wichtiger als die Lesbarkeit war offenbar die Sichtbarkeit der Satzung im konkreten Sinne, nämlich als Symbol und Garantie ihrer unabänderlichen und dauerhaften Geltung").

[3] Whitley 1997: 660 (and similarly in Whitley 2001: 250–1).

[4] For a text that combines visual and textual effects, one might cite the Vietnam Memorial in Washington DC, which makes a powerful visual impression and at the same time provides a text, and most visitors stop to read at least a few of the names on it.

[5] "Whereas in sixth-century Attica, both the number and variety of inscriptions steadily increase, the opposite appears to be true in Crete" (Whitley 1997: 651–2).

more widespread in sixth-century Crete, literacy became more restricted and "scribal literacy" prevailed, much as it did in the Near East at this time. From this he concludes (as noted above) that the inscribed laws would have been read by the ruling elite, who could probably read, but by few if any others, and the effect of inscribed monuments such as the Gortyn Code would have been to impose laws favorable to the ruling class on the rest of the population, who would not be aware of the inequalities contained in such legislation (Whitley 1997: esp. 649–61).

Whitley does well to stress that different parts of the Greek world may have experienced different levels of reading and writing during the archaic period; we cannot assume that the Attic model was valid for all other parts of Greece. But the evidence he cites for Crete does not fairly represent the situation. In a careful examination of forty-two Cretan private inscriptions dated to either the eighth and seventh centuries or the sixth and first half of the fifth century, Perlman concludes that private writing actually increased after 600, suggesting that reading and writing were not confined to the elite members of the community, and that a significant number of people outside of the ruling elite could have read the archaic legislation of Crete.[6]

This still leaves the question, who actually read these texts, either in Crete or any other archaic polis, including Athens? The ability to read did not necessarily mean that a person did in fact read laws; social patterns and expectations could have discouraged or encouraged access. In our own day of widespread literacy, for example, the texts of laws are widely available in libraries, and more recently on the internet, but hardly anyone outside the relatively small number of legal professionals actually reads the text of a law. Was this the situation in Crete? Perlman concludes with reference to Cretan laws, "although there is no reason to reject *a priori* the possibility that both officials and ordinary members of the community consulted the laws, either on their own or those unable to do so having the laws read aloud to them, the officials who judged cases and those who enforced the penalties were perhaps their primary audience."[7]

---

[6] Perlman 2002: 194–6 (with Table pp. 218–25); more recently published material (*SEG* 52.861, 862 and 868) has added slightly to her figures but does not affect her conclusion. As she puts it (p. 196): "The chronological distribution of public and private writing on Crete which indicates an increase in both categories during the sixth century BC, the evidence for writing practice and for pride in the skill on the part of at least one individual, perhaps a shepherd or soldier, who had time to kill in the hinterland of Itanos, and the emerging pattern of writing used for private purposes by members of those communities where the public use of writing is also attested combine to suggest that literacy was not the exclusive possession of a narrow scribal class as Whitley argues."

[7] Perlman 2002: 197, with reference to Davies 1996: 54–6; see also Hölkeskamp 2000: 87.

Perlman argues that this group of current and potential officials was relatively large, but even so, I see no reason to omit litigants, actual or potential, from this group. Unlike modern legislation, which is accessible to anyone but is not a presence in most people's lives, the texts of laws in archaic Crete were prominently displayed in public places where most members of the community would encounter them regularly during the ordinary course of events. If these inscriptions were intended only for officials or potential officials, there would have been little reason to display them in such prominent public places. Moreover, most of us today rely on representatives (i.e. lawyers) to read laws for us if necessary, but nothing suggests the presence of similar legal professionals in archaic or classical Greece. The easy accessibility of a text may not guarantee that those who can read it will, but when texts are easily accessible, people with an interest in them – whether because of impending or potential litigation or for some other reason – are likely to read them if they can. And because of the relative ease with which the Greek script could be read, there was a fairly large number of potential readers of laws in Greece – certainly larger than in other comparable societies.

We may conclude that in addition to officials, who would need to read the laws in order to learn some of their obligations and duties, ordinary citizens would also need to read them if they wanted to know how to proceed when they had some dispute or thought they had been harmed in some way. Families with property, for instance, might want to read an inheritance law, and of course laws about an "heiress" (see Chapter Seven) would be of special interest to families in which a man died leaving only a daughter. We will never have precise numbers, but it is likely that many, perhaps most of those who were or might be involved in legal matters as officials or litigants would have been able to read the relevant laws, some perhaps with help from friends, and that many of these would actually have done so. Presumably, the wealthier segment of the community would be more interested in some of these laws (such as property laws), and would also probably be best able to read them, but we cannot exclude the possibility that ordinary citizens, and even slaves, read these texts too.

Beyond this, we can only guess what percentage of the community could read in archaic Crete. It may have been around 5 percent, but, as Whitley (1997: 639) rightly notes, there is a very significant difference between such a society and one in which less than 1 percent is literate. And even if only a few of the non-elite could read these texts, their public display for the benefit of these readers would have created very different assumptions from those in the ancient Near East or in the Greek Bronze Age, where written texts were never meant to be accessible outside the circles of professional scribes or other royal officials. By contrast, the Greeks assumed that written texts should be widely available to the community, and thus they wrote them in large clear letters, and included features of style and organization intended to make the texts easier to read, and they displayed them prominently in public places.

Turning now from reading to writing, we must ask two separate questions: who enacted the laws and thus caused them to be written, and who actually carved the inscriptions? It is possible, of course, that some early lawgivers inscribed their legislation themselves, but the earliest text from Dreros is explicitly enacted by the polis, and the actual inscription of the law was almost certainly not a group effort. Moreover, although the earliest laws show considerable variation in the forms of letters, the letters soon become more regular, indicating that the work of inscribing texts on stone soon became more specialized. Thus, it is likely that professional masons cut most, if not all, legal inscriptions.

I do not call these masons "scribes," since this title, from its use in Near-Eastern and other cultures, suggests an elevated status and degree of authority that goes beyond the mere ability to write, and as far as we know, most inscribers of inscriptions in Greece had no special status or authority. The one possible exception we know of is Spensithios,[8] who is called a "writer" (*poinikastas*) and clearly did have a high status. But as we shall see (Chapter Five), Spensithios does not have the duties generally associated with ancient scribes. Rather, he is directed to "write and remember" for the city in all public matters; this probably included writing laws (and perhaps little else), and his high status may have been derived as much from his remembering as from his writing. Thus, I will call Spensithios a writer not a scribe, and those who inscribed texts on stones inscribers or masons, not scribes.

As for those who enacted these laws, most archaic laws say nothing about their enactment, leaving us to speculate, but the main law at Dreros and one other (Dreros 3) begin by saying, "the polis decided," and similar expressions at the beginning of three other laws from Dreros and several other archaic laws indicate enactment by a group. Later authors, on the other hand, generally attribute early laws to an individual lawgiver, who in one way or another was appointed or authorized (or perhaps seized the power) to enact laws. Draco and Solon at Athens are the best known examples of this, but other traditional lawgivers probably also enacted

---

[8] We will examine the agreement with Spensithios (*SEG* 27.631, *Nomima* 1.22) in Chapter 5.

laws with the authorization of the city. In other cities, legislation may have been enacted by an anonymous official who, like the early lawgivers, probably had some sort of authorization from the community. Thus, archaic legislation was enacted in different ways in different cities, and sometimes by different groups or individuals in the same city (as at Dreros), but in most cases the ultimate authority for these laws was the community, either directly through a body comprising some segment of the community or indirectly through the community's appointment or approval of a lawgiver.

Why, then, did these communities decide to write laws? The Greeks had been familiar with writing for more than a century before anyone wrote a law; during that time they apparently were satisfied with a system of oral law such as that portrayed in Homer and Hesiod (Chapter One). What impelled them suddenly to start writing down laws? The Greeks themselves tended to frame their answers to this question in political terms, and many scholars have followed their lead. The Athenians proposed a democratic answer, formulated most famously by Theseus in Euripides' *Suppliants* (429–34), who as part of a rousing endorsement of democracy as opposed to the evils of monarchy, hails the democratic effect of writing laws. "There is nothing more detrimental to a polis than a tyrant. First of all, when there are no public laws (*nomoi koinoi*), one man holds power by keeping the law all for himself, and there is no more equality. But when the laws are written, the weak man and the rich man have equal justice (*dikē*)."[9]

Stirring as these words are, the Greeks also held less sanguine views of the effect of writing laws. In a story that is undoubtedly fictitious but that must have its source in earlier Greek ideas about law, Plutarch reports a conversation between Solon, who was in the process of drawing up his laws, and the Scythian wit Anacharsis (*Solon* 5). The Scythian laughed at Solon for thinking he could restrain the injustice and greed of citizens with written texts. These were just like spiders' webs: they caught and held the weak and the delicate, but were torn to pieces by the powerful and the rich. Solon's response was that if laws were written, as he was writing his laws, to be beneficial to all, then everyone would abide by them because there would be no profit in breaking them. In this version Solon's view is

---

[9]   οὐδὲν τυράννου δυσμενέστερον πόλει,
ὅπου τὸ μὲν πρώτιστον οὐκ εἰσὶν νόμοι
κοινοί, κρατεῖ δ' εἷς τὸν νόμον κεκτημένος
αὐτὸς παρ' αὑτῷ. καὶ τόδ' οὐκέτ' ἔστ' ἴσον.
γεγραμμένων δὲ τῶν νόμων ὅ τ' ἀσθενὴς
ὁ πλούσιός τε τὴν δίκην ἴσην ἔχει.

utterly unpersuasive, and Plutarch notes that in fact things turned out as Anacharsis had predicted, not as Solon had hoped.

Until recently many modern scholars adopted a view along the lines proposed by Theseus.[10] Bury and Meiggs (1975: 104), for example conclude that "one of the first demands the people in Greek cities pressed upon their aristocratic governments, and one of the first concessions those governments were forced to make was a written law." In recent decades, however, scholars have reacted against this view, noting that most early legislation comes from cities with aristocratic not democratic governments, and arguing instead that written laws enabled the ruling class to maintain their control over the people. For example, Stratton argues that the state could not control the earliest writing in Greece, and this made necessary "the development of a state system based on repressive written laws created and amended by the government" (1980: 118). Eder sees the codification of law as "a reaction of the few aiming at preserving their political influence as completely as possible"; it thus served the political interests of the ruling class and preserved the control of the few over the many (1986: 264). And for Stoddart and Whitley, "the purpose of law codes [in Crete] was not to make public, and thereby 'democratize' the laws but to mystify them ... In a society where few could read or write, the monumentality of such inscriptions would appear all the more imposing." Thus, "writing remained the preserve of a scribal class, and the skills of literacy were put to conservative, not revolutionary ends" (1988: 766, 771).

Other, less political motives have been suggested for the earliest legislation, such as the needs of colonies (which were first settled in the late eighth century) or the needs of trade. New colonies may have wanted written laws if the colonists were assembled from several different cities, in which case they would not have had the same common heritage of traditional rules and customs as a long established city. But some colonies were sent out by a single city,[11] and (more important) many of the earliest laws, notably those from Athens and Crete, were not written for colonies, so this cannot be a primary explanation for first writing down laws, though it may have been a factor in some cases. As for trade, we noted earlier (Chapter Two) that not only are relatively few archaic laws connected with trade and commerce,[12] but in Greece very little early writing of any sort is concerned

---

[10] For a review of earlier views with further references, see Gagarin 1986: 121–30; Whitley 2001: 188–90, with n. 97.

[11] This is the traditional view; it is challenged by, e.g., Osborne (2004: 31–2), who argues that few colonies followed the traditional pattern of a single city sending out its own inhabitants.

[12] Solon wrote at least one law concerning export (Ruschenbusch 1966: F 65).

with matters of trade. Of course, traders may have written on perishable materials, but if laws about trade had been written down, they presumably would have been published just like other laws, and so the argument from silence carries some weight.

More recently, the question has been raised, whether archaic legislation consisted predominantly of large-scale legislation and even codification, culminating in legislation like the Gortyn Code, or whether it consisted primarily or entirely of single laws enacted piecemeal as *ad hoc* responses to specific situations. Stories about the earliest lawgivers tell of several – Zaleucus, Charondas, Solon, Lycurgus, and others – who enacted large-scale legislation, but as Hölkeskamp has correctly (and repeatedly) noted,[13] the surviving archaic inscriptions are mostly short texts directed at specific issues. The Gortyn Code, which he insists is not a code at all, is relatively late and appears to be exceptional. He concludes that archaic laws were generally written as specific, *ad hoc* responses to crises that regularly arose throughout Greece at the time. Hölkeskamp's studies have helped correct the tendency of earlier scholars to accept too readily the traditional stories,[14] and he has given us a better understanding of archaic legal inscriptions, but his conclusions need to be qualified in several respects.

First, as we noted (Chapter Two) both the inscriptions and reports in later authors like Aristotle tend, for different reasons, to present specific laws in isolation, but both sources are probably not representative of the full range of actual archaic legislation (Osborne 1997). The surviving legislation may not include large-scale collections earlier than the fifth century, but the Greeks certainly enacted much more legislation than survives today. And when, in the case of Solon, we have fairly reliable historical evidence for one legislator, it strongly supports the conclusion that he wrote a large set of laws together and that these were inscribed and displayed as a group on numbered *axones* (Rhodes 2006).

The method by which Solon arranged his laws on the *axones* is uncertain,[15] but it seems unlikely that they were arranged in purely random order. More likely, he arranged them in some coherent order, perhaps according to magistrate, that would have provided guidance to a litigant or a magistrate who wished to locate a specific law. We do not have complete

---

[13] Hölkeskamp 1992, 1994, 1995, most fully in 1999, and most recently 2005.
[14] Szegedy-Maszak 1978 already shed doubt on these stories.
[15] The *axones* numbered at least sixteen (Plutarch, *Solon* 23) and probably at least 21 (Harpocration, O 43 Keaney); see Ruschenbusch 1966: 64 (T8 and T9). Ruschenbusch 1966: 27–31 argues against the common view that they were arranged by magistrate.

enough remains from Solon's legislation to enable us to assess fully Hölkeskamp's claim (1999: 263–4) that Solon's laws are not a systematic codification, but a "series of concrete single provisions (*Einzelgesetze*)," but the evidence we do have indicates something between these two poles – a large collection of laws on many different subjects with at least some of these subjects (such as inheritance) being addressed by several laws that may well have been organized in some fashion. Hölkeskamp is undoubtedly correct that "we cannot speak of an abstract, logical systematization of all substantive law and legal procedure,"[16] but no one writing about ancient law uses "code" in this sense, for it would be futile to expect this degree of organization in the legislation of any premodern legal community. In ordinary usage, the terms, "code" and "codification" are broad and flexible concepts, and there is no good reason to insist on a narrow definition. Thus, in line with most other scholars,[17] I will continue to use "code" to designate a large-scale collection of laws with some degree of coherence, but will not speak of Solon's legislation as a codification since we do not have clear evidence for the arrangement of his laws.

Unfortunately, this focus on codification has diverted attention from other, important features of early legislation. Although they are far from being codes, Draco's homicide law, which we will discuss in Chapter Four, and several early inscriptions from Gortyn contain legislation that extends beyond a single concrete problem or crisis. Evidently the Greeks recognized the value of addressing and displaying on the same inscription laws relating to different aspects of a single subject. One of the early inscriptions from Gortyn (4.3) contains provisions arranged in what may be a chronological order. As we shall see, Draco's law, one of the earliest pieces of archaic legislation, already reveals an ability to organize provisions concerning different aspects of a subject into a substantial and coherent whole. And it is reasonable to assume that if more survived of archaic legislation in Greece, we would find more instances of such large-scale organization. To be sure, much archaic legislation consists of relatively short texts addressing a single issue. It thus appears that rather than try to fit all archaic legislation into a single mold, we should recognize the diversity of archaic

---

[16] "Von einer 'logisch-abstrakten Systematisierung des gesamten materiellen Rechts und des Verfahrenrechts kann dennoch keine Rede sein" (Hölkeskamp 1999: 263). He not surprisingly concludes that "Solon's laws – though they do cover an extraordinarily broad range of matters, from inheritance to debt, substantive as well as procedural – do not constitute a 'code' in a meaningful sense of the concept" (2005: 287).
[17] See the papers in Lévy 2000b, in particular van Effenterre and van Effenterre 2000.

legislation and accept that it varied from place to place and, at some places, from law to law.

The question remains, why did the Greeks first write laws? In fact, there are several questions here: why did Greek communities first enact laws, why did they write these laws down, and why did they display them publicly? I will begin with writing: what did the first lawgivers think they would accomplish by writing down a law rather than communicating it to others orally? We cannot simply say that they took the idea from the Near East.[18] As we shall see in Chapter Seven, Near-Eastern laws were written down for very different reasons than the Greek laws, and so even if the Greeks did take the idea of writing laws from the Near East, they almost certainly had different motives for doing so. Nor can we rely on later reports about the motives of early legislators, since these reports are almost certainly influenced by later ideas. To understand early legislation we must look primarily at the laws themselves, and in examining these, we must be open to the possibility that different laws had different aims or effects.

We can begin with the main law from Dreros, one of a group of early laws inscribed on the temple of Apollo at one edge of the agora or public gathering area. This area is in a saddle between two hilltops that had probably been inhabited since late Minoan times (Prent 2005: 283–4). The hilltop location was undoubtedly selected for defensive purposes, and the construction of the temple, probably in the second half of the eighth century (Mazarakis Ainian 1997: 217; Prent 2005: 284–6), and the careful organization and construction of this public area of which the temple was an integral part probably coincided with the expansion of Dreros' control over the surrounding territory. About a century after the temple's construction, the eight laws we now possess were inscribed on its wall, where they could easily be seen by the inhabitants when they gathered in the agora.[19]

The main law at Dreros begins with its enactment clause ("the polis has decided"), then states the rule that "when someone has been *kosmos*, within ten years the same person will not be *kosmos* again," prescribes the penalties for a *kosmos* who violates this rule, and ends with the names of three groups

---

[18] This view was most strongly argued by Muhl 1933. For more recent scholarship, see Westbrook 2005: 3–4 with the works cited at 4 n. 4, and cf. Cantarella 2005b: 26–7.

[19] Forrest observes that the agora at Dreros was not a market-place but a speaking-place or assembly-place: "There, about or a bit before 700, was prepared a little area with benches along one side, a formal meeting-place . . . that is, there is a debate going on, with a plurality of opinion expressed on a regular basis" (2000: 288).

of oath-swearers, the *kosmos* and the *damioi* and the twenty of the city. We might call this a constitutional law, though it does not establish a *politeia* or form of government but rather presupposes the existence of a certain form of governance and merely modifies one element of it. Very likely it modifies an earlier situation in which there was no restriction or perhaps a different time limit on repeating as *kosmos*. Whatever the previous rule, it had probably been in place for a long time and must have been a matter of unwritten custom not written law. And the Drerians undoubtedly had other customary rules and traditions concerning officials and other matters that were communicated orally.

Whatever the precise changes implemented by this law, it would have had little direct effect on the lives of most ordinary citizens, who would never become, and probably never aspired to become, *kosmos*. Why then did someone decide to write this law down and display it in a prominent, public place rather than communicating the rule orally to the relatively few individuals or families who would be directly affected by it, perhaps to all who had been *kosmos* during the past ten years, and to each new *kosmos* on entering office? Current or potential *kosmoi* could easily follow the rule if it were communicated to them orally, and if someone were going to violate the rule, it seems unlikely that a written version would be a more powerful deterrent than an oral version. As we shall see below, writing may help ensure the accurate preservation of details, but in this case the details (the penalties for a violation and the list of the oath-swearers) are not especially complex or unusual, and they too could probably have been remembered without difficulty, though writing them down would help. Nor would these details have been of direct interest to most members of the community. So even if a written text was thought necessary to preserve details, why was it written in stone and publicly displayed?

The decision to write down and display the law publicly was very likely made by the same body that initially enacted the law, namely the polis. This means that the rule, if not its details, must have been of interest to this group not just to the few who would be directly affected by it; and the law's larger interest is confirmed by the presence of the enactment clause at the beginning. Strictly speaking, this clause is unnecessary: a written law would derive its authority from its being publicly displayed, as do other early laws without enactment clauses. But right at the beginning the law boldly proclaims itself a decision of the polis, and this must indicate that those who made this decision felt it important to commemorate their participation in the enactment process as well as to state the rule itself.

Who, then, comprised the polis of Dreros at this time? At the very least, the expression in the last line of this law, "the twenty of the polis" (*ikati oi tas polios*), must mean that the polis consisted of no fewer than twenty members,[20] and the fact that "polis" without qualification is sufficient to designate this body in line 1 implies that the specification of "the twenty of the polis" is a different body, namely a subsection of the larger group, perhaps a representative body like the "five from each tribe" who approve the agreement with Spensithios (see Chapter Five). We cannot know just how large a group comprised this polis, but if it had twenty representatives, then it probably numbered at least several hundred, certainly a larger group than just those who held or might hold magistracies. Whether membership in this polis depended on land ownership or participation in hoplite warfare, or some other factor, most members are likely to have come from the middle segment of the population, neither the very rich nor the very poor.[21]

There are at least two reasons why the members of the polis may have wished to have this law publicly displayed. First, after enacting the law, they may have wished to remain involved in its implementation, especially in case of violations. Publication of the law suggests that the oath-swearing mentioned in the final clause was a public ceremony, perhaps occurring at the installation of a new *kosmos*, where he would swear to obey the law and the others would swear to enforce the law if he violated it. Other members of the community, including many who had taken part in the enactment of this law, would presumably attend such a ceremony and would feel reassured to know that the rules they enacted were being followed precisely. Second, public display of the law with its enactment clause would continually remind members that they had imposed this law on their officials, and this in turn would reinforce the members' sense of their own authority as a group (the polis) at a time when this body's sense of its authority as a group was probably still quite weak. In other words, even though this law did not directly affect most members of the polis, the law was an expression of their authority as a group and it was thus in their interest to have that authority memorialized in a publicly displayed text.

---

[20] Davies (2004: 20) seems to think that the polis and the twenty of the polis are equivalent, which seems unlikely. Otherwise, Davies makes some good points in this interesting article, but it is puzzling that in discussing terms for members of the community he says nothing about the early use of collectives, such as "the Gortynians."

[21] Estimated by Donlan 1997: 45–6 at 50 percent of the total population in the archaic period, with the rich elite at 20 percent and the very poor at 30 percent. At a guess, perhaps a few thousand people lived in the fortified hilltop area of Dreros.

The Dreros law thus seems to mark a stage in the development of a communal self-awareness, which was emerging all over Greece at this time, though in different forms and going by different names – *polis, dēmos, laos*, etc. (Davies 2004). At the time when this law was enacted, the population of Dreros was expanding and its territory was probably growing. Its well-fortified position would have given it influence over neighboring villages, whose inhabitants would take refuge there in times of danger; over time, they probably began to think of themselves as members of the Drerian community, and some might even have been allowed membership in the polis. The bilingual text from about the same time (Dreros 8) indicates that at least one Eteocretan community was part of the larger Drerian community. In such circumstances, towns like Dreros faced the challenge of creating a unified sense of community. The prominent display of this law with its enactment clause would advertise this accomplishment and would strengthen the sense among the members of the community who constituted this polis, including perhaps some members of these neighboring communities, that they comprised a single unified group, the polis of Dreros.

None of the seven other inscriptions that were inscribed on the same temple wall at Dreros appears to hold nearly the same degree of public interest. Although at least four of these begin with an enactment formula – one enacted by the polis, two by different bodies, and a fourth by some group whose name is lost – they all appear to treat relatively minor matters. None seems to have much detail, which might have required that it be written, nor does any appear to address the sort of issue that is likely to have caused a crisis. Nonetheless, each was published and prominently displayed along with the first law, which was of real public interest. A possible explanation is that once the non-iteration law was written and displayed and the Drerians experienced the satisfaction of regularly seeing visible evidence of their authority, they were pleased with the result and wished to continue enacting and displaying laws, even on matters of less public interest.

At Gortyn, in the early seventh century a small iron-age community moved from a nearby acropolis down to a site at the northern edge of the large fertile Mesara plain in southern Crete, around which were scattered a number of small villages. The move was probably motivated in part by an increase in population, but the Gortynians may also have wanted easier access to the plain and the communities around it. And of course they must have felt secure enough to do without the natural protection of an acropolis. At this new site they built several large temples, including the temple of Pythian Apollo, on whose exterior walls all of the forty archaic texts at Gortyn were probably inscribed.[22] These temples are one indication of Gortyn's growing influence; by the end of the seventh century when the earliest laws were written down, the city was prospering economically, its population was increasing, and its influence over neighboring settlements was expanding.

The temple of Apollo was undoubtedly a site of frequent public activity, and Gortynians must regularly have encountered the texts inscribed on it, which, as Perlman (2004: 182) notes, "were meant to attract an audience." The earliest laws address a wide range of issues and may have been displayed here for different reasons, but many of them were longer and more complex than the Dreros laws, and the need to preserve details may explain why these were written down. Oral communication can preserve general rules and maxims for generations without significant alteration, but as many studies of oral cultures have shown, details in oral texts are unstable and often change with successive retellings. Only in exceptional circumstances do orally transmitted details perhaps remain constant over time,[23] and because orally transmitted rules are unable to preserve details without change, they normally do not include much detail. Accordingly, the rules preserved in the poems of Homer and Hesiod have nowhere near the degree of detail we find in the early laws, as a direct comparison of texts will show (Chapter Four). 4.14 is not overly detailed, but it is complex enough and important enough that the community would not want to rely on oral preservation.

At Gortyn, one part of 4.14 closely resembles the main law at Dreros[24] and may have been inscribed in part for the same reason, to reassure the people that this restriction on holding office was being enforced and to remind them of their ability to regulate their highest officials. But 4.14 is more complex than the Drerian law: it specifies three different periods for the iteration of three different offices and imposes different fines on at least two officials.[25] Since it would be more difficult to preserve and transmit

---

[22] The temple was built a short distance from the later agora (whose date is uncertain). It is usually dated to the second half of the seventh century, largely because of the dating of the inscriptions associated with it (Prent 2005: 274–5; see also Perlman 2000: 60, 83 nn. 10–12). But the two dates need not be so closely connected; at Dreros, for example, the first laws were inscribed on the temple about a century after its construction.

[23] These might involve a small religious community transmitting a sacred text. See Goody 1987: 110–22; Finnegan 1992: 139–53, especially 150–2. Both scholars express doubts, however, about the accurate oral transmission of the *Vedas*, which are often cited as an extreme case of exact memorization of a large body of material.

[24] Line 2: "The same person is not to be *kosmos* again for three years; for the *gnōmones* ten years and for the foreigners' (*kosmos?*), five years."

[25] Line 1: "The *kosmos* in charge, if he does not exact full payment, shall owe it himself, and the *titas*, if he does not exact full payment, [shall pay] double."

this amount of detail orally, one reason to write down the law was probably to ensure its accurate preservation and consistent enforcement.

The need to preserve details accurately is even clearer in 4.3, a list of sacrifices which is notable for the amount of detail it presents even in the relatively short fragments that have been preserved. The subject matter here seems uncontroversial, and as we noted before, these rules were probably not displayed on the temple of Apollo because of their religious nature: the sacrifices listed involve other gods in addition to Apollo and nothing else about the inscription differentiates it from the many other laws with no religious content inscribed on the same temple. Of course, priests and other officials at Gortyn must for a long time have been remembering which sacrifices were to take place to different gods on different occasions. But as the population of Gortyn grew, and as smaller villages were integrated into the Gortynian community, the number of sacrifices probably increased to the point that memory would no longer be able to preserve accurately all the details of a sacrificial calendar such as 4.3. And since the details of religious rites are usually of great importance to people who participate in these rites, it would be important to ensure the accuracy of these details. The full text of 4.3 must have contained much more detailed information than survives today; the only way to preserve this information accurately would have been to write it down.

Why, then, write it on the temple for all to see? Why not let the officials in charge of sacrifices record the details on papyrus for their own consultation? Public display, I would argue, must be an indication of public interest, and the same reasons for displaying an important constitutional law like Dreros 1 must have been one reason for displaying this list of sacrifices at Gortyn, which would be of interest to the many members of the community who would participate in the rites, not just to a few priests and officials. Thus, the list was displayed in a prominent public place rather than being kept privately by priests for their own use.

At Dreros, I suggested that once the important constitutional law had been written down and publicly displayed, the community continued to treat other less significant laws in the same way. At Gortyn, it seems, the same practice emerged and the community decided to display many different laws in the same public area, not only constitutional laws like 4.14 but many different sorts of laws – the sacrificial calendar in 4.3, rules about herd animals and injuries in 4.1, and rules about inheritance disputes involving an adopted son in 4.21. These Gortynian laws are complex and detailed, and would need to be written down in order to be accurately preserved, but in addition, once the practice of public display was established for some laws, others would automatically be displayed in the same way so that members of the community affected by them would be able to read them.

All these considerations point to a larger public interest, not the interests of a small ruling elite, as the main motivation for the writing and public display of these laws. Public interest explains why masons made an effort to make these texts easier for readers to understand, and why the enactment clause was displayed together with the law in Dreros 1. Public interest also explains why so many texts were inscribed on the same wall both at Dreros and Gortyn. Some of these texts are quite short and many concern minor issues, and yet all were written down and displayed. Public display of these minor texts next to the more important laws can hardly have served the interests of the ruling elite, and the additional visual impact must have been negligible. And if visual impact was one motive for displaying some of these texts, the group that sought this visual impact was just as likely to be the community (the polis) as a ruling elite. We will address the question of the elite's role in archaic legislation at some length later, but first we should consider the reasons for writing the other archaic laws in Chapter Two.

Like Gortyn and Dreros, Chios seems to have expanded its territory and grown in population and prosperity during the eighth and seventh centuries. It had sent out a colony during the eighth century, and by the sixth century its trade was flourishing and the city controlled not only the whole island of Chios but also some agricultural land on the nearby mainland (Cook 1982, C. Roebuck 1986). Under these circumstances, perhaps in the 570s, the text of an important constitutional law was inscribed on a freestanding stele. We do not know where it originally stood,[26] but it is hard to imagine that it was not in a public area. The law protects the ordinances of the people, imposes penalties on certain officials, and directs a people's council (*boulē dēmosiē*) to conduct public business and in particular to hear lawsuits. The text places a heavy emphasis on the people – *dēmos* or *dēmosios* occurs five times – who very likely had a role in enacting the law and in its public display. Exactly who comprised the demos and how this group might have approved legislation is unclear, but it is reasonable to suppose that they would want to have the text displayed publicly for the same reasons as the polis at Dreros. And some members of the demos would surely have wanted to read the text, which included more details than the Dreros law, even if others may have been content just to know that it was publicly displayed.

---

[26] The stele was discovered built into a modern wall in a small village in the southern part of the island.

Eretria was also a prosperous city in the eighth and seventh centuries. It sent out several important colonies, either by itself or together with its neighbor Calchis, it was a major center of trade and commerce, and it had connections with cities all over Greece. By the mid sixth century, it exerted its influence over the whole island of Euboea and over parts of coastal Boeotia and Attica.[27] In the third quarter of the sixth century, at the height of its power, Eretria enacted a law and inscribed it on two sides of a stone block that formed the corner of a building probably located in the harbor area. The provisions of this law appear to concern trade and navigation, and they may not have affected or been of interest to some members of the community. But the many Eretrians involved in trade and commerce would have wanted to know the details of these rules. Thus, this law was probably written down and publicly displayed for the same reasons as laws elsewhere, to preserve its details and communicate them with certainty and consistency to the inhabitants of a diverse and increasingly prosperous community.

The laws from Elis and Argos that we examined in Chapter Two fit the same pattern. By the late sixth century, both cities controlled a relatively large territory and played important roles in Greek affairs. Elis, the dominant city in the western Peloponnesus, supervised the shrine and festival at Olympia. Argos exercised its authority over much of the surrounding territory in part by its control of the great shrine and temple of Hera, the Heraion, and was one of the most important cities in the Peloponnesus and the main rival of Sparta (Piérart 2003). Of the three provisions of the law from Elis, *A* is religious (prohibiting intercourse in a sanctuary), but *B* and *C* regulate litigation and legislation generally, specifying that no judgment can be contrary to written law, but the people, presumably in the form of an assembly, can overrule a law, and that a law can be emended by three successive votes of the council and the assembly. There would be an obvious public interest in having these provisions publicly displayed. The text also indicates that the people (*damos*), who must have been a much larger group than the 500-member council, have considerable power in the city; they were probably the body that enacted the laws (perhaps together with the council), and they would presumably have wanted to see the results of their work publicly displayed.[28]

---

[27] See K. Walker 2004: esp. 183–206. The Athenian tyrant Peisistratus stayed in Eretria in between the periods of his rule in the mid sixth century.

[28] On democracy in Elis, see further Robinson 1997: 108–11.

Finally, the use of *graphos* ("writing"), singular and plural, to designate laws at Elis tells us that already by this time all laws were written and presumably readers of this law were also able to find and read other laws from Elis. The law from Argos is too fragmentary for us to speculate about reasons for its inscription, but since it too uses the word "writing" (*grathmata*) for its own laws, it seems that here too, it was taken for granted that all laws were written and available (and thus publicly displayed).[29]

The regulations for Naupactus are the only legal text we have examined that was written for a colony, but it does not seem that this factor entered into the motivation for writing this law, since it clearly dates from a period later than the initial foundation. Even if the original settlers came from different cities and thus lacked common customs and traditions, this would no longer have been a factor when this law was written. The law addresses two matters: the inheritance of land and the need for additional settlers. We cannot tell if there were any special motives for writing and displaying this law, but it clearly was not the first law in Naupactus to be written, since it refers (lines 12–13) to a homicide law as a *tethmos* (*thesmos*), a word otherwise used only of written law. This homicide law does not survive, but it must have set out the punishments mentioned in the surviving law (curse, confiscation of property, and demolition of the house) and may have also specified more details about these punishments. More important, the expression "according to the homicide law" (*kat ton andrephonikon tethmon*) is the first cross-reference we have encountered in these laws, though this is a common feature of later legislation. By itself a single cross-reference may not be highly significant, but as we shall see, cross-referencing implies that a city's laws have a coherence and unity of purpose, and it may be that when this law was inscribed, Naupactus had already developed the sense that all its laws formed a coherent unit.

Cleonae, though small, was moderately important because of its location near the road between Corinth and Argos and its traditional control over the panhellenic sanctuary of Zeus at Nemea and the Nemean Games. The inscription, which addresses the issue of pollution and purification for homicide, may have been displayed at or near the sanctuary of Zeus at Nemea, though this is just a guess. If there were other written homicide laws at Cleonae, as may be implied by the expression "against the law"

---

[29] We cannot firmly date the beginning of democracy in Argos before the fifth century, but it is possible that the people were already exercising power in the sixth century (Robinson 1997: 82–4) and thus had the same motives for publicly displaying their laws as the people at Dreros and Chios.

(*para nomon*), we do not know where these were displayed. But it is not surprising that this law was written, since any homicide law would have been of interest to many in the community. Otherwise we can only speculate, but a law concerning pollution and purification might have been of special interest to the priest or priests who administered the sanctuary and who may have caused the law to be written and displayed nearby.

Finally, despite the oddness of the inscription from Tiryns and our lack of information about this town and its inhabitants in the archaic period, it is notable that we find in the text both a regulation punishing officials who do not carry out their duty and another that requires an official to follow the decision of the *damos*. Whatever the explanation for this curious law, in exercising popular control over their officials the people of Tiryns resemble those in several other cities with early legislation.

This survey of archaic laws from Dreros, Gortyn, Chios, Eretria, Elis, Argos, Naupactus, and Cleonae, has suggested a number of different motives for writing down and publicly displaying these texts, but two factors are especially important: the desire of the larger community, however broadly or loosely defined, to memorialize itself and its accomplishment in enacting these laws, and the need to preserve the details of increasingly complex rules without change over time. The important role of non-elite groups like the polis in these laws means that these groups, whose role is documented in Greece as early as the assemblies and mass armies that we find together with kings and heroes in the poems of Homer (Raaflaub 1997b, Davies 2004: 23–4), must have been growing in power along with the elite groups which, as archaeologists have shown, began emerging in the iron age. Ordinary citizens often leave little or no mark on the archaeological record, but these laws document the existence of collective bodies, as well as whole communities like "the Gortynians," an expression found in two of the earliest (very fragmentary) texts from that city (4.10, 4.23). Elite groups undoubtedly played a large role in the governance of all these archaic cities, but collective bodies evidently had no qualms about asserting their own authority too.

Most cities from which we have significant remains of archaic laws were relatively large and important cities which controlled or strongly influenced a large amount of surrounding territory. From the eighth to the sixth centuries, these cities were generally growing in both size and population, and were becoming more prosperous. Such growth would have had significant consequences for the legal system, including an increase in the number of disputes and in the variety and complexity of issues raised by these disputes.[30] An increase in the number of disputes would increase the demand for judges who could help resolve them, and this would put a strain on traditional procedures and increase the likelihood of inconsistency in judgments. At the same time, as cities extended their control over smaller, formerly independent towns and villages in the near vicinity, they would become more diverse. Small villages coming under the influence of nearby towns might not share the same customs and traditions, and as intercourse among all the inhabitants of the larger territory increased, there would be more occasions for uncertainty or disagreement about how to handle alleged violations of traditional rules and a greater likelihood of inconsistent judgments.

These two factors – the emergence of more powerful collective bodies and the increase in the size and diversity of populations – lay behind the two main motives for writing down and publicly displaying laws in the archaic period: the memorialization of collective authority and the specification of details. Simple traditional rules that were widely agreed on may not have needed to be written down, since almost everyone would know these and there could be little doubt about their meaning. But when traditional rules differed among different parts of the community, or when new rules were enacted (especially if these were complex), it would be necessary to put these rules in writing.

One other factor influencing the writing down of laws would probably have been contact among different cities. We do not know exactly where or when the first law was put in writing, but we may assume that people in other cities would soon hear about the use of this new technology for preserving and communicating their rules, and would realize that this could be helpful in their own cities. News of this development appears to have spread rapidly, since, like writing itself, we find the practice of writing laws emerging all over the Greek world at about the same time.

In sum, the increasing need for detailed rules in cities that were growing larger and more diverse and the desire of a body of ordinary members of the community to confirm their own authority were the most important factors behind the rapid spread of publicly displayed, written legislation. Both factors also provided a reason to display these laws prominently in public places and to make the texts as readable as possible for people whose reading skills may have been limited. These written laws had the advantage

---

[30] Growth "will have driven ... an increased need to deal with quarrels to do with property, inheritance, debt and crime" (Davies 2004: 25–6).

of being fixed and, especially if written in stone, not easily changed. The sense of permanence that resulted would help give these rules the kind of authority that previously resided in the traditional rules and values of the community. The authority of written laws would also have been strengthened by the strong visual impression some of these texts would have made on those who encountered them regularly. But some of the texts we have examined (in particular those from Naupactus, Elis, and Argos) are not particularly impressive and probably had little visual impact. And as we have seen, even texts that made a strong visual impression were nonetheless intended to be read by members of the community beyond the ruling elite.

The emphasis I have been giving to the role of non-elite bodies in enacting and publicly displaying this early legislation goes against the recent trend to see archaic legislation as the product of competition among the elite.[31] By the beginning of the archaic period elite groups had emerged in most parts of Greece and probably held most, if not all, public offices. As far as we can tell, moreover, the early lawgivers mentioned in later accounts all belonged to these elite groups. But there are obstacles to connecting archaic legislation directly with intra-elite competition. First, the main evidence usually cited in support of this view are the laws against iteration of office (Dreros 1, Gortyn 14). But as far as we can tell, out of the hundred or so archaic laws that survive, only these two restrict the iteration of office.[32] Perhaps many other laws like these have perished, but it is more likely that only a few such laws were ever enacted.

More widely attested are laws imposing fines or otherwise punishing officials who do not properly carry out their duties (Gortyn 14, laws from Eretria and Tiryns, and probably the law from Chios and Gortyn 1).[33] Since it seems unlikely that the elite would often impose penalties on themselves, the impetus for these regulations probably came from non-elite groups. Laws imposing penalties on officials are especially significant because no surviving archaic law grants greater authority to an official. Laws specify the

---

[31] See Osborne 1996: 185–90; Papakonstantinou 2002: 135 ("written legislation in archaic and classical Crete can partly be explained in the context of inter-aristocratic strife for political power within the Cretan *poleis*"); Forsdyke 2005: 26 ("both formal public offices and early written law were, at least in part, responses to the problem of intra-elite conflict in the early polis").

[32] Forsdyke (2005: 26 n. 50) cites in addition a very fragmentary sixth-century law from Eleutherna (*ICret* 2.12.4 = *Nomima* 1.83, *IGT* 110), in which the words "the same" (τὸν ἀϝτόν) are evident, but van Effenterre and Ruzé's speculation that this law may conceivably have concerned the iteration of some office is no more than a guess. Forsdyke also cites a more complete law from Erythrae prohibiting anyone from being a secretary more than once, but all other scholars date this to the fifth or early fourth century and it can hardly be as early as the mid sixth century, as she claims.

[33] E. Harris (2006) sees the control of officials as one characteristic of Greek as opposed to Near-Eastern law.

duties and responsibilities of officials, but officials are never exempted from the legal consequences of their actions. Members of the elite may have played a role in formulating legislation that controlled their conduct in office, but the main motivation must have come from elsewhere.

More important, there is clear evidence in the Dreros law and elsewhere that non-elites participated in the enactment of legislation. Not only is this law explicitly enacted by the polis, but the oath-swearers include "the *damioi* and the twenty of the polis." As suggested above, the latter group may be twenty representatives; the *damioi* are apparently officials, whose duties are unknown but they may be some sort of people's officials (if *damos* = "people") who served the people's interest in some way.[34] Finally, the ten-year limit on iteration might indicate that ten or more elite families devised this means to ensure that the office rotated among them, but in view of the significant role played by the polis and its representatives at Dreros, it may also have been a way for the non-elite to open up this office to wider participation. And even if the position of *kosmos* was held only by elites, there is no reason to think that members of the polis were any less interested than the elite in ensuring its orderly rotation. In short, the Dreros law, together with others that show the presence of collective bodies (polis, *damos*, Gortynians), provides stronger support for the view that non-elites were responsible for early legislation than that the elites were regulating their own competition by means of legislation.

Participation by non-elites does not mean that written laws had a democratic effect. The cities that wrote laws in the archaic period, many of them in Crete, were more often oligarchies than democracies (to use traditional terminology). Even some tyrants were lawgivers (e.g. Pittacus of Mytilene).[35] And laws that provide evidence of democracy, such as the law from Chios, may be testimony after the fact, since the law itself does not enact a democratic change but confirms the presence of already established democratic institutions, such as a popular council (Robinson 1997: 100 n. 30). But the most interesting feature of archaic legislation from a political perspective is the number of cities that provide evidence of the combined presence of popular and elite elements in the city.

The Dreros law, to begin with, not only expresses the authority of the polis, but also confirms the position of *kosmos* as (probably) the chief

---

[34] Van Effenterre (1985: esp. 394–6) makes an interesting argument that because *dēmos* in Homer and other early texts regularly means "country" as opposed to the urban area, the *damioi* are the landholding elite. I am not persuaded by this, but "the *damioi* and the twenty of the polis" may be those officials who represent country people and city people respectively.

[35] On tyrants as lawgivers, see Salmon 1997: 63–5.

official in the city, and indicates that he had considerable power, which the law does nothing to diminish (unless he violates the ten-year limit). At Gortyn the positions of *kosmos* and others are confirmed, but other laws (4.10, 4.23) mention "Gortynians," who are presumably a collective body of non-elite. At Chios there are "kings" (*basileis*), but also a people's council. The Naupactus inscription mentions a council of elders, the polis, and an elected body (*apoklēsia*). And at Tiryns we find several officials including a *hieromnamōn*, together with the *damos* and an assembly. Many of the cities that wrote archaic legislation, in other words, had forms of government that combined elite and popular elements in different ways. In this regard they are following the general parameters found in Homer, where various councils exist together with "kings," and even lowly figures like Thersites have the opportunity to speak (*Iliad* 2.211–77). This suggests that elite and popular forces in a community may have often worked together, presumably not always in harmony, within political structures that combined both elements; and the legislation they produced was presumably approved by both sides. Elite competition was undoubtedly an important factor in the development of many archaic poleis, but much archaic legislation appears to be a community-wide endeavor, not simply an outgrowth of elite competition.

There is no evidence, then, that early legislation regularly strengthened the position of one side of the elite/popular pair, but the enactment of legislation probably helped strengthen the whole community's sense of itself as a single political entity. This is perhaps clearest in texts that explicitly mention the people as a group, a polis, a demos, or a collective like *Gortynioi*, since this would convey to most readers that they were members of this group, and that they together with the others in the group were regulated, but also protected, by this law. A similar sense of privilege might be suggested by the mention of foreigners, which we find at Gortyn in the sixth century (4.14 speaks of "the foreigners [*kosmos*?]'). And simply by being displayed in a central public space, even laws that do not mention a collective body would probably have conveyed the sense that the rules contained in the inscribed text applied to all those who, like the reader, participated in that public space and were thus members of the political community. This strengthened sense of community could, in turn, reinforce the sense of the authority not only of the laws, but also of all the elements of the community, popular and elite.

Finally, what led communities to enact these particular laws, that is to decide that there should be a rule on a particular subject, and to formulate the precise wording of that rule, which would then be written down? We have already suggested motives, such as the desire to regulate an area of conduct not regulated by traditional rules and customs or to clarify a regulation when traditional rules and customs were ambiguous or conflicting, or to change the rules governing a particular subject. All such motives are in some sense responses to the recent past, since the need for clarification of rules or for new regulation generally becomes evident only through experiencing the limitations of current rules. But the laws that result are not necessarily responses to a crisis. Many archaic laws addressed more than one issue or regulated several aspects of one subject. Indeed, perhaps the most striking feature of archaic legislation is the variety of issues it addressed. Laws might address a single issue (Dreros 1), several issues (Chios), or several aspects of one issue (Gortyn 3). A constitutional law may be enacted in response to a crisis, but there could be other reasons why, for example, the Drerians regulated the *kosmos'* term of office; and the list of sacrifices in Gortyn 3 was almost certainly not enacted in response to a crisis. And although large-scale legislation (whether or not one calls it codification) is not attested in the inscriptional record before the fifth century, it is well documented in Athens in the early sixth century (Solon). We cannot easily generalize about the content or nature of archaic legislation.

The process by which archaic laws were enacted probably also varied, though in many cases we can only guess what this process was. Even when a law's enactment clause survives, we do not know exactly how the polis or other group actually gave their approval. The early lawgivers either already held some office which gave them authority or were appointed for the specific task of legislation; then they probably enacted legislation without further approval. Certainly Solon did not need *post facto* approval for his legislation; on the contrary, he prohibited Athenians from tampering with his laws after he wrote them. It has been suggested that early laws were a compilation of judicial verdicts (Várhelyi 1996: 41–2; Davies 1996), but there is no good evidence that verdicts were written down during the archaic period.[36] And some laws, like Dreros 1, that is explicitly enacted by some body, or the list of sacrifices in Gortyn 3, cannot be verdicts. Many laws were probably influenced by recent litigation and some may have echoed or reproduced recent verdicts, but others probably diverged from recent verdicts. There was no direct path from the text of a verdict to the text of a law. And there probably was no single method of legislation that was followed in all archaic cities. In some cities, single lawgivers enacted

[36] For the Thesmothetae possibly writing down verdicts at Athens, see Chapter Five.

laws, but in others, groups were responsible. In some cities a single official may have been authorized to legislate; in others it may have been a group of officials. Most likely each city proceeded in the way that best suited its own political situation.

Similarly, the diversity of subjects covered by archaic legislation – the conduct of officials, property, family and inheritance, public sacrifices, homicide and others – indicates that the Greeks as a whole did not have a single view of the kinds of subjects deserving of legislation. Rather, each city used the new technology of writing to produce laws on matters that particularly concerned them, and these would vary from city to city. Some issues, such as the conduct of public officials, were of concern to several different cities, and cities may sometimes have borrowed ideas or specific rules from other cities. But each city made its own decisions about the subjects of its early laws and developed its own set of written laws.

Cities even differed in the terms they used for written laws. In Homer, traditional rules and practices are referred to as *themistes*, and after Homer *nomos* is often used to designate a rule, custom, or tradition (not until the fifth century does *nomos* designate a written law).[37] The archaic Greeks used different terms for their written laws: *graphos* ("writing," from *graphō*, "scratch, draw, write"), *thesmos* ("ordinance," from *tithēmi*, "put, place"),[38] and *rhētra* ("proclamation," from *erō*, "speak"), to which we may add related words and expressions, such as *grammata* or *tethmos*.[39] The choice among these terms was apparently a matter of local preference, but only rarely does a city use more than one of them. Use of any of the terms would have marked these new written rules as different from the community's traditional oral rules and customs, but this effect would be especially clear if *graphos* or a related term was used, since this would make explicit the bond between law and writing. *Graphos* would also suggest that everything that is written (and presumably publicly displayed) is a law, as in the law from Elis (*IvO* 7, discussed above): "if anyone judges contrary to the writing (*graphos*), the judgment will be void." At Elis, writing was law. But even *thesmos* and *rhētra* would mark these rules as special.

The Elis law illustrates the final effect I will note of writing early laws, the creation of the idea of a law as a statute and also law as an institution. Even if a written law was identical with traditional practice, the act of putting this rule in writing separated it from its traditional oral context and

---

[37] The law from Cleonae discussed in Chapter Two is a possible exception.
[38] *Thesmos* does occur in Homer (*Odyssey* 23.296), but probably in the sense of "place, location."
[39] See further R. Thomas 1996; Hölkeskamp 2000: 83–7.

gave it a separate existence. It might be marked as the law of some legislator or group, but it derived its authority primarily from its being written down and publicly displayed, often together with other texts. These texts then formed a group of texts that were recognized (in Hart's sense) as comprising the community's laws. By means of writing, then, an oral rule could become separated from a body of undifferentiated rules like the *Works and Days* and be given a special authority that lay immediately in the fact that it was written (often in a special place) and ultimately in the authority of the community which agreed to write or allowed someone else to write it down. Writing would make the rule a law.

Over the course of the archaic period, then, the new technology of writing allowed Greek law to develop from a preliterate, oral process relying on traditional communal norms, to a more formal institution supported and defined by a body of written legislation regulating both substance and procedure. Some cities enacted many laws, others only a few. The subjects of each city's laws varied, as did their methods of enactment. But in almost all cases the new written laws were displayed in a prominent public place so that they could be read by members of that community. Some were displayed in a sacred place, or written on a temple, and in these cases the location in itself probably invoked the authority of the god or gods. And even laws not so located sometimes began by alluding to or invoking the gods (Pounder 1984). But the ultimate authority behind archaic legislation was always the community, in whose interest and for whose use these texts were written down and displayed.

CHAPTER 4

Why Draco Wrote his Homicide Law

None of the inscriptions surveyed thus far comes from Athens, but we do have later information about archaic legislation in Athens; in particular, the text of Draco's homicide law was reinscribed on a stone stele at the end of the fifth century (*IG* I³ 104, dated to 409/8).[1] The text from this stele provides no evidence for the original physical appearance of Draco's law, but it does tell us much about the content, style, and organization of the law, and this can help us understand why the law was enacted and why it was written down and displayed in public. After examining this law in some detail, we will look briefly at archaic Athenian legislation after Draco.[2]

Tradition holds that Draco wrote the first Athenian laws in 621/0 (*Ath. Pol.* 4.1, 41.2). Best attested is his homicide law but he may have written laws on other subjects too. A generation later, in 594, Solon wrote a new set of laws covering many different issues, but he kept Draco's homicide law. The Athenians reinscribed this law in 409/8 as part of their attempt to republish all valid laws (Chapter Eight). Part of this later reinscription survives, from which scholars have reconstructed a fragmentary text that, in the opinion of many, accurately reproduces the original text of Draco's law, though it is uncertain whether we have the original beginning of the law.[3] In what follows, I will assume that the fifth-century reinscription preserves

---

[1] Republished with commentary in Stroud 1968. I discuss some of the issues in this chapter in Gagarin 2007b.

[2] Another archaic law for which we have only later evidence is the *rhētra* attributed to the seventh-century Spartan legislator Lycurgus (Plutarch, *Lycurgus* 6.1–2, 7–8), setting out the basic structure of Sparta's government. Although this text probably was written down at the time it was enacted, there are too many uncertainties about the text and its interpretation, and about Lycurgan legislation in general, to allow us to draw any conclusions about why it was written down (see further MacDowell 1986: 3–6, Millender 2001: 127–41; cf. Gagarin 1986: 53–54 n. 9).

[3] Indications that Draco's text was not revised before being reinscribed include the fact that the fifty-one are to choose ten members from the phratry by rank (*aristindēn*) and that the text refers to itself as a *thesmos*. In the first case, a more democratic process would surely have been implemented if the law had been revised in the fifth century, and in the second, a later writer would have referred to the law as

the original beginning of Draco's law (though this is not essential for my conclusions), and that the surviving text adheres closely to Draco's original words.[4]

We do not know whether Draco was one of Athens' annual officials when he wrote his law or was specially appointed for this task, but in either case he created his law for a community that did not yet have written laws. He may have known about written laws elsewhere in Greece, but he probably had little or no precedent for writing a homicide law. So why did he write down this particular law? The most common answer is that he was trying to resolve a crisis that stemmed from an attempted coup by a certain Cylon in 636. The story is told in different versions by Herodotus, Thucydides, Plutarch, and others. All agree that the coup failed to gain the support of the people and that the Cylonians were trapped on the Acropolis or in some other sanctuary, where many of them were killed sacrilegiously. The opposition was probably led by the family of the Alcmeonids, and as a result of this killing, many members of this prominent family later went into exile, and the family itself was long thought to be under a curse or in a state of pollution.[5]

No ancient source connects Draco with Cylon, but because of the temporal proximity of the two events, scholars usually make the connection. Humphreys presents the most detailed case for a connection, arguing that fifteen years after the killing of the Cylonians, their descendants were voicing claims on behalf of their dead kinfolk and some of the killers who were in exile wanted to return. Since many of the killers were only indirectly involved, or acted unintentionally or in self-defense, she argues, Draco felt the need to address these particular factors in his new legislation.[6] One difficulty with this thesis is that no source suggests that any of

a *nomos*, the term used in the fifth-century prescript to the inscription (line 5). In addition, the provision for retroactivity would have been without force by the time a generation or so had passed, yet it is still preserved in the reinscribed text; and the frontier markets mentioned in provision 10 no longer existed by 409. Finally, the copy preserves the original spelling with aspiration indicated by an *h*, whereas in the prescript aspiration is not marked.

[4] For the first assumption, see Gagarin 1981a; for the second, see the preceding note, and also Gallia 2004: 456, who, following the arguments in Stroud 1968: 60–4, calls the inscription "a painstakingly accurate transcription of the original Draconian law." See also Lewis 1967 on *IG* i^3 105 (=*IG* i^2 114), the companion inscription to ours, which he sees as the work of "a careful man transcribing a damaged original with such fidelity that he preferred to mark three blank spaces which he could not read rather than make what appears to us the easiest of conjectures."

[5] Attempts to select details from among conflicting ancient sources for this episode seem to me futile, and so I have tried to present only those elements that all or most agree on. For a more detailed account see, e.g., Thür 2002: 633–4. The date of 636 for Cylon is not certain, but is generally accepted; for details see Rhodes 1981: 79–84. For full details about the ancient sources, see Stroud 1968: 70–4.

[6] Humphreys 1991: 21–2; see also Stroud 1968: 70–4 with references, Thür 2002, and most recently Forsdyke 2005: 84–90.

those who killed the Cylonians acted unintentionally or in self-defense. On the contrary, the massacre of the Cylonians was evidently carried out quite intentionally, as one would expect during a period of civil strife. Another difficulty is that the killing of the Cylonians had political and religious aspects, in that Athens traditionally allowed anyone to kill a tyrant or would-be tyrant like Cylon with impunity, but killing someone who was either in a sanctuary or, as a suppliant, was protected by the gods was considered a very serious crime. The killing of the Cylonians probably presented a dilemma, pardonable as a political act but not as a religious act. Draco's law as we have it, however, says nothing about either aspect of homicide. If the law was motivated by this episode, Draco would surely have addressed these factors, but there is no evidence that he did.

Furthermore, if Draco's law was aimed at resolving the Cylonian conflict (or some other conflict or crisis), one question never asked by scholars is, how would the act of writing down this law accomplish that goal? Could a written law be expected to resolve a conflict that could not be resolved by traditional methods of dispute-settlement that did not use writing? Oral procedures for resolving disputes, including conflicts arising out of homicides, were well established by the time of Homer. Athens must long have had its own procedures for resolving homicide cases and other disputes; these probably resembled procedures illustrated in Homer. For instance, the fact that some of those who killed the Cylonians apparently went into exile suggests that exile was one possible response to homicide in Athens, though the sacrilegious nature of their crime may have been an additional reason for this. We do not know whether any of the killers had been reconciled with their victims' families, or whether still others, perhaps the more powerful of the killers, may have refused to submit to traditional procedures for dispute-settlement, perhaps claiming that they had not been directly involved (so Thür 2002: 634–5). But in any of these cases, how would Draco's law change the situation?

If relatives of the victims were refusing to accept compensation and allow a killer to return from exile, Draco's law would not change this; if anything, by requiring unanimity, the law would make reconciliation less likely. And if accused killers were refusing to submit to traditional procedures, Draco's law could not force them to do so now. It might allow the victims to pursue the killer with impunity, but if a killer had thus far avoided trial, presumably he was powerful enough to resist such pursuit. A new law would not change this. It is possible that Draco created new rules and procedures that were more attractive to people who were still engaged in disputes, but if so, why could he not simply make these same

changes in existing oral rules and procedures? Why would changes need to
be put in writing? In fact, as we shall see, some of the rules in Draco's law
resemble traditional Homeric rules and practices quite closely; it is particularly hard to see why he would need to put these in writing.

To understand the reasons for writing this law, we must first examine
the law itself. As we have it, the prescript with the decree authorizing
the republication of the law is followed on a separate line by a heading,
First *Axōn*.[7] The law then begins on a new line with six provisions that
I will designate as Section One:[8]

1. Even if someone does not kill someone intentionally, he is to go into exile.
2. The kings (*basileis*) are to judge (*dikazein*) guilty of homicide the killer
   or the planner, and the *ephetai* are to decide (*diagnōnai*).
3. Reconciliation, if there is a father or brother or sons, [is to be by] all of
   them; or the objector is to prevail.
4. But if these are not (alive), up to the degree of first cousin once removed
   and first cousin, if all are willing to reconcile, [they are to be reconciled,
   but] the objector prevails.
5. But if not one of these is (alive), and he killed unintentionally, and the
   fifty-one, the *ephetai*, decide he killed unintentionally, let ten phratry
   members admit him if they wish; and let the fifty-one choose these by rank.
6. And let those who killed earlier be bound by this ordinance (*thesmos*).

Provision 1 is a simple concise statement of the traditional practice of exile
for homicide.[9] Provision 2 also follows Homeric practice in declaring that
an accomplice would be treated just like an actual killer. It also briefly states
the procedure for deciding cases. The provision implies that the kings and
the *ephetai* already existed in Athens. If so, both may have had judicial
duties before this time (as the kings regularly do in Homer and Hesiod),
but the particular division of duties between the kings and the *ephetai*
specified here may (or may not) represent a change from their earlier

---

[7] The law is clearly being copied from the *axones* (revolving blocks) on which it was inscribed by Draco
or by Solon when he incorporated the law into his own legislation.

[8] The English translation is mine, as is the division of the text (Greek and English) into separate
sections and provisions. The Greek text, located in Appendix II, is from Stroud 1968: 5–6. See also
Nomima 1.02, *IGT* 11. I have preserved the spelling of the inscription but have removed most of the
epigraphical notation. In provision 2 (line 12) and provision 11 (lines 30–1) I include supplements
exempli gratia to illustrate the generally agreed sense of the missing words. I omit the prescript (lines
1–9) and the heading.

[9] I have argued (Gagarin 1981a: esp. 96–110) that the first words of the opening provision ("even if
someone kills unintentionally") imply that the provision applies to all homicide, intentional and
unintentional. Most scholars think it only applies to unintentional homicide and that the law on
intentional homicide was either omitted in this later version or written elsewhere, perhaps lower
down on the same inscription.

division of duties, about which we know nothing. After these two clauses come three provisions concerning reconciliation, which the killer presumably arranged by paying compensation to the victim's relatives; the requirement for unanimity may be an innovation, since the rules in Homer say nothing about disagreements among relatives, which in practice may have been a source of conflict.[10]

The first section then ends by stating that this law is retroactive. This must mean that the entire law up to this point (and probably beyond) is retroactive, since without any qualification, the expression "this ordinance" (*tōide tōi thesmōi*) cannot designate just some provisions and not others. Note that the rules about reconciliation become longer and more detailed as the contingency becomes more remote. Provision 3, which reaffirms a traditional practice (reconciliation with the immediate family), is brief and uses the same concise style as 1 and 2. Provision 4 has a little more detail than 3. And in provision 5, which addresses the remote contingency of someone with no relatives, for which almost certainly no earlier rule existed, Draco spells out the procedures in considerable detail. We do not know if any of these details reflect traditional practices, but in some places at least, Draco is very likely writing new rules. His method thus seems to be to state well-known, traditional rules briefly and concisely, but to provide more details for rules that are new.

This first Section (provisions 1–6) contains the essence of the homicide law. It states the basic penalty, specifies who judges, puts accomplices in the same category as killers, allows for reconciliation no matter which relatives (if any) remain, and designates itself as retroactive. The next five provisions (7–11), which I designate Section Two, specify the procedures that the accuser and the accused must follow in homicide cases.

7. There is to be a proclamation against the killer in the agora [by relatives] up to the first cousin once removed and first cousin.

8. Cousins and cousins' sons and sons-in-law and fathers-in-law and phratry members are to share the prosecution.

9. [A gap in the text here may have contained provisions giving the accused killer protection before trial, or the convicted killer safe passage into exile, or both.[11]]

---

[10] The dispute on the shield of Achilles may have resulted from a disagreement among relatives about how much compensation (if any) is acceptable, but this is only speculation (Gagarin 1981a: 13–16).

[11] In lines 23–6 only a few letters can be read: "is responsible for a homicide," "the fifty-one," and "they convict of homicide." If these last words were part of a conditional clause, provision 9 may have regulated the killer's journey into exile after he is convicted, perhaps specifying that he not be harmed on the way. There was probably another provision before this one.

10. But if someone kills the killer (in exile) or is responsible for his killing
    while he is avoiding a frontier market and athletic contests and
    Amphictyonic sacrifices, he is liable to the same treatment as someone
    who kills an Athenian; and the *ephetai* are to decide.
11. To kill or summarily arrest killers in the territory is to be allowed.

In this Section, Draco sets out procedural rules for homicide cases in the
same order as a case would normally proceed. He first specifies who is to
make the initial proclamation (7), which was the first step in a prosecution
for homicide. This would normally be followed by the actual prosecution,[12] and so Draco next specifies which relatives share in the prosecution
(8). The next provision (9) may have specified how a convicted killer was
supposed to go into exile and granted him protection if he followed the
proper procedure; it may also have granted him protection before the trial.
After this comes a rule protecting a killer in exile, provided he avoids
certain places and events (10). The section ends by stating that a killer who
does not leave or who returns to the territory can be arrested or killed with
impunity (11).

All these rules reflect traditional practices we can observe in Homer,
where a victim's relatives take the lead in pursuing a killer and will kill him
if they find him in their territory, but they no longer pursue the killer after
he goes into exile. If provision 9 granted protection to an accused killer
before his trial, then this too reflected traditional practice when the two
sides sought a trial; in the scene on Achilles' shield, at any rate, the accused
killer is evidently in no danger before his case is heard by the elders. But in
all these provisions, Draco specifies a number of details that almost
certainly were not fixed in traditional rules and practices. Perhaps most
important, he specifies exactly where a killer would be protected in exile. If
one of the main reasons why a killer had to go into exile was to prevent
contact between him and the victim's family and friends, it was vital that
both sides know exactly how far this protection extends. Frontier markets,
athletic contests and Amphictyonic sacrifices were international events
outside of or on the borders of Attica, where a killer and his victim's
relatives might encounter one another. It would be essential to know
whether the killer would be protected if he attended them. Draco's new
law provides this information.

Two more provisions constitute what is left of the third section, which
may have dealt with the general topic of justified homicide. After a gap of

---

[12] Prosecution did not follow automatically: the trierarch in Demosthenes 47.68–73 is advised to make
a proclamation at the dead woman's tomb but not to prosecute.

three lines come three fragmentary lines (12) that apparently concern killing someone who began a fight, and a provision about justified killing (13), which can be restored from a citation in Demosthenes 23.60:

12. ... beginning a fight ... he kills [someone who?] begins a fight ... and the *ephetai* are to decide.

13. ... or is free; and if someone kills defending himself immediately against someone who is forcibly and unjustly plundering or seizing him, the death shall be without recompense.

After these provisions, only a few letters and one or two words are visible, but seventeen lines later we can read another heading, Second *Axōn*, written in the same larger letters as the initial heading, First *Axōn*. Evidently additional provisions continued up to this point and beyond, and a few traces of letters can be seen after this. We do not know how much more text the original law may have contained, but it was certainly more than twice as long as the text we now have, and it may have been much longer.[13]

Draco, then, wrote a fairly substantial homicide law with at least twenty or twenty-five provisions arranged in several sections. We do not know whether the original seventh-century inscription contained physical features that would have made the text easier to read, but if it was written on *axones* or *kyrbeis*, as tradition reports, these probably were intended to make it easier for a reader to consult the text. The *axones* were blocks of wood that somehow revolved, enabling someone to read more of the text while remaining in one place.[14] The *kyrbeis* may have been bronze bases with pyramidal tops that, if inscribed on four sides, would have presented four columns of text that could be read with relatively little movement.[15]

Whatever the physical features of Draco's original inscription, the republished text contains organizational and stylistic features that would make it easier to use. To begin with, the arrangement of provisions is clear and logical: first come the basic elements of the law – the crime and its punishment, together with procedures for judging and reconciliation – followed by a statement of its retroactivity. Then come procedures for litigation, arranged in the order in which a case would normally develop, from the initial proclamation announcing the homicide to protection of the convicted killer in exile but not in Attica. And these appear to be

---

[13] Sickinger (1999: 17–18) calculates that the first *axōn* had about 2,250 letters (perhaps 400 words) and subsequent *axones*, of course, would have added to this total.

[14] At least this must be the idea behind this device. But the *axones* may not have been as practical as intended, since as far as we know, they were not used for any other texts.

[15] See Ruschenbusch 1966: 24 and Stroud 1979: 46 for two possible reconstructions, and Robertson 1986 for further considerations.

followed by a group of rules concerning justified homicide. This arrangement can only have resulted from a conscious effort on Draco's part, and
since it would have made the law easier for a reader to use, and since Draco
was probably not seeking clarity and order simply for their own sake, ease
of use was almost certainly one of Draco's aims in writing this law.

Also of help to a reader would be certain stylistic features (Gagarin 1981a:
153–9). First, several provisions have a chiastic arrangement of subjects and
verbs.[16] This marks the beginning and end either of a provision (2, 3) or of a
clause within a provision (5, 10). Second, Draco begins provisions 2, 3, 7, 8,
and perhaps 11 with an infinitive (with the force of an imperative) followed
by *de* ("but, and"). In these provisions the initial infinitive is a kind of
heading stating at the beginning the subject matter of that provision –
dikazein ("judgment"), *proeipein* ("proclamation"). And 4, 5, and 10 begin
with *ean de* ("but if" or "and if"), indicating that these provisions add a
further qualification to the preceding clause. Like the numbered sections
and subsections of modern legislation, these features would help readers
more easily understand the arrangement of provisions and find those that
they wished to read.

Now, if Draco was trying to make his law easier for people to read and
use, this still does not explain why he decided to enact the law and write it
down in the first place. We can first look to the same motives already
suggested for other archaic laws, in particular the need for new, more
detailed rules. Athens in the seventh century was experiencing some of
the same trends we saw in Crete and elsewhere at the time of the earliest
written laws. The city had expanded its reach over neighboring towns and
villages in Attica by the process of unification or *synoecism* (Diamant 1982).
Athens' population was growing,[17] and the city was becoming more
prosperous. And the incorporation of formerly separate villages into the
Athenian community together with a significant influx of immigrants,
meant that the population was becoming more diverse, as well as larger.[18]

Elite competition notwithstanding, the growing prosperity suggests that
Athens was a fairly peaceful community and thus that traditional procedures for dispute-settlement were functioning fairly effectively. On the

---

[16] Chiasmus is an arrangement whereby the order in which two elements first appear is reversed when
the elements occur again. In this case the order, subject–verb, is followed by verb–subject (or vice
versa). Provision 2, for example, begins *dikazein de tous basileas* (VS) and ends with *tous de ephetas
diagnōnai* (SV).

[17] Osborne 1996: 70–81 speaks of "slow and steady growth" (80); see also Whitley 2001: 98–9.

[18] Manville 1990: 55–78 has a good summary of what we know about the social organization of Attica
and its development up to Draco's time.

other hand, growth and diversity would have increased the number and complexity of disputes, and would also have created more uncertainty about traditional rules and practices, thereby straining the traditional procedures for dispute-settlement, which had evolved in a smaller, more coherent community. In this context, the need for clarification of rules and procedures, and in some areas for entirely new rules, would become evident, and would provide the motivation for Draco to undertake legal reforms. Whether he intended from the beginning to write down his new law is uncertain, but once he began to develop new rules, he would soon have seen the need for including many details in these rules, especially in his procedural rules, and for making them as clear as possible in order to prevent misunderstanding or disagreement in the future. It would also have become clear that the amount of detail being included would make it impossible to preserve and transmit the law accurately and without change by oral means alone, and that the rules would thus need to be written down in order to ensure the accuracy and the stability of their details.

The need for writing and its value in preserving details can be seen especially clearly if we contrast some of the rules Draco wrote with similar rules about the treatment of homicide preserved in Homer. In Chapter One we noted two conflicting rules about homicide: Odysseus' statement that a killer flees into exile and Ajax's statement that reconciliation occurs after a homicide.

A man who kills another man in his community, even one who leaves only a few avengers behind, that man flees into exile, leaving behind family and fatherland. (*Odyssey* 23.118–20)

A person accepts from the killer the blood-price (*poinē*) for his dead brother or son, and when he has paid a large compensation, the killer remains in his land, and the person's heart and manly anger are curbed, when he has received the blood-price. (*Iliad* 9.632–6)

The first is an adequate statement of the rule that a killer must go into exile,[19] but it says nothing about the procedure by which this would happen, whether a killer in exile or going into exile is protected, and other matters addressed by Draco. And Ajax says nothing about which relative can or must agree to compensation if there is more than one present, what happens if no father or brother is alive, and other details.

---

[19] The fact that Odysseus and Telemachus do not observe the rule is probably not significant, since this is determined by the special needs of the plot and would probably not be seen as invalidating the general rule.

As general oral pronouncements, the Homeric rules have the virtue of being easily remembered and communicated to large audiences. But as the community became larger, more diverse, and more complex, the lack of detail and the contradictory nature of the two rules would have increasingly become a source of confusion and conflict. A rule clarifying the situation and specifying the necessary details, would be difficult, however, if not impossible, to compose in a version that could easily be remembered and transmitted orally. One would, in effect, have to put the text of Draco's law into Homeric verse, a nearly unimaginable task. And even if one could create a detailed rule in a form that could be easily remembered, it would be nearly impossible to communicate this oral version to a wide audience with all the details intact over time. As we noted above (Chapter Three), studies of oral cultures have shown, details in oral texts are unstable and often change with successive retellings (which is why orally preserved rules are usually quite general).[20] Thus, the only way Draco could ensure the accurate transmission of the details of his law was to put the law in writing.

Now, if the need to preserve details led Draco to put his law in writing, what motivated him to create a homicide law in the first place? First, he must have realized that the traditional rules and procedures for homicide cases were inadequate, and this realization must have come from observing actual cases, probably over a long period of time. Some of these cases may have arisen out of the Cylonian conspiracy, but there must have been other homicide cases in the intervening years, and it seems unlikely that this fifteen-year-old event was his main concern. And although some of Draco's new provisions may have helped settle previously unresolved disputes, this cannot have been his main purpose, since the law (which was originally at least twice its present length) covers a wide range of matters, many of which would be of no relevance to most cases. It is clear even from the provisions that survive that Draco set out not just to address one or two contentious issues but to write a very broad law covering many aspects of homicide, including some quite remote contingencies.

In approaching his task, Draco decided first not to address only the most urgent aspects of homicide, but to write a comprehensive law. He also decided to keep the two traditional (Homeric) rules providing for both exile and reconciliation, but to organize them into a coherent structure (first exile, then reconciliation), and to provide greater clarity and specificity for the rules about reconciliation. He could keep the basic traditional rules brief and concise – exile for homicide, reconciliation by the father or

---

[20] See above, Chapter 3, n. 23.

brother or sons all in agreement – but he would have to provide more detail for rules that were new or might not be well known. He included rules concerning many different issues – some that may never have been raised before – and he organized them into a logical and coherent whole. Past conflicts or recent crises may have guided his thinking on some of these issues, but his aim in writing this law was not to resolve specific conflicts, but to provide a comprehensive and detailed set of rules that could easily and effectively be used in whatever homicide cases might arise in the future. To that end, he arranged the provisions of his law with an eye toward their use by members of the community, and presented them in an order and style that they could most easily be read and used by potential litigants.

This does not necessarily mean that the law would have been of no help in resolving past conflicts. But people in exile for homicide (to take one group sometimes proposed as benefiting from Draco's law) would not easily have achieved reconciliation with their victim's family, given the requirements for unanimity in the law. And many of Draco's rules address points of detail that are unlikely to have caused serious conflict in the past. Surely few disputes could have gone unresolved because of disagreement about which relatives were to make the initial proclamation or join in the prosecution. These rules would help the relatives of homicide victims bring cases to court, but would do nothing to resolve past crises. Draco was trying to write a comprehensive law; he was looking to the future, not the past.

Moreover, disputants who had not been able to resolve their differences under traditional rules would not necessarily be any more likely to succeed under Draco's law, since, as far as we can tell, his procedures were not significantly more compulsory than traditional procedures had been. It remained up to the victim's relatives to initiate any homicide prosecution and to enforce any punishment. We do not know whether a court could convict an accused killer *in absentia* if he chose not to appear when summoned (as it could in the fourth century), but even if it could, no public official or body could compel the killer to go into exile; only the victim's relatives and any support they could muster in the community could ensure this result. And more or less these same means had been available to plaintiffs before Draco.

Draco's law represents a stage in the gradual development of a more compulsory judicial procedure.[21] Even in the Hellenistic period Greek procedure depended on the participation of its citizens (Rubinstein 2003),

---

[21] For objections to the influential theory of Wolff (1946), that procedure became compulsory in clear stages, beginning with Homer, see above Chapter One.

and cities never had institutions like a police force that are taken for granted in modern societies. But from the beginning there was community pressure to submit to the legal process, and this pressure increased over time, creating a more compulsory process, but one that still depended on voluntary prosecution and enforcement. To the extent that Draco's new law was seen as fair and effective, it would have been used by an increasing number of Athenians, and this would add even more pressure for others to abide by the new rules. Certainly by the fourth century, when prosecution and enforcement still remained largely in the hands of individual citizens, it was rare for citizens openly to flout the law, though it was probably not uncommon for someone voluntarily to go into exile in order to avoid a trial and probable death sentence. Draco's law may have inspired a similar acceptance of the rule of law, even in the seventh century. One sign of this, perhaps, was that in the sixth century even the tyrant Peisistratus appeared in court to answer a charge of homicide (*Ath. Pol.* 16.8).

There is nothing in Draco's law, moreover, to suggest that he aimed to further his own interests or those of a small ruling class by imposing his authority on ordinary people who would not have been able to read his law. On the contrary, the law would have been useful to all members of the community. And as I suggested in Chapter Three, the mere fact of writing and displaying rules that applied, by implication at least, to all Athenians and only to them would have conveyed a sense of political unity (Manville 1990: 79–82; Forsdyke 2005: 88–9). This sense of inclusion was not just implicit in the opening *tis*, "someone" – that is, some Athenian – but would be especially evident in provision 11, where Draco provides that anyone who kills a killer in exile "is liable to the same treatment as someone who kills an Athenian." By using the word "Athenian" for all members of the community (or at least all free adult males), and by making it clear that the killer of an Athenian was subject to special treatment (presumably more severe than for other killers), Draco's law would convey to the reader that, as an Athenian, he was a privileged person, protected by this law as others were not.

The law would also convey this sense of political unity by indicating, perhaps for the first time, that Athens, or Attica, was a territory with clear, demarcated boundaries.[22] Provision 10 suggests this concept of a territory with known boundaries when it speaks of a frontier market, as does

---

[22] As Manville 1990: 80 notes, "probably such boundaries were not carefully surveyed demarcations but primarily natural limits and marginal lands." We cannot be certain that the territory mentioned by Draco coincided exactly with the territory of Attica in the classical period (Anderson 2003: 21), but it was probably not much different.

provision 11 when it allows a killer to be killed or arrested "in the territory." Thus, by writing a law for all inhabitants of Attica, by speaking of an Athenian as a privileged person, and by implying that Athens is a bounded and unified territorial unit, Draco would have fostered a growing sense of Athenian political unity. This may not have been his conscious aim, since these details are inserted almost by the way in later provisions of the law, but it was probably one of the effects of writing this law. And the desire to clarify rules for an increasingly diverse community indicates a general interest in creating a more closely unified political community.

The fact that at this early date Draco could create such a comprehensive and skillfully organized law without precedent is truly remarkable. In Chapter Seven, we will see that parts of the Gortyn Code are organized in ways that resemble the organization of Draco's law, with general rules followed by more specific provisions often in an order that reflects the stages of actual litigation. But the Gortyn Code was preceded by a century and a half of legislation at Gortyn, whereas Draco was the first to write a law in Athens. Did his skill in organization have any precedent? Presocratic thought may offer a parallel, with its search for a single unifying element in the world, but this movement appears to have begun shortly after Draco's time and was confined at first to Miletus.

More relevant parallels may be found in pottery. The geometric vases produced in Attica and elsewhere in the ninth and eighth centuries assemble many geometric patterns, often together with human or animal scenes, into a well organized, symmetrical whole, as is particularly clear in the Dipylon amphora.[23] By the seventh century, when Draco wrote his law, the proto-Attic orientalizing style was dominant. These painters continued to use geometric patterns, but primarily to frame the more substantial human and animal scenes, some of which portray episodes from myth.[24]

A good example from the second quarter of the seventh century is the well-known Eleusis amphora, with a large scene of Perseus beheading Medusa on the body and a smaller scene of Odysseus blinding Polyphemus on the neck, both framed by geometric patterns. The overall effect is that two scenes of extreme violence are contained within an orderly whole that suggests the possibility of rational control of violence in the world. One could argue that Draco similarly arranges his treatment of the most violent of human acts, homicide, within an orderly set of rules and

---

[23] Boardman 1998: 23–82, with figures 26–162; the Dipylon amphora is fig. 44.
[24] *Ibid.* 83–140, with figures 163–282; the Eleusis amphora is fig. 208, for discussion of which see S. P. Morris 1984: 43–6.

procedures that promise to bring order and stability to human affairs. Thus, the systematic and logical arrangement of provisions in his law suggests the same confidence in the ability of reason to control violence as the Eleusis amphora. The parallel cannot be pressed too far, but both Draco's law and Attic vases of the period may reflect the same spirit of confidence in rational means of organizing and controlling the violent forces in the world. Thus, the large-scale, rational organization evident in Greek geometric pottery long before Draco suggests a systematic and logical thought process that seems to be reflected in other areas of Greek culture, including Draco's homicide law.

One could also argue that the Greeks' interest in writing laws for the practical use of the community in itself stimulated them to explore ways of expressing rules clearly, so that they could be most easily used, and of organizing groups of rules systematically and logically, and that in this way, the very act of writing laws contributed to the development of rational thought. At the very least, the process of creating laws that would be available for public use was a way of making them available for the sort of open public discourse that Lloyd (1979) has argued was the original stimulus for Greek rationality.[25]

Organization on an even larger scale may have been undertaken by Solon, a generation later. Although Draco's homicide legislation was so successful that Solon retained it for his legislation, economic conditions in Attica worsened. When internal turmoil threatened to destroy Athens in 594, Solon was asked to intervene. One part of his response was to write laws for the city. As he tells us in his own words, "I wrote laws (*thesmous egrapsa*) for the lowly and the well-to-do alike, securing a straight justice (*eutheian dikēn*) for each" (fragment 36 West, lines 18–20). In later years the Athenians were quick to attribute laws to Solon that he could not have written himself, and so considerable uncertainty remains concerning just what laws he did write. But his use of the archaic term for law (*thesmos*) in the quotation above – the same word Draco used to refer to his own law in provision 6 – assures us that Solon really did legislate for Athens, and later sources indicate that his laws covered a wide range of topics. These sources also consistently report that Solon kept Draco's homicide law intact while

---

[25] Asper 2004 argues that the actual use of written laws forces litigants in court to use processes of induction and deduction and thus contributes to the development of abstract reason. His interesting argument is flawed by various misconceptions about Greek law, such as the assumption that litigation involved arguments over such matters as whether certain acts fall under a certain law. Such arguments are not characteristic of Athenian litigation and they do not appear to have played a role at Gortyn either.

writing new laws for all other matters. And Ruschenbusch (1966: 1–58) has made a strong case that Solon's original legislation on wooden *axones* survived into the Greco-Roman period and that many of the later quotations of Solon's laws are likely authentic.

Solon probably wrote at least some of his laws in response to the economic crisis he was facing.[26] We know of several laws he wrote concerning economic matters that could have had this aim and that apparently contained benefits for both sides. For example, one law apparently restricted the amount of land one could hold, but another allowed whatever rate of interest a lender wished to charge (Ruschenbusch 1966: F66, F68). But Solon also legislated on many matters that had nothing to do with the economy, including such matters as personal injury, pederasty, and slander. Thus, although a crisis may have provided the immediate impetus for Solon to write his laws, his legislation (like Draco's) went far beyond an immediate response to a crisis. We do not know just how he arranged his laws, though it appears that the homicide law came first (on the first *axōn*). After this, Solon could have written the laws down as they occurred to him or in some other arbitrary order, but it seems more likely that he arranged them in some manner, though we can only guess what this might have been.

Solon's legislation endured through the classical period and probably beyond, though new laws and modifications were, of course, added. But as effective as they apparently were, it is still surprising that the tyrant Peisistratus, who ruled Athens for several decades not long after Solon, did not change his laws, and even appeared in court to answer a charge of homicide.[27] It is a testimony to the legislative abilities of both Draco and Solon that their laws continued in effect through this sometimes turbulent period.

In sum, the factors motivating Draco to write and display his law were some of the same factors that we noted in the preceding chapter. These included the need to clarify and make permanent a detailed set of rules for an increasingly large and diverse community, so that the members of this community who might need to use them could do so, to convey to the people the idea that in some sense these rules belonged to them, and to foster in readers a sense of communal unity. It would be especially

---

[26] Solon's statement that he wrote laws follows immediately after his report of two other steps he took to resolve the crisis, removing boundary markers and thereby freeing the earth, and freeing Athenians who had been enslaved for debt at home and abroad.

[27] Herodotus 1.59.6, Thucydides 6.54.6, *Ath. Pol.* 16.8, Plutarch, *Solon* 31.3. *Ath. Pol.* 16.5 also reports that Peisistratus created deme judges so that people in the country could have their disputes settled without having to journey to the city.

important to write down procedural details,[28] which tend to be of little
interest to those who pronounce traditional rules orally (or to later writers
who report on the activities of early legislators).[29] We have already noted
the advantages of written laws over oral pronouncements: they could
specify the content of as many rules as one might wish in precise detail,
they could ensure the relative permanence and consistency of these rules
over time and space, and they could make these rules available for use by
members of the community whenever and wherever they might need
them.[30] Draco's law demonstrates especially well the role of writing in
preserving details when we contrast it with the more general, orally
preserved rules in Homer. Oral texts tend to eschew details,[31] and the
rare cases of oral transmission of highly detailed rules, such as (perhaps) in
medieval Iceland of the sagas, have no parallels in ancient Greece.

Another factor we noted in Chapter Three is that once written, a law can
become independent of any personal propounder or spokesman. When the
law is displayed in a public space, the community, to which that space
belongs, becomes the authority behind the law; even if it is closely associated with its legislator ("Draco's homicide law"), when written and
publicly displayed, the law stands apart from its creator. Thus, the act of
writing down laws in archaic Greece created for the first time depersonal-
ized, authoritative rules – laws as opposed to the oral rules of the traditional
authorities, the poets. Amid all this written legislation, however, the legal
process in Greece remained oral throughout the archaic period. Litigation
was regulated by written rules but it must also have continued to be guided
by unwritten customs and traditional rules of procedure, and litigants
must have continued to appeal to general norms and values that were not
written, just as they did in the fourth century. Draco's law addressed many

---

[28] The same connection between writing and procedural rules is found in Anglo-Saxon laws: "the text
of Æthelberht is the closest extant equivalent to Germanic law as it was transmitted in a preliterate
period, while the laws of Hlophere and Eadric and Wihtred testify to the expansion of customary law
when laws were first cast in the medium of writing. The text of Hlophere and Eadric concentrates on
legal procedure and process, discussion of which is almost entirely lacking in the tersely worded
clauses of Æthelberht" (Oliver 2002: xi).

[29] This may explain why so little of Solon's surviving legislation is procedural in nature (Gagarin
2006a).

[30] Except for treaties, copies of which might be displayed in both cities, there is no evidence that
duplicate copies of laws were made in the archaic period. But it is not impossible that copies were
written, perhaps on less permanent materials, and made available to people, especially in the
outlying areas of the city's territory.

[31] Of course, oral texts contain details, most notably in the catalogues, such as the catalogue of ships in
Iliad 2, but this catalogue appears to belong to one of the latest stages in the creation of the poem and
it has probably not endured very many transmissions. Moreover, the catalogue contains much
anecdotal information of no direct relevance to the detailed listing of ships and manpower.

aspects of homicide, but oral rules and principles continued to play a role in litigation. In this sense, written law supplemented oral law but did not replace it.[32]

Finally, the effects of writing down laws in archaic Greece both conform with and differ from the general effects of writing and specifically of writing laws that some scholars have identified in other cultures.[33] First, writing imposes standards: standards for language, education, commercial practices, even morality. In law, writing standardizes rules and procedures, and helps make them uniform and stable over time and space. Second, writing depersonalizes information; that is, it divorces the written text from its personal source. We have already noted all these effects in Greece, but writing Greek law did not result in some of the common effects of standardization and depersonalization, such as the centralization of authority in the form of a state, which in many societies gains complete control of all public writing.

In addition, writing Greek law differed from writing law elsewhere in its inclusion of details. Goody has argued (1986: 166) that "the process of putting laws, rules, or norms in writing is also a process of universalization, of generalization." There is some truth to this as regards Greek law, for as we have seen, Draco begins with two or three brief general rules about homicide. But Goody neglects the fact that writing laws also allow rules, especially rules of procedure, to be much more specific and detailed than does oral transmission. And universalization and generalization, in fact, are also characteristic of the orally preserved rules we find in Homer. As we saw, Draco's law devotes very little space to the most general rules, while focusing primarily on more detailed rules, especially procedural rules. So too, some of the early inscriptions we examined earlier appear to have been written specifically in order to record details of rules, as, for example, the list of sacrifices in *ICret* 4.3. In this respect, writing law in archaic Greece differed significantly from writing law in many other early legal systems, and writing Greek law continued to differ in the classical period and later, as we will see. A key factor, already evident in writing archaic laws, is that, unlike the laws of most other premodern legal systems, Greek laws were written for members of the community to use in actual litigation. Draco's homicide law is a clear example of this.

---

[32] R. Thomas 2005. Cf. Derderian's argument (2001: 76) about early (written) epitaphs and (oral) laments: "the epigram represents a new type of communication at the gravesite which supplements rather than replaces lament."

[33] These remarks rely primarily on Clanchy 1985 and Goody 1986: esp. 127–70.

CHAPTER 5

Oral and Written in Archaic Greek Law

As we have seen, during the archaic period laws were written down and publicly displayed in cities all over Greece, but almost nothing else of a legal nature was written and publicly displayed. One consequence of this was that terms like "writing" (*graphos, grammata*) could be used without qualification to designate a written law. In addition to examples from Elis (*IvO* 7) and Argos (*IG* IV 506) noted in Chapter Two, other texts from Elis and Eleutherna also use expressions designating writing in this way.[1] Another inscription from Elis (*IvO* 9; *Nomima* 1.52, ML 17) begins by designating itself a *rhatra* or "pronouncement,"[2] one of the other terms by which archaic cities designated written laws, but later warns against destroying "these writings" (*ta graphea*). Here, as in *IvO* 7 (Chapter Two), *rhatra* designates the pronouncement of the people in assembly enacting the law and *graphos* (singular and plural) designates the text of that pronouncement after it is written down as the law. And a law attributed to Solon provides that any agreement made by the members of certain organizations is valid "as long as no public writing (*dēmosia grammata*) prohibits it" (Ruschenbusch 1966: F76a). Although Solon elsewhere calls his laws *thesmoi*, it appears that here he uses the expression "public writings" to designate the city's laws, perhaps to emphasize that these are written and publicly displayed.

This use of expressions for writing to designate written laws (which becomes even more common in fifth-century Gortyn) was only possible because of the nearly total absence of other sorts of written texts of a legal nature during this period. Indeed, before 500 we have no clear example of or reference to a written legal document other than a law except in the case of Athens, for which we have indirect evidence that writing may have been

---

[1] Elis: *IvO* 3 (= *Nomima* 1.108, *IGT* 38), lines 5 and 6; Eleutherna: *ICret* 2.12.13.
[2] "[This is] the pronouncement [i.e. agreement] for the Eleans and the Euaeans" (ά ϝράτρα τοῖρ ϝαλείοις καὶ τοῖς Ἐυϝαοίοις).

used in the legal process in the archaic period. The sixth-century agreement with Spensithios, which we will examine at the end of this chapter, may be an exception, but the texts that Spensithios is supposed to write, according to this agreement, may have been mostly, or even entirely, laws.

The best evidence for writing in archaic law other than for legislation is the report that one of Solon's legal reforms was the creation of a new kind of procedure in which anyone who wished could prosecute.[3] In classical Athens this procedure was called a *graphē* ("writing") and it was distinguished from the traditional lawsuit or *dikē*, which could only be brought by the victim of an offense or by a person related to the victim.[4] The verb *graphesthai* in the middle voice ("to have something written") was used to denote the act of filing a *graphē* ("written indictment") against someone. We have no direct evidence for the terms *graphē* and *graphesthai* in connection with this new procedure before the second half of the fifth century;[5] thus they may have been introduced some time after Solon's reform. But in view of the generally conservative nature of legal terminology in Athens,[6] it is more likely that the terms go back to the sixth century, if not to Solon. A *graphē* must somehow have involved the use of writing, and even if the procedure was not given this name by Solon but acquired it only in the fifth century, it is likely that writing was part of the procedure from the beginning.

In the classical period, a *graphē* or indictment was filed at the beginning of the case. The fact that *graphesthai* and other verbs used for bringing a charge against someone are in the middle voice indicates that a would-be plaintiff would have someone else actually write the complaint; most likely he would go to the magistrate in charge of this type of case (or his clerk) and have this person write down the complaint.[7] The indictment spelled out the particulars of the alleged offense, sometimes in considerable detail. For example, Diogenes Laertius (2.40) preserves one of the most famous indictments in Athenian history, that of Socrates for impiety (*asebeia*) in 399.

---

[3] *Ath. Pol.* 9.1, Plutarch *Solon* 18 (= Ruschenbusch 1966: F 40). On the nature of this procedure, see Rhodes 1981: 159–60, with references to earlier work.

[4] *Dikē* could also designate a judicial case in general, even one that was technically a *graphē*.

[5] The terms occur in [Xenophon] *Constitution of the Athenians* (the "Old Oligarch") 3.2, Antiphon 2.1.5, etc. and Aristophanes, *Wasps* 892, etc., all probably written in the period 440–420. *Ath. Pol.* does not use the term *graphē* in describing Solon's reform as "allowing anyone who wishes to seek retribution for those who are wronged." Plutarch does use the term *graphesthai*, but he is not quoting Solon directly and may be using an anachronistic term.

[6] Cf., e.g., the widespread use in the classical period of the verbs *diōkein* ("pursue") and *pheugein* ("flee") to designate prosecution and defense.

[7] See Calhoun 1919: 178–80, whose conclusion on this point is generally accepted.

Meletus son of Meletus of Pitthos indicted and swore an oath against Socrates son of Sophroniscus of Alopece. Socrates does wrong by not recognizing the gods the city recognizes but introducing other new divinities, and also by corrupting the youth. The proposed penalty is death.

Litigants in this type of case often refer to the specific wording of the *graphē*, and in some cases they have the *graphē* read out to the court.[8]

It is not certain why the complaint in this type of case had to be put in writing when, at least in the classical period, the complaint in an ordinary *dikē* was probably not written. It is also puzzling that writing was used at this initial stage of the procedure and apparently nowhere else, and that the written nature of the complaint was so significant that the whole procedure was called a "writing." With regard to the name *graphē*, first, even if writing was only used to initiate the litigation, writing could have become associated with the whole procedure, even if this was not the procedure's original name. Second, a written indictment may have been the clearest difference (or the only clear difference) between a *graphē* and a *dikē*, so that when people thought of this new procedure they thought first of the requirement of a written accusation.

One reason why Solon (or some later official) required writing at this initial stage of the procedure may be that the complaint in this new *graphē* procedure would have been more complex than the complaint in a traditional *dikē*. The earliest preserved text of a *graphē* is in Aristophanes' *Wasps* (produced in 422). Bdelycleon, who is trying to cure his father Philocleon of his addiction to jury duty, stages a mock trial of the dog Labes for stealing a cheese. The whole trial is a farce, but procedurally it does seem to adhere quite closely to a real Athenian trial, and the indictment, though a parody, probably echoes the kind of complaint that would be written in a real *graphē*. Bdelycleon first asks someone to fetch "the notice boards (*sanides*) and the indictments (*graphai*)" (848).[9] *Sanides* served in many contexts as whitened boards on which temporary notices were written or posted. Before a trial began, the *graphē* in the case would be posted on these boards, first in front of the statues of the ten eponymous heroes in the agora, so that people could see which cases were coming up,[10] and then on a *sanis* outside the courtroom so that people could, if they wished, see the

---

[8] For example, in his discussion of the indictment against Ctesiphon in his speech *On the Crown* (18.53–9), Demosthenes has the *graphē* read out to the court (18.54–5).

[9] The plurals here presumably echo the call at the beginning of an actual court day, when preparations were being made to hold several successive trials in the same court.

[10] See, e.g., Dem. 21.103 with MacDowell's note (1990: 326); cf. Dem. 47.42.

indictment before the trial started. Then the *graphē* would be brought into court and read out as the trial began.

In *Wasps* (894–7), the indictment is quoted as follows: "Cyon ["Dog"] from Cydathenaeum indicts Labes from Aexone[11] for wrongdoing (*adikein*), in that by himself he ate up the Sicilian cheese. The proposed penalty is a figwood collar." As this example shows, in a *graphē* the indictment not only specifies the procedure and the general category of offense (theft, impiety, hybris, etc.) – here a *graphē* for wrongdoing[12] – but also provides specific details of the indictment. This same combination of general category and specific allegations is found in the indictment of Socrates, quoted above. A *graphē* thus set forth the type of case and the specific allegations that the litigants then had to prove or refute.

The accusation (*enklēma*) in a *dikē* had the same structure (type of case followed by specifics), and in the fourth century it could have a similar amount of detail[13] and was therefore put in writing, as in a *graphē*. But in Solon's time the accusation in a *dikē* could be very simple. Our earliest evidence is from homicide cases in the late fifth century, at the beginning of which both litigants swore formal oaths which included a brief statement of the accusation and the defense. In Antiphon 6 the defendant reports, "They swore that I killed Diodotus by planning his death (*bouleusanta ton thanaton*), but I swore I did not kill him either by my own hand or by planning."[14] If the speaker is accurately recalling the initial oaths, the accusation in this case was "X killed Diodotus by planning his death," and in the more common cases of killing with one's own hand, the accusation might be as short as "X killed Y." An accusation like this was

---

[11] Cydathenaeum and Aexone are Athenian demes, or "precincts." A person's deme was regularly used as part of his name in formal contexts (note Pitthos and Alopece in the indictment of Socrates cited above).

[12] We might expect the specific charge in Labes' case to be theft rather than the more general wrongdoing (see MacDowell 1971: 250–1, note on 896), but the cheese was not stolen from the prosecutor (Cyon), and so he could not bring a private suit (*dikē*) for theft, but had to prosecute on behalf of the victim (the household). Aristophanes clearly intends the dog Labes as a stand-in for the Athenian general Laches, who was alleged to have profited personally from a campaign he led in Sicily in 427, and so he makes the case – theft of a (Sicilian) cheese – a public *graphē* on behalf of the community rather than a simple private *dikē*.

[13] See for example, the very detailed charge brought by Dinarchus (late fourth century) in a suit for damages (*dikē blabēs*), quoted by Dionysius of Halicarnassus (*Dinarchus* 3). Dionysius refers to the detailed accusation as an indictment (*graphē*), but the case was almost certainly a *dikē*. See also the detailed *enklēma* in a similar suit cited in Dem. 37.22, which begins, "Nicobulus has damaged me by plotting against me, etc."

[14] Ant. 6.16. If, as I have argued (Gagarin 1990), cases of having planned (*bouleusas*) an intentional or unintentional homicide were tried at the Areopagus and Palladium respectively, then the prosecutor in Antiphon 6 would not have needed to specify that the accused killed unintentionally, since the fact that the trial was taking place in the Palladium would make this clear.

easily stated and remembered, and did not need to be written down, and if accusations in other early *dikai* were similarly concise – such as "X stole a cheese from me" – then they too would not need to be written down. Thus, accusations in *dikai* may have remained entirely or mostly oral until the fourth century, when writing became more widespread in legal matters. At this time, the accusation in a *dikē* was also put in writing, and some accusations in *dikai* became quite detailed.[15]

The *graphē*, on the other hand, was instituted to allow others to prosecute in cases where the victim normally could not.[16] Thus, instead of a simple accusation such as "X assaulted me" or "X killed Y," the indictment in a *graphē* would have to include the names of the prosecutor, the accused, and the victim, together with some description of the crime: e.g., "X indicts Y for insolence (*hybris*) toward Z, because he did such and such." Even if the case concerned a public crime with no individual victim, besides naming the prosecutor and the accused the *graphē* would have to specify the nature of the offense (as in the indictment of Socrates). This need for a longer, more detailed accusation may explain why the accusation in a *graphē* was put in writing. We cannot say for certain that this happened in the sixth century or that Solon was responsible for it, but he seems the most likely person to have made this significant change.

Besides the indictment in a *graphē*, we have no reason to think that any other written texts were used during a trial in the archaic period, but we do have possible evidence for one other use of writing in early Athenian law. This is the puzzling report in *Ath. Pol.* 3.4 concerning the establishment of the offices of the nine archons, who were the most important magistrates in the Athenian democracy. According to this report, the three named archons (the Archon, the Basileus, and the Polemarch) were the first to be established, followed later by the six other archons, who were collectively known as the Thesmothetae. "The Thesmothetae were established many years later, when the selection for these offices [the other three archons] had already become annual, in order that they might write down the *thesmia*

---

[15] See Calhoun (1919: 188–9): "in the earlier period the litigant's responsibility for the content of his pleading is established by the oath, whereas in the time of Demosthenes the outstanding fact is that the statements in the pleading are written by his own hand."

[16] The first victims for whom Solon allowed anyone to prosecute may have been those enslaved for debt and children sold into slavery by their parents; he may also have allowed others to prosecute on behalf of orphans and elderly parents. In all these cases the victim would probably have been unable to bring suit himself. Only later did the *graphē* come to be used for offenses against the community as a whole, such as impiety or embezzlement of public funds. See Glotz 1904: 369–82, Calhoun 1927: 72–87, Ruschenbusch 1968: 47–53. Solon also instituted other procedures such as *eisangelia* by which anyone could prosecute.

and keep them for deciding disputed cases."[17] Many scholars doubt there is any historical basis to this report (e.g., Rhodes 1981: 102–3); they argue that the author of *Ath. Pol.* had no external information about the Thesmothetae and was probably guessing about their duties on the basis of their name, *thesmothetēs*, which, like *nomothetēs* ("lawgiver, one who establishes *nomoi*"), would also mean "lawgiver" ("one who establishes *thesmoi*"). But in that case one would expect the report to say that the Thesmothetae wrote down *thesmoi*, not *thesmia*, which is not an archaic term for a law, but on the analogy with *nomima* ought to mean something like "established rules and practices."[18] The use of *thesmia*, then, may indicate that *Ath. Pol.* had another source for this information.

Even if this information has a basis in fact, however, it is not clear what the Thesmothetae would have been writing. The word *thesmios* is not attested as a noun (*thesmion*) before the fifth century,[19] though it occurs as an adjective in the preamble to a law of Solon against the establishment of a tyranny (see below). In the classical period the Thesmothetae were closely associated with the law courts. If they had a judicial role from the beginning, they may have been writing down established practices and procedures, not for publication but just to keep them for use in the future. If so, the Thesmothetae were not writing legislation,[20] but something like notes for their own use. If, then, the report in *Ath. Pol.* has any historical basis, the six Thesmothetae may have been judges, probably before Athens had any written laws, who decided cases on the basis of *thesmia*, traditional, unwritten rules, which had developed over time in part through the judgments reached in these cases. The Thesmothetae would write down these *thesmia* – probably general rules and procedures underlying or implicit in their decisions – and keep these notes so they could consult them in future cases.

This hypothetical reconstruction may gain support from another report in *Ath. Pol.*

They [the Athenians during the time of Peisistratus] had the following law (*nomos*): "These are ancestral ordinances of the Athenians (*thesmia tade Athēnaiōn kai patria*): If any people set up to be tyrants in a tyranny, or if anyone

---

[17] ὅπως ἀναγράψαντες τὰ θέσμια φυλάττωσι πρὸς τὴν τῶν ἀμφισβητούντων κρίσιν.

[18] *Nomima* was used of traditional rules in the fifth century (e.g., Sophocles, *Antigone* 455) at a time when *nomos* commonly designated a written law. Like *nomima*, *thesmia* is almost always used in the plural.

[19] Aeschylus, *Eumenides* 491; cf. Herodotus 1.59.

[20] "It is in any case not very likely that such a duty would be given to six annual magistrates" (Rhodes 1981: 102).

joins in establishing a tyranny, both he and his family (*genos*) will be outlawed (*atimos*)."[21]

This report cites an Athenian law (*nomos*), usually dated to the fifth or late sixth century (Rhodes 1981: 222–3), which officially enacts into law long-established (*thesmia*), ancestral (*patria*) rules, that anyone establishing or helping to establish a tyranny will be outlawed. If these *thesmia* are an example of the *thesmia* that were reported to have been written down by the Thesmothetae (*Ath. Pol.* 3.4), then this would support the historicity of that report. It would also suggest that the office of Thesmothetae and this method of writing down *thesmia* were probably intended to give some consistency to judicial decisions. And if this practice preceded the enactment of written legislation by Draco,[22] as is likely, then the Thesmothetae may have stopped writing down *thesmia* when he wrote his law. But all this is speculation, and it is perhaps more likely that the report is mistaken and the Thesmothetae did not use writing in the archaic period.

Even if we accept that indictments in *graphai* had to be written down in the sixth century and that the Thesmothetae wrote *thesmia* in an early period, the vast majority of legal writing at this time was legislation, which as far as we can tell was always displayed in public where it could be seen and read by the inhabitants of the city. On the other hand, with these possible exceptions, the judicial process remained entirely oral. Draco's law gives no hint of writing in connection with procedure, but says that family members should speak (*proeipein*) the initial proclamation, and the rest of the process was almost certainly oral too, as it was in Homer and in the fifth century. Similarly, the trial in a *graphē* remained oral, as far as we know, except for the indictment. In other words, archaic procedure at Athens was almost entirely oral.

Outside of Athens, as far as we know, the legal process was also entirely oral (Gagarin 2001). In sixth-century Cretan laws, all the verbs relating to litigation imply speaking: *mōlen* ("contend") and its compounds are used of litigants contesting a case in several texts from Gortyn and one from Eleutherna, *pōnēn* ("say, declare" usually in court) occurs once or twice at

---

[21] *Ath. Pol.* 16.10 (Ruschenbusch 1966: F 37a). The pleonasm ("to be tyrants in a tyranny") and abrupt shift from a plural to a singular construction have caused most scholars to emend this text, usually by deleting the expression *epi tyrannidi* as redundant (see Rhodes 1981: 223), but the text is defended by Ostwald 1955: 121 n. 97, who sees similar pleonasm in Draco's law. See also Gagarin 1981b.

[22] Ostwald (1955: 106) and others maintain that because the law cited in *Ath. Pol.* 16.10 was written, it cannot antedate Draco, who wrote the first laws (*thesmous*) for Athens (*Ath. Pol.* 41.2). But if the conclusion suggested above is correct, the Thesmothetae could have written *thesmia* for their own use before Draco, and these would not have been considered laws.

Gortyn, and *proeipein* ("proclaim") appears in an early text from Lyttos.[23] In addition, with the possible exception of the agreement with Spensithios (see below), there are no references in archaic inscriptions to any kind of written documents other than laws. Such documents begin to appear only in fifth-century texts,[24] but even in the fifth century such references are rare, and fifth-century inscriptions from Crete contain no references to writing except for written laws. There remains much that we do not know about archaic procedure, but everything indicates that it was just as oral in the sixth century as in the fifth.

One consequence of the absence of writing was the need for an official who could remember what happened during judicial proceedings in case this information was needed later. For this purpose some cities (mostly Doric) used an official called a *mnamōn* (*mnēmōn* in Attic), literally "rememberer"[25] (discussed briefly in Chapter One). Although the simple noun is not found in inscriptions before the fifth century,[26] officials called *hieromnamones* ("sacred rememberers") are mentioned the an early sixth-century law from Tiryns (Chapter Two) and a somewhat later text from nearby Mycenae,[27] and scholars reasonably assume that the position of *mnamōn* dates from the archaic period. In the Tiryns law the *hieromna-mones* have some supervision of public properties; at Mycenae they are to serve as judges "according to what has been said," implying that they judge on the basis of what they remember was said. Of course, the duties of the archaic *mnamōn* may have been different from those of the *hieromnamones*, but the implications of the Mycenean text are consistent with the fifth-century evidence, that the *mnamōn* remembered earlier proceedings. In addition, the sixth-century agreement with Spensithios informs us about the activity of remembering (*mnamoneuein*), though we do not know if Spensithios was also called a *mnamōn*. We will examine this agreement

---

[23] *Mōlen*: Gortyn 4.1, 4.9, 4.13 (4x), and 4.2121 (3x); Eleutherna *ICret* 2.12.15. *Pōnēn*: Gortyn 4.9. *Proeipein*: Lyttos *ICret* 1.18.1.

[24] E.g., a reference to the record of a debt in the regulations for the port of Thasos from the mid fifth century (*SEG* 42.785 = *Nomima* 11.95, lines 13–14).

[25] Some translations of *mnamōn* wrongly imply that he needed to write. Willetts, for example, translates it "recorder" (record in his memory or in writing?) in 9.32 of the Great Code, and "secretary" in 11.16 and 11.53. Simondon 1982: 293–301 also wants to see the *mnamōn* as more of a writer than a rememberer: "il est surtout un *grammateus* qui consigne, un dépositaire d'archives écrits" (p. 301). Cf. R. Thomas 1996: 19–25.

[26] *Mnēmōn* is an adjective in Homer (*Odyssey* 8.163, 21.95) describing someone who remembers well or is mindful of something, but in inscriptions before 400 it is only a noun designating an official.

[27] *IG* IV. 493 (*Nomima* 1.101, *IGT* 24), dated ca. 525: "if there is no *damorgia* (Board of Demiurges?), the *hieromnamones* concerned with Perse (?) are to be judges for parents, according to what has been said."

below, but it will help to look first at the evidence of several fifth-century texts.

The best evidence for the fifth-century *mnamōn* is a passage from the Gortyn Code (9.24–37):

> If someone dies who has given surety (for a debt), or has lost a lawsuit, or owes money from securing a loan, or is involved in litigation, or has promised repayment, or who faces the reverse situation with another, a suit concerning this matter must be brought within a year; and let the judge rule according to the testimony. If someone who has won a case brings suit, the judge and the rememberer, if alive and a full citizen, and the appropriate witnesses [should testify]; in cases of surety, or money owed, or (previous) litigation, or promise, let the appropriate witnesses testify.

The precise nature of most of the dealings mentioned at the beginning of this passage is unclear, but all must have involved a debt owed by or to the deceased. If the debt resulted from a legal judgment and is now the subject of litigation involving the deceased's estate, then the *mnamōn* is called to testify. Presumably he attests to the earlier judgment, and he (and the judge) must therefore have attended the earlier trial and be able to remember the proceedings, or at least the verdict.[28] The judge is surely the judge from the earlier case, and the *mnamōn* apparently an assistant, whose task was to remember the proceedings of the earlier trial. Thus the *mnamōn* must have existed at Gortyn earlier in the fifth century, and the office was very likely created in the sixth century, if not earlier. This provision also implies that there was no written record of the proceedings, since if there were, the law would surely allow the introduction of this written evidence in case the judge and *mnamōn* were both unable to testify.[29]

Another, slightly earlier fifth-century text from Gortyn (*ICret* 4.42.B6 = *Nomima* II.5, *IGT* 129) also implies an oral process: the law states that "the

---

[28] The qualification "if alive and a citizen," which I take to apply to both the judge and the *mnamōn*, is puzzling. It goes without saying that both must be alive in order to testify, and it is hard to see why, if these officials could be non-citizens in the first place (as this proviso implies), they could not testify later.

[29] So Gernet 1968: 286. Simondon 1982: 297–8 resists this conclusion, holding open the possibility of a written record in addition to memory. The *mnamōn* is also mentioned in two other places in the Code, neither very informative: in 11.10–17 he is to receive a deposit from someone who renounces an adoption and deliver it to the person renounced, and in 11.46–55 he is to be present together with the judge when someone states a charge against a woman involved in a dispute about property during a divorce.

judge and the *mnamōn* will have preference in their oath" with regard to whether something has been done in fifteen days. There is no provision for introducing a written record, only memory. And another Gortyn text (4.87), if the usual restoration is correct, mentions "the *mnamōn* of the *esprattai*"; here too he seems to be an assistant to another official. *Mnēmones* also appear in a fifth-century inscription from Halicarnassus, which records a decision about real property that is to take effect during the time when four named individuals are serving as *mnēmones*.[30] It specifies that from this time on, the *mnēmones* are not to receive (abandoned?) property, but people have eighteen months in which to challenge the status of property in court, and "what the *mnēmones* know is to prevail" (lines 20–2). As in the Great Code, there is no mention of writing, and the *mnēmones* appear to rely solely on their memory of earlier proceedings. And here too, the position of *mnēmōn* must have existed for some time before this inscription was written.

After the fifth century, the duties of the *mnamōn* and *hieromnamōn* increasingly involve writing (though still in connection with judicial proceedings) and by Aristotle's time their main task is to record (*anagraphesthai*) such matters as contracts, verdicts of courts, and indictments.[31] But in the fifth century, and *a fortiori* in the archaic period, they rely on memory (as their name implies) and do not use writing. Thus the importance of remembering did not diminish with the introduction of writing in the archaic period, but only much later, when the use of writing had become widespread in legal and other public matters.

Perhaps the most important piece of evidence for writing and remembering in archaic Greece is a recently discovered semicircular bronze *mitra* (a piece of armor covering the abdomen) from Arcades in Crete, written near the end of the sixth century.[32] The text is an agreement between the city and a certain Spensithios, who is called a *poinikastas* (A 11–12, B 1), which most scholars interpret as "writer" or "scribe."[33] The relevant parts read (A 1–13, B 1–7):

---

[30] ML 32 = *Nomima* 1.19, *IGT* 84. The verb *mnēmoneuein* ("serve as *mnēmōn*") occurs in lines 11–12, 13–14, and 31; the noun occurs in lines 8, 10, and 21.

[31] *Politics* 6.8, 1321b34–50; for the Hellenistic *mnēmōn*, see Lambrinudakis and Wörrle 1983: 328–44.

[32] The text (= *SEG* 27.631) was first published in Jeffery and Morpurgo-Davies 1970; they date it around 500. *Nomima* 1.22 gives a date "near 550," but at the end of the commentary (p. 106) the editors appear to accept a date near 500. For the text, see the Appendix below.

[33] *Poinikastas* is almost certainly connected with *phoinikēia*, which in a fifth-century inscription from Teos clearly designates "letters" (ML 30 = *Nomima* 1.104, *IGT* 78, B.37–8); cf. *phoinikographos* in another contemporary Tean inscription. (*Nomima* 1.105, *IGT* 79), and the fragmentary

Gods! It was decided by the Dataleis and we, the polis, five from each tribe, pledged to Spensithios subsistence and exemption from all taxes for himself and his descendants, so that for the city they may write and remember (*poinikazein te kai mnamoneuwein*) public business, both divine and human. And no one else except for Spensithios and his family is to write for the city or remember public matters, either divine or human, unless Spensithios himself shall urge and say (to do this) or the majority of his sons who are adults. And every year (the city) will give the writer fifty jugs of must wine.

The writer shall have an equal share and shall be present and participate in divine and human affairs everywhere, and where the *kosmos* is, so too shall be the writer. And to whatever god a priest does not ... the writer shall make the public sacrifices and shall have the precinct revenue; and there is to be no seizure nor is the scribe to take security.

Most of the interest in this text has focused on Spensithios as a writer whose primary duty was to write. The agreement does not specify exactly what kinds of things Spensithios was to write or remember, and it has been suggested that "write and remember" describe essentially one function: Spensithios must first remember what was said and then write it down (Raubitschek 1972: 48). But if this were the case, *mnamoneuwein* would be superfluous (and should also be the first verb of the pair). It seems more likely that the verbs designate separate activities, and that Spensithios is supposed to write some things and remember others. And since as far as we know, the only written public texts in the sixth century were laws, Spensithios' writing would probably include the texts of laws approved by the city.[34] And the events that Spensithios would be expected to remember would probably include judicial proceedings (as at Gortyn). The text implies that he would have to attend all public gatherings, including religious events, a time consuming task that would not leave him much time for writing. But laws were not enacted every day, and there

---

poinika[... in a late sixth-century text from Eleutherna (*ICret* II.xii.11 = *Nomima* 1.14, *IGT* 112). The meaning may come from the color red, *phoinix*, which was used in some inscriptions to paint letters for greater visibility, or from the Phoenician origin of Greek writing; see Jeffery and Morpurgo-Davies 1970: 132–3. Not until the fifth century do we find words related to *graphō* ("write") used to designate a "writer" (*grapheus, gropheus*) or secretary (*grammateus*); see, e.g., *IvO* 2 (= *Nomima* 1.23, *IGT* 37); *IvErythrai* 1 (= *Nomima* 1.84, *IGT* 74). I do not use the common translation "scribe" for Spensithios for reasons explained in Chapter Three, p. 71.

[34] Van Effenterre 1973: 39 suggests "mettre par écrit les textes de lois ou les règlements religieux, les calendriers de sacrifices, etc." – the same sorts of matters we find in archaic laws.

may have been little else the city wanted him to write. On the other hand, writing was apparently seen as his most important task, since he is called a writer (*poinikastas*) at least five times but never a rememberer (*mnamōn*), at least not in the surviving text.

The agreement with Spensithios is our only evidence for this dual employment as both writer and rememberer, but it is not inconsistent with the other evidence we have examined that indicates that in the archaic period legislation was written down but judicial procedure was conducted orally and needed to be remembered. In fact, the coexistence of writing and remembering in Spensithios' position illustrates nicely the coexistence of written legislation and oral procedure we have been examining in archaic Greece.

CHAPTER 6

Writing Laws in Fifth-Century Gortyn

In the fifth century, Greek cities everywhere continued to inscribe laws on stone and other materials and display them in public. Judging from the surviving inscriptions, the most active city in this regard continued to be Gortyn, and it is here that we can best study developments in the organization and presentation of legal texts. The crowning glory of fifth-century legal inscriptions is the Great Code (*ICret* 4.72), probably from about the middle of the century, with almost twelve full columns of text. We also have a second large inscription, the so-called Little Code (4.41, probably before 450), which treats damages done to and by animals, runaway slaves, and indentured servants; parts of seven columns of this text survive, and originally there must have been more. In addition, four (incomplete) columns of text survive on 4.75, traces of three columns can be seen on 4.77, and several other inscriptions originally had at least two columns of text.

The Great Code is a unique document, and its laws cover a far broader range of subjects than any other Greek legal inscription. Because of this, it will be treated separately in the next chapter, where we will also explore some of the similarities and differences between it and the Babylonian Code of Hammurabi. But even leaving aside the Great Code, Gortyn is exceptional in the quantity and diversity of inscribed legislation in the fifth century. In this chapter I examine a selection of fifth-century inscriptions from Gortyn (4.41–140), paying particular attention to features of style and organization. As we shall see, though the Code may be unparalleled in size and scope, it shares some of the features of other fifth-century inscriptions from Gortyn, and its large-scale organization builds on methods of organization in these other texts.

The fifth-century inscriptions from Gortyn share several general characteristics (Guarducci 1935–50: vol. IV 87). Laws are no longer written on the wall of Apollo's temple but on stones that either formed part of the walls of other buildings or in some cases were free standing. They are written boustrophedon, in letters that are slightly smaller than those of earlier inscriptions, but also neater, more upright, and written in straighter rows. One can sometimes see traces of the fine lines that the masons used to keep their rows straight. Masons no longer use dividing lines to mark words or groups of words, but they sometimes leave a gap of a letter or two at the beginning of a new clause or provision.[1] There are also occasional instances of asyndeton,[2] either after a gap or without a gap. Both asyndeton and gaps usually signal a shift in subject or in focus with respect to the same subject. On some inscriptions (e.g. 4.41) gaps mark the more important shifts, on others like the Great Code, asyndeton is more important. There is also a growing tendency to organize texts in relatively narrow columns. Because these features are so widely shared, I will often not remark on them, but will focus primarily on matters of presentation and organization, paying particular attention to the ways in which laws on different subjects are arranged on the same inscription and to the large-scale organization of provisions on the same subject into coherent units.

Dating this group of inscriptions (4.41–140) on the basis of letter forms is an imprecise art at best. Most scholars follow Jeffery (1990: 315), who tentatively dates 62–4 to "*c.* 525–500?," 41–61 and 65–71 to "*c.* 500–450?," 72 to the "mid-5th c.?," and 73–140 to "*c.* 450–400?" In view of the uncertainties, I will treat this whole group (41–140) as simply fifth-century, except for 62–4, which show several signs of being earlier than the rest and may perhaps date to the late sixth century. Like sixth-century texts, 62–4 have no gaps; they are written in fairly long rows, on blocks that are 1/3 to 2/3 meters high and in their original state were perhaps two meters long.[3] Thus, although they are not as long as the early long inscriptions like 4.14, most later texts are narrower. All three inscriptions are fragmentary, but enough remains to see that 62 is a law dealing with disputes concerning a slave, 63 is an agreement between Gortyn and Leben (a port on the south

---

[1] These gaps are not found in sixth-century inscriptions, except at the ends of lines. Some of the gaps on the Great Code and occasionally on other inscriptions are filled with a painted design, which some scholars have treated as significant. But the painting probably has no special significance, because in all likelihood all the gaps originally had such painted signs. By now, most of the paint has worn off, as has most of the red paint that originally marked all the lettering (Gagarin 1982: 138 n. 35). Thus I do not distinguish gaps in which the original painted signs happen to survive today from other gaps.

[2] Asyndeton is the absence of a connecting particle ("and," "but," "therefore," etc.) at or near the beginning of a new sentence, which usually designates a break in sense (see above, Chapter Two, and see further Gagarin 1982).

[3] 4.62 is currently only half a meter long but we know the text continued to the left on the same stone and to the right on a separate stone, so the original inscription may have resembled 4.64, which survives on two long rectangular blocks, side by side.

coast probably controlled by Gortyn), and 64 is a decree awarding rights and privileges to a certain Dionysius.

62 is particularly interesting because even though only about a dozen words survive, several of these words (notably the words for "free" and "slave") also occur on the first column of the Great Code, though in no place is what survives of 62 identical to the wording of the Code.[4] Thus, 62 may have contained an earlier version of the regulations we find in the Code, or it may have regulated other matters involving free men and slaves. In either case, this is one of several indications we have that the legislation of the Code may have in some way modified earlier legislation, though too little remains of 62 to know just what the relationship was between it and the Code. We should also note the apparent mention of "the Gortynians," which also occurs on earlier inscriptions (4.23 and perhaps 4.10.*x–y*).

63 represents an agreement between Gortyn and Leben, a port city directly south of Gortyn. The legible text consists of fragments of five lines: "to carry ... twelve *medimnoi*[5] of barley ... [the Lebenian?] against the Gortynian, and the Gortynian (?) against the Lebenian ... for the Lebenian, a witness is to prevail ... bread (?), five staters per day and." Most scholars consider this a treaty between independent cities, but it seems that at this time Leben, located on the southern edge of the large plain of Mesara, was already dependent on Gortyn, which was on the northern edge of the plain and had expanded its influence extensively over the plain during the sixth century. In the process Gortyn had also established hegemony over other nearby cities, such as Rhitten, Amyclae, and Aulon (see 4.64 below), and probably controlled Leben too.[6] Thus, the treaty probably records an agreement establishing the relationship between the dominant community and one of its subordinate villages.

64 is the best preserved of these three inscriptions. We have its left-hand edge, which is where the inscription begins with the word "gods" (*thioi*), followed by "good luck" (*tycha agatha*), and the text may have extended only some 10–12 letters on the missing block on the right. We almost certainly have the decree's end in line 6, since the text ends in the middle of the line, the rest of which is blank. Strictly speaking, this text is not a law

---

[4] All that remains of 62 is a short bit of text from the middle of nine lines: 2. the Gortynians (?) ... free (?) ... but if someone (?) ... a slave ... being *kosmos*, or another ... should release ... divine matters ... but if he does not wish ... to drink. For the Greek text of this and the other inscriptions, see Appendix IV.

[5] A *medimnos* is a dry measure of grain equivalent to about 62 liters.

[6] Perlman 1996: esp. 258–70 and, for Leben, 248 and 255.

but a decree honoring an individual; I include it here because it helps shed light on the kind of concerns that occupied the Gortynians at this time.

1. Gods, good fortune. A gift was given to Dionysius the son of (?) Ko[...

2–3. ... because of his valor in war and his benefactions, by all Gortyn and those living in Aulon, exemption from taxation in all matters (?) for himself and his descendants (?)...

4–5. ... a citizen's justice[7] and a house in Aulon inside of Pyrgos and a piece of land outside ...

6. ... and of the gymnasium.

The inscription is remarkable in that the honors are awarded by "all Gortyn and those living in Aulon." Aulon was a community close to Gortyn, perhaps a suburb (Perlman 1996: 266–8). The precise reference of "all Gortyn"[8] is unclear, but since it is paired with "those living in Aulon," it can hardly designate anything less than "those living in Gortyn," and it may be intended to include those members of the larger Gortynian community who reside outside the city. The other remarkable expression is "citizen's justice" or "civic justice" (*wastian dikan*), which presumably designates access to the same judicial system as a full resident (*astos*) of Gortyn. Evidently the Gortynians had by now developed the idea of citizenship or official membership in their community, and were willing on occasion to grant membership to others.

These three inscriptions indicate that matters concerning civic status were a major concern of Gortynians at the end of the sixth century: 62 apparently treats free and slave status, 63 concerns the relations between dominant and subordinate communities, and 64 grants something like citizen status to an outsider. Moreover, the presence of the collective "the Gortynians" in 62 suggests that like 64 and probably 63, it represents a decision made by the entire community. As we noted, this collective also occurs in earlier laws (4.23 and perhaps 4.10), and like "all Gortyn," it must designate a fairly large percentage of the inhabitants of the city. It appears, then, that as Gortyn expanded its control over the Mesara plain and the smaller communities in and around it, it was also defining itself as a civic entity and establishing the relationship between this civic body and other smaller communities. And in view of the prominent place this community has in these laws, and its role in awarding citizen status in 64, this

---

[7] *Wastia dika* probably means that Dionysius would have the same access to justice as a citizen.

[8] The expression is unparalleled at Gortyn or in any other Cretan city (Perlman 1996: 267).

legislation cannot have been enacted and publicly displayed by a small group of elites primarily serving their own interests.

As far as we know, none of the laws at Gortyn before the fifth century has an explicit enactment clause,[9] which might shed light on the decision-making process there, but if the entire civic body somehow authorized an award of a civic honor, they must have made other decisions about significant civic matters, and we can hardly suppose that the enactment of legislation was not one of these matters. Thus, by the end of the sixth century, if not earlier, a civic body referred to as "the Gortynians" or "all Gortyn" was almost certainly enacting legislation and making other decisions for the community.

As Gortyn moves into the fifth century, the quantity of inscribed legislation increases substantially.[10] The most important physical development in this period is that the texts are written in narrower columns, generally between half a meter and a meter wide; inscriptions with several columns tend to have narrower columns, and the widest columns are found on stones where the whole text is written in just one column.[11] Apparently the Gortynians were learning that columns of about this width were the easiest to read. The writing is always boustrophedon, it may start from either the right or the left, and the beginning of the first line often coincides with the top edge of the stone.

A notable feature of texts that are divided into columns is that fifth-century masons make an effort to avoid dividing a word, or in some cases a phrase, between the end of one column and the beginning of another. For example, the last line of the first column of 4.47 ends about two letters before the end of the line, apparently so as not to divide the next word between this line and the next, which is the top line of the next column. This same feature is evident at the bottom of five of the seven columns in 4.41 (1–3, 5, 7). The end of 41.7 (for the text, see below) is especially notable since the bottom line ends in mid sentence with the word *kai* ("and") about

---

[9] For most early laws, of course, the opening words are not preserved, but we probably have the beginning of one (4.21). The one fifth-century enactment clause that survives (4.78) is discussed below. The beginnings of other fifth-century laws are preserved (including the Code), and some of these, like 64, begin by invoking the gods.

[10] The number of surviving inscriptions may not be an accurate index of legislative activity in the sixth and fifth centuries, but we have more than twice as many fifth-century laws (41–140, less 62–4) as earlier laws (most of which were inscribed on the Pythion and so would have been preserved even if obsolete), and many of those we have are longer than the earlier laws, some much longer.

[11] 4.78 and 4.80 are each written in one column (4.80 spans two stones) with a width of about 1.20 meters. Of course, some of the columns that are now fragmentary may also have been wider than a meter.

six letters before the end of the line, leaving a relatively large gap.[12] Similarly, nine of the eleven columns of the Great Code probably ended with the end of a word (2–9, 11),[13] and in two of these (7 and 8) the bottom line ends well before the end of the line (4 and 8 letters short, respectively).[14] Masons did not always end a column with a complete word, but the coincidence of column end and word end is clearly much greater than would occur by mere coincidence, indicating once more that those who carved laws in Gortyn paid attention to the needs of the people who would read them.[15]

Another interesting feature of the fifth-century laws is that some inscriptions (e.g. 47) show traces of earlier writing that has been erased.[16] Only a word or two can be made out from these earlier traces, but the implications of the traces are interesting. Since almost all early inscribed texts at Gortyn were laws, it is likely that the erased texts were also laws. But erasing the text from a stone cannot have been easy, and the large size and unruly appearance of the erased letters that are still visible suggests that they are at least half a century (and perhaps more) older than the new texts inscribed over them. Thus, although the practice of erasing texts might convey the message that laws written on stone were not stable and permanent, the texts erased here were probably considered obsolete and their erasure would do little to diminish the sense of the law's permanence. Of course, the early texts inscribed on the temple of Apollo remained intact, perhaps out of respect for the god, even though undoubtedly some of these were also obsolete.[17]

---

[12] The top of the next column no longer survives, but I assume that the first word (or the phrase of which it was part) was too long to fit in this gap at the bottom of column 7.

[13] Column 9 ends with the letters *syn*, which are probably a complete word, though we cannot be certain since the beginning of column 10 is missing. Column 11, the bottom of which consists of several short addenda, ends with a complete provision, the last two words of which are written on the stone below what is normally the bottom of a column. I exclude column 12, which ends less than half way down the stone. For comparison, if we consider all 620 lines of the Code, line end and word end coincide only 27 percent of the time.

[14] In both these cases, the first line of the next column begins with an article that is short enough to have been written at the end of the preceding column, but this would have meant that the article would be divided from its noun.

[15] A different strategy seems to be at work in 78, where the mason stretched out the letters at the end of the last line in order to fill the line and not leave a large gap. Here the concern seems to be appearance rather than readability.

[16] In one text (42B.3) part of a line has been erased and new text written in the gap. The letters in this part are slightly smaller than the rest, so that the new text might fit into a space that is slightly too small. Evidently, a mistake was discovered, the error was erased, and the correct text, which was slightly larger, was inscribed in its place.

[17] The Gortyn Code, in fact, was taken down and reassembled in a new place during the Roman period, though it is not certain whether it was still considered valid law.

These erasures are yet another indication that these texts were written to be used, since this is the likely explanation why a law that had become obsolete was erased and then replaced by a new text. If the primary reason for inscribing laws was to impress an illiterate population, there would have been no need to erase obsolete laws; one could much more easily write the new law separately, which would make an additional visual impact. If the laws were displayed in order to be read and used by the community, however, then the removal of obsolete laws would be imperative.[18] The Gortynians knew that laws could change over time, and when one law replaced another, it was vital to display only the new version in public. Some early inscriptions, however, were left standing, even though they treated subjects covered later, such as adoption in 21 and 72.10.33–11.23, because the later legislation supplemented but did not replace the earlier,[19] which was thus left standing because it had not been rendered invalid.

Of the fifth-century texts that survive, the longest and most interesting with respect to the organization of its provisions is 4.41 with more than seven columns of text. The bottoms of each column are preserved with about 17 lines of text each, but each is missing an unknown amount of text above this. Originally, there was at least one more column of text on each side.[20]

The preserved columns treat damages done to and by animals (1–3), runaway slaves (4), and damages done to and by indentured servants (5–6); the subject of column 7 is uncertain. These topics may have been thought of as loosely related, in that they all concern agents owned or controlled by someone else, and they may have been inscribed together for that reason. Of course, still other subjects might have been treated in the columns that are now missing, and there may have been other reasons, not evident to us, for inscribing these provisions together. But if we begin with the first three columns and perhaps the first lines of the fourth, which treat injuries done to and by animals, together with the rest of column 4, which deals with fugitive slaves, we can study some of the methods by which the legislator organized a group of provisions on the same subject.

---

[18] By contrast, copies of Hammurabi's laws (Chapter Seven) continued to be made centuries later in diverse parts of the Near East, where they could not possibly have been the actual law of the land.

[19] We have no evidence of direct overlap between surviving laws on the same subject. Some scholars think that 4.41, col. 7 is superseded by 7.10–15 of the Great Code, but it probably treats a different subject (see below, n. 31). And I will suggest a reason why much of 4.75A is identical to the text of 4.81.

[20] A few letters are visible before col. 1, and since col. 7 ends in the middle of a sentence, there must have been at least one more column after this.

[Col. 1] It is possible for the injured party, if he wishes, to give up his own and take that of the other party.#[21] If he does not wish to have it, he will be paid the simple price. *vac.* And if he does not lead[22] his wounded animal or does not take his dead animal [to the offending animal's owner], or does not display it as is written, he shall have no recourse to legal action. *vac.* And if a pig wounds or kills an ox, the pig shall belong to the owner of the ox, and the . . .

[Col. 2] . . . he shall pay the equal amount. *vac.* If possible, a horse or a mule or an ass shall be driven [to the offending animal's owner] as is written. But if it is dead or cannot be driven, then [the injured animal's owner] shall summon [the other] in the presence of two witnesses within five days in order to display it, wherever it is; and the summoner and his witnesses shall have the preference in swearing an oath as to whether he drove or took it or summoned him so as to display it.# *vac.* If someone wards off the attack of dogs . . .

[Col. 3] If[23] both the different ones are following, there shall be no legal action; but if both are not, he [the attacking dog's owner?] shall pay the simple price.# *vac.* If someone has been entrusted with an animal or bird either as a loan or for some other reason and is not able to return it, he shall pay the simple price. But if while pleading in court he denies [having received it], he shall pay double and a fine to the city . . .

[Col. 4] . . . fourfold. *vac.* But whenever someone returns it safe and sound, he shall pay the simple price. *vac.* The fugitive slave[24] is not to be sold if he has taken refuge in a temple or for a year after he has run away. If the fugitive belongs to someone who is *kosmos*, he is not to be sold while he is *kosmos* or for a year after he has run away. But if he is sold before this time, [the seller] shall be convicted. Concerning the time, after swearing an oath [the judge will decide] . . .

---

[21] I use # in the translation to indicate the presence of asyndeton (the absence of connection between sentences – see above, n. 2) and *vac.* to indicate a gap between the end of one sentence and the beginning of the next. The significance of these is discussed below.

[22] For the meaning of *epidiomai* and 4.41 in general, see Bile 2000.

[23] The sense of this sentence is uncertain. I (hesitantly) understand it as referring to an attack by two dogs belonging to different owners, the wounded dog's owner and another; the other owner is not liable for injuries to the wounded dog if the two dogs attack together, but is liable if his dog alone attacks. Guarducci (ad loc.) and others take it, perhaps correctly, as referring to dogs hunting (see *Nomima*, ad loc.).

[24] This may refer to a slave who has caused some injury or damage and is fleeing to avoid having to pay for it.

The first three columns concern domesticated animals: first (1, 2 and the beginning of 3) liability for an animal that has been wounded or killed by another person's animal; then (3) failure to return an animal that has been entrusted to a person. Column 1 begins by providing alternate ways by which an injured animal's owner may receive compensation: he may either receive the offending animal in exchange for his injured one or accept money equal to the amount of the damages, in which case he presumably keeps his injured animal. Since the next group of provisions apply to a pig attacking an ox, these initial rules probably apply only to cases involving the actions of a different kind of animal that was named earlier, perhaps attacks by an ox on other animals. The next provision specifies the consequences for not taking or showing the dead or wounded animal "as is written." This expression and variations of it occur regularly in fifth-century inscriptions from Crete, and in all cases they refer to a law that is written down elsewhere on the same inscription or a different inscription. Here the rules specifying how the animal was to be taken or shown to the responsible party were probably written earlier in this same inscription.[25] Column 1 ends with a special rule about compensation if the injured animal is more valuable than its attacker (specifically, if a pig injures an ox); in such a case the injured animal's owner receives the injuring animal together with something additional (in lines now lost).

Thus, column 1 probably contained rules on (at least) three related topics and part of a fourth: first (and now lost), that in order to receive compensation, an injured animal's owner must take and show the animal to the responsible party together with rules on how to do this; second, that the victim's owner can choose between two types of compensation, taking the injuring animal in exchange or accepting a monetary payment; third, that if the injured animal is not taken and shown as specified, the owner cannot bring suit in the matter; and finally, that in a special case the compensation should be greater than a simple exchange. This arrangement is clear – first the procedure for requesting compensation, then the kinds of compensation allowed, then the prohibition on suing if the proper procedure is not followed, and finally a special situation – the rules are reasonable, and where the text survives, a gap marks the beginning of each new topic. A person whose animal is injured would be able to understand his rights and responsibilities and the options available to him and could

---

[25] "As is written" might refer forward to column 2, which has rules for summoning the offending animal's owner, but since nothing is said there about bringing the animal to the other owner, it is more likely that there were rules about this before the text on column 1.

relatively easily take the necessary steps to receive proper compensation. The arrangement is more complex than what we saw in sixth-century inscriptions, where specification of a penalty is followed by the consequences of non-compliance, but here too the order is clear and coherent.

The next three columns do not yield as much information about the organization of topics, but they do confirm the use of gaps to separate one from another. Most of column 2 is devoted to one topic, the requirement that the injured animal be taken and shown to the injuring animal's owner or, if this is not possible, that the owner be summoned to view the dead or injured animal. A different topic preceded this (followed by a gap), and the column ends (after a gap with asyndeton) with a new topic, defending oneself against a dog. It is possible that this topic continued down to the preserved text on column 3, which concerns attacks, perhaps by dogs, or perhaps by other animals. In either case, column 3 ends (after a gap with asyndeton) with the topic of persons who do not return a borrowed animal: if they admit the borrowing, they pay simple compensation, but if they deny it, and presumably if the lender proves otherwise (probably by means of witnesses), the fine is more than doubled.[26] Column 4 seems to have begin with a related topic, perhaps the theft of an animal, for which the fine is fourfold, unless the animal is returned safe and sound, in which case the fine is simple. These alternatives are separated by a gap, but the larger arrangement of provisions on this topic is unclear. Column 4 ends (after another gap) with an apparently unrelated topic, protection for a fugitive slave who takes refuge in a temple. The connection may lie in the fact that the slave has caused injury to an animal and is fleeing to avoid having to pay for it, but this is just a guess.

Before examining the last three columns, it is worth remarking on the overall organization of 4.41.1–4. These four columns alone contain more legislation than any sixth-century text, and whoever created the legislation must have made a conscious effort to organize these rules. In the sixth-century texts we noted some fairly rudimentary forms of organization: for example, a simple list of sacrifices (4.3), perhaps arranged chronologically by days of the month with each entry beginning on a new line, or the statement of a rule followed by the consequences of non-compliance (in 4.14). This structure continues to be used,[27] but fifth-century texts generally rely on more complex arrangements.

---

[26] His denial apparently makes this in effect a theft (Cohen: 1983: 67).
[27] E.g., in column 4: "... he is not to be sold ... but if he is sold ..."

We can see this in 4.41. First, rules concerning animals occupy at least the first three columns, with rules concerning injuries in columns 1, 2, and the beginning of 3. These are arranged in groups (injuries by an ox (?), injuries by an animal of lesser value, injuries to a horse, mule, or ass, attacks by a dog). Each group is separated from the others by a gap, and within some groups further subgroups of rules are also marked by gaps. Provisions are commonly paired with alternatives, which are regularly introduced by the words "but if" (*ai de ka* = Attic *ean de*), with the first provision addressing the common situation followed by a less common alternative. Finally, we should note that in two places a gap together with asyndeton marks the beginning of a new topic: at the end of column 2, where the topic changes from displaying an injured animal to an attack by a dog, and then at the beginning of 3, where it changes from dog attacks to the loan of an animal. Thus, gaps with asyndeton seem to indicate a stronger break than gaps without asyndeton.[28]

I will not analyze the rest of column 3 and column 4, but they show similar arrangements which are considerably more complex than anything in the sixth-century texts. By the fifth century, then, legislators at Gortyn were enacting larger groups of provisions on one subject and were seeking ways to organize these provisions in a clear and coherent whole. This desire for clarity and coherence on a large scale, which we also noted in Draco's homicide law, might be explained as the result of intellectual or aesthetic sensibilities, but this would not explain why these sensibilities are evident in Greek laws but not, say, in Near-Eastern laws. The main factor, as I have been stressing, is that Greek laws were written to be read and used by members of the community. Legislators therefore not only had to devise rules for the community, but when they wrote and displayed these rules, they also had to attend to the needs of those who would be reading and using them. This forced legislators to strive for clarity and coherence by means of those organizational features we have been examining.

A similar attempt to organize provisions is evident in columns 5–6 of 4.41, though the arrangement here is slightly different from that of the earlier columns. 5–6 treat damage caused by or to an indentured man (*katakeimenos*) – one who is temporarily working for another man in order to pay off a debt. For the sake of completeness, I translate column 7 here,

---

[28] There is one example of asyndeton without a gap, after the first sentence in column 1, but this is atypical. Since there is no apparent reason why there should be asyndeton here – the asyndeton comes between one conditional sentence ("if he wishes") and its contrary ("if he does not wish") – the mason may have omitted a connective by mistake.

but because its interpretation is uncertain and it probably does not treat the same topic as 5–6, I will omit if from the discussion.

> [Col. 5] . . . And if he does not swear, he shall pay the simple fine. *vac.* And if on the orders of the one to whom he belongs [i.e. his temporary master] the indentured man has done or taken something, he is not liable. But if [the temporary master] testifies that he did not so order, the judge is to decide after swearing an oath, unless a witness testifies. *vac.* And if the indentured man criminally wrongs another man,[29] then he himself is to be liable. And if he does not have the means to pay, the man who won his case and the temporary master . . . [will arrange a settlement?]
>
> [Col. 6] *vac.* But if someone criminally wrongs the indentured man, the temporary master shall bring suit and shall exact the penalties as for a free man, and whatever penalty he exacts, the indentured man is to have one half and the temporary master the other [half]; and if the temporary master does not wish to bring suit, let [the indentured man] himself bring suit when he has paid his debt; and if the indentured man . . .[30]
>
> [Col. 7] . . . drives or brings possessions to a temple or . . . (line 7) the buyer is to pay the fine to those who have a claim on the possessions, as is written in each case, and the man (*andra*) himself[31] is to belong to those who have a claim on the possessions if he does not complete [the transaction] within thirty days after the purchase; but if they agree within ten days not to complete it, [he is to return?] the surety and . . .

After the first sentence of column 5, which refers to the issue that preceded (perhaps still on the subject of the fugitive slave), the provisions in 5–6 envision two main issues: injuries done by an indentured man and injuries done to him. The first of these is subdivided according to whether he was

---

[29] The verb *adikein* ("wrongs") may imply that the crime is more serious; I have added "criminally" to try to capture this sense.

[30] The missing text at the end of this column may have contained further specifics concerning the outcome of a suit by the servant himself, perhaps something to the effect that any fine levied at this later date is to be retroactive (as in 4.72.1.53–5).

[31] Scholars often take "the man" here to refer to a slave who has been purchased, and then go on to discuss what relation these provisions may have to a short provision in the Great Code (72.7.10–15) giving the buyer of a slave sixty days to terminate the agreement (see Davies 1996: 46–7). But the use of *andra* to refer to a slave would be very unusual, and since nothing else in this column indicates that it treats specifically the purchase of a slave, it seems more likely that *andra* designates the buyer who receives the goods but does not pay the agreed price within thirty days. This buyer would then be indentured (*katakeimenos*) to the seller until he paid the agreed price.

acting on orders or acting on his own, a distinction not relevant to the issue of injuries done to the man. The result is three different sections separated by gaps:[32] first, if the indentured servant does wrong on his temporary master's order, second, if he does wrong acting on his own, and third, if he is wronged himself. Each section, moreover, begins with the general rule governing the situation and then adds a supplementary rule (if the master denies, if the man cannot pay, if the master declines to bring suit). These two columns thus treat the whole subject of injuries and indentured servants in a clear and coherent manner evident to any reader.

In sum, 4.41.1–6 address several large subjects with a number of provisions devoted to each. These are arranged in different ways, but always clearly and coherently. In addition, the placing of these three subjects (and probably more) together on the same inscription was almost certainly not arbitrary, since the first and third concern injuries involving animals (1–3) and indentured servants (5–6), and the second, runaway slaves (4), may also have somehow involved injuries. Thus, two and perhaps all three of these sections concern the question of legal liability in the rather mundane affairs of daily life (cf. *Nomima* II: pp. 234–5).

The rules, moreover, are fair, reasonable, and practical. Someone who claims compensation for injury to his animal must first show the injured animal to the other party for inspection, or, if this is not possible, he must summon the other party (before witnesses) to see the injured or dead animal. Thus one cannot claim compensation for the injury without providing verification. In column 4, a slave is allowed to take refuge in a temple for a reasonable period of time (generally one year) but not permanently. In columns 5–6, a man acting on his master's order is not liable for the damages he causes, but he is liable if acting on his own; and if the two disagree about the master's orders, the judge uses his own judgment, unless there is a witness.

In sum, in 41 the legislator combined a number of related topics into a logical and coherent unit with rules that are rational, fair, and easily understood. This is no small accomplishment. It must have required the legislator's careful attention, and his aim must have been to create legislation that would be most easily read and used by the community.

Let us now examine several of the shorter fifth-century inscriptions where related subjects may be treated together, beginning with two (43 and 47) from the group generally considered earlier than the Great Code

---

[32] The top part of column 6 may have addressed a fourth topic, or it may all have been devoted to the topic at the end of 5.

(41–71), followed by two (78 and 75) from the slightly later group (73–140). We can begin with 4.47, which is very likely a complete text neatly inscribed on one and one-half columns of a single stone.[33]

> (A) If an indentured male or female slave wrongs (someone), in that he does wrong on the orders of his current master, the case is to be brought against the current master, but in that he himself (does wrong) on his own, the case is to be brought against his old master and not his current master. And if the one who indentured him [i.e. his old master] loses the case, he is to give to the current master what he owes. *vac.* But if someone else wrongs the indentured (slave), if both [masters] plead the case and win, they shall each have half (of the penalty). And if one of the two does not wish (to plead), if the other pleads and wins, he shall have (the whole penalty) himself. And if the indentured (slave) should disappear, let (the judge) rule that the current master should swear that he is not to blame, neither himself nor with another, nor does he know (that the slave is) with someone else. And if he (the slave) should die, let (the current master) show (him to the former master) (B) before two witnesses. And if he does not swear as is written or does not show him, he shall pay the simple value (of the slave). And if (the former master) accuses him truly of selling or hiding away (the slave), if he loses the case, he shall pay double the simple value. And if (the slave) takes refuge in a temple, he is to show him clearly (to the former master).

The close resemblance between this law and 4.41.5–6 concerning indentured free men is evident. In both, the law addresses first wrongs done by the indentured person and then wrongs done to him, with a gap separating the two. The temporary master is responsible for any actions he ordered, but not for those he did not order, though in the latter case it is the former master who is liable, not the slave himself.[34] If the slave is injured, both current and former master may bring suit, or one of them alone if the other

---

[33] Since the first line of column *B* is certainly the top of the column, we must also have the top of column *A*. Van Effenterre and Ruzé (*Nomima* II.26, ad loc.) suggest that column *A* may have been preceded by another column on another stone, which is not impossible, but the existing text can be satisfactorily understood as is, and seems to be complete as it is. The first word in the law is *katakeimenos* ("indentured"), which I understand as marking the general subject. There is room for two or three letters before *katakeimenos*, but the only possible supplement is an article, and it is better to take *katakeimenos* as an adjective. It appears that the legislator moved *katakeimenos* to the beginning of the sentence to mark the general subject of this law as "the indentured" person.

[34] In Greek law generally, liability for the actions of a slave rests with his master.

declines. Added to these provisions (but not separated by a gap) are rules concerning other possible contingencies, which might cause conflict between the current and former master – if the slave disappears, or dies, or takes refuge in a temple. Each contingency is regulated together with other potential issues related to it before the next contingency is addressed. Since this text is complete, the overall organization, which also resembles parts of 4.41, is readily apparent, clear and logical (though unlike 4.41, it makes little use of gaps to separate provisions).

4.43,[35] with four separate texts inscribed on one stone, raises different questions.

(Aa) If someone who has obtained as a pledge a threshing floor (?)[36] unjustly[37] fails to harvest the grain (?), he shall pay the value of the pledged products as is written for each case.

(Ab) If someone unjustly obtains as a pledge a male or female slave or strips him/her of clothing or takes his/her jewelry, he shall pay half the amount that is written for a free person and triple[38] the value of the clothing and the jewelry as (is written?) for a free man (?).

(Bb) Gods, the polis has given the fertile land at Keskora and Pala for planting. If someone buys it or accepts it as a mortgage, the purchase is not to be valid for the purchaser nor the mortgage (for the mortgager). A person cannot accept a pledge unless he calculates the amount of produce (it will bear?).

(Bb) Gods, if someone diverts water from the river in its median flow[39] to flow over one's own land, there is to be no penalty for the diversion. But he is to leave as much water flowing as the bridge by the agora has[40] or more, but not less.

The four provisions of 43 are inscribed in two columns with two provisions in each, clearly separated from one another by clear vertical and horizontal spaces. Each text begins with asyndeton. The left column (B) is approximately twice as wide as the right (A). All four texts run right up to the right

---

[35] The four texts of 4.43 are printed together as *Nomima* II.70, but the third (Ba) is discussed separately as *Nomima* I.47. *IGT* treats them as four separate texts (130–3).

[36] *Alōs* ("threshing floor") could also designate the product of the *alōs* ("grain"), and "harvest the grain" (*karpoomai*) could also mean "deliver, or thresh, grain (or other products)."

[37] "Unjustly" is usually taken to go with "obtained," but this implies that there would be no penalty for unjustly obtaining the *alōs* as long as one harvests the grain, but unjustly obtaining something ought to be punishable in itself.

[38] Scholars disagree about whether *ta tritra* means "one-third" (Guarducci *et al.*), "three times" (Koerner *et al.*), or even two-thirds (van Effenterre and Ruzé). Cf. Chapter 7, n. 42.

[39] Lit. "the middle" but it probably means the median amount of water that flows. The river is probably the modern Mitropolianos which runs through Gortyn.

[40] I.e. as flows under the bridge by the agora.

or left edge of the stone. Despite making the bottom two lines of Ab a letter longer than the preceding line, the mason could not fit the whole provision on the stone; he must have continued it on the stone below (or possibly to the right). By contrast, Bb ends well before the bottom of the stone. This may indicate (Guarducci, *ICret* ad loc.) that column B was inscribed first, leaving too little room for the laws in column A.

Each of the four texts appears to be a complete provision, but none is easy to interpret. As best we can tell, the first concerns the unjustified failure to use a threshing floor (or to deliver grain) which one has obtained as a pledge; the second concerns the unjust treatment of a slave whom one has obtained as a pledge; the third regulates the possession by purchase or mortgage of a public field set aside for planting; and the fourth regulates the diversion of water from a public stream. If there is a relationship among the four texts, it is not easy to discern, though there are clear verbal links between them: Aa and Ab both begin with nearly identical language, differing only in what was obtained by pledge, they impose fines relative to the value of an object, and refer to something written elsewhere. Ba and Bb both begin with the invocation *thioi* ("gods") followed by a noun that conveys the subject of the provision, which in both cases is a public resource (public land, the river). And Ba is loosely linked to Aa and Ab in that it too involves obtaining a pledge. But there is no clear overall relationship among the four texts and we can only speculate why someone decided to inscribe them together on one stone.[41]

One possibility is that, as Guarducci suggests, column B was inscribed first. In this case, the first law to be inscribed (Ba) would have allowed private individuals to use certain public lands but not to sell or mortgage them. Bb would then allow private access to river water, another communal resource, but also with restrictions on the amount that can be used. Aa and Ab were then inscribed on the same stone because, like the first two provisions, each was understood to regulate a resource that the public had an interest in protecting. Perhaps some threshing floors were public property, and although the slaves probably did not belong to the city, this provision may have concerned a certain group of slaves who for some

---

[41] Van Effenterre and Ruzé treat Aa and Ab as part of the same series of regulations concerning ownership by pledge and the resulting damages, but they treat Ba and Bb as separate laws, unrelated to the first two texts or to one another. Koerner treats all four texts separately, while acknowledging that the first two have some relationship. Davies (1996: 50–3) concedes that the two texts in each column might somehow belong together, but argues that the four are more likely to be separate enactments that were inscribed together, and that the similarity in subject matter of the first two texts is mere chance.

reason were a matter of public concern. Some support for this view may lie in the fact that both Aa and Ab refer to written laws inscribed somewhere else; this indicates that the use of threshing floors (or the value of commodities) and the treatment of slaves had already been regulated by the city, and this suggests that the Gortynians (or the polis, which acts in Ba) had a special interest in these two matters. Thus, these four texts may not have been inscribed together arbitrarily, and the connections among them may be more than verbal.

In any case, the four texts indicate that the polis has become actively involved in several aspects of the lives of the inhabitants of Gortyn. An increasing amount of legislation was being enacted in the fifth century, and we have already noted evidence for the involvement of "the Gortynians" in this legislation. If some sort of public approval was required for this legislation, as seems likely, then the polis was clearly becoming increasingly concerned to regulate the lives of its citizens.

4.78 is a decree granting full rights to a group of immigrants (or less likely a group of freedmen) who are called Latosians (or who reside in a part of Gortyn called Lato).

> Gods.# The following was decided by the Gortynians voting.# *vac.* Of those who have returned (?),[42] whoever wishes is to settle as a Latosian on equal and similar terms (viz. as a Gortynian), and no one is to enslave him or plunder him.# If anyone enslaves him, the foreigners' *kosmos* is not to allow it.[43] And if anyone plunders him, the *Titai* are to make each pay one hundred staters and are to exact [from them] double the value of the (plundered) goods and return it. And if the *Titai* do not act as is written, each of them is to pay a double amount (half) to the person who has a claim and (half) to the polis.

4.78 is the only fifth-century inscription from Gortyn which we know opened with an explicit enactment clause, using the same expression, *tade ewade* ("these things were pleasing"), as several of the laws from Dreros. We have encountered "the Gortynians" before, though this is the first time they enact a law or are said to vote. They must constitute a fairly large body, and voting suggests some sort of assembly, even though Gortyn was not a

---

[42] The lost end of line 1 can be restored as *tōn apeleu[samenōn* ("of those who have returned"), or *tōn apeleu[therōn* ("of those who have been freed"). Parts of lines 2–3 and 7–8 could also be restored differently.

[43] The normal meaning of *lagaiō* is "release, dismiss," and some editors translate "shall not release him." But this seems to go against the sense of the decree and most editors translate as I have.

democracy, as that term is generally understood (Robinson 1997: esp. 13–34.). The presence of an enactment clause in this text and as far as we can tell no other might suggest that only this law was enacted by this group. But it seems unlikely that this measure offering protection to a group of immigrants would be the only law that needed to be ratified by this body. Many other laws appear to be of equal, if not greater, public interest. It seems more likely, then, that the body that ratified this decree also enacted other laws in Gortyn, but for some reason unclear to us, a statement of the enactment was only inserted into this text.

The organization of the decree is straightforward. The enactment clause is followed by the substance of the decree, probably marked off by a gap with asyndeton. The decree grants equal rights to immigrants and specifically prohibits anyone from enslaving them or plundering their property. The prohibition is followed, after an asyndeton, by measures to remedy violations, and, as often in archaic Greek laws, officials who do not enforce the law are themselves fined. The third asyndeton is unusual in that it marks a break between a prohibition and the statement of penalties for a violation, which elsewhere are not separated in this way, but as we have seen, the use of asyndeton to mark a new topic, like the use of gaps, was not systematic. A gap or asyndeton, or both virtually always mark a break, and there is some regularity to their use, but actual practice remains flexible.[44]

In my last example, 4.75, several columns of text may all concern the same subject, giving security for a debt. But this law is of greater interest to us for the fact that the text of column *A* is (with minor variations) identical to another, contemporary inscription, 4.81.4–15. Four columns of 4.75 are preserved but originally there was probably at least one more column on either side of these. An unknown amount of text is missing at the top and bottom of each column. Only about half of column *A* survives, but the text can be restored from 4.81.

> *A* And he is to summon the man who is taking security before two witnesses three days in advance in order to measure (the property). And if the man does not come when he is summoned as is written, let him (the summoner) measure it himself and declare to him four days in advance before two witnesses that he should be

---

[44] Other examples of gaps besides those in the texts examined in this chapter are 42B.9 (where there is little or no break), 42B.11 (a slight break but a related subject), 76.2.7 (a new subject), 77.2.4, 77.2.10, 83.7, and 83.9. In 81.22, Guarducci posits a gap between two now missing letters in a break in the stone, although no previous editor had done so and examination of the stone casts doubt on her restoration at this point.

present in the agora. And he (the summoner) shall swear that indeed (the land?) was his without fault and lawfully before the case was tried, and the man from whom they took security (is to swear) that it was not.

B . . . the arms of a free man which he has for war, except for a cloak, jewelry, a loom, wool that has been worked [i.e. woolen cloth], iron tools, a plow, a team of oxen, an implement (?), the lower and upper millstones, from the men's club (*andreion*) whatever the director provides for the club, the bed of a man and a woman, a free man's . . .

C . . . each man . . .# *vac.* If someone is old or for some other reason unable to come where he is supposed to receive the security, another man who receives the security for him is not to be liable. But let him name the (man's) name . . . witness to whom . . .

D . . . to the *esprattēs* or the judge and one who . . . witnesses . . . and whatever is written shall be collected without a trial . . .

Columns *A* and *C* are clearly related in that each concerns security for a debt; after *A* specifies the procedure for giving land as security, *C* allows someone else to receive the security on behalf of a lender who, because of age or other disability, cannot receive it in person. It is thus tempting to understand *B* (as most scholars do) as also concerned with some aspect of security; most likely it is a list of a family's possessions that cannot be pledged as security. If *D* is also related, it may then specify procedures for recovering the security one has given after the debt is discharged. If this interpretation of the four texts is correct, the legislator has arranged the parts of his law clearly and reasonably: *A* prescribes the process for giving security, *B* exempts certain items from being pledged as security, *C* states that a proxy may receive the security in special circumstances, and *D* gives rules for recovering the security. If this partly hypothetical picture is correct, this inscription illustrates a fairly complex form of organization we will also see in the Gortyn Code, where provisions on one general subject may be arranged partly temporally (first the procedure for giving security then for recovering it) and partly hierarchically (the general rule followed by exceptions and a specific contingency).

The repetition of *A* in 4.81, lines 4–15 raises interesting questions. The entire surviving text is as follows (for the Greek text, see Appendix IV.9):

(1–4) [In a case where ?] nine of the neighbors, those who possess the
closest land, swear regarding trees and a house, he [the mortgager?] is
to bring suit;

(4–16) and he is to summon the man who denied in court [that the land belonged to the mortgager?] before two witnesses three days in advance in order to measure (the property). And if the man does not come when he is summoned as is written, let him (the summoner) measure it himself and declare to him four days in advance before two witnesses that he should be present in the agora. And he (the summoner) shall swear that this indeed was [done?] without fault and lawfully before he pleads his case, and the man who is taking security [is to swear] that it was not (done). And whatever the majority swear, (that side) is to win. *vac.*

(16–23) And if they take something from a house as security, if the one who is providing security says that he does not live in it, three of the nine neighbors, whom he notified earlier, are to swear together with him that the man providing security does not live in the house; if it is one of the neighbors. *vac.*

Davies (1996: 47–50) assumes that essentially the same law was written on two inscriptions, but there is one significant variation: in 75A.2–3 one is to summon "the man who is taking security" (*ton enekyraksanta*), but in 81.5–6 the summons is for "the man who denied in court" (*ton apololesanta*). The law in 81 addresses a dispute over whether the man giving security actually owns the land and perhaps also whether the land is adequate, but 75A simply specifies the procedure for giving security in the form of land. Instead of an exact duplicate, therefore, 81 may address a contingency (that the mortgager does not own the land) not mentioned in 75. If so, when the legislator enacted this new law, he repeated the basic provision for giving security from 75. I cannot say why he did not simply provide a cross-reference ("as is written"), but we need not understand 75A and 81 as exact duplicates.

I have focused in this chapter on the organization of laws on different inscriptions. Although the fragmentary and difficult nature of many texts creates the risk of circularity in the argument, as assumptions about the coherence of subject matter may influence assumptions about the restoration of texts, it is possible, nonetheless, to perceive some of the organizational methods Gortynian legislators were using at this time to organize their laws both at the macro level (the organization of subjects on inscriptions that treat more than one subject) and at the micro level (several provisions addressing one aspect of a subject). Already in texts like 4.41 and 4.75, we can see a considerable advance in macro-organization when we compare these to a very early inscription like 4.3, with its list of rules about sacrificing animals, where separate provisions, each related to and closely resembling the others, are inscribed together, simply one after the other. In a rudimentary way and on a small scale, sixth-century legislators were already confronting the problem of collecting and organizing several provisions on the same subject, but fifth-century legislators are clearly becoming more skilled at meeting this challenge. In Athens, to be sure, Draco had already anticipated several of these techniques in his seventh-century homicide law. The organization of archaic laws outside Athens develops more gradually, but there is no doubt that legislators are concerned with it and are taking steps to organize laws effectively.

Finally, the presence of cross-references in many of these fifth-century laws suggests that some thought was being given to the overall organization of the city's laws. Cross-references of the sort "as is written" abound in fifth-century legislation at Gortyn and other cities in Crete.[45] At Gortyn, more than two dozen cross-references are scattered throughout the fifth-century texts other than the Code, and there are many more there.[46] All these references occur in one of two contexts, procedural or penal. That is, someone is directed either to follow a certain procedure or to pay a certain penalty "as is written" or "according to what is written." For example, a law may direct someone, to display an animal "as is written" (41.1.11) or swear an oath "as is written" (47.23–4), or it may specify, for example, that the offender should pay the value "as is written in each case" (43. *Aa*.7–9), or "pay one-half as much as is written for a free man" (43. *Ab*.7–9).[47]

This system of cross-referencing is fairly rudimentary, particularly in that it often does not make clear where the law being referred to is written. In some cases we can be quite certain that the reference is to a provision that was part of the same inscription (47.23–4, 75. A.4–5 = 81.7–8, 78.7), but in others it is clear that the reference is to a provision inscribed somewhere else (43. *Aa*.7–9, 43. *Ab*.7–9, 80.10), and in many cases we cannot be sure. In one text, however, the cross-reference specifies the place where it is written with precision. This is 80.10 ("he shall pay twice the simple fine as is written *en tai porai*"), where the reference is almost certainly to a specific place. We do not know where this

---

[45] There is no explicit mention of writing in the sixth-century inscriptions from Gortyn (*ICret* 4.1–40, 62–4), though of course writing may have been mentioned in parts of these or other archaic texts that are now lost. Several laws referring to writing from Lyttos (*ICret* 1.18.4, 1.18.6) and Eleutherna (2.12.4, 2.12.13) may date from the sixth century, but they are too fragmentary to allow any conclusions to be drawn.

[46] I do not count the reference to writing in 80.12 (see below), which is not really a cross-reference.

[47] In fifth-century texts at Gortyn I note the following examples (not including 80.12). Procedure to be followed: 41.1.11, 41.2.6, 47.23–4, 75. A.4–5 = 81.7–8, 76.5, 78.7. Penalty to be paid: 41.7.10–11, 43.1.7–9, 43.2.7–9, 77.2.10, 80.10, 83.8–9. Too fragmentary to determine the context: 45.2.3–4, 56.4, 56.6, 60.1, 75.D.4, 77.3.8–9, 86.3, 86.5–6, 90.2.14, 92.8, 136.

place is, but presumably it was known to readers of the law. We can only guess why a specific place is named here and not elsewhere, but it may be that since this is the text of a treaty between two cities, the inhabitants of one city might not know exactly where the written laws of the other city were displayed. Or perhaps some legislation specifically regulating relations between people in these two cities had been displayed in some place apart from the other laws of either city, and the author of the treaty wanted to make the location clear. In any case, only here, but nowhere else at Gortyn, did the legislator feel a need to specify the precise location of another law.

To the modern legal mind, the lack of precision in "as is written" would be a serious fault. Modern law normally makes such cross references very precise (e.g., "see Article 6.5, subsection 12"). The Greeks also knew how to avoid this vagueness in cross-referencing by referring to the law on a specific subject. They rarely used this method until later, but in the sixth-century law from Naupactus (Chapter Two) we have the expression "as in the homicide law" (in a penal context), and the sixth-century law from Cleonae provides that "there is to be purification (*katharsis*), just as when someone dies and is purified according to the law." The Gortynians, however, do not seem to have been troubled by the potential vagueness of "as is written." It would have helped that, despite the relatively large amount of legislation in this city, it had many fewer laws than any modern state, and the laws they did write were generally much shorter than modern laws. It would also have helped that the Gortynians inscribed and displayed in public almost no texts other than laws and decrees, and these were probably all displayed in just a few places in the city. Thus, when a Gortynian read that something should be done "as is written," he knew this meant "as specified in the law," and he also knew the general location, at least, where the relevant law might be displayed.

The extensive use of these expressions to refer to other legislation at Gortyn and some other cities would implicitly convey to the reader the sense that all the laws of the city formed a body of rules ("what is written") separate from other rules that were not written, and that these written rules were all related to one another, so that a law on one inscription could draw on a procedure or penalty written on a different inscription. They were all part of a single, unified body of texts, "what is written," which comprised the laws of the city. As a treaty between Gortyn and Rhitten puts it, "The things that are written, but nothing else" (4.80.12).[48] In other words, all the written statutes of each city are to be valid, and only these.

---

[48] τὰ ἐγραμμέν' ἄλλα δὲ μέ. The sentence is marked by gaps with asyndeton before and after.

We may conclude from all this that legislators paid attention to the ways in which their laws were assembled and arranged on inscriptions and made at least some effort to provide a clear and logical organization that would be helpful to the reader. The results, as far as we can see them, were uneven and in many cases rudimentary from a modern perspective. But it is clear that the degree of organization we will find in the Code (Chapter Seven) is not an isolated or unique feature but a continuation and expansion of developments evident in Gortynian laws from the beginning.

The fact that legislators paid attention to the physical, stylistic, structural, and organizational features, thereby making their laws easier for readers to read, understand, and use, confirms that this legislation was meant for practical use by some moderately large part of the community. Laws written solely for magistrates could be presented on a much smaller scale and would not need to be prominently displayed in public spaces. And if the texts were conceived as monuments intended for visual impact alone, the Gortynians would hardly have needed to continue inscribing so many texts and displaying them all over the same public space, nor would they need to concern themselves with making texts easier to read and use. This is not to say that the visual impact was not important. Tourists today who gaze at the Great Code without understanding a word of it are nonetheless impressed, as undoubtedly the Gortynians themselves were, simply by knowing that this city had such an extensive collection of laws. But the message, that these texts were invested with the full authority of the polis, was joined with the message that these texts belonged to their readers and were intended for their use. These readers formed a body that could be designated "the Gortynians"; and the sight of dozens of texts displayed all around them in public areas of the city must have made members of the community, especially but not only those who could read them, feel themselves part of a group that acquired special authority by being the possessors of, the beneficiaries of, and (probably) ultimately the authority behind "the things that are written."

CHAPTER 7

Writing the Gortyn Code

If, as I have argued, the frequent use in fifth-century inscriptions at Gortyn of expressions like "as is written" to refer to laws written elsewhere conveyed the sense that the text was part of a larger, interconnected set of legal texts, this sense of a unified set of laws may have been part of the inspiration for one of the grandest legislative achievements of ancient Greece, the Gortyn Code (GC),[1] sometimes called the "Queen of Inscriptions" (Willetts 1967: vii). The scale of GC puts it in a class of its own. In eleven and a half columns of text, with 621 lines and more than 3,000 words, it presents rules on a range of subjects, primarily related to family and property law, but also concerning many other issues. The large clear letters are generally well preserved and with few exceptions, the text is easy to read.

Many interesting questions have arisen about the nature of this extraordinary inscription: Why were these particular laws inscribed together? Is it properly called a code? How are the laws on GC related to those on other inscriptions at Gortyn? Are all these laws the work of a single magistrate? The work of a succession or group of magistrates? Or decisions of some assembly or group of citizens? Or are they verdicts rendered in court cases?[2] I do not expect to answer all these questions, and most of them will never be answered with certainty. But they provide a starting point for exploring the nature of writing and law at Gortyn.

---

[1] *ICret* 4.72 – I will refer to specific passages only by column and line number. Willetts 1967 provides a convenient text with facing English translation and commentary; van Effenterre and Ruzé 1994–5: vol. 11, 357–89 have a complete text with facing French translation, but their commentary on individual sections is scattered throughout (mostly in vol. 11). Koerner also divides the text into separate provisions (*IGT* 163–81).

[2] Among the more extensive treatments of some of these questions are Lemosse 1957, Gagarin 1982, Camassa 1988, Lévy 2000a, van Effenterre and van Effenterre 2000, Perlman 2002, and the studies in Greco and Lombardo 2005. Of special note is the very interesting study of Davies 1996, which has influenced my thinking on many points. The question, whether the document is a code, is to my mind the least important. I use the term for convenience (cf. van Effenterre and van Effenterre 2000), while recognizing that it is not a code in the full modern sense (complete, systematic, etc.).

A different sort of insight into these matters can come from comparison of GC to another ancient inscription with a large collection of laws, those of the Babylonian king Hammurabi inscribed around 1750 BCE, which I will refer to by its traditional abbreviation CH.[3] Although these two collections come from different civilizations and are separated in time by more than a millennium, the fact that they are similar in length and in the broad range of subjects they treat makes them natural candidates for comparison. I will be particularly interested in how the two codes treat writing and written texts, and how they organize their material.[4]

Like the other fifth-century laws from Gortyn, GC regularly uses words and expressions for writing like "as is written" (*ai egrattai*) to refer exclusively to laws. Take, for example, 12.1–4: "If a son has given money to his mother or a husband to his wife *as was written before these writings*, the matter shall not be brought to court; but for the future, gifts should be given *as is written*." The italicized expressions clearly differentiate between two versions of a law, before and after revision, "as was written" and "as is written" being equivalent to "the previous law" and "the current law." As we have seen, the law so designated may be written on the same inscription or elsewhere.

By contrast, even though CH has about the same number of references to writing and written documents as does GC – thirty-four in GC[5] vs. twenty-five references to documents in CH (nine of which explicitly mention writing), and six mentions of writing in the Epilogue[6] – the kinds of written texts it refers to are different. In CH the only references to written law are the six instances in the Epilogue where Hammurabi refers in the first person to texts in the main body of CH – e.g., "the commands I have written on this stela" (E15; cf. E8, E11, E14, E18, E19) – and every such reference is to CH as a whole, never to a specific provision, as at

---

[3] Since I cannot read cuneiform script and do not know the language of these laws (Akkadian), I have relied on translations, primarily Richardson 2000, but also M. Roth 1995 (which also contains other Near-Eastern collections of laws), as well as the earlier edition of Driver and Miles 1952. I will only note differences between the translations of Richardson and Roth when they might affect my argument.

[4] Some of the material in this chapter is treated more briefly in Gagarin 2001 and 2006b (with Westbrook 2006).

[5] Thirty-four instances in GC: 1.46, 1.55, 3.20–1, 3.29–30, 4.11, 4.30–1, 4.46, 4.48, 4.51, 6.14–16 (3x), 6.31, 7.47–8, 8.10, 8.25–6, 8.29–30, 8.35–6, 8.40, 8.54, 9.16 (2x), 9.24, 10.45, 10.46, 11.20 (2x), 11.27–9 (2x), 12.2–3 (2x), 12.5, 12.9, 12.14.

[6] Identifying references to writing and written texts in CH is not always easy without knowledge of the language. I have used Richardson's translation (2000) here and (unless otherwise indicated) in the citations below, checking it as far as possible against words in the Akkadian transliteration he provides. Using M. Roth 1995 would change the numbers slightly but would not significantly affect my conclusions.

Gortyn. In the body of CH, however, all references to written texts are to documents other than laws.[7] Sometimes the specific word for "contract" (*riksu*) is used (7, 47, 52, 122, 123, 128, 264), but more often the word used is simply "tablet" (or "sealed tablet"), which indicates a written document. Otherwise the type of document is only clear from the context, which reveals the following: a judge's verdict (5), transfers of property (37, 150, 151, 165, 171b, 178, 179, 182, 183), records of debts (48, Fragment a), contracts (Fragments m?, v, w, 177?), and receipts for payment (104, 105).

Several provisions in CH require a person to have a written document, which would presumably have to be presented in court in the event of litigation.[8] And the provision that mentions a judge's written verdict (5)[9] suggests that verdicts were commonly recorded on a tablet and sealed, in part to prevent anyone from changing them. Even if CH was not intended to be used in actual legal affairs (see below), these references to writing indicate that written documents were important in the judicial system, and actual documents representing most of the types mentioned in CH have been found.[10]

Since it is generally agreed that when writing began to be used in Mesopotamia, it was primarily for commerce (C. B. F. Walker 1987: 7, 11), it is not surprising that the references in Hammurabi's code are primarily to commercial documents. Most of these were probably written by professional scribes, who in addition to their writing skills, must have been knowledgeable in financial and legal matters and in particular must have known the rather formulaic language of most documents.[11] Thus, in most cases someone who wanted to enter into a contract or get a receipt for payment probably had the document written by a scribe. In this respect, the Near East differed significantly from Greece, where although the masons who inscribed laws and other public documents may have been professionals as early as the sixth century, their role was probably limited to inscribing a prepared text; there is no reason to think that they had any

---

[7] Roth twice translates a word (*simdatu*) as "royal edict" (51, gap u), but Richardson translates this as "decision of the king" and explains (p. 279) that it means "the official rate agreed by the king."

[8] E.g., 104 requires an agent to receive a sealed document as a receipt for silver he has given a merchant; 105 then specifies that if he fails to obtain this, "any silver without a sealed document may not be counted in the reckoning." See also 128, 178.

[9] "If a judge has conducted a trial, given a verdict, had a seal placed on the document, but some time later modifies his verdict, they can show that that judge is guilty of changing the verdict he has reached, and he shall pay 12 times the amount of the loss which had occasioned that trial."

[10] Most of these documents are not readily available to non-specialists; but a selection from different periods are translated in Joannès 2000.

[11] C. B. F. Walker 1987: 33–6 briefly describes the education and work of scribes.

legislative expertise,[12] and they do not appear to have played any further role in legal or commercial affairs. And there is no evidence in Greece before the fifth century for the types of written commercial documents that were common in the Near East.

The fact that CH regularly recognizes the role of written documents in court but never mentions written laws being used in litigation suggests a different understanding of the nature and use of its laws than we have observed in Greek legislation. Why then were these laws collected, written down, and displayed? Are they meant to be used in actual legal affairs? If not, what are they and why were they inscribed here? And who were the intended readers? These questions have been debated almost since the Code was discovered a century ago, and in recent decades most scholars have come to think that this collection was not intended for use in litigation, and thus that the text should not be treated as legislation but as a kind of legal science.[13] This position is perhaps most fully articulated by Bottéro,[14] who notes first, that CH was often copied, even 1,000 years after Hammurabi's death, when his rules could no longer have had any authority. In itself, this proves nothing,[15] but it may suggest that CH is not the normative text it was originally assumed to be. Bottéro's next point, that the text is not complete but is rather an "anthology" (*florilège*) of 282 "articles" grouped according to different sectors of communal life, could also describe GC. But when Bottéro points to three other features of the laws in CH – their particularity, illogicality and ineffectiveness[16] – his arguments become more compelling.

On the first point, Bottéro observes that CH treats some very particular situations but says nothing about many others that would be just as common, as, for example, 229–30:

---

[12] The Athenian Nicomachus may be an exception (Todd 1996).

[13] In addition to Bottéro 1992 [1987], Westbrook 1989, and M. Roth 2000 (all discussed below), Kraus 1960 and Finkelstein 1961 were influential early proponents of this view. French scholars are the primary dissenters from this view: e.g., Leemans 1991: col. 416 ("Les Lois de Hammurabi sont une pièce de législation réelle, destinée à être mise en pratique"). Lafont 2000 argues that CH contains positive law, but its rules are "subsidiary," in that they were intended to apply only in the absence of a local community rule on the matter. See also Charpin 2003: 210–18.

[14] Bottéro 1992 [1987]: 156–84. The English translation of this work must be used with caution (see below n. 16).

[15] Many centuries after its enactment, GC was reassembled for display during the Roman period, when some, if not all, of its provisions were obsolete.

[16] Bottéro 1992: 162–4. "Ineffectiveness" is my translation of *inefficacité*, perhaps better rendered as "lack of practical effect"; to render the term as "inefficiency" (Bottéro 1992: 162) is completely misleading.

229. If a builder has built a house for a man but does not make his work strong enough and the house he has made has collapsed and caused the death of the owner of the house, that builder shall be killed.
230. If it has caused the death of a son of the owner of the house, they shall kill that builder's son.

The second article presupposes that a builder with a son builds a house for a client with a son and that the house's collapse kills the client's son. The two provisions could be read as an incentive for builders to do good work (also an incentive for builders not to have children?), and they can, of course, be extended by analogy: for example, if the owner's daughter is killed, the builder's daughter is put to death. But this does not help one decide a case where the builder has no equivalent relative or where the house collapses but no one is injured. Articles 229–30 are obvious examples of the general principle of the *lex talionis* ("an eye for an eye"): the death of one person's son is compensated by the death of another person's son. But like the *lex talionis* itself, which gave rise to various academic disputes about one-eyed men and the like, such rules are more effective as general principles than as working law. Thus, Hammurabi is not writing legislation regulating the building trade but providing a neat illustration of an appropriate response in selected cases.

For his second point about illogicality Bottéro notes striking differences between articles amounting at times to a contradiction. For example, article 8 specifies the penalty for the theft of a boat from a workman as ten times the value of the stolen object, and death if the thief cannot pay, whereas 295 specifies only the modest fine of five shekels for the theft of a plow. Such discrepancies in collections of laws are not uncommon, however, and do not necessarily tell us anything about the legislator's intent. Third, Bottéro argues that the many other legal documents that survive from this time make no reference to the authority of CH, even when this collection contains relevant rules. In actual legal situations, if an authority is sought, the parties appeal to "decisions of the king" not these rules (unless these are the same, as some think). Some of the provisions in CH may reflect verdicts that Hammurabi rendered in particular cases, but this would not make them true legislation, which often reflects litigation but is never a simple record of verdicts. And even if many of these rules were derived from verdicts, Bottéro's conclusion seems reasonable: "in the eyes of its author the 'Code' was not at all intended to exercise by itself a univocal normative value in the legislative order. But it did have value as a model; it was instructive and educative in the judicial order" (1992: 167).

Other scholars have provided additional arguments for this view. First, Westbrook 1989 makes a compelling argument that CH is not true legislation because, by contrast with actual legislation, which must address the issue of retroactive application whenever a piece of legislation significantly changes existing law, CH gives no evidence of being temporally situated or coming into existence at a specific time and place, and it never mentions the possibility of retroactivity.

Second, Roth examines two letters written about the same time as CH which might be thought to reveal a connection with it, but concludes that they do not, and that the Code "had no demonstrable impact on the law of the land" (M. Roth 2000: 30). Roth then reexamines a controversial passage from the Epilogue to CH, which is sometimes used to support the idea that the Code was meant to be of practical use:

> (E11) Let any wronged man who has a lawsuit come before the statue of me, the king of justice, and let him have my inscribed stela read aloud to him, thus may he hear my precious pronouncements and let my stela reveal the lawsuit for him; may he examine his case, may he calm his (troubled) heart.[17]

From this passage Roth concludes first, that the oppressed man is not someone who is currently a litigant in a case but someone who has already lost his case and is troubled by this, and second, that the man is not instructed to take action to correct the wrong he has suffered but only to listen to the law being read to him, from which he will understand the issue and feel better and (in E12) will praise the king. Thus, the Epilogue does not say, as has often been thought, that someone wishing to pursue a legal case should read the Code and learn what the law is so that he can apply it to his case, but rather that someone who feels he has been treated unjustly should be comforted by listening to the Code being read out to him by someone else (the implication being that he cannot read the text himself).

To these arguments we may add some simple observations about physical features of the two inscribed texts. The famous stele, now in the Louvre, with the text of CH topped by a relief of Hammurabi apparently receiving his laws from the god Shamash, is an impressive monument

---

[17] This is Roth's translation. Richardson's translation differs slightly but agrees with Roth's on relevant points: "Let any man oppressed, anyone who has a complaint, come before this statue of the king of justice and let him have the message on the stone read aloud, and let him listen to the treasured words I have written, and may my stela resolve his complaint, and may he understand his problem, and may he be content in his heart."

indeed,[18] but it presents difficulties for the potential reader beyond the fact that, as most scholars agree, only a relatively small class of scribes and perhaps a few other elite persons knew how to read the cuneiform script. The text is inscribed all the way around the column-shaped stele, so that a person cannot read the full text without walking around the stone. There is no obvious physical indication, moreover, where on the circular stele the text begins. The Gortyn text, by contrast, obviously begins at the top of one edge of the inscription, and its twelve columns are inscribed on a slightly concave wall, making it easier to move from one column to the next. The inscription is currently enclosed so that visitors must stand about two meters away and view it from behind protective bars, but even at that distance the letters are easy to make out, and red paint would originally have made the letters even clearer. By contrast, it requires very sharp eyes to make out the incised wedges on Hammurabi's stele from the same distance.

Direct comparison of the size of the two very different scripts may not be meaningful, but we may observe that the cuneiform script of CH is about the same size as on many other inscriptions in the Louvre and elsewhere, but the text is engraved in shallow incisions on hard diorite stone and is considerably less easy to read than contemporary cuneiform inscriptions carved on softer stone. The letters of GC, by contrast, are a little larger (2.5–3 cm.) than those of most of the contemporary inscriptions from Gortyn (4.72–140), and their neatness and clarity are striking. These physical features suggest that whoever inscribed CH was not primarily aiming to assist readers, and this would be another indication that these laws were not written primarily in order to be read and used in actual litigation.

We should note that similar views have recently been proposed for several other premodern collections of laws, especially those from medieval Europe, where there is growing resistance to the straightforward use of these collections by legal historians as if they were legislation in the modern sense.[19] Thus far there is little consensus, but Wormald 1999, for example, has argued that the law collections of the Anglo-Saxon kings are expressions

---

[18] Although many other fragments of CH have been found, the copy in the Louvre is the most complete and is generally agreed to date from the time of Hammurabi, when a number of copies were probably made and set up in different parts of the kingdom. See Driver and Miles 1952: vol. 1, 27–30, M. Roth 1995: 73.

[19] I claim no expertise in the area of medieval law; works that I have found helpful include Green 1994, Wormald 1999, Wickham 2003, and the essays in Davies and Fouracre 1986 and McKitterick 1990.

of an ideal law, derived ultimately from a biblical model of justice.[20] The Anglo-Saxon collections may have incorporated laws from actual cases at the time, but they appear to have had little practical authority or influence on actual litigation. Instead, their purpose was at least in part ideological: to present an image of the king as just legislator, heir to a tradition going back to Moses. The best known of these texts, the laws of King Alfred (871–99) preserved in the *Domboc* (Book of Dooms or Laws), was apparently not aimed at the people who had to live under them but at the relatively small group of royal officials, clergy, and intellectuals who then and in the future would be judging the character of Alfred and the success of his regime. Thus, we can use these laws to learn something about actual law at that time, but they are not actual legislation in the sense of rules enacted to control or influence people's conduct under the law. It has similarly been suggested that some of the medieval law collections from the continent, such as the Frankish collection known as the *Lex Salica*, may also have been written for ideological purposes rather than as legislation.[21]

Now, if premodern collections of laws from medieval Europe and the ancient Near East were not true legislation intended for use in actual legal affairs, why should we think that GC was different? Perhaps it too was not meant to be used in actual litigation but served primarily as a visual sign of authority, which few people actually read or used. For its monumental visual impact, GC certainly has few rivals. On the other hand, physical, stylistic, and organizational features of other inscriptions indicate that they were in fact meant to be read and used by members of the community beyond the ruling elite, and these same features are found in GC.

I have already noted the large, clear, (originally) painted letters, conveniently arranged in columns. Another clear indication that GC was intended for actual use is the inclusion of several provisions concerning retroactivity (Westbrook 1989).[22] In contrast to CH which lacks any

---

[20] *Contra* Keynes 1990, who grants the written law some authority in Anglo-Saxon England; he sees it as primarily intended for the king's reeves, who had the primary responsibility for enforcing order, but notes that the king's (oral) word was still the supreme law. Griffiths (1995: 11–19) also adds a note of caution about Wormald's views.

[21] "The Franks, then, were not so much creating law for subject peoples as coaching them in the value of having written law ... Frankish *lex* was to all appearances as inert as it was anonymous ... Its subsequent fossilization implies that it soon became more a symbol than a tool of Frankish ascendancy" (Wormald 1999: 44–5). Similarly, Wickham argues that to understand how dispute-settlement worked in practice in medieval Europe one must start with records of actual cases, which "are as close as we get to how things happened – certainly far closer than the idealizations of written law" (in Davies and Fouracre 1986: 228). On early codes, see also Diamond 1971: 47–54 (the Anglo-Saxon law collections "are literature rather than law," p. 53); Goody 1986: 135.

[22] Recall that Draco's law also contains an explicit provision of retroactivity.

concept of a historical moment for legislation, the author of GC understood the need to situate his legislation within a historical process in which
a law becomes valid at a specific moment in time. The clearest evidence of
this is 5.1–9:[23]

> A woman who does not have any property, either as a gift from her
> father or her brother or as a pledge or inheritance as of the time
> when the Aithalian *startos*, Kyllos and his colleagues, formed the
> *kosmos*, these women shall obtain their share [of the inheritance];
> but for women before this time no legal action shall be taken.

This provision specifies the date when it takes effect, thereby acknowledging that it belongs to a historical moment in time. The clause just cited
also recognizes and addresses the potential conflict between this legislation
and previous laws or customs that may differ from it, specifying that the
old rules govern cases up to this time, but after this date these new rules are
in effect. This and the other provisions concerning retroactivity show
conclusively that the Code was intended to guide the conduct of members
of the community and provide practical rules for resolving disputes.

5.1–9 is the first of five provisions in the Code, where a rule is specified as
not being retroactive (the others are 6.9–25, 9.7–17, 11.19–23, and 12.1–5);[24]
this is also the only such provision with a date, and it probably represents
the date on which the whole Code takes effect. As the only date in GC,
moreover, it probably was intended to stand as the effective date for all the
other provisions of GC, and more specifically to apply to the other
provisions for non-retroactivity. It is understandable that the legislator
would insert a date for the Code at the earliest point where the question
of retroactivity is explicitly addressed, since a date would not have been
needed before this point; and once the date had been given, there would be
no need to provide it again. This date, then, probably stands as the date for
the entire Code.

The practical purpose of GC is also indicated by the fact that it pays
much more attention to procedure in court than does CH.[25] CH and most

---

[23] Unless noted, translations of GC are my own, sometimes based loosely on Willetts 1967. I do not
normally cite the Greek, since the text of GC is for the most part unproblematic.

[24] See further Gagarin 1994. The provision in 4.52–5.1 – "Any (daughter) to whom he gave or promised
(something) before is to have these things, but from the paternal property she is not to receive (by
inheritance) anything else" – reads a little like a provision of retroactivity, but I understand "before"
here to mean before the father's death, not before the enactment of this law.

[25] I treat this matter more fully in Gagarin 2001. The other premodern codes I discuss there are, in
addition to CH, the *Lex Salica*, the Lombard laws in Rothair's Edict, and the nineteenth-century
Chinese Code of the Qing Dynasty.

other premodern collections of laws are primarily concerned with setting penalties for crimes and otherwise providing rules of conduct; they pay little attention to procedures for settling disputes and when they do, the procedure mentioned is commonly an automatic procedure such as an oath or an ordeal. By contrast, GC is less concerned with fixing punishments for crimes but contains many provisions about judicial procedures. In legislation intended for actual use procedural details are as important as substantive rules (some would say more important), since those using the legislation must know how they should proceed to prosecute a case or defend themselves. But procedural details are of little significance in a set of laws intended to show its readers the norms and values of the society or of its ruler.

Moreover, the procedures commonly specified or alluded to in GC and other laws from Gortyn all indicate that litigants pleaded their cases orally before a judge who decided the case on the basis of these pleadings. One indication of the oral character of procedure is the frequent occurrence (more than a dozen times each in GC) of two verbs designating the activity of litigants or witnesses in court: *mōlen*, meaning "plead, contend in court," is always used of a litigant, and *pōnēn*, meaning "say, declare," usually in court, is used of either a litigant or a witness.[26] By contrast, the non-Greek codes make almost no reference to anyone speaking in court. This does not mean that judicial procedure was not important in practice or that litigants in other cultures did not speak in court; we know from other documents that they did, but the portrayal of litigation in CH does not reflect this reality.[27] But since these non-Greek collections were not intended for practical use, it was not important that they include information about procedure in court. Thus, the inclusion of rules for litigation in the Code is one more indication of the practical aims of its author, just as the absence of such rules in CH is another sign of Hammurabi's lack of interest in the practical use of his laws.

This different approach to legislation also corresponds to a different understanding of justice. Legislators in these other cultures aimed to portray justice as a matter of the appropriate punishment for each crime;

---

[26] These verbs with their compounds also occur regularly in earlier fifth-century laws from Gortyn (4.41–71): *mōlen* occurs eight times (41 (3x), 42 (2x), 47 (2x), 57), *pōnēn* four times (41 (2x), 42, 46). For *mōlen* and *pōnēn* in sixth-century laws at Gortyn and elsewhere, see Chapter Five, n. 23.

[27] In Egypt, on the other hand, complaints had to be submitted in writing, probably as early as the Old Kingdom (2700–2200); if the complaint was accepted, the defendant responded in writing, and further arguments of both litigants were also submitted in writing (Versteeg 2002: 130). This system recalls the use of writing by Deioces after he has become king of the Medes.

they saw no need to address the practical difficulties of determining the guilt or innocence of the accused. By contrast, the Gortynian legislator, even in the sixth century, considered it important to include information about procedure in his legislation. This is in keeping with the deeply rooted Greek view, going back to Homer, that a fair procedure for litigation is an essential requirement of justice.

Lack of concern with procedural justice is only one way in which Hammurabi's justice differed from Greek views. The provisions about building a house cited above illustrate a vicarious justice: in 230 the builder's son, who evidently is totally innocent, is put to death, not the builder (cf. 210, cited below). The Greeks might at times subscribe to principles of strict liability – in Homer unintentional killing appears to be treated no differently from intentional killing (Gagarin 1981a: 11) – or even joint liability – Hesiod warns that whole cities will be destroyed for the evil deeds of kings (*Works and Days* 260–2), and Agamemnon sees nothing wrong with destroying the city of Troy to avenge Paris' theft of Helen (Aeschylus, *Agamemnon* 810–28). But vicarious justice, where an innocent person is punished instead of the guilty party (though Hammurabi presumably thought a son's death would punish the father too) is foreign to Greek thinking about justice, though sometimes resorted to in practice, as when Medea kills Jason's children. Hammurabi does not often resort to such punishments, and when he does, he seems primarily concerned to find a clever illustration of "poetic justice." But the difference between his and the Greeks' views of justice is significant.

Besides retroactivity and oral procedure, another important difference between GC and CH is the organization of laws in the two collections. Given the length of both collections, I will limit my examination to a few sections from each collection.

As we noted, Bottéro describes CH as an anthology of articles grouped together according to subject: false testimony (1–5), theft (6–25), tenure of royal fiefs (26–41), agricultural work (42–66), places of dwelling (67–?),[28] commerce (?–111), deposits and debts (112–26), wives and the family (127–94), assault and battery (195–214), free and subordinate professions (215–77), and slaves (278–82).[29] Bottéro also claims that these "chapters" (as he calls them) are organized in a linear fashion in which one chapter follows

---

[28] A gap in the preserved text prevents us from being certain about the extent of this set of provisions and the next.

[29] Bottéro 1992: 159. Others would group the laws of CH differently (see, e.g., Richardson 2000: 25–7), but all would agree that they are grouped together loosely according to subject.

another because it begins with a provision that is related to the last provision in the preceding chapter (though his first example, assault and battery following the family does not seem to support this conclusion). In this respect, the overall organization of GC is quite similar: provisions are grouped together into what I will call sections, generally marked off by asyndeton (almost always accompanied by a gap), and many (but not all) of these sections are placed next to other sections on related subjects.[30] In terms of macro-organization, the author of GC does not appear to have progressed much beyond the accomplishment of the earliest Gortynian legislators, who already gathered laws on similar subjects together.

In terms of micro-organization, however, when we examine the arrangement of provisions within these sections or chapters, the two collections reveal important differences that are directly related to their different aims. Two common tendencies in the arrangement of articles in CH at this level are first, that laws stating penalties for different instances of the same kind of offense are listed roughly in decreasing order of severity, and second that closely related provisions, especially those that address contrary situations, are often grouped in pairs. Both tendencies are evident in 209–14:[31]

209. If a man has struck the daughter of a man and has made her lose her unborn child, he shall pay ten shekels of silver for the foetus.
210. If that woman has died, they shall kill his daughter.
211. If he has made a commoner's daughter lose her unborn child by the violence, he shall pay five shekels of silver.
212. If that woman has died, he shall pay half a mana [= 30 shekels] of silver.
213. If he has struck a man's slave-girl and made her lose her unborn child, he shall pay two shekels of silver.
214. If that slave-girl has died, he shall pay a third of a mana [= 20 shekels] of silver.

These articles further illustrate Hammurabi's view of justice as a matter of fitting the appropriate punishment to the crime, in some cases (such as 210) according to the principle of the *lex talionis* (see above on 229–30). The punishments generally follow a linear order according to the severity of each, which depends on the status of the victim. Here, the second member of each pair is a more serious offense than the first and is published more severely, but the three pairs are arranged in descending order of severity.

---

[30] Gagarin 1982. The main modification I would now make to that study would be to recognize that, as we saw in other fifth-century texts from Gortyn, the use of asyndeton and gaps in GC may not follow quite such strict rules as I assumed at the time.

[31] 229–30 (quoted above) and the rules on adoption discussed below also reveal many of these tendencies.

This arrangement is well suited to illustrating Hammurabi's justice, for when offenses are arranged in order of severity (whether increasing or decreasing), one can easily see that the punishments are also so arranged. This group of provisions also illustrates other features of CH, such as the repetition of nearly identical language in closely related provisions. And in keeping with the particularization that Bottéro notes, Hammurabi does not say what should happen if the assailant has no daughter, or if he kills another man's son.

The desire to find the appropriate penalty is particularly evident in the chapters of CH we would call criminal law, the laws on theft (6–25) and assault and battery (195–214). By contrast, GC seems less interested in establishing appropriate penalties for such crimes, for it has only one section, at the beginning of column 2, where several rules stating an offense and a penalty follow in close succession (2.2–45):[32]

1. If someone rapes a free man or free woman, he shall pay a hundred staters.
2. If it is someone from the *apetairos* class,[33] (he shall pay) ten (staters).
3. And if a slave (rapes) a free man or woman, he shall pay double.
4. And if a free man (rapes) a male or female serf, (he shall pay) five drachmas.
5. And if a serf (rapes) a male serf or female serf, five staters.
6. If someone should forcibly overcome a household slave woman, he shall pay two staters.[34]
7. But if she has already had intercourse, (he shall pay) one obol by day.
8. But if at night, two obols.
9. And the slave woman shall be preferred in the oath.
10. If someone attempts to have intercourse with a free woman who is under the guardianship of a relative, he shall pay ten staters, if a witness should testify.
11. If someone is caught committing adultery with a free woman in her father's, brother's or husband's house, he shall pay a hundred staters.
12. And if in someone else's house, fifty (staters).

---

[32] For ease of reference, I have numbered these provisions as single laws, in the same manner as the articles in CH are normally numbered, though this is not normally done for GC. A stater is worth 2 drachmas and a drachma is worth 6 obols.

[33] An *apetairos* is apparently a free person but not a full citizen. In provision 4, the "serf" (*woikeus*) was apparently a free person, but the category was often assimilated to that of slave. See Lévy 1997, Willetts 1967: 12–17.

[34] The difference between "rape" and "forcibly overcoming" appears to be that the latter refers to a master who pressures a slave to have intercourse, though he does not necessarily use physical force. Davies (1996: 40) considers it a fault that the difference between these acts is not defined, but the meaning of the words was probably clear to readers at the time.

13. And if (he is caught committing adultery) with a woman belonging to [i.e. the wife, sister, or daughter of] an *apetairos*, (he shall pay) ten (staters).

14. And if a slave (is caught committing adultery) with a free woman, (he shall pay) double.

15. And if a slave (is caught committing adultery) with a slave, (he shall pay) five (staters).

This is the only passage at Gortyn with a list of crimes and punishments, and a number of differences from CH are evident. First, the provisions are grouped according to the nature of the crime – rape, forcible intercourse, attempted seduction, adultery – but not according to severity, at least not if the amount of the penalty is an indication of the severity of each offense.[35] Second, provisions in GC are rarely structured as a pair of alternatives (only 7 and 8 above). Third, although similar circumstances and penalties are repeated in many of these laws, GC mostly avoids the word-for-word repetition common in CH, preferring ellipsis (the omission of words) rather than repetition.[36] Fourth, the penalties in GC consist entirely of fines and do not match the crimes in specially appropriate ways, as they do in CH (e.g. a daughter for a daughter). Fifth, these provisions are more complete in their coverage than similar provisions in CH, though some possible offenses (such as the rape of an *apetairos* by a slave) are missing.[37] Finally, and perhaps most important, some of the provisions include procedural rules together with penalties for offenses.

Procedural rules are first introduced after the rules setting penalties for forcible intercourse (6–8), which are followed by a provision (9) that the oath of a slave woman will be preferred. This provision must envision a case where the facts are disputed,[38] and its inclusion shows that the legislator gave some thought to difficulties that might arise during actual litigation. The rule about attempted intercourse (10) also contains a clause about

---

[35] If we convert all the payments into obols (cf. Willetts 1967: 10), the results are 1200, 120, 2400, 30, 60, 24, 1, 2, 120, 1200, 600, 120, 2400, 60.

[36] See further, Gagarin 1999. In my translation I have tried to suggest the Greek style by bracketing words omitted in Greek, but I have not tried to replicate the conciseness of the Greek by omitting these words entirely (e.g., 15: "if a slave with a slave, five").

[37] Davies (1996: 42) is quite critical of the fact that not all possible circumstances are addressed. I suggest this is a question of whether the glass is half empty or (more than) half full. It is impossible for any code to cover every possible situation, and in contrast with CH, the presence of so many cases in GC is more impressive than the absence of some possible cases. We might note that medieval codes sometimes go to ridiculous extremes in attempting to cover every possible case, for example, listing the compensation owed for every possible injury down to each finger and toe.

[38] The dispute would probably center on whether or not the woman was a virgin at the time, for which it might be difficult to find any evidence other than the two sides' statements.

procedures ("if a witness should testify"). And the last provisions I have cited (11–15 on adultery) are followed by an extensive group of procedural regulations (2.28–45).[39] CH, by contrast, and the other non-Greek collections almost always simply state the facts, as if they were undisputed, and show little concern for disputes that might arise about the guilt or innocence of the accused.[40]

The laws at Gortyn and elsewhere often include procedural rules; as in Draco's homicide law, these provide guidance to litigants who otherwise might not know how to proceed. Similarly in GC, the addition of procedural regulations to a list of offenses and punishments shows that the legislator was concerned not just to let judges and others in the community know the consequences of certain actions, but to help judges and litigants manage the actual litigation that might result from these rules. This, then, is another indication that the Gortynian legislator intended his laws to be read and used by actual litigants.

No other section of GC presents such a list of offenses and penalties. The organizational structure of other large sections varies but most show clear signs of conscious organization and in most the arrangement is logical and hierarchical: a general principle may be followed by rules concerning its implementation or punishing non-compliance (or both); groups of provisions may follow one another in the order in which actual disputes would evolve; and within such structures sub-sets of provisions may be arranged in various ways, such as providing alternative courses of action. We will examine in some detail the organization of one large section of GC (disputes about persons) and will then look more briefly at two others (inheritance and "heiresses"). Finally, we will compare the section on adoption in GC with the treatment of the same subject in CH.

I begin with the first section of GC (1.2–2.1), which has perhaps the most sophisticated structure in the Code.[41]

1. (1.2–14) Whoever is going to contest (the status of) a free man or (the ownership of) a slave is not to seize him before trial. If he does seize him, let (the judge) sentence him to pay ten staters for a free man and five for a slave because of the seizure, and let him rule that he release him within three days. And if he does not release him, let him sentence him to pay a

---

[39] "Let (the captor) declare to the relatives of one who is caught before three witnesses that he is to be ransomed within five days; and to the master of a slave before two witnesses; etc."

[40] Of course, in most legal systems many laws prescribe consequences for many offenses without saying how disputes over the facts might be handled. In modern systems such procedural matters are often addressed in provisions entirely devoted to procedure, but this is not the case with CH.

[41] The division and numbering of paragraphs in this section and the others I examine below are my own.

stater for a free man and a drachma for a slave for each day until he
releases him. And the judge is to decide about the amount of time after
swearing an oath. If he should deny he seized him, the judge is to decide
after swearing an oath, unless a witness should testify.

2. (1.15–24) If one party contends that he is a free man and the other that he
is a slave, whichever ones affirm that he is a free man shall prevail. And if
they contend about a slave, each affirming that he is his, if a witness
testifies, (the judge) is to rule according to the witness; but if they testify
either for both sides or for neither, the judge is to decide after swearing
an oath.

3. (1.24–39) When the person in possession (of the disputed person) loses
the case, he is to release the free man within five days and return the slave
into the hands (of the proper owner). And if he does not release (the free
man) or return (the slave), let (the judge) rule that (the successful party)
win, in the case of a free man fifty staters and a stater for each day until
he releases him, and in the case of a slave ten staters and a drachma for
each day until he returns him into the hands (of the proper owner). And
when the judge has ruled, after a year (the winner) is to exact a triple
fine[42] or less, but not more. And the judge is to decide about the amount
of time after swearing an oath.

4. (1.39–49) And if the slave concerning whom (a litigant) has lost the case
takes refuge in a temple, (the loser) shall summon (the winner) in the
presence of two free adult witnesses, and either he himself or another for
him shall point him out at the temple where he is taking refuge. But if
he does not summon him or point him out, let him pay what is written.
And if he should not give him back even in a year, he shall pay the single
penalties.

5. (1.49–51) If (the slave) dies while the case is being tried, he shall pay the
single penalty.

6. (1.51–5) If a *kosmos*[43] seizes (someone) or another (seizes someone)
belonging to a *kosmos*, it shall be tried after he leaves office, and if
(someone) loses, he is to pay what is written from the day (he seized him).

7. (1.56–2.2) There is to be immunity for one who seizes a person who has
lost a case or has indentured himself.

---

[42] The meaning of *ta tritra* is uncertain. In 4.43.*Ab* the context implies "one-third" (Chapter Six, n. 38),
but here a reduction of the fine after a year makes little sense, since this would encourage a
delinquent not to pay the fine until a year had passed.

[43] The *kosmos* is the highest official in Gortyn. We do not know if there was more than one at a time, or
how long his term was (most likely a year). An early law at Gortyn (4.14) prevents a *kosmos* from
serving another term until ten years have passed.

This section of GC deals with two sorts of disputes about persons, whether a person is slave or free, and whose slave a person is. It begins with the general rule that someone who disputes a person's status must not seize that person by force but must take his dispute to court. The next provision specifies the consequences of non-compliance with this rule – the violator is fined and must release the person he seized. Then the law specifies the consequences of not complying with the injunction to release the man. Then, only after completing the rules for punishment of illegal seizure, does the legislator return to the initial prohibition against seizure and specify the procedure to be followed if the person accused of seizure denies it. And only when all aspects of the subject of illegal seizures have been addressed, does the law finally turn to the dispute itself (paragraph 2), since whether or not there was an initial seizure, sooner or later there will need to be a trial to decide the issue of status or ownership. The two kinds of cases, status and ownership, are taken up in turn, with procedures provided for each kind of case that depend primarily on the availability of witnesses. Next (3) come rules stating the consequences when the possessor of a disputed person has lost the case: he is to return a slave or release a free person, and penalties are stated for failure to comply in each case. Two further provisions then address enforcement of these penalties. Finally, the section ends with four additional rules (4–7) covering special situations – a disputed slave who seeks asylum in a temple, a disputed slave who dies, a dispute when one party is *kosmos*, and disputes about a person who has been convicted or is indentured.

As in Draco's law, the rules in this section are arranged logically and hierarchically, and to some extent chronologically (Lévy 2000a: 196–7), so as to provide a systematic and comprehensive treatment of the subject. The section as a whole has two main objectives: to prevent anyone from seizing a person whose status or ownership is in dispute before trial and to punish anyone who does (1), and to prescribe rules for trying disputes and for punishing non-compliance with judicial verdicts in these cases (2–3). The first of these (illegal seizure) is fully treated before the rules for deciding status or ownership are given, presumably because a seizure would need to be redressed before a trial took place. After these two parts, the legislator added a miscellany of rules for special situations that might arise (4–7). In paragraphs 1, 3, 4, and 6 provisions are arranged chronologically, but 5 and 7 are single provisions that stand alone. In paragraph 2, the rules for deciding cases are arranged by subdivision: first disputes about status and then disputes about ownership, the latter being further subdivided according to the availability of witnesses for one side, or for both or neither.

Some of the methods of organization here, including the addition of consequences for non-compliance and the juxtaposition of alternatives, are found elsewhere at Gortyn, but the scale and complexity of organization in this section is unparalleled, and must be the work of a legislator with exceptional ability and experience, who devoted time and effort to the task of creating a clear, well-organized, and practical statement of the rules for these kinds of disputes. He must have been motivated in part, at least, by a desire to assist litigants who would need guidance in managing these sorts of disputes and judges who would handle the cases.

This degree of systematic organization is unparalleled in Near-Eastern laws, and I am not aware of any other premodern legislation that is organized in this fashion. In fact, even the small methods of organization found in earlier laws at Gortyn are rare in non-Greek collections. In only one of the laws in CH (178), for example, is a provision requiring something followed by another stating the consequences of non-compliance, which is one of the basic elements of organization at Gortyn. And although there are examples of this arrangement in Middle Assyrian Laws and Palace Decrees and in the Hittite laws (see M. Roth 1995), in general the consequences of non-compliance are of little interest to the authors of premodern law collections outside of Greece. Any such concern, as with procedural rules, would be practical, and thus foreign to the aims of Hammurabi and other Near-Eastern legislators.

Finally, beyond the clear and coherent organization of this first section of GC, we must note the reasonableness and relative liberality of its rules.[44] The insistence on law not force, and the provision that the judge should be guided by witnesses where these provide guidance but should otherwise decide himself are generally consistent with our own view of law and legal procedure. In a society where slavery was taken for granted, moreover, the law creates a surprising bias in favor of free status, and allows slaves to take refuge in a temple with no penalty for his previous owner as long as he points out the refugee.[45] And, it seems both reasonable and wise that the legislator decided that trials involving the *kosmos* should be postponed until after his term in office has ended, though any fines levied at that point are to take effect from the original time of the dispute. The U.S. Supreme Court would have done well to adopt such a rule in the case of former President Clinton.

---

[44] "Reasonable" and "liberal" are, of course, loaded terms. I understand them in the context of classical liberal theory and the common-law standard of reasonableness and the "reasonable man."

[45] Recall also that in a case of alleged rape (# 9 above), a slave woman's oath is given preference over that of her free assailant.

No other section of GC is organized in quite this way, but logical and systematic organization is also evident in several other sections of the Code, including the two largest, inheritance and "heiresses." The rules concerning inheritance (4.23–5.54) are relatively straightforward and were probably less difficult to organize than the rules on disputed status. The first part of this section (4.23–5.9) provides the ground rules, as it were; these specify what comprises the (separate) estates of the husband and wife, state the basic formula for division of an estate at Gortyn ("the sons, however many there are, are each to receive two shares, while the daughters, however many there are, are to receive one share each," 4.39–43),[46] and allow an alternative means of providing for a daughter by giving her gifts equivalent to her share of the inheritance before her father dies, probably as a kind of dowry when she is married.

After dealing with these matters, the law specifies the order of inheritance, beginning with the direct descendants and continuing with the other groups who will inherit if there are no heirs with higher priority: "if there are children, or children of children, or children of children of children, these are to have the property" (5.9–13); and "if none of these is alive but there are brothers of the deceased and brothers' children, or children of these, these are to have the property" (5.13–17). After this come three more groups – sisters of the deceased with their children and grandchildren, other relatives, and other members of the household[47] – who will inherit in that order (5.17–28). The rest of this section (5.28–54) then consists of five rules about how the estate is to be divided among the heirs: (1) if some heirs wish to divide the estate and others do not, those who wish to divide have control; (2) anyone who takes property after the judge has ruled is to be fined; (3) the judge will decide about movable property; (4) if the heirs cannot agree about the division, the property is to be sold and the proceeds divided; (5) three or more witnesses must be present.

Here too, the overall arrangement is clear and logical: first come general rules specifying what comprises the estate and that males inherit twice as much as females. These are followed by rules specifying in detail the order of inheritance, which are so extensive as to provide an heir for almost any estate. The section ends with rules about dividing the estate in case of

---

[46] The male bias in this rule is less severe than at Athens, where daughters inherit nothing.

[47] The precise composition of the last two groups is uncertain, though it was probably clear to Gortynians.

disagreement among heirs. The arrangement of provisions within these three parts varies from strictly logical in the second ("X inherits; if no X, then Y; if no Y, etc.")[48] to moderately cohesive in the other two. The five rules in the third part appear to have been devised as separate provisions rather than a systematic treatment of disputes about division; they come in a reasonable order but several other arrangements would be equally reasonable. The first part addresses three topics (the composition of estates, the formula for division, and alternative gifts for daughters), but these are not made clear by the organization, since after the first rules about the composition of the estate come (a) the formula for division between sons and daughters, followed by (b) the rule that a mother's property should be distributed like the father's, after which comes (c) the rule that daughters receive their share "as is written" even when there is only a house. A clearer order might be to put (b) first together with the general rules about distribution; then (c) would follow immediately after (a), the provision to which it refers ("as is written"). In sum, the organization of the section is clear and coherent but not quite as logical as in the section concerning disputes about persons.

The laws concerning the so-called heiress[49] form by far the most extensive section of GC (7.15–9.24). These rules are particularly complex because their main purpose is to ensure that an heiress will marry and produce an heir to whom she can transmit her father's estate, and they must remain flexible in view of the many special situations that could arise in such cases. Behind the rules lies the tacit understanding that many claimants will want to marry a rich heiress but few if any will want to marry a poor one.

More than half the section (7.15–8.40) contains rules for the marriage of an heiress to the appropriate male (cf. 5.9–28):

> The heiress is to marry her father's brother, the oldest of those living. And if there are more heiresses and father's brothers, they are to marry the next oldest in turn. But if there are no father's brothers but sons of the father's brothers, she is to marry the oldest brother's (son). And if there are more heiresses and brothers' sons, the others are to marry the sons of the next oldest in turn. (7.15–27)

---

[48] The rules on reconciliation in Draco's homicide law have the same form.

[49] Like the Athenian *epiklēros*, the "heiress" (*patrōiōkos*) at Gortyn is a daughter whose father has died and who has no brothers (or brothers' sons). Thus she, along with any sisters she may have, is to some extent a vehicle through whom her father's estate is transmitted to future generations.

After these come rules providing for contingencies: the claimant or the heiress is too young to marry, the claimant does not want to marry her or she does not want to marry him, or there is no claimant. Then the legislator addresses the possibility that a woman who is already married might become an heiress: if she wishes to leave her husband or if she is a widow, she must marry the claimant unless she already has (male) children, in which case she need not marry. Finally, if a married heiress's husband dies or leaves her, if she already has (male) children, she is free to marry as she pleases, but if she does not, she should marry the claimant "as is written."

Up to this point (8.40), the rules governing an heiress are systematically organized to ensure that, unless she is already married or has male children, she will marry the closest possible relative of her father, as long as they are both of age and willing. The rest of the section (8.40–9.24) contains a diverse set of rules only loosely related to one another, beginning with the definition of the heiress (8.40–2) as "one who has no father or brother from the same father." It may seem odd that the definition of an heiress is not placed at the beginning of the section, but most readers would probably know what an heiress was, and so the precise definition could be taken for granted at first. Here the definition stands alone, marking a transition from rules about the heiress's marriage to rules specifying how the estate should be managed while the heiress is not of age and what to do if someone marries an heiress "otherwise than is written" (inform the *Kosmos*). The rules allow the sale of part of the estate to satisfy a debt but not otherwise. The section ends with rules about procedure in court in disputes concerning an heiress's property.

Like the section on status disputes in column 1, this section first addresses its main concern, the heiress's marriage, in a well-organized set of rules occupying the first two-thirds of it (7.15–8.40); these first treat unmarried heiresses and then those who are already married. These rules are followed by additional provisions, (8.40–9.24), in no particular order, including the definition of an heiress and other matters that did not fit easily into the earlier rules. Although the organization as a whole is looser than on column 1, mostly because of the greater number of provisions and the greater complexity of the situations that might arise, the legislator has nonetheless produced a clear and reasonable structure that anyone who wished to know what to do with an heiress could read and follow with relative ease.

Our last example of organization in GC is a shorter section, on adoption (10.33–11.23). Although the arrangement of provisions here is not substantially different from what we have already seen in other sections, it is worth citing them in full as a basis for comparison with the rules on adoption in CH, which are roughly the same length:[50]

1. (10.33–4) Adoption can be made from whatever source one wishes.
2. (10.34–9) Adoption is to take place in the agora when the citizens are gathered, at the stone where proclamations are made. And the adopter should give his own *hetaireia* ("cohort") a sacrificial victim and a measure of wine. *vacat*
3. (10.39–45) If (the adopted son) receives all the property and there are not also legitimate children, he is to fulfill all the adopter's religious and secular obligations and is to receive the property just as is written in the case of legitimate children.
4. (10.45–8) If he does not wish to fulfill these as is written, the next-of-kin are to have the property.
5. (10.48–52) If the adopter has legitimate children, among the male (heirs) the adopted son (is to receive a share) in the same way as the females receive a share from their brothers.[51]
6. (10.52–11.5) If there are no males, but females, the adopted son is to have an equal share, and he is not required to fulfill the adopter's obligations and accept the property that the adopter leaves.
7. (11.5–6) But the adopted son is not to have any more. *vacat*
8. (11.6–10) If the adopted son dies without leaving legitimate children, the property is to revert to the adopter's next-of-kin.
9. (11.10–17) If the adopter wishes, let him renounce [the adoption] in the agora from the stone from which proclamations are made at a gathering of citizens. And he is to deposit ten staters with the court, and let the rememberer (*mnamōn*) of the magistrate concerned with foreigners pay it to the person renounced.
10. (11.18–19) Let not a woman adopt, nor a minor. *vacat*
11. (11.19–23) These rules are to be followed from the time he wrote these writings, but in matters before this time, in whatever way someone has (property), whether by adoption or from an adopted son, there can no longer be any legal action.

In this section I have recorded the gaps on the stone (*vacat*) because more than in some other sections they provide a guide to its structure. It has four parts: 1–2 state the general rule that adoption can come from any source and

---

[50] For an earlier, somewhat different analysis of this section, see Gagarin 2006b; for discussion of some of the issues raised in this section, see Maffi 1991.
[51] I.e. the one-half share of the inheritance that a daughter receives compared to a son (4.39–43).

specify the procedure for adopting. 3–7 give rules for inheritance of the property depending on whether or not the adopter has other legitimate children. 8–10 then give three separate rules relevant to adoption: inheritance of the adopted son's property if he dies without children (this could also be grouped with the rules in 3–7), the procedure for revoking an adoption, and a prohibition on women and minors adopting. The section ends (11) with a statement that these rules take effect immediately but are not retroactive.

Once more, the arrangement is logical and partly chronological, similar to what we have seen elsewhere but perhaps more tightly organized, possibly because there are fewer provisions.[52] The legislator's first concern is general: to allow adoption and specify the proper procedure for it. He then addresses what appears to be the law's main concern, division of the adopter's property after his death (3–7); the rules in this part follow a logical order of division (there are or are not legitimate children) and subdivision (there are legitimate children but they do or do not include males). Three more rules address additional concerns, and a statement of non-retroactivity ends the section. This arrangement is clear and coherent, with the law's main concern, inheritance, coming right after the basic rules for adoption. The three rules after this are also in a reasonable order, though the rule that women and minors cannot adopt might have been put somewhere else. But like the definition of the heiress, it makes explicit something most readers would take for granted, that an adopter would be an adult male, and so it does not need to be featured more prominently. Finally, the provision for non-retroactivity naturally comes at the end.

The rules on adoption in CH (185–93) take a different approach to the subject.[53]

185. If a man has taken in a tiny child at birth as a son and has brought him up, that ward shall not be reclaimed.

186. If a man has taken in a tiny child as a son and then soon after he has taken him in his father and mother search him out, that adopted child shall return to his father's house.

187. The son of an official with a position in the palace and the son of a priestess shall not be reclaimed.

---

[52] Davies 1996: 40 singles out this section on adoption as an extreme example of systematization in the Code: "This really is codification: a general principle is enunciated, whether enabling or prohibitory (here enabling), a cross-reference to existing law is inserted, and the likely circumstances arising from its application are envisaged and systematically provided for – altogether a model of a modern major general law." I do not disagree, but I think Davies exaggerates the difference between this and other sections of the Code.

[53] Richardson puts 192 and 193 in a separate section on child care problems, but the problems these rules address nonetheless involve adopted children; see the detailed study of Westbrook 1993.

188. If a professional craftsman has taken in a child as a ward and has instructed him in manual skills, he shall not be reclaimed.

189. If he has not instructed him in manual skills, that ward shall return to his father's house.

190. If a man has not counted together with his own sons the child whom he has taken in as a son and whom he has brought up, that ward shall return to his father's house.

191. If a man has established his house after taking in a child as a son and bringing him up, and then has his own children and reaches a decision to expel the ward, that child shall not go away empty-handed. The father who brought him up shall give him as his inheritance one-third of his wealth, and then he shall go away. He shall not give him any field, orchard, or house.

192. If the son of an official or the son of a priestess has said to his father or mother who has brought him up, "You are not my father. You are not my mother," they shall cut out his tongue.

193. If the son of an official or the son of a priestess declares he knows his father's house, and he hates the father and the mother who have brought him up, and he has gone away to his father's house, they shall pull out his eye.

All these rules essentially address one kind of concern: the conditions under which an adopted child must or may or may not return to his natural parents. The Babylonians may have considered this the most important issue concerning adoption, but from the Greek perspective, it seems odd that Hammurabi included only these rules. Clearly he does not have the same aim as the Greek legislator, who produced a more comprehensive set of rules. Instead, these are highly particularized rules (as Bottéro would say), each addressing a specific situation.

If we look more closely at the arrangement of these rules some patterns appear. Eight of them form four pairs (185–6, 188–9, 190–1, 192–3), the ninth (187) being a supplement to the first pair. In each pair, moreover, the two rules between them present a contrast or opposition. The first pair (185–6) allows the natural parents to reclaim their child soon after he is adopted (as a baby) but not after he has been reared, a reasonable distinction. 187 then adds an exception to 186, prohibiting children of certain parents from being returned after they have been adopted.[54] The second pair (188–9) contrasts two craftsmen who adopt: the one who teaches his

---

[54] It is not clear to us, but probably was to people at the time, why children of these parents are treated differently – perhaps because these people were forbidden or unable to have natural offspring.

adopted son his craft should keep his son, but the one who fails in this duty may rightly lose his son; again, the consequence in each case seems fair. The third pair (190–1) appears to contrast the adopter who has natural children when he adopts with one who only has children after he has raised the adopted son. It is not clear why the first child receives nothing, whereas the second receives a share of the estate. Finally, the last pair (192–3) adds rules that support 187 (prohibiting an adopted son from returning to certain types of natural parents).[55] Here there is only a slight contrast between a son who verbally renounces his adopted parent (who will lose his tongue), and one who simply leaves his adopted home out of anger (who will lose an eye). The first penalty obviously embodies the rule of *lex talionis*, the second is puzzling.

The rules in CH are thus arranged in four successive groups, each with two contrasting provisions. For the most part, the different treatments seem reasonable and appropriate, but there is no obvious reason for the inclusion of only these particular rules or the order they come in.[56] And because the rules address only the issues concerning the adopted son leaving (or not leaving) his adopted father's house and disregard many other situations that adopters and adoptees must have faced, beginning with the general procedure for adoption, they would have been of limited practical value. Indeed, the narrow focus of the section suggests that it was not intended to provide practical guidance, but rather to illustrate once again the lawgiver's principles of justice.

The differences in organization between the rules on adoption in GC and CH confirm the essential difference in the aims of those who wrote and displayed the two collections. In GC we see the same practical goal that had motivated Greek lawgivers from the beginning: the rules are organized in such a way as to be easily used by those who wished to adopt or had disputes about adoption. Hammurabi's adoption rules, on the other hand, may contribute to making CH a lasting monument of his reign, in which later generations can read examples of his outstanding sense of justice, but these rules also show clearly that CH was not created for practical use but, as Bottéro puts it (1992: 167), is "instructive and educative in the judicial order."

As for questions about authorship and the source of the laws in GC, the scale and complexity of organization in at least some of its sections strongly

---

[55] One might expect this pair to follow immediately after 187; it is not clear why it does not.
[56] There might be a progression from general conditions under which the adopted son may return to his natural parents (185–7) to the special case when a craftsman adopts (188–9) to a later time (190–3) when the fully reared adopted son wishes to leave the house, but this is not at all clear.

suggest that a single legislative mind was the guiding force behind the Code. Such a sophisticated organization of some of the larger sections, cannot have been achieved by a committee, let alone an assembly. A larger group may have participated in the selection of laws to be included in the Code, and may have ratified the final draft, but this organization points to a single, unusually talented legislator as the one who envisioned the grand scale of GC, selected the general areas to be covered, and arranged specific provisions within these.

Some of the provisions may reflect recent (or not so recent) court decisions, but all of them cannot have been based on "case law," as Davies (1996) argues. Even if a large number of cases concerning heiresses, for example, had recently been decided in court, it is hardly possible that all the situations envisioned in the section on the heiress had been the subject of recent court decisions. Moreover, provisions that are explicitly said not to be retroactive must have differed from traditional practices and must therefore represent new ideas. Thus, the legislator must have supplemented case law from other sources, including earlier legislation and custom. And the comprehensiveness of some sections also indicates that the legislator himself created some of these rules in an effort to anticipate potential points of dispute that had not previously arisen. Surely a legislator interested in producing a systematic arrangement of provisions must have used his experience and intelligence to fill gaps he perceived in case law and traditional rules and procedures. All these considerations, then, suggest that a single legislator most likely drafted the full text of GC, drawing on earlier laws and custom, on the results of earlier litigation, and not least on his own sense of fairness, reasonableness, and practicality.

Before leaving the question of organization one more feature of GC remains to be considered, the six amendments inscribed at the end (11.24–12.19). These provisions were added after the main body of the Code was inscribed. They may have been inscribed by a different mason, but any differences in writing are within the realm of normal variation, so that whoever inscribed the main text may also have inscribed some or all of the addenda. We cannot know when these addenda were added, but it was probably not more than a few years after the body of the Code, and they may even have been inscribed as soon as the mason finished the main text. In any case, the mason clearly demarcated the addenda from the main text, the last line of which (11.23), written from right to left, occupies only half of the line, leaving the rest blank. The next line (11.24) then begins again from the right, interrupting the boustrophedon pattern and indicating a separate text. From here, the boustrophedon pattern is maintained, but each addendum begins on a new line and is marked by asyndeton and a gap, three of which (11.26, 11.45, 11.55) are much larger than most other gaps.[57]

Five of the six addenda are amendments to different sections of the main text, but the second (11.26–31), a general statement of the procedure judges must follow in deciding cases, is not directly related to a single section but applies to the whole Code. Davies (1996: 43–6) sees in these amendments a movement away from the codification and systematization evident in much of the body of the Code, and argues that they provide a "subversive" effect that counteracts and corrupts the process of codification. But physical constraints made it very difficult to change a text once it was inscribed on the stone. The Greeks could erase an entire text, and we have cases where a few words were erased, either to correct a mistake or perhaps revise a rule.[58] But if a new provision supplemented or altered an existing law without invalidating it, then one must either erase the old law entirely and inscribe the revised version in its place (which was totally impractical for a text the length of GC), or add the amendment at the end of the text, leaving it to the reader to understand that the old law is valid only as modified. Greek readers undoubtedly became accustomed to this practice and could without much difficulty combine the amendment with the main text.

This process of amendment would not affect the organization of the original law, though it might modify its content, as we can see, for example, in the new rules about heiresses that are added in 12.6–19:

> If there are no orphan-judges, one is to treat heiresses according to what is written, as long as they have not reached puberty. And when, in the absence of a claimant or orphan-judges, the heiress is brought up by her mother, the paternal uncle and the maternal uncle who are specified in writing are to administer the property and the income (from it) in the best way they can until she marries. And she is to marry at the age of twelve or older.

Davies (1996: 44–5) sees this addendum as making three changes which "remuddle" the section of laws on the heiress (7.15–9.24, see above): it introduces orphan-judges but does not say what these officials do (only what should be done if there are not any); it replaces two earlier provisions for administering the heiress's property before she is married with a single

---

[57] There is a similar gap of half a line in the main text at the end of 10.32, which scholars have largely ignored. It may indicate that the section on adoption (10.33–11.23) was also an addendum. This would not significantly affect the following discussion.

[58] See, e.g., *IG* XII.9 1273/1274, line 4 from Eretria (Chapter Two, esp. n. 48).

provision; and it sets the minimum age for marriage. This analysis is misleading. First, orphan-judges must already exist; they are not being introduced by this amendment, which merely specifies that if there are no such officials, the rules for treating heiresses remain the same "as is written" – i.e. as in the main body of the law. The position of orphan-judge may have been created between the inscription of the main text and the amendment, and it was probably understood that if there were such officials, they would take care of the heiress before puberty. Second, the addendum corrects a relatively minor and obviously flawed provision, that an unmarried heiress (who might be only an infant) living with her mother shall administer her property herself (8.47–53), directing instead that her uncles shall administer it. Third, it specifies an age for marriage, which is probably not a change but a clarification of a point omitted in the main text. The addendum, in other words, corrects one small flaw in the main law and clarifies two other points; far from muddling the law, it clarifies and modestly improves it.

The other addenda work in similar fashion. The first (11.24–5) supplements the prohibition on seizure before trial in 1.2–3, allowing anyone to receive a man who was seized before trial.[59] Whether this is a supplement or new law (Davies 1996: 43) seems to me a distinction without a difference. The second (11.26–31) does not amend any specific rule, but clarifies the procedure for judicial decision, by providing a default process for use when no instruction is given. 11.31–45 supplement the rules in 9.24–40 for litigating claims against an estate, by adding an alternative procedure for settling such claims without going to court. 11.46–55 specify precise conditions for taking the oath prescribed in 3.5–9. And 12.1–5 provide that the rules in 10.14–25 are not retroactive. Thus, these later additions to GC introduce one entirely new rule (11.24–5), one minor change (12.9–17), and several clarifications.

A modern legislator could easily integrate such changes into the original text of the Code, but the technology of stone inscription made it necessary to add provisions at the end. This is not a move away from codification and systematization, even if provisions on the same subject end up separated from one another. The aim of the Greek legislator is the same as that of a modern codifier, to organize the laws as clearly and coherently as possible, but the constraints of his writing materials make his final text different. Davies may be right that the source of these changes was "feedback" but

---

[59] I follow the common view of these lines (Guarducci, Willetts, Koerner, *et al.*); for a different view see van Effenterre and Ruzé 1994–5: vol. II, 49.

I would not limit this to feedback from the political arena. Judges, litigants, advisers and the legislator's own experience may all have influenced him to add these provisions; or he may simply have had further thoughts after writing the main text.

Looking back over the long process of writing law at Gortyn, we can see a steady progress in the physical presentation of material and the organization of the contents of these laws. Greek masons began by writing in large crude letters, in lines that alternated direction, with dividing marks to set off groups of words. Gradually they learned to write more clearly in neat block letters, to shorten their lines, and to form the text into columns. They also developed more sophisticated means of organizing their laws, particularly in sections treating the same issue, in ways that would make the laws easier to read, understand, and use in actual litigation. In this respect, Draco's homicide law, one of the earliest pieces of legislation we have, matches GC in the clarity and complexity of its organization, though it only addresses a single subject. These two legal masterpieces, Draco's law and the Gortyn Code, display a skill in organization unparalleled in other premodern cultures, one that even a modern legislator can admire.

Comparison with CH reveals especially clearly the practical nature of legislation at Gortyn. It also confirms the significance of the orality of judicial procedure at Gortyn by contrast with Babylonian procedure, which made much use of written documents. If written laws, publicly displayed, were essential to making law available to many members of the community, the consequences of keeping writing out of judicial procedure were just as significant. We will return to this aspect of writing law in more detail in Chapter Nine, but for the moment, we should recall the story of Deioces, which (as we saw in Chapter One) encapsulates the transition from an oral, public, communal legal process to an institution based on writing. Recall that once Deioces became king of the Medes he shut himself off from the people, who now had to bring their disputes to him (and no one else). They had to put their pleas in writing (which in practice would mean paying a scribe to write them), and Deioces would then make his decision in private, indeed in isolation, and convey it to the disputants in writing through intermediaries (Herodotus I.100). As an oriental monarch, Deioces employs writing as a tool to control the legal process, and we can see in the story the roots of the full bureaucratic and scribal organization that in fact controlled the law in fifth-century Persia, as in Hammurabi's Babylon. The story leaves no doubt that writing can be a tool to control the judicial process, but that this is an oriental practice, foreign to Greece.

In sum, the Greek use of writing in law – writing legislation but keeping procedure unwritten – was just the reverse of Near-Eastern practice. This fundamental difference makes it *prima facie* very unlikely that GC was significantly influenced by CH or other Near-Eastern codes,[60] and the long history of written law at Gortyn makes direct influence even less likely. To be sure, the Greeks borrowed the alphabet from the Near East, and they may have known of large-scale Near-Eastern legal inscriptions, but the Gortynians had been writing and displaying laws for more than a century before GC in ways for which there are no parallels in the Near East. Starting with relatively short texts, they gradually produced longer and more complex legislation, culminating in GC. It is easy to see from this that the idea of inscribing a large collection of laws like GC came out of local experience not from foreign influence.

Finally, if we look to explain the difference between Greek and Near-Eastern approaches to writing law, we might begin by connecting it with the number of people who could read in each country. The consonantal cuneiform script could probably be read only by a small class of professional scribes and high officials; the new Greek alphabetic script, on the other hand, was considerably easier to read, and reading and writing in Greece were thus never restricted to a small professional class. And even a novice reader could read the text of a Greek law to some extent, though he might need assistance in understanding just what it meant. Thus, Greek written laws were available to members of the community, whereas laws in Babylonia, or for that matter in Anglo-Saxon England or medieval Europe, were not.[61]

A more general explanation for the differences between writing law in Greece and the Near-East lies in the fundamentally non-authoritarian nature of Greek communities from the beginning. As we noted earlier (Chapter Three), from as early as Homer "kings" (*basileis*) in Greece do not have the same authority and power as Near-Eastern and other monarchs. In Homer, a place is always reserved for public discourse, in which a broad segment of the population sometimes participated, and the public (oral) discourse of law is particularly valued, as we see in the crowd of vocal onlookers attending the trial on Achilles' shield. After Homer, the

---

[60] Muhl 1933 remains the fullest statement of this view; more recently Gehrke 2000: 144. *Contra* Whitley 1997: 659.

[61] Anglo-Saxon and early European laws could probably have been read only by clerics and high court officials (many of whom were also clerics). Even as medieval laws came to be written in the vernacular rather than in Latin, it still appears that few outside the church and the nobility could read them, and even among these, few would have cared to do so.

governments of most early poleis in which legislation was written can be described as oligarchies. Most were governed by a small group of officials, but again and again, beginning with the earliest law from Dreros, we see signs of a larger group with considerable authority, whether this is a Council, an assembly, a polis, a *damos*, or simply "the Gortynians." All these terms indicate that at least some non-elite members of the community participated in government and in legislation in archaic Greece, and their participation ensured that laws would be written and accessible to the community from the beginning. This unique approach to writing law thus reflects the non-authoritarian and inclusive nature of Greek social and political structures in oligarchic and democratic poleis alike. Written legislation in Greece from the beginning was a public discourse, just as the oral judicial process portrayed by the poets had been since pre-literate times. And as we shall see, this public discourse, involving both written legislation and oral procedure, persisted into the classical period (and beyond).

CHAPTER 8

Writing Law in Classical Athens

Thus far our study of writing in Greek law has focused largely on the texts of laws, these being practically the only legal texts that were written in the archaic period and fifth-century Gortyn. When we turn to law in classical Athens, however, we find evidence of many more kinds of written documents. Much of the evidence for these comes not from inscriptions but from speeches written for actual trials ca. 420–322. This evidence is in some ways more problematic than a collection of statutes like the Gortyn Code, but the speeches not only provide information about written texts in Athenian law; they also shed light on the actual operation of law in classical Athens, and they inform us about attitudes toward writing and written texts at this time.

Before the fifth century, the only written texts in Athenian law besides the laws themselves were the written indictments in cases prosecuted by means of the *graphē* procedure (Chapter Five). During the course of the fifth and fourth centuries, however, written texts are increasingly present in judicial procedure. In fact, the amount of writing in general, as well as the number of people who knew how to read and write, increased steadily. We cannot speak of mass literacy, but literacy went "far beyond the circle of the wealthy" (W. Harris 1989: 114). For the fifth century Harris suggests that about 10 percent of the total population was literate, but others would put the figure much higher.[1] For the fourth century it was undoubtedly higher. In Athens' participatory democracy, several hundred magistrates (at least) were appointed each year to handle public business,[2] and most of these would have been required to submit their accounts at the end of their terms, a task that required at least a minimal level of literacy.[3] And literacy

---

[1] Most recently Pébarthe (2006: 23–67) argues for widespread literacy in Athens in the fifth century and earlier (without giving a precise figure); he would include at least some women and slaves in this group.

[2] See Sinclair 1988: 69. Wallace 2005: 152–3 gives a long list of offices, which is undoubtedly incomplete.

[3] Aristophanes, *Wasps* 960–1: "I wish he would not have known letters (*grammata*) either, so that he would not have cheated when he wrote his accounting (*logon*) for us."

was not confined to the upper and middle levels of society, from which most magistrates presumably were drawn; as early as the sixth century and perhaps earlier rural shepherds were writing short texts on stones (Chapter Two). Rustic Athenians like these shepherds may not have been able easily to read the texts of laws or decrees inscribed in the city, but even they could probably get the gist of an inscribed text and with help could probably read it.

In addition, forensic oratory conveys the clear impression that those involved in public life to a significant extent – that is who did more than occasionally attend the assembly or serve as a juror – could read. The orators portray a wide range of people as reading and writing, and no orator ever speaks of someone as unable to read or write, or as needing to have someone else write a text or read a written text for him.[4] The only group that speakers do not normally portray as able to read are jurors. Jurors are never explicitly said to be unable to read, but reading is not an activity they are assumed or required to engage in. Nowhere are jurors spoken of as reading a text, nor are they told that they are familiar with the details of some written text.[5] And the jurors as a group are never portrayed as actually reading a text in court.

A possible exception occurs in Demosthenes 43.18, an inheritance case, where the speaker, a certain Sositheus, says,

At first, gentlemen of the jury, I intended to write on a tablet (*pinax*)[6] the names of all Hagnias' relatives, and thus to display them to you one by one. But since I realized that not all the jurors would have the same view, for those sitting far away would be disadvantaged, it is perhaps necessary to instruct you with my speech (*logos*), since this is the same for all of you. So we will try as best we can, to make clear to you as briefly as possible the family of Hagnias.

It is unlikely that Sositheus ever intended to write out all these names. Since he later mentions about forty members of this extended family by name, or

---

[4] As we saw in Chapter Five, the use of the middle voice, *graphesthai*, for filing a complaint indicates that in a *graphē* procedure litigants did not write the complaint themselves but had someone else write it. This may suggest that when this particular aspect of the procedure was instituted, perhaps in the early sixth century, some potential litigants could not write (Calhoun 1919: 178–80).

[5] In Dem. 37.18 Nicobulus tells the jurors, "I think you know, without my telling you, that the laws do not allow suits to be brought again concerning matters that have been dealt with in this way." This assertion does not assume any close familiarity with the text of the law on the part of the jurors, who would likely have learned about the law from experience, not from reading it. In the next sentence Nicobulus asks the clerk to read them the law.

[6] *Pinax* could designate a personal writing tablet, commonly used to take notes or for other short messages. It is sometimes identical to a *sanis*, which commonly designates a whitened writing board on which public texts were written and posted for all to see (see below n. 19).

if they are unnamed women by the name of their father or brother, and since several of the people have the same name in different generations, one suspects that writing out all the names, whether in the form of a family tree or just as a list, would not have been of much help to the speaker or his audience. Rather, this sounds suspiciously like a ploy on the part of Sositheus to appear fully knowledgeable himself by indicating that he could have written them all down if he had wished, but also to excuse himself in advance, if in his speech he does not make all the complex relationships clear to the jurors by implying that if he had been able to write down the names, everything would have become clear.[7] On the other hand, Sositheus' statement implies that those jurors sitting close enough to see the names would have been able to read them. And the connection between writing and clarity and accuracy is common in forensic oratory (see below).

Another hint that the jurors might read comes toward the end of Demosthenes 25, where the speaker asks rhetorically how, if they vote for acquittal, they can leave the court without feeling ashamed: "And how will you walk to the Metroon,[8] if you so wish? For surely each one of you individually will not visit (*poreusetai*) the laws as if they were valid if you leave now without collectively having confirmed them" (25.99). Although the precise implication of *poreusetai* ("will visit") is not certain, the speaker implies that the jurors would no longer be able to go and consult – that is read – the laws, if they acquit the defendant in the present case, for this would render the laws no longer valid. This suggests that at least some jurors would on occasion ("if you so wish") read texts, and it should not surprise us that the texts they might potentially read would be laws, but we should note that their reading would not occur during the trial.

Two other passages may be relevant. In Dem. 45.17, Apollodorus recalls a will that was supposedly produced at the arbitration hearing: "if it was genuine, they should have put the document (*grammateion*) in the jar (*echinos*) and the witness to it should testify, so that the jurors would have decided the matter on the basis of the truth and of seeing the seals (*sēmeia*)." Jurors who saw the seals might be expected to read a name, but more likely they would only recognize someone's mark; and they are not envisaged as reading any of the will itself. Jurors are also envisaged as

---

[7] Even if Sositheus had written out the names, it is not clear that the jurors would have been required to read them. If he had simply had a list of names, reading them would have done the jurors little or no good; and even if he had managed to write them in some sort of family tree, he may have wished to convey only the structure of connections, emphasizing perhaps the closeness or distance between two people, without having anyone actually read the names.

[8] The public archive, where among other things were kept copies of laws.

literate in Plato's *Apology* (26d–e): "Do you [Meletus] scorn these people (the jurors) so much and think they are so unskilled in letters (*apeirous grammatōn*) as not to know that Anaxagoras' books (*biblia*) are full of these ideas (*logoi*)?" The obvious irony of this statement (few Athenians of any class would have read the books of Anaxagoras) undercuts its value as evidence for the literacy of jurors. But many jurors probably were literate, and at least some may have read substantial texts outside of court.

By contrast with jurors, litigants and others are commonly portrayed as reading texts, most often the texts of laws.[9] In what is perhaps our earliest preserved speech, Antiphon 6, delivered in 419, the defendant tells us (6.38) that the Basileus to whom the plaintiffs presented their first complaint accusing the speaker of homicide refused to accept the case since too little time remained in his term of office. "The Basileus read them the laws (τοὺς νόμους ἀνέγνω) and showed them that there was not enough time to register the case and issue all the necessary summonses." It is possible that the speaker envisages the Basileus reading the law to illiterate plaintiffs, who only listened, but more likely at least one of the plaintiffs could also read the law to make certain the Basileus was reading it correctly.

Two decades later, Andocides (1.115–16) reports an interesting exchange between Callias and Cephalus shortly before his trial. Callias first cites as evidence the provisions of a "traditional law" (*nomos patrios*) that his father had interpreted as prescribing immediate death if someone placed a suppliant branch in the Eleusinium. Cephalus responds, "you speak of a traditional law, but the stele you are standing next to prescribes that if someone places a suppliant branch in the Eleusinium, he is to be fined 1,000 drachmas." The *patrios nomos* Callias appeals to is evidently an orally preserved custom, against which Cephalus cites the written text of a law on a stele, that would be available to Callias and anyone else to read. Cephalus then challenges Callias, who is called before the Council, where "the stele was read out," after which Callias withdraws his claim. This episode shows quite clearly that by 399, at least, written legislation, available to all to read, took precedence over oral customary law.[10]

Another early example (around 400) is Euphiletus in Lysias 1, who bases his case on a law that (he claims) required him to kill Eratosthenes when he found him in bed with his wife: "This is the reason, in my opinion, why every city enacts its laws, so that whenever we are uncertain about some

---

[9] On the availability of laws for litigants and others to read, see Sickinger 2004.

[10] For the official prohibition on using unwritten laws, which was part of the legal reforms at the end of the fifth century, see below.

matter we can go to the law and find out (*skeptomai*) what we should do" (1.35). It is safe to say that, just as today, few Athenians who were uncertain how to conduct themselves in a particular situation would actually go and read a statute in order to find out, and the jurors may not have accepted Euphiletus' argument. But they must have found it plausible that a relatively modest farmer could, if necessary, find and read the law relevant to his situation.

Later in the fourth century, several other litigants note that they have had occasion to read the laws. The trierarch in Demosthenes 47 says he did not know how to proceed when faced with a possible homicide case, and so he first consulted a group of religious "interpreters," the Exegetes, asking whether he should bring an action for homicide even though he was not directly related to the victim. He adds that when he had heard their advice, "I examined the laws of Draco on the stele and consulted with my friends about what I should do" (47.71). In Demosthenes 54.17, Ariston gives the jurors a lesson on why the laws are organized in the way they are: there are laws against minor offenses like slander so that harmful talk does not lead to blows; there are laws against fighting so that this does not lead to wounding; and so on. He prefaces this lesson by explaining that "you see, because of the defendant it was necessary for me to investigate and learn these things" – that is, to read the laws. Similarly, the speaker in Hyperides 3 *Against Athenogenes* 13, who is only moderately well off, reports, "You [the defendant, Athenogenes] have made me so fearful of being brought to ruin by you and your cunning that I have been studying and examining the laws night and day and neglecting all my other affairs." Even if in all these cases it was the logographer (or speechwriter, e.g., Lysias) not the litigant himself, who read the laws, it cannot have been thought unusual that even citizens of moderate means would read and study the laws.

In short, throughout the classical period, litigants report that they and others involved in litigation read laws. Moreover, no speaker ever reports that someone was unable to read or needed help from a friend in order to read. To be sure, most litigants in Athens probably came from the middle and upper levels of the community, and the speeches we have were written for a relatively elite group of these litigants, all of whom must have been able to read. But some of those who speak of reading laws present themselves as men of modest means, and the examples thus seem to confirm that literacy had spread well beyond the small circle of rich Athenians.

Litigants never speak of reading laws, however, merely out of interest or as a routine matter. Rather, they present themselves as having been forced, usually by their opponent, to read and study the laws. Someone who read the laws on his own without being compelled by circumstances could be criticized as one who "knows the laws more than is proper" (Dem. 57.5). As a character in a late fourth-century comedy observes, "the laws are indeed a fine thing, but the man who looks too closely (*lian akribōs*) at the laws shows himself to be a professional litigator (*sykophantēs*)" (Menander fr. 768 K–A). Thus, reading laws was something that many people were capable of doing if necessary, but did not do otherwise.

Finally, the laws that these people read are regularly presented as authoritative. The Basileus reads the law to the plaintiffs to justify his conduct after they have questioned his refusal to accept their case; Cephalus points to the written text of a law to refute Callias, whose view is based on a traditional custom (*patrios nomos*) reported to him orally; Euphiletus treats the text of the law as the ultimate authority for his conduct; and the trierarch seeks the advice of the Exegetes but checks the written text to confirm that they have correctly stated the law. As we shall see below, other sorts of written texts are treated differently; but whenever litigants speak about reading laws, they treat these texts as authoritative.

The fact that Athenian litigants could, if they wished, read and consult the texts of laws means that these texts must have been publicly available in Athens, as they were in other cities. No inscribed laws from archaic Athens survive;[11] later sources indicate that the laws of Draco and Solon were written and publicly displayed, but we do not know for certain where they were displayed. Euphiletus asks the clerk to read Draco's law "on the stele from the Areopagus" (Lysias 1.30, see above), and it would have been reasonable to have a copy of this law (perhaps the only inscribed copy) at the meeting place of the Areopagus, the court that judged most homicide cases.[12] The evidence for Solon's *axones* and *kyrbeis* is scanty and inconsistent; all scholars agree that these were set up in a public place, but they disagree where.[13] But wherever they were, Solon's laws, like Draco's, were

---

[11] The earliest inscribed Athenian law is the fragmentary *IG* 1³ 2 from ca. 500.

[12] M. B. Richardson 2000 shows that copies of *IG* 11² 244 (on rebuilding the Piraeus wall) were placed where they would be most accessible to the officials and contractors who needed to consult them. We have scattered reports of other laws being set up in relevant places; e.g., *Ath. Pol.* 35.2: the Thirty "took down from the Areopagus the laws of Ephialtes and Archestratus concerning the members of the Areopagus." (Todd 1996: 123 n. 28 notes that this report implies the essential identity of the law and stone on which it is inscribed.) Sickinger 1999 argues that as early as the sixth century other copies were made of texts inscribed on stone.

[13] Stroud (1979: 11–13, 42) accepts the late report by Didymus that the fourth-century historian and rhetorician Anaximenes of Lampsacus wrote that "Ephialtes [probably in 461] transferred the *axones* and *kyrbeis* down from the acropolis to the council chamber and the agora." Ruschenbusch (1966: 31–2), however, dismisses this report and also suggests (32 n. 67) that Didymus mistakenly wrote

publicly displayed, and the reason for this must have been, at least in part, so that litigants and others could read them.

The only evidence suggesting that a law may not have been easily accessible is a puzzling remark in Dem. 59.76, where Apollodorus cites an old law about the qualifications for holding the position of Basilinna, the woman who was the wife of the Basileus and presided at one of the rites during the annual festival of the Anthesterion.[14]

> After they wrote this law on a stone stele, they put it in the sacred precinct of Dionysus in the Marshes, next to the altar; the stele itself still stands there today, displaying its writing (*ta gegrammena*) in faint Attic characters (*grammata*)[15] . . . And they put it in this most ancient and holy sanctuary of Dionysus in the Marshes so that not many people would see the text, since the sanctuary is open only once each year, on the twelfth day of the month Anthesterion.

Even if we are skeptical of Apollodorus' explanation of the motive for displaying this law in an out-of-the-way sanctuary, the effect of placing this law in a place open to the public only one day a year would have been to restrict access to it. On the other hand, since this was a religious law concerning a rite that took place only on that day, few would have needed to consult it at all, and the limited access was probably sufficient. It is also possible that the priest and perhaps a few other officials could enter the sanctuary on other days too. In any case, this evidence is not inconsistent with our conclusion that Athenian laws were accessible to litigants who needed to consult them. Indeed, the fact that this law, which was probably of interest to only a few people, was nonetheless inscribed on a stele and displayed, even in this restricted manner, confirms the importance the Athenians attached to making the texts of laws publicly available.

We know little about legislation in Athens between Solon and the late fifth century, but the Athenians continued to enact laws, either to address new concerns or to modify or even repeal older laws. Not surprisingly, the increase in the number of existing laws and the fact that laws were inscribed in various places around the city resulted in considerable confusion over just what the law was on various matters (Todd 1996: esp. 107, 125–6).

"acropolis" instead of "Areopagus." Perhaps the most plausible proposal is Robertson 1986, that the *kyrbeis* were put in the agora and the *axones* in the Prytaneum; but even this is largely speculative. See Sickinger 1999: 29–31 for a review of the issue.

[14] The law required, among other things, that the Basilinna be a citizen; this rule would probably have been unnecessary after 451, when Pericles' marriage law prohibited citizens from marrying non-citizens. Thus the law cited by Apollodorus is probably earlier than 451 (*pace* Kapparis 1999: 337).

[15] I.e. in writing older than the Ionic characters that were used in Athens after 403.

When democracy was restored in 410 after a brief coup by an oligarchic council of 400 in 411, a measure was approved to appoint a group of Anagrapheis ("Recorders, Inscribers") of the laws, who, were supposed to record the laws of Solon.[16] Just what the Anagrapheis were supposed to do is disputed, but since we hear of no other official with authority to decide what texts to inscribe, the Anagrapheis themselves probably decided this, though they probably had to submit their decisions to the assembly for approval.[17]

The task of writing down the laws that were valid before 411 required considerably more work than most people initially expected. Laws were scattered around the city; some of these may have repealed others or parts of others without necessarily ensuring that the original and its copies were removed or erased; others may have been clearly or potentially inconsistent with one another without this having been recognized. Not surprisingly, the work dragged on for the rest of the decade, interrupted only by the short-lived oligarchic coup of the Thirty in 404/3. Some of the difficulties the Anagrapheis encountered and some of the controversy surrounding their work can be gleaned from Lysias 30, a speech that is highly critical of one of these, a man named Nicomachus (Todd 1996). But for our purpose, the controversial details of their appointment and their work are less important than their final product.

In 399 the Anagrapheis produced a set of laws[18] that had been valid before the Thirty, together with new laws that had been approved since. The Athenians also instituted a new procedure for enacting legislation that relied primarily on a board of Nomothetai, whose work was authorized by the decree of Teisamenus (Andocides 1.83–4):

Such additions as are needed shall be recorded (*anagrapsantes*) on boards (*sanides*)[19] by the Nomothetai appointed by the council, and shall be displayed in front of the eponymous heroes[20] for anyone who wishes to see (*skopein tōi boulomenōi*) and handed over to the officials in this month. The laws handed over

---

[16] The following account of the legal reforms of 409–399 is based primarily on Robertson 1990, Rhodes 1991, Todd 1996, and Sickinger 1999: 94–105. On several points these accounts differ from one another. I present what seems to me the most reasonable reconstruction with particular attention to developments in the writing of legislation.

[17] At least, this was the procedure for reinscribing Draco's law in 409/8 (Chapter Four). The law is preceded by a decree of the assembly instructing the Anagrapheis to "record the law of Draco concerning homicide on a stone stele" (*IG* i[3] 104 lines 1–9).

[18] It is misleading to speak of this as codification; see Thür 2002.

[19] For *sanides*, see above n. 6; they were commonly used for temporary texts, since they could easily be reused. Some uses of *sanides* and other writing tablets are illustrated in the *testimonia* in Boegehold 1995: 236–7, 240–1. See further Fischer 2003.

[20] Statues of the ten heroes after whom the ten Athenian tribes were named stood in the agora.

are to be examined first by the council and the five hundred Nomothetai chosen by deme members, who have sworn an oath. And any individual who wishes is to be allowed to come to the council and offer any good advice he may have about the laws. When the laws are enacted, the Council of the Areopagus will oversee the laws and make sure the officials obey the laws that are in force. And the laws that are approved are to be recorded on the wall where they were written before for anyone who wishes to see.

In the process laid out here, the Nomothetai first propose new laws, then the council and the Nomothetai consider them, together with any public response they receive; then after the council ratifies the final text, the new laws are written on the wall. The decree does not mention permanent publication of a systematic code of laws, but speaks only of writing proposed laws on boards, so that anyone who wished could read them. After this, when the council has given final approval, they "are to be written on the wall where they were written before for anyone who wishes to see." Scholars traditionally have taken this last directive to refer to the comprehensive publication of Athenian laws on a wall in the Stoa Basileos; fragments of such a wall have been found, most of which concern a calendar of state sacrifices, and it is possible that the wall originally contained all Athenian laws approved in 403 (see, e.g., Dow 1959). But it is more likely that this directive refers only to the display of new laws that were in the process of being approved.[21]

In the last decade of the fifth century, then, the Athenians were concerned to collect in some central place texts of all the valid laws of the city that had been passed during the previous two centuries, to remove conflicts among them and delete provisions no longer in force, and to add any new laws that these changes might require or that might otherwise be advisable. They did not, as far as we know, revise the texts of older laws, nor did they attempt to produce a comprehensive or systematically organized code. Their concern was to make the existing laws of the city more readily accessible and more usable than they had been in their chaotic state before 411, and again after 403. At the same time they established a new process for enacting legislation, in which the Nomothetai played a large role, and they also added five new laws concerning litigation and

---

[21] So Robertson 1990: 46–9, approved by Rhodes 1991: 98–9; *contra* Sealey 1994: 46–8. There is no indication in the decree itself of a shift in focus from the new laws proposed by the Nomothetai to the entire set of the laws of Athens, though some indication of such a shift would be easy to include and would be expected. Sickinger 1999: 103–4 suggests that many but not all valid laws were published on stone, but that they were all written on papyrus and kept in the Metroon.

legislation. Andocides quotes these five provisions (1.85–7) right after he cites the decree of Teisamenus, though it is unclear how closely they were connected to it:

1. The magistrates are not to use any unwritten law (*agraphos nomos*) on any matter whatsoever.
2. No decree (*psēphisma*), either of the Council or of the Assembly, is to have more authority than a law (*nomos*).
3. No law can be enacted concerning a single man unless the same law applies to all Athenians, unless it is approved by 6,000 in a secret vote.
4. Any trials and arbitration hearings that took place while the city was a democracy are to be valid.
5. These laws are to be used from the archonship of Eucleides [403/2].

In addition to distinguishing between a decree and a law, with the latter having clear priority, these laws also affirm the continuing validity of litigation that took place before the rule of the Thirty and establish the effective date from which these new laws are valid. Thus, as in Draco's law and the Gortyn Code, this legislation conveys a clear historical awareness and understanding of the need to clarify the status of earlier litigation.[22] The first, and perhaps most important, provision prohibits authorities from using any unwritten law (*agraphos nomos*). Andocides' discussion makes clear that this expression does not refer to a general category of unwritten laws, like Antigone's *agrapta nomima* (Chapter One) but rather to any law that has not been recorded by the Anagrapheis or Nomothetai during the archonship of Eucleides or officially enacted after this.[23] Laws that had been enacted and written down in the past would be considered "unwritten" unless they had been reinscribed at this time.

Taken together, these five laws make clear precisely which laws now constitute the official statutes of Athens, and thus provide Athens with an explicit "rule of recognition" (to use the terminology of Hart 1994 – see Introduction) – the first such rule we know of in Greece. Before this, the implicit rule of recognition in Athens, as elsewhere in Greece, had been that a law was a rule that was written and publicly displayed, perhaps in a specific place or a few specific places. Henceforth, in Athens all valid laws must either be included in this publication of laws or must be enacted by the new process for legislation described in Teisamenus' decree.

---

[22] Todd 1996: 120–5 argues that the Athenians had a relatively ahistorical attitude toward law before 403, but he may be overstating the case. Sickinger 2004: 98 disputes the traditional view that the Athenians did not date their laws before the last decade of the fifth century.

[23] MacDowell 1962: 125–6; Ostwald 1973: 91–2; Thür 2000: 92.

None of these new rules explicitly provides rules of adjudication (Hart's third category of secondary rules), but the fourth provision in Andocides' list, accepting the results of trials and arbitration hearings under the earlier democracy, implicitly confirms the traditional Athenian rules of adjudication that provided for trials and arbitration hearings in the case of disputes, including disputes about the meaning and applicability of a law. In addition, this provision may have been the basis for the new procedure of *paragraphē*, established shortly afterwards,[24] that allowed the accused to block the case against him on the ground that the issue had previously been decided. Only after a trial on this question could the original trial proceed.

Finally, Teisamenus' decree provides a rule of change (Hart's second category) by establishing the process whereby the Nomothetai are to consider new legislation. This process seems to have been altered from time to time in succeeding decades in ways that are not entirely clear,[25] but the role of writing in enacting legislation apparently did not change: proposed laws had to be written down, at least temporarily, before they were ratified so that people could read and comment on them. This procedure for writing down laws, set forth in the decree,[26] seems to have remained constant during this period; and this same procedure was included in three of the four fourth-century laws concerning the process for enacting new legislation for which we have clear evidence: (1) the Old Legislation Law (Dem. 20.89–99), (2) the Review Law (Dem. 24.20–3), (3) the Repeal Law (Dem. 24.33), and (4) the Inspection Law (Aeschin 3.38–9).[27]

(1) The Old Legislation Law is the old procedure for legislation, described in Demosthenes 20.94: "(Solon) ordered that before this (the proposer) is to display (the proposed law) before the eponymous heroes, and hand over (a copy) to the clerk," who will read it in the assembly. Although writing is not mentioned here, what will be displayed is clearly the written text of the proposed law. Note that in addition to being written, the law will be read out by the clerk before passage in the

---

[24] It was proposed by Archinus, probably in 401/0; see Rhodes 1981: 473. For the uses of *paragraphē*, see Todd 1993: 136–8.

[25] See Hansen 1985, with references to earlier work of MacDowell and Rhodes. According to Todd 1996: 129, "the general effect [of the changes in the first half of the fourth century] seems to have been to make it progressively easier to change the law."

[26] "Such additions as are needed shall be written on boards by the Nomothetai appointed by the council, and shall be displayed in front of the eponymous heroes for anyone who wishes to see" (Andocides 1.83).

[27] I follow the terminology of MacDowell 1975. He also lists a fifth law, the New Legislation Law, but this depends on inferences from Dem. 20.91 which, even if valid (they are rejected by Hansen 1980), contain little detail about the law.

assembly. Not every Athenian will be able to read the posted text or will take the trouble to read it, but all who are in the assembly meeting must know what the law says before voting to approve it, and this is accomplished orally.

(2) The Review Law, cited in Dem. 24.20–3, provides procedures for approving a new law. Among other things it specifies (24.23) that "before the Assembly meeting, any Athenian who wishes is to write the laws he proposes and display them before the eponymous heroes, so that the people (*dēmos*), considering the total number of proposed laws, may vote on how much time the Nomothetai will have. Someone who proposes a new law is to write it on a whitened board before the eponymous heroes every day until the Assembly meets."

(3) The Repeal Law, cited by Demosthenes (24.33) does not mention writing. It focuses on the penalties for introducing a new law that violates an existing statute.[28] Nothing in this text, however, is incompatible with the process of writing prescribed in the other laws.

(4) The Inspection Law is said by Aeschines (1.38–9) to provide for annual inspection of the laws by the Thesmothetai to see "if any law is written that contradicts another law, or an invalid law stands among the valid ones, or if more than one law has somehow been written down concerning each act. And if they find such a law, (the lawgiver) requires that they write it on boards and display it before the eponymous heroes."

The law cited in Dem. 24.23 and the descriptions of legislation in Dem. 20.94 and Aeschin 1.38–9, like the decree of Teisamenus, all state in identical language that proposed laws must be displayed before the eponymous heroes, and two of the passages also include the detail that the text of the law should be displayed on a whitened board, where it would be available to any person who wished to read it (not just look at, Hedrick 2000), before he would have to vote on it.

The five new laws together with Teisamenus' decree thus provide Athens with a full set of secondary rules for recognizing, changing, and (at least by implication) adjudicating among its substantive laws. This recognition that in order to be fully authoritative in practice, a set of rules of conduct had to be supplemented by certain kinds of secondary rules that were first analyzed by Hart (1994) is quite extraordinary, and is unparalleled in premodern law. And writing was now not only the explicit means of validating a law, it

---

[28] Hansen 1980 93–4 rejects MacDowell's argument that there are discrepancies between this law and the Old Legislation Law, and suggests instead that these are probably parts of the same law.

had also become an integral part of the process of legislation, a process that presumed that a substantial portion of the Athenian people, or at least of all adult males, could read these texts that were publicly displayed for their benefit.

Writing also played a role in the enactment of decrees in the fourth century, which only required a vote of the assembly. The expression for proposing a decree remained "X spoke (*eipe*)," as it is in the preamble to Draco's law (*IG* I³ 104, line 4); this refers to the fact that the proposer would present the text orally in the assembly, and we regularly find this expression in the preamble to fourth-century decrees (e.g., Dem. 18.73, 24.39). Thus, forensic speakers can speak of a decree as an oral proposal rather than a written text (e.g., Dem. 18.75). But Demosthenes and other later orators also regularly refer to writing decrees and speak of decrees as written by someone,[29] and the common expression for the activity of public figures in the assembly is "speaking and writing" (e.g., Dem. 18.66), that is giving oral advice and proposing decrees orally, but also putting those decrees in writing before they are approved.

During the fourth century, the use of writing in the legal system also begins to expand beyond legislation. Although laws and decrees make up the largest category of written texts mentioned by the orators, speakers also refer to many other kinds of written documents, including public documents such as treaties, lists of public debtors, deme and tribe registers, and other sorts of public registers. But private documents comprise the large majority of texts cited in the orators; these include wills, contracts (*syngraphai*), other kinds of agreements (*synthēkai*), depositions of witnesses, letters, accusations, oaths, challenges, and various unspecified documents (often called *grammateia*, "writings").[30] And the existence of a written contract was a prerequisite for bringing suit in the special maritime courts (Lanni 2006: 149–74). References to all these types of documents become more frequent during the course of the fourth century,[31] as writing was increasingly used not only for legal matters, but in many areas of Athenian life. This is not to say that what we might call oral proofs disappear; unwritten agreements of all sorts continue to be cited throughout the

---

[29] E.g., Dem. 18.75, "the decree Eubulus wrote (*egrapse*)."

[30] On written documents in classical Athenian law, see R. Thomas 1989: 38–45; she notes (p. 41) that the earliest reference to a written agreement (*synthēkē*) is in Isocrates 17.20.

[31] A very crude index of this growth is to compare the frequency of words from the root *grap-* (*grap-*, *graph-*, *graps-*, *gram-*). Using the *TLG* Disk E, we find about 2 1/2 times as many such words in Demosthenes 36–59 as in the works of Lysias (excluding Lysias 2 and 33), which have roughly the same number of total words.

classical period (Lanni 2006: 157–61). But forensic speakers often discuss written texts in their speeches, and the way they do so is significant. A brief examination of the use of written texts will help us understand the place of these texts in the legal process. Later in the chapter we will look more closely at Athenian forensic discourse about written texts.

When a litigant wanted to cite a written text as evidence in court, he could, of course, quote (or paraphrase) it in his speech, but he often found it more effective to supplement his own discussion by having the text read aloud in court. The speaker simply asked the clerk (*grammateus*) to do this and, in private cases at least, the water clock was stopped while this happened so that the reading did not shorten his time for speaking.[32] In the fifth century, evidence was commonly presented to the court orally by witnesses, but by around 375, all such testimony and any other documents to be presented to the court had to be put in writing.[33] In most cases, moreover, all these written texts had to be submitted in advance at a preliminary hearing, so they could be sealed in a jar and kept for use at the trial; a litigant could not use any document in court that was not in the jar.[34] This was presumably done to prevent a litigant from gaining an advantage by surprising his opponent with evidence for which he was not prepared.

The process for presenting these documents in court underlies the fundamental division Aristotle establishes for forensic rhetoric between "artistic proofs" (*pisteis entechnoi*), which are the arguments the speaker has devised himself, and "non-artistic proofs" (*pisteis atechnoi*), which (says Aristotle) the speaker simply finds and uses.[35] In *Rhetoric* 1.2, 1355b35–1356a1 he explains,

By non-artistic proofs I mean those that we do not supply ourselves but that already exist, such as witnesses,[36] interrogations under torture (*basanoi*), contracts, and the like; by artistic proofs I mean those that can be devised by our own skill and methods. Thus we only need to make use of the former, but we must discover the latter.

---

[32] The water clock was not normally stopped for reading texts in public cases (Rubinstein 2000: 61–2, n. 99 and 74–5).

[33] Bonner 1905: 46–7; Calhoun 1919: 190–3; Rubinstein 2000: 72–5 (with n. 143 on the date).

[34] *Ath. Pol.* 53.2–3. A fragment of such a jar has been found; see Boegehold 1982 and the comments of Wallace 2001.

[35] I use traditional translations for the Greek expressions *pisteis entechnoi* and *pisteis atechnoi*, though in this context "arguments" would be a better translation of *pisteis*, and "artistic" only partly captures the meaning of *entechnos* and *atechnos* – "with or without *technē* (art, skill craft)."

[36] Instead of "witnesses" (*martyres*), we often find "testimony" (*martyriai*), in the speeches. Though the terms may suggest oral and written testimony respectively, in fact this distinction does not hold and the two terms can be used interchangeably, sometimes in the same speech (e.g., Andoc 1, Lys. 16).

Later Aristotle expands the number of non-artistic proofs, adding laws and oaths (*Rhetoric* 1.15, 1375a24).

Aristotle does not say so explicitly but he and his audience certainly knew that the artistic proofs were the litigant's oral arguments which he or his logographer had constructed, and the non-artistic proofs were those written documents that were brought into court and read out by the clerk during the speech. By far the most common of these non-artistic proofs are laws (and decrees) and witnesses; contracts and oaths are relatively rarely read out in court, and no example survives of a *basanos* being read in court.³⁷ But in addition to these five categories, many other kinds of documents are introduced in court by litigants and read out by the clerk.³⁸ At one point Demosthenes even introduces his own notes (*hypomnēmata*) listing Meidias' offenses and (probably) has the list read out by the clerk (21.130, see below).

By describing the non-artistic proofs as already existing, so that we only need to make use of them, Aristotle is suggesting that these written texts presented in court have an objective existence that does not depend on the speaker's rhetorical skill; they simply exist as material artifacts. And this analysis reflects a common sentiment in forensic discourse, that these non-artistic proofs and the written texts in which they reside are independent of the speaker and thus, in contrast to the speaker's arguments, are objective and true and not subject to rhetorical manipulation. The speaker simply goes and finds these proofs and then brings them into court to be read.

Aristotle must have been aware that the actual use of these non-artistic proofs by the orators does not correspond to the simple description he gives in 1.2, for when he returns to the subject in 1.15 (1375a22–1378a11), he makes clear that the speaker does not simply go out and find these proofs, but

---

³⁷ In several cases a challenge (*proklēsis*) is cited which is in fact the *basanos* ("interrogation") which the challenger had proposed but was not accepted, so that no interrogation ever took place.

³⁸ In the surviving forensic speeches, in addition to those already noted, we find (in no particular order) the following kinds of documents (and others were presumably cited in speeches that are now lost): judgment (*gnōsis*), inventory (*apographē*), list of public services (*leitourgiai*), a litigant's sworn statement (*antōmosion*), objection (*diamartyria*), will (*diathēkē*), a challenge (*proklēsis*), answer to questioning (*anakrisis*), oath of denial (*exōmosia*), letter (*epistolē*), indictment (*graphē*), resolution (*dogma*), epitaph (*epigramma*), preliminary decree (*probouleuma*), alliance (*symmachia*), agreement (*homologia*), curse (*ara*), poetry (*iambeia, elegeia, rhēsis*), oracle (*manteia*), motion to dismiss (*paragraphē*), accusation (*enklēma*), reversal of judgment (*antilēxis*), report (*apophasis*), lease (*misthōsis*), denunciation (*phasis*), inscribed marble slab (*stēlē*), reconciliation agreement (*diallagai*), date (*chronos*), pleading (*synēgoria*), question and answer (*erōtēsis*), various lists (*katalogos, arithmos, dialogismos, biblion, onomata, praxeis*), and miscellaneous texts (*grammata, hypomnēmata*) and copies (*antigrapha*). Isocrates puts a new twist on this practice by citing his own speeches as evidence in *Antidosis* (e.g., Isoc. 15.59, see Gagarin 2002b).

must also be creative in using them. In using laws, for example, if the law is favorable to the speaker's case, he should remind jurors to vote according to the law, whereas if the law is opposed to his case, he must urge the jurors to use their own best judgment. Similar advice is given about the other non-artistic proofs, that speakers should use them if they support his case, but if they do not, then he should use other arguments. This reflects the practice of actual speakers, who emphasize these non-artistic proofs when they support their case, but ignore them when they do not. In either case, the use of non-artistic proofs clearly requires a degree of rhetorical skill.

But we can go further, for it is misleading (and in some cases simply wrong) to say that a speaker just finds these non-artistic proofs. Some of them such as laws do exist independently of any specific litigation, and certain other documents, such as contracts, also existed before the litigation concerning them began. But a speaker (and his logographer) had almost complete freedom in deciding not only whether to use these documents, but which parts of which documents to cite. Many laws are cited in the orators but, as is often noted, laws can be cited in support of many different arguments, and some of the laws cited are only marginally relevant to the speaker's case.³⁹

In addition to selecting which law or laws to include in one's plea, litigants and logographers must also select the specific excerpts they wish to cite, and must then coordinate these citations with their artistic proofs or arguments. Some of the ways litigants may exercise this skill in citing laws are suggested by a brief exchange between Aeschines and Demosthenes in their pleadings in the famous case "On the Crown" (Aeschin 3, Dem. 18). The case stems from a decree proposed in the assembly by a certain Ctesiphon that a crown should be awarded to Demosthenes for his service to the city; Aeschines then brings an action against Ctesiphon, charging (in part) that his decree violates existing laws regarding when and where crowns can be awarded. In *Against Ctesiphon*, Aeschines, speaking first, has the text of a law read out in court that appears to restrict where the proposed crown can be awarded (3.32). After citing the decree and arguing that it violates this law, he then warns the jurors that the defense (i.e., Demosthenes speaking on behalf of Ctesiphon) "will provide a law (*nomos*) that has no bearing on this indictment, and will say that the city has two laws concerning decrees, one that I now cite ... and the other (they will

---

³⁹ See Carey 1996, De Brauw 2001–2. A well-known example is Demosthenes 54, where in the course of a suit for assault (*dikē aikeia*) the speaker Ariston cites two other laws (54.24), in part to show his own modesty and restraint, but never cites the law concerning *aikeia*.

say) is a law that is opposed to it" (3.36). He then goes on to argue that the city cannot have two such contradictory laws.

In response, Demosthenes does indeed cite a different law (18.120) and then accuses Aeschines of suppressing that part of the law that allows the award: "Are you not ashamed to bring a charge prompted by envy not by any actual wrong, altering laws and removing parts from them when they should rightly be read out in their entirety to those who have sworn to vote according to the laws [i.e. the jury]?" (18.121). We do not have the actual text of the law cited by either speaker, but we know that Demosthenes himself sometimes cites only parts of laws.[40] More to the point, each speaker is free to cite just that law or that part of the law that he can best use in constructing his argument. Litigants probably did not simply fabricate the texts of non-existent laws since they had to make the texts available to their opponent before the trial and the penalty for citing a non-existent law was death (Dem. 26.24). But they certainly controlled which texts were read to the jurors, and they may have rearranged clauses and made other small changes in wording to suit the needs of their argument.[41] Thus, the effective citation of these texts in court required considerable skill, even though in a technical sense the texts already existed and one only had to find them.

Even more creative artistry was needed in order to use most of the other non-artistic proofs (Carey 1994). A contract, like a law, may have existed before the litigation was planned, but in most cases, one or both litigants had written the contract, and each presumably took care to make the text most helpful to his side in the event of litigation. Furthermore, the citation of a contract, like a law, may have required excerpting the text and arranging it for effective use. A further degree of creativity was needed for the testimony of witnesses, or the challenge to swear an oath, or the testimony of slaves under torture, for these texts were normally not written until litigation either was in progress or at least was being planned. And in most cases it was the speaker himself (or his logographer) who wrote the text that was read out in court. This is clear in the case of challenges: one litigant would, for example, offer to swear an oath or request that his opponent interrogate a slave, and he would write down the offer or request,

---

[40] In 23.22–60, Demosthenes cites a series of excerpts from Draco's homicide law, but there are many parts of the law that he does not cite. In Greek, as in English, a large group of provisions can be called a law (*nomos*) – "Draco's law on homicide" – but a single provision from this group can also be called a law.

[41] For example, in a case having nothing to do with homicide (Dem. 43.57), the speaker rearranges the provisions he cites from Draco's homicide law and makes one or two small changes in the wording.

including the oath he wanted sworn or the question he wanted asked. He expected his proposal to be rejected, but he could then introduce this written text in court and argue that rejection of it was a sure sign of his opponent's guilt or the speaker's own innocence.[42]

In the case of witnesses (see Thür 2005), in earlier days, a witness may have testified orally or read from a prepared (written) statement, but by 375, if not earlier, a written version of the testimony was included among the documents submitted before the trial and was then read out by the clerk. Each litigant selected his own witnesses and he would regularly write down for the witness exactly what his testimony would be. The litigant could also draft a statement for a hostile or reluctant witness, who would then have to agree to the truth of the statement or swear an oath disclaiming knowledge of the matter.

Litigants do not normally tell the jury that they themselves have written the testimony of their witnesses but they do not try to conceal this either. In Dem. 43.48, for example, the speaker tells of an earlier case in which "we did not write witness depositions (*martyriai*) concerning matters that were agreed upon, nor did we summon witnesses (*martyres*), but we thought that we were safe on these points." In other words, if they had summoned witnesses for these matters, they would also have written their depositions. And in the speech against Conon (Dem. 54.26), Ariston complains about his opponents' behavior at the arbitration hearing: they dragged out the hearing past midnight, in part by "writing witness statements (*martyriai*) that had nothing to do with the case." Evidently it was normal, at least by the middle of the fourth century, for litigants (or logographers) to write depositions for witnesses. Thus, the written texts of non-artistic proofs that are introduced in court are in many cases created and always manipulated by litigants using some of the same rhetorical strategies and techniques they use for constructing their artistic proofs.

Another important use of writing in connection with law that obviously required rhetorical skill was logography – the writing of a speech by a logographer for someone else to deliver or by a litigant for his own use. All the speeches that survive today were, of course, written down, probably at the time they were composed, but the practice of logography only began in the late fifth century. Before that, litigants spoke without written texts, though they presumably planned what they would say beforehand and may have used some notes. We may assume that after the invention of

---

[42] E.g., Dem. 59.124–5, where Apollodorus cites the complete text of his challenge. See further Thür 1977; Gagarin 1996.

logography, many litigants continued to do without written texts, either by preference or because they could not afford a logographer's fee. But we have no idea what percentage of pleadings were written by logographers. The practice is often criticized,[43] but it must have been effective, since logographers not only made a living but many became rich from the practice (Dinarchus 1.111).

Other sorts of written texts were used in the administration of Athenian law.[44] First, we have seen (Chapter Five) that in the *graphē* procedure the indictment was written. In the fourth century this indictment was then posted before the statues of the eponymous heroes in the agora, where it could be read by anyone interested, and on the day of the trial, after the case had been assigned to a specific court, the *graphē* was also posted outside this court. The same procedure was probably followed in a *paragraphē* or "counter-suit" (i.e. a motion to dismiss), and an *apographē* required a written list of property that would serve as the basis for legal action. By the mid fourth century, in fact, most accusations were probably put in writing, whatever the procedure used. The orators mention a written accusation (*enklēma*, e.g., Dem. 32.4), and also the defendant's written response to the accusation (*antigraphē*),[45] and these were probably both read out at the beginning of the trial, either by the clerk or by the litigants themselves.

In cases of *graphē paranomōn* ("indictment for an illegal proposal"), where someone is accused of proposing a decree that violates an existing law, the use of writing was adapted to the specific circumstances of these cases: both the text of the decree under attack and the text of the law or laws it is alleged to have violated were written down next to one another on a board, which was displayed at the entrance to the court (and probably also by the statues of the eponymous heroes), the idea being that one could read the two texts side-by-side and see for oneself whether the decree violated

---

[43] Demosthenes and Aeschines both accuse the other of being a logographer (Dem. 19.250, Aeschin 2.180). The latter (Aeschin 2.165) also accuses Demosthenes of writing a speech for Phormio (Dem. 36) and revealing the contents to Phormio's opponents, and Plutarch even reports that Demosthenes wrote speeches for both sides in this case (*Demosthenes* 15), but these accusations may not be true.

[44] I limit myself here to writing that is specifically concerned with judicial matters, passing over the considerable amount of writing in other areas of government in Athens. *Ath. Pol.* 47 gives a good picture of some of the ways writing was used in administration.

[45] Only one *antigraphē* is actually cited by a litigant: in Dem. 45.46 Apollodorus has the clerk read out the defendant Stephanus' *antigraphē*, though this does not mean that the *antigraphē* had not already been read at the beginning of the trial. If the document preserved in our manuscripts is authentic (which is debated), it shows that the *antigraphē* contained the accusation and the accused's response, both of which are simple and to the point ("Stephanus gave false testimony against me, etc." "I gave true testimony, etc.").

the law. Both texts would then be read out to the court by the clerk at the beginning of the trial (Aeschin 3.192).[46]

As for the verdict, we find little evidence of the practice attributed to the early Thesmothetae (see Chapter Five) of preserving previous judgments in writing. In the classical period, verdicts were only written down in certain cases, for instance, when an important political figure was convicted (Lanni 2004: 169 n. 26). We have the verdict, for example, condemning Antiphon to death for his part in the oligarchic coup in 411.[47] A verdict would also have been recorded when it involved a fine payable to the city (unless it was paid immediately) or a public punishment such as disenfranchisement (*atimia*). In the case of unpaid fines, the debtor's name was written on a list of public debtors until the debt was paid, and the names of other sorts of criminals may also have been posted.[48] But verdicts in general were not officially recorded.[49] The decision reached in an arbitration hearing, on the other hand, was written down so that it could be sealed in a jar with the other non-artistic proofs and read out at the trial.[50]

We have seen that many different kinds of written texts were brought into court and read out by the clerk, either at the beginning of the trial or during the litigants' speeches. Other written texts are alluded to or quoted by a litigant (as, for example, the juror's oath sometimes is), and writing was used in several ways in the administration of law before and after the trial. But the only means by which any of these written texts gained a presence in court was by being reported by one of the litigants in his speech or read out by the clerk. Hypothetically a litigant may have been able to bring a writing tablet and write names on it for the jurors to see, but to our knowledge this never happened. In short, all the written texts that played a role in the trial were presented to the jurors orally. Jurors are never given

---

[46] Some jurors may have read these texts before entering the courtroom but most jurors probably did not, and in most cases it would not have done them much good if they had, since the bare texts often do not make clear just how the speakers will argue their cases.

[47] [Plutarch] *Moralia* 834a–b. The report says that the text of the verdict was appended (*hypogegraptai*) to that of the decree proclaiming that Antiphon and two others should be arrested and tried for treason, but it is not clear whether the verdict was actually written below the decree on the stele that was inscribed at the time of the trial, or was just written after the decree in [Plutarch]'s source, Caecilius.

[48] Isocrates (*Antidosis* 15.237) says that the names of various wrongdoers are posted on *sanides* around the city, but we cannot trust his claims in this speech.

[49] This conclusion depends in part on an argument from silence, but it is striking that although speakers often mention the result of a previous case, sometimes, because their opponent has refused to comply with an earlier verdict, no speaker mentions writing in connection with the verdict in a private case.

[50] *Ath. Pol.* 53.2. Demosthenes claims (21.85) that Meidias offered the arbitrators fifty drachmas to change and rewrite (*metagraphō*) the verdict, but they refused.

these texts to read, and no other reading takes place during the trial. Writing continues to have an important presence in legal matters outside the court, especially in the many laws and decrees that continue to be written and displayed in public, but when this writing is introduced into the trial, the written text is always converted into oral speech.

One reason for this is that in Athenian law, after the preliminary hearing before the arbitrator or other magistrate, the rest of the procedure consists entirely of a jury trial in which no judge (in the modern sense) participates. Even today, when juries are much smaller than in Athens and jurors are presumed to be literate, the proceedings in the jury's presence are for the most part conducted without writing, though the jurors may occasionally be shown notes or other written documents to read. Of course writing infuses all other aspects of the U.S. judicial process, particularly the procedural hearings and appeals that take place before a judge and for which both sides regularly prepare written briefs. But the practical difficulty of using written texts with even a small group of jurors, combined with the fact that jurors in the U.S.A. (like Athenian jurors) do not have any specialized training, tends to keep writing out of the jury phase of our judicial process. And the large juries used for Athenian trials would have made the use of writing in court even more impractical.

But this was not the only reason for the complete orality of Athenian trials. Official arbitration hearings, for instance, were held before three or fewer arbitrators in their fifty-ninth year. We do not know much about procedures in these hearings, but nothing suggests that written documents had a much larger role at this stage than in the subsequent trial. Written documents were presented in the arbitration hearings, and were probably read over by the opposing litigant and by a clerk before being sealed in a jar for trial, but as far as we know, the arbitration procedure was conducted entirely orally, by means of question and answer. And although the verdict in an arbitration hearing was written down so that it could be introduced at the trial, this writing took place after the hearing ended and did not interfere with the hearing itself. It would not have been difficult to require litigants at the arbitration hearing, at least, to submit a written account of their case, as is often done in Ptolemaic Egypt not long afterwards (Chapter Ten), but Greeks in the classical period never take this route. Practical reasons alone, therefore, cannot explain why even these arbitration proceedings before a small group of experienced judges were conducted orally.

It seems then that the Athenians restricted the amount of writing in the legal process as far as was practical for other reasons, which we shall consider in the next chapter. For now, we should recall that the judicial process revealed in the Gortyn Code also appears to have been entirely oral even though there cases were heard by a single judge. This confirms that the exclusion of writing from trials was a feature of Greek law in general, and was not motivated primarily by the democratic use of large juries, as at Athens. Similarly, we have seen that the substantial use of writing for recording and displaying laws so that they could be read by all concerned persons was characteristic of Greek law in general, and not a result of Athenian democratic ideology. Classical law in democratic Athens thus embodies the same fundamental duality as archaic law in oligarchic Greek cities: widespread use of writing for legislation but restricted use of writing in litigation. This duality may explain the ambivalent attitudes expressed toward law by, on the one hand, Herodotus' story of Deioces, in which writing becomes a tool by which a monarch establishes complete control over the legal process, and Euripides' Theseus, on the other, for whom written laws are an essential component of democratic government.[51]

Athenian litigants participated fully in this ambivalence, sometimes praising, at other times questioning the value of written documents of all sorts,[52] and in the rest of this chapter we shall consider the different attitudes litigants express toward written texts. We have already noted that written laws are often said to be authoritative, but these are not the only texts to be so treated. Litigants often stress the value of witnesses, *basanoi* (slave interrogations), and other non-artistic proofs, usually without calling attention to the fact that they were written. But their status as written texts is sometimes signaled explicitly and is probably implicit in most other cases. For example, Demosthenes (30.35–6) tells of asking Onetor to let him interrogate three slave women,

so that we would have not only reports (*logoi*) about them but also *basanoi*. When I made this request, which everyone present said was fair, he was unwilling to have recourse to this precise information (*touto to akribes*) but, as if there were other clearer proofs (*saphesteroi elenchoi*) on these matters than *basanoi* and witnesses, they did not provide witnesses or hand over for interrogation the women who knew.

---

[51] Herodotus 1.96–100 (Chapters One and Seven); Euripides, *Suppliants* 429–34 (Chapter Three).
[52] Their ambivalence may also stem in part from the ambivalent status of a written text, which can either be viewed as a material object and construed as factual, hard evidence, or can be characterized as (mere) words, and thus as a subjective expression of thought or argument subject to manipulation and distortion (Gagarin 2002b).

Demosthenes does not explicitly say that the witness depositions and *basanoi* are written, but he contrasts them with his *logoi* (oral arguments) and characterizes them as "precise" (*akribes*) and "sure proof" (*saphes elenchos*), all terms that frequently characterize written, non-artistic proofs.[53]

Demosthenes is more explicit about writing when he accuses Aphobus of destroying his father's will (28.5), "which would have enabled us to know with precision (*to akribes*)," and expecting others to believe whatever he says about the will. Instead of destroying the will, Aphobus and his colleagues should have sealed it in front of witnesses so that, "if there was any dispute about it, it would have been possible to refer to the written text (*ta grammata*) and discover the entire truth." Similarly, in Demosthenes 36.18–21, both sides recognize the value of written texts: the plaintiff, Apollodorus had argued that his mother had done away with the written documents (*ta grammata*) he needed, and had claimed that without these he could not "prove his case precisely" (*exelenchein akribōs*). The defendant asks, "on the basis of what written documents (*grammata*), then, did you bring your suit? . . . if these *grammata* disappeared, on the basis of what *grammata* did he bring his suits?" The demand for written documents here echoes the language of proof (*elenchos*), precision (*to akribes*), and clarity (*to saphes*) in the other passages just cited, all of which depend on written texts.

Contracts (*syngraphai*) too are often cited for their authority, especially in maritime cases, where a contract specifying the terms of the maritime loan was required in order to have the case heard in the special maritime courts.[54] As one speaker says (Dem. 33.36),

When men make contracts with one another, they seal them and give them to people they can trust for the following reason, so that if there is a dispute about something, they can refer to the written text (*ta grammata*) and they can find proof (*elenchos*) in it concerning the disputed point. But when someone has removed the precise information (*to akribes*) and tries to deceive you with an argument, how could you in all fairness believe him?

In Demosthenes 35, the plaintiff has the entire contract read out in court (35.10–13), and then later has it read again (35.37).[55] After the first reading, he takes up the provisions of the contract one by one, laying emphasis on the

---

[53] For the connection of precision (*akribeia*) with writing, see Gagarin 2002a: 28.

[54] For the arguments in maritime cases, see Lanni 2006: 149–74, and on attitudes toward written contracts in maritime cases and this case in particular, see Cohen 2003: 92–6. Some litigants in these cases may have attacked the validity of the contract, but most litigants accept the contract and claim that they have adhered to its terms, but their opponent has not.

[55] If genuine (as many think it is) this is the only full text of a contract we have preserved in the orators. Kussmaul 1969 has a useful collection of contracts in inscriptions.

fact that they are written: "First it is written (*gegraptai*)"; "this is explicitly written (*diarrhēdēn gegraptai*)"; and so on. He then concludes (35.25), "they gave not the slightest heed to the text (*ta grammata*) written (*gegrammena*) in the contract, but regarded the contract as mere stuff and nonsense."

Contracts were not required and may not have had the same degree of authority in non-maritime cases. Hyperides 3, *Against Athenogenes*, shows that in an ordinary suit a contract could be disputed, but not easily. Both parties would have signed the contract, making it difficult to claim the document was a forgery, and in Athenian law, as the plaintiff Euxitheus admits (Hyp. 3.13), whatever two people agreed to was valid. Thus, Euxitheus admits signing the contract, but claims he was deceived and then argues by analogy with several other laws that deception should invalidate a contract.

This is just one of many cases where a speaker rejects the evidence of written documents and affirms the superiority of spoken words (see Cohen 2003). In a well-known example, Aeschines explains to the jury why they should rely on rumor or report for proof of Timarchus' misdeeds rather than seeking written evidence in the form of contracts (1.127–31). Citing Homer, Hesiod, and Euripides, he praises Rumor as a goddess who proclaims the truth about people. He adds a bold elaboration of the reasons why he should not be expected to produce a written contract between Timarchus and a client: what everyone talks about is a surer guide to the truth than any writings (1.160–5).

Aeschines also denies the value of written documents in the celebrated case "On the Crown," where he challenges not just Ctesiphon's decree honoring Demosthenes, but the need for written honorary decrees in the first place. The great men of the past like Themistocles and Miltiades, he argues, were highly esteemed by the people but they did not need confirmation of this in a written decree (3.182):

Let Demosthenes show if it is anywhere written (*gegraptai*) that any of these men should be given a crown. Well then, was the *dēmos* ungrateful? Not at all. They were great-hearted, and these men were worthy of the city. But they did not think their honor should lie in written texts (*grammata*) but in the memory of those who had benefited from their deeds – a memory that has endured, immortal, from that time down to the present day.

Aeschines here claims that honor and fame are better preserved in a collective memory which, transmitted orally, will spread the immortal renown of these men and their deeds, rather than by written documents.[56]

---

[56] Pericles expresses the same idea in his funeral oration (Thucydides 2.43.2–3); see Gagarin 2006c.

In response, Demosthenes ignores Aeschines' arguments against written decrees and has several earlier decrees honoring him for his service to the city read out in court as evidence of the honors he has received from the city in the past (Dem. 18.222–3).

Aeschines' depreciation of writing as a medium for conveying honor echoes a long tradition in the orators that oral communication of important information is superior to written communication. This assumption underlies an early passage (Antiphon 1.29–30) in which the speaker recalls how, when he was a boy, his dying father directed him to avenge his death. The speaker observes that dying victims, if they are able, summon family and friends, ask them to bear witness, and direct them to avenge the crime. "If victims lack these means," he continues, "they write things down (*grammata graphousi*), and they summon their own servants as witnesses and reveal who is causing their death." Here, direct, oral communication is the norm; writing is only a fall-back. Similarly, in Antiphon 5.53–6, Euxitheus challenges the evidence of a note (*grammateidion*) he is accused of writing that allegedly proves he killed Herodes: he would not have needed to write a note, he says, since a messenger could give a clearer report of the crime orally. People only use writing if there is a special need to keep the message secret from the deliverer, or because it is too long to remember.[57] To be sure, this argument fits the needs of his case, but Euxitheus must think that the jury will find it plausible that oral communication would be considered the norm.

Assertions such as these form the background for many passages in fourth-century oratory in which written documents are challenged on the grounds that they are forged or otherwise falsified, or that they misstate the writer's intentions, or that they have been misinterpreted or wrongly cited by the opponent. The speaker in Lysias 32.22 accuses a guardian of falsifying his account books in order to cheat his wards out of their inheritance: "it's as if he had been appointed guardian of the children so that he could show them writing (*grammata*) instead of money (*chrēmata*) and thus reveal that they were impoverished, not rich." This is almost the exact opposite of the argument in Demosthenes 36.18 (quoted above), that to bring a case one must have written documents, but it illustrates the contrast speakers regularly draw between false or deceptive writing and real objects and facts.

Especially prone to challenge are wills, which are often at issue in inheritance disputes. One speaker, in challenging the will presented by

---

[57] Cf. Nicias' decision to write a letter back to the Athenians describing his dire situation, because he was worried that a messenger who reported this orally might distort the truth (Thucydides 7.8).

his opponents as a forgery, elaborates a view of wills in general as impossible to verify without the confirming evidence of family and friends (Isaeus 4.11–14). Another speaker describes in detail the steps someone should take to ensure that his will will be upheld in case of a challenge: he should "first summon his relatives, then the members of his phratry and deme, and then as many of his other friends as he could. In that way if anyone should dispute the estate by either kinship or bequest [i.e. in a will] he would easily be proved a liar" (Isaeus 9.8). In both cases the testimony of family and friends is presented as more important than a written will in determining the wishes of the deceased and ensuring that these are carried out after his death.

In cases like these, of course, the speaker on the other side must have asserted the validity of the will in question.[58] As we saw above, Demosthenes emphasizes the importance of his father's will in his attempt to recover his rightful inheritance, and other speakers too base their cases on wills. But even when a speaker bases his claim on a will, he always tries in addition to show how close and familial his personal relationship was with the testator and how devoted he was to him both when he was alive and after his death (e.g., Isocrates 19.16–33). If possible, he will introduce the testimony of family members and others with personal knowledge of this relationship. Thus, even when a litigant has the support of a written will, other arguments that do not depend on a written document usually play a large role in his plea.

Dozens of other kinds of written texts are mentioned in the orators – rental agreements, inventories, memos, and others. In most cases speakers express no particular view about the fact that a text is written. When they do address this aspect, they tend to affirm the value of a written text a bit more often than they dispute it. But regardless of numbers, any forensic speaker can, if he wishes, present written documents as hard evidence as opposed to subjective arguments, or conversely as subject to falsification, concealment, and destruction, and thus of no value in contrast to speech, which can reveal and clarify the truth.

These two views are directly opposed in a pair of passages from "On the Crown." As noted above, this case is a *graphē paranomōn*, or indictment for an illegal decree, in which the text of the decree under attack was written next to (the verb is *paragraphō*) the law or laws it allegedly violated, and these were posted on a board outside the court. In this case, Aeschines had

---

[58] Cohen 2003: 90–2 is one-sided in discussing only Isaeus 4 and 9 and ignoring cases (e.g., Isaeus 6) where the speaker defends a will. But his point that a person's social identity depends largely on the testimony of friends and relatives is nonetheless valid.

asserted in his indictment that Ctesiphon's decree violated two laws,[59] and he refers to this arrangement in a striking simile (3.199–200):

For the issue of justice (*to dikaion*) is not something imprecise but something defined by your laws. It is like in carpentry: when we want to know what is straight and what is not, we apply a ruler (*canōn*), which decides[60] the issue. In the same way, in indictments for illegal decrees we have at hand as the ruler of justice (*canōn tou dikaiou*) this board here containing the decree and the laws written side by side (*paragegrammenoi*). Just demonstrate [he says to Demosthenes] that these agree with one another and then step down.

Aeschines' simile emphasizes the purely objective nature of the jury's decision. A simple physical comparison of these two sets of written texts, the decree and the laws, will provide a conclusive and objective decision about what is just: either they will agree or they will not.

Aeschines' argument is perhaps the strongest statement in the orators of the certainty of written evidence, and as we might expect, Demosthenes rejects the challenge (18.111):

Since he thoroughly jumbled the arguments he made about the laws that are written side by side (*paragegrammenoi*), by the gods, I don't think you understood most of them, nor was I able to make sense of them either. So in a simple fashion, I will discuss the correct understanding of the issue of justice (*ta dikaia*) in the case.

Demosthenes then proceeds to attack Aeschines' interpretation of the legal issues in detail. To be sure, he cites other written texts – a law and several decrees – in support of his own position. But the message of the passage just cited is clear: the aim of this trial is justice (*ta dikaia*), and the correct (straight) means of reaching this goal is by oral argument. Demosthenes does not reject the value of written texts entirely, but argues that simply citing the laws, as Aeschines has done, produces confusion, not certainty, and that only a clear and simple (oral) discussion is the straight road to justice.

Demosthenes' challenge to the unmediated authority of the texts of laws is uncommon. A litigant may occasionally attack his opponent for quoting the wrong law or the wrong part of the law, as Aeschines and Demosthenes both do elsewhere in this case, but as a rule, litigants do not question the authoritative force of the laws. And even in this passage, in fact, Demosthenes is not questioning the authority of the laws Aeschines cites so much as attacking his way of using these texts. His point is not that

---

[59] Most scholars agree with Aeschines' conviction that the decree violates these two laws (Gwatkin 1957), but Harris (1994: 140–8) argues that Demosthenes is correct that the decree does not violate the laws.
[60] *Diagignōskein*, "decide," also means "judge." Cf. Lycurgus 1.9 for the idea of using the law as a *canōn* in deciding a case.

the laws lack authority, but that the meaning of a law is not self-evident. A litigant must use oral argument to clarify just what the law means and how it relates to the justice of this particular case, and this Aeschines has not done. In other words, even an authoritative law needs to be interpreted and clarified by means of oral discussion.

Forensic speakers, then, never deny the value of written laws,[61] but they do argue that laws have their limitations and by themselves may not be an adequate path to justice. This view is elaborated in an often quoted address to the jury at the end of Demosthenes' speech against Meidias (21.223–4):

> If you wish to examine and investigate why you, who at any time are judging cases, have power and authority over all the affairs of the city, [it is not because you are armed or physically strongest or youngest,] but because of the strength of the laws. And what is the strength of the laws? Is it that when one of you is wronged and cries out for help, they will come running up and be there to help you? No. They are simply letters that have been written down (*grammata gegrammena*) and they could not do that. So what then is their power? You are, if you support them and make them authoritative every time someone asks you to. Thus, the laws are strong through you and you through the laws.[62]

Here too, Demosthenes does not question the authority of the laws but reminds the jurors that written texts are only authoritative with their help.

Just a few months earlier, Lycurgus had added another element to this view of the laws' authority (1.3–4):

> Three things are most important for preserving and protecting the democracy and the city's well-being: first, the system of the laws; second, the vote of the jurors; and third, the prosecution which puts crimes in their hands. The law exists to prescribe what must not be done, the prosecutor to reveal those who are subject to the penalties provided by the laws, and the jurors to punish those whom both of these have revealed to them. Thus, there is no force in either the law or the jurors' vote without a prosecutor who will put criminals in their hands.

Lycurgus was known as a religious reformer and a severe punisher of criminals,[63] and his view, that the prosecutor is as important as the jury and the laws, is well suited to this prosecution speech, though it would not be appropriate for Demosthenes' defense speech.

---

[61] But cf. below, n. 67. Like laws, decrees (which were not clearly distinguished from laws until the late fifth century) are usually assumed to be authoritative. But Aeschines disparages the value of written decrees in 3.182 (discussed above), and when a decree conflicted with a law, the law had greater authority.

[62] The point that written laws need the support of the jurors is also alluded to at the beginning of Demosthenes' plea "On the Crown" (18.6): "the laws, which Solon ... decided must draw their authority not only from their being written down (*tōi grapsai*) but also from the fact that those who are judging have sworn an oath."

[63] According to [Plutarch] *Moralia* 841e, he dipped his pen "not in ink but in death."

These examples should caution us not to be misled by Aristotle's advice about how a speaker should use the evidence of the laws (*Rhetoric* 1.15, 1375a26–34):

It is clear that if the written (*gegrammenos*) law is opposed to the facts (*pragma*), one must rely on the general law (*koinos nomos*) and what is more reasonable[64] and more just, and also that the expression "according to my best judgment"[65] means not relying entirely on written laws. Further, one should argue that reasonableness always remains the same and never changes, nor does the general law (for it is in accord with nature), but the written laws change often.

Aristotle then quotes Antigone's famous defense of unwritten laws (Sophocles, *Antigone* 454–5, see Chapter One).

Despite Aristotle's logical and persuasive advice about the use of laws in forensic pleading, we have no actual example of a litigant following this advice. No litigant ever suggests that written laws are opposed to what is reasonable or to the general law (which is largely synonymous with unwritten law), nor does anyone say that written laws change often, implying that they have less authority. On the contrary, when general or unwritten laws are mentioned, they either reinforce written rules (Dem. 18.275), or have authority (in matters of impiety) only in the absence of written laws (Lys. 6.10), or they work together with written laws, as when Demosthenes exclaims, "Is it not terrible, O Earth and Gods, and clearly against the law (*paranomon*), not only against the written law but also against the general law of all humans?" (23.61; cf. 23.70, 45.53). In other words, speakers never present unwritten law as in conflict with written law.[66] They may argue, as we have seen, that written laws by themselves are not enough but require clarification by the speaker, assistance from the prosecutor, and support from the jury, but they never suggest that written laws are not authoritative. In short, forensic litigants always accept the authority of written laws and regularly enlist it in support of their plea.[67]

---

[64] For the idea of "reasonableness" (*epieikes*, often translated "equity") and its relationship to written law, see *Rhetoric* 1.13; Meyer-Laurin 1965.

[65] In the oath that Athenian jurors swore at the beginning of each year, they pledged to judge according to the law but in the absence of a law to judge "according to the most just judgment" (*gnōmē tēi dikaiotatēi*).

[66] See Carey 1994, Thür 2000: 98–9; see above on the legal reforms in which the Athenians specifically prohibited the use of any unwritten law (Andoc. 1.85–9), by which they meant any statute not included in the republication of Athenian laws.

[67] Outside of forensic oratory, written laws may sometimes be criticized. In his *Areopagiticus* (7.39–41), for example, Isocrates argues that virtue makes written law unnecessary. One polis can borrow written laws from another, but this will not produce virtue among its citizens.

In sum, forensic orators express many different views about the validity of written documents, and actual use of such documents varied widely. In most cases, litigants had broad leeway in their pleadings to use or to ignore written documents, including laws, and except for laws, most documents could be, and were attacked almost as often as they were defended.[68] Some public documents like deme registers appear to be more easily manipulated and corrupted than others (Whitehead 1986: 104–9; Cohen 2003: 80–90); among private documents, wills are the most often challenged. However, most attacks on a written will or deme register or other document were probably matched by a defense of the same document by the opposing litigant. On the other hand, litigants who accept the validity of a will always add the same sorts of arguments as those advanced by litigants who deny the validity of a will about their devotion to the deceased and so forth, and the same is often true of litigants who draw support from other sorts of written documents. A litigant would rarely base his case entirely on written documents.[69]

There are differences, however, in the degree of acceptance of different written documents, with only written laws having an unquestioned authority in forensic discourse. This is surely in part because of their long history, beginning in the archaic period when laws were the only legal texts to be written. We may also speculate that because many of the jurors in court probably also attended the assembly when it voted to approve new legislation, they would not be sympathetic to a litigant who questioned the validity of these texts. And in their oath, the jurors swore to judge "according to the laws" – the only mention of written texts in the oath. Laws, in short, are in a class by themselves, except that contracts have a similar authority in maritime cases. Other written texts could be construed as having varying degrees of authority depending on the speaker's need. Thus, the basic duality in the use of writing in Greek law – broad use of writing for legislation but restricted use for litigation – is well reflected in the complexity of attitudes expressed toward writing and written documents in forensic oratory.

---

[68] The forensic speeches may give a misleading picture of the degree to which written texts were challenged in court, since when a document was not challenged, there may have been no litigation. In addition, litigants may not bother to mention a written document that has not been challenged.

[69] In general, because litigants have only one, or in some cases two, speeches in which to plead their case, they normally include every argument that might support their case in this speech, even if they feel especially confident about one argument.

CHAPTER 9

Writing Athenian Law: a Comparative Perspective

In Chapter Seven, we contrasted the use of writing in connection with law at Gortyn, where legislation was routinely written down and displayed in public, but writing had little or no presence in judicial procedure, with the very different use of writing in the laws of Hammurabi. Now that we have established a similar pattern in the use of writing in Athenian law, we can extend this contrast to two other premodern legal systems, early Roman law and early English common law. But first, let me extend the observations made in Chapter Eight about the use of writing to other features of Athenian law that are related to the ways in which writing was used.

As we have seen, from its very beginning in the late seventh century, Athenian legislation was written down and publicly displayed. Moreover, Draco and his successors strove to make the laws as accessible as possible to all members of the community who might wish to make use of them. In other words, Athenians always assumed that legislation was a matter of public interest and should be available to the public. Athenian law also displays from the beginning a reluctance to use writing for procedural matters or to insert writing into the traditionally oral trial process. This may at first sight appear to be a contrary tendency, but in fact it would have had a similar effect, and I suggest that it resulted from similar motivation: to make the legal process as open and accessible as possible to members of the community. In the archaic period writing began to be used in the administration of law, and in the classical period this use of writing increased, as litigants were required to provide written texts in connection with their litigation; but these procedural uses of writing had relatively little effect on the course of the trial, since evidence brought into court in written form was always communicated to the court orally by being read aloud, and was then interpreted and manipulated by the litigants in their oral pleadings using the same techniques used for their other arguments. The clear line Aristotle draws between (oral) artistic argument and (written) non-artistic evidence was considerably blurred in practice, and trials remained in essence oral competitions, as they had been from earliest times.

Limiting the role of writing in judicial procedure had several important results. First, it helped keep formalism out of Athenian law. An oral legal process can accommodate very simple formulae, but any substantial degree of formalism can only be enforced if rules and procedures are written. There is no evidence that Greek law was ever inclined toward formalism,[1] but by restricting the use of writing, the Athenians prevented any possibility of the law becoming more formal. Litigants remained free to present their arguments and proofs in court in any way they wished, using ordinary language familiar to the untrained jurors. Obscure or obsolete expressions are rare in forensic speeches and are normally explained to the jurors in ordinary language.

Another often noted feature of Athenian law is the restricted role of professionals, who tended in any case to be treated with suspicion by the Athenians.[2] For example, as we saw (Chapter Eight), although litigants may mention studying the laws, they usually claim to have been forced to do so by their opponent. If they had been studying the laws simply out of interest, they could be suspected of being a professional litigant, or *sykophantēs*. Among the quasi-professionals who came under suspicion were logographers, the speechwriters who wrote most of the pleadings that survive today. Logography was not a formal profession and logographers had no formal legal training or professional code of conduct. To the extent that they developed an expertise, it was skill in forensic pleading. With respect to law, logographers were amateurs, and when they declare an interpretation of a law, or of the lawgiver's intent, their opinions have no more authority than anyone else's, except to the extent that they can persuade a jury to accept their view. In no way were they legal professionals of the sort that exist in most of the world's other legal systems.

Besides the logographers, a group of religious authorities called the Exegetae (Expounders) could give opinions about legal matters that had a religious dimension, including homicide, but as we see in Demosthenes 47.71, their opinion is treated as advisory not authoritative. Indeed, the

---

[1] One might see a hint of formalism in the oath Menelaus proposes to Antilochus: "Put your hands on the horses and by the earth-embracing, earth-shaker swear you did not intentionally impede my chariot by trickery" (*Iliad* 23.584–5, above Chapter One). But the only formulaic elements in this are the epithets of Poseidon; the specific content of the proposed oath is not at all formulaic. Similarly, when an oath of denial is required at Gortyn, the place is specified, but not the content of the oath (*ICret* 4.72.3.7–9).

[2] Todd 1996 argues that distrust of experts in Athenian law (and in general) underlies the case against Nicomachus (Lys. 30).

Exegetae themselves seem to recognize that they are primarily religious advisers not legal authorities, since they ask the speaker who is consulting them if he wants them only to expound the law or also to advise him Dem. 47.68–70). When he responds that he wants both, they first simply paraphrase the provision in the homicide law concerning the preliminary step to be taken in a homicide case, with little or no elaboration: "First, if anyone is related to the woman, he is to carry a spear at the funeral and make a proclamation at the tomb and then guard the tomb for three days."[3] Next the Exegetae give him their advice which is much more extensive and which he decides to follows. Thus, the Exegetae know the laws concerning religious matters and give advice about them, but they do not provide authoritative interpretations of the law, and as far as we know, they have no expertise apart from religious matters.

Besides the logographers and Exegetae, numerous magistrates helped administer judicial proceedings from the initial accusation to the final verdict.[4] With the help of one or more clerks these magistrates would oversee a case from start to finish: they would receive and record the accusation, schedule preliminary hearings and then a trial date, oversee the random assignment of courts and jurors, and oversee the trial itself (including such tasks as tending to the water clock, reading the documentary evidence, and counting the votes). But none of these magistrates had any significant authority, and since they served only a one-year term, they would not have developed any special expertise. They could affect litigation by refusing to allow a case to proceed, but as far as we can tell from the two surviving examples, their authority in this regard was quite limited. In Antiphon 6, the first Basileus to whom the plaintiff brings his complaint refuses to accept the case, claiming there is not enough time left in his term of office. This ruling may or may not have been strictly mandated by the law (see Gagarin 2000a), and in any case, it only delays the trial for a few months. And in Lysias 13, the Eleven apparently refused to accept the plaintiff's accusation until he had inserted the phrase *ep'autophōrō* ("caught in the act") into the indictment (see further below), but when he agreed to do this, they allowed the case to go ahead, even though the added phrase patently misrepresented the facts. Thus, the only control these officials had over litigation was in the relatively minor administrative details and rules of

---

[3] Draco's law states that a homicide victim's relatives are to make a proclamation; we do not know whether the law in its original form or as later amended also mentioned carrying a spear and guarding the tomb.

[4] See the survey of the duties of various magistrates in *Ath. Pol.* 50–9, where the types of cases that came within the jurisdiction of each are listed.

procedure. Their task was to facilitate the proceedings, not make significant rulings.[5]

In the absence of any significant control by trained professionals, the Athenian legal process was in essence a contest (*agōn*) between litigants in front of a jury who decided the winner. A litigant had almost total freedom to present his case in whatever manner he wished. He was free to choose the procedure, the arguments, and the words he wished to use. He could bring whatever written texts he wanted to court, submitting them first at the arbitration hearing, and he could make whatever use he wished of them in his pleading. If he needed to introduce laws that were relevant to his case, these were readily available to be read by anyone who wished. And he could, if he wanted, do without written texts entirely, except in maritime cases, where he would need to present a written contract. His choices might or might not be effective, but as long as the procedure he chose was even remotely plausible, these choices would not be wrong in a technical or formal sense. A litigant may complain that his opponent has used the wrong procedure (as, e.g., in Antiphon 5), but no one could make an authoritative or conclusive decision on this matter except the jury, and it did not vote separately on such questions.[6] Thus, their decision about the correctness of the procedure used could only be expressed in their vote on the verdict, which would also be conditioned by many other considerations.

In this way, the restricted role given to written texts in Athenian trials had a similar effect as the abundant use of writing for recording and displaying substantive law, namely to help keep the legal process open and accessible to ordinary citizens. Even if most litigants were relatively wealthy and even if many of these received help from a logographer,[7] the system was fundamentally open to all. Thus the essentially oral nature of the legal process, like the abundant use of writing to display the texts of laws, facilitated use of the legal system by ordinary citizens.

---

[5] It is possible that there were professional judges at Gortyn, where we know of no other duties for the *dikastas*. The *dikastas* either gives a verdict directed by the law or decides the case on his own; neither task would require specialized training. Dreros 1, on the other hand, speaks of the *kosmos* judging cases.

[6] The procedure of *paragraphē* may be an exception, if the jury decided the purely procedural issue of whether the suit was admissible first; but this is not certain.

[7] We have no real evidence that either of these assumptions is true. The surviving speeches were all written by a logographer or a fairly experienced litigant for his own use, and most litigants in these speeches are relatively well off. But there are notable exceptions (e.g., Lysias 24), and we simply do not know how many litigants pleaded their case without the help of a logographer, whether because they could not afford one or for some other reason.

The widespread publication of laws that would be accessible to ordinary citizens also meant that laws were generally written in broad terms using common, everyday language. Most laws apparently designated an offense by means of an everyday term and provided little or no further precision about the exact nature of the offense. *Klopē* was theft, *asebeia* was impiety, and it was left to individual litigants and jurors, guided by common usage and understanding, to determine whether any specific conduct fell into this category.[8] As a result, there was considerable room for disagreement whether an act fell within the scope of a specific offense.[9] This feature of law is often called "open texture" (Hart 1994: esp. 128–36); all laws have it to a certain degree, but the "fringe of vagueness" (*ibid.* 123) possessed by all rules was considerably wider in Athenian laws than in most others. A more precise definition of the offense such as we might expect today might reduce this open texture (and would be welcomed by many modern scholars, who fiercely debate just what crimes like *asebeia* entailed), but it would not help most Athenian litigants. In fact, it would reduce their ability to argue that a wrong they had suffered was covered by the law. The limited use of writing for verdicts had a similar effect on the use of precedent in Athenian law. Since verdicts were not normally written, and since the reasons for a verdict were never formally stated, precedent in the strict sense (as in common law) was impossible. Athenian litigants do argue from precedent (Lanni 2004), but without written verdicts precedent necessarily has a more open texture than it does in common law (Hart 1994: 134–6).

In contrast to the brief, general designation of offenses, Athenian laws often devoted considerable space to the details of legal procedure. The law against *hybris* provides a good illustration of both features (Demosthenes 21.47):[10]

If anyone treats with *hybris* any person, either child or woman or man, free or slave, or does anything unlawful (*paranomon*) against any of these, let anyone who wishes, of those Athenians who are entitled, submit an indictment to the Thesmothetae. Let the Thesmothetae bring the case to the Eliaia within thirty days of the submission of the indictment, if no public business prevents it, or otherwise as soon as possible. Whoever the Eliaia finds guilty, let it immediately

---

[8] As we noted (above, Chapter Five), the indictment in a case would normally give further particulars about the alleged offense.

[9] For example, the defendant in Lysias 4.6–7 argues that his actions do not qualify as "intentional wounding."

[10] Most (but not all) scholars accept this text, that is preserved in our manuscripts of the speech, as authentic; see MacDowell 1990: 263–4.

assess whatever penalty it thinks right from him to suffer or pay. Of those who submit indictments according to the law, if anyone does not proceed, or after proceeding does not get one-fifth of the votes, let him pay one thousand drachmas to the public treasury. If he is assessed to pay money for his *hybris*, let him be imprisoned, if the *hybris* is against a free person, until he pays it. (translation MacDowell)

Here the substance of the offense is conveyed in the first sentence by "treat with *hybris*" and "do something unlawful." There is nothing in the law to indicate more precisely what kinds of behavior are designated by these expressions, or what constitutes an act of *hybris* (an issue modern scholars have debated for decades), but a prospective litigant would not have considered this a problem. Every Athenian had a general idea what *hybris* was and could judge for himself whether he thought someone had acted with *hybris*. As a prospective plaintiff, he would find as much substantive information in the law as he would need or could easily use. On the other hand, most plaintiffs would need to know the detailed information about the procedure the law provides in order to prosecute a case. Thus, the law does specify the magistrate to whom he should present his accusation, the time limit for bringing a case, and other procedural matters.

Unlike the substance of the offense, some of these procedural details are expressed in semi-technical language – "submit an indictment" (*graphesthai*), "introduce the case" (*eisagontōn*), "assess the penalty" (*timatō*), "prosecute" (*epexelthēi*). Some technical language is probably inevitable in any system that has developed a number of different procedures for litigation, since these procedures will at the very least require names. But despite the details, the wording of these procedural regulations is simple and clear, and for the most part the Athenians used terms for their legal procedures that are fairly obvious extensions of the ordinary meanings of words. For example, the word for introducing a case or bringing a suit is *eisagō*, which in ordinary language means "bring or lead in."[11] And even the more technical procedural terms are sometimes interpreted rather loosely by litigants.

Take, for example, the phrase *ep'autophōrō*, which roughly means "caught in the act" or "red handed" (E. Harris 1994). When relatives of a certain Dionysodorus wanted to prosecute Agoratus for his murder (Lysias 13), they

---

11 For more on the language of Athenian law, see Todd 2000. He does not explicitly discuss differences between procedural and substantive language, but the examples he cites (pp. 32–3) of "specialist vocabulary" are procedural terms.

could not use the normal homicide procedure (*dikē phonou*), because the amnesty agreement reached shortly after the fall of the Thirty a few years earlier had prohibited all prosecutions for homicide unless the accused had killed with his own hand, and Agoratus had not actually killed Dionysodorus but only informed against him (which led to his death). The relatives therefore decided to use a special procedure (*apagōgē*) normally used against common criminals (*kakourgoi*) such as thieves. But this procedure required that the accused be caught "in the act" (*ep' autophōrō*).[12] Since Agoratus was certainly not caught in the act of murder, the addition of this phrase would have made the accusation false, in a strict sense, and so the relatives did not originally include the expression in their accusation. But the officials overseeing the case (the Eleven) refused to allow the case to proceed without the inclusion of this expression. The prosecutor therefore added it, even though it was not strictly true, and the Eleven allowed the case to proceed.

The speaker confronts this issue toward the end of the speech (13.85–7), arguing that Agoratus was in effect committing an act of murder when he gave a deposition against Dionysodorus, but the weakness of this argument is transparent. We do not know the outcome of the case, but it is significant that the Eleven allowed the case to proceed, even though they must have known that Agoratus had not been caught *ep' autophōrō* in the normal sense of that term. The case illustrates the open texture of even semi-technical expressions in Athenian law, as well as the limited powers of magistrates to control litigation. Clearly, the Athenian legal system was more concerned to allow citizens access to litigation than to enforce strict procedural rules.

In short, Athenian laws were written for ordinary citizens, not for specialists, and were intended to help Athenians have their day in court without the intervention of a specialist. The non-specialist nature and ready accessibility of the texts of laws are one reason for the wide variety of arguments Athenian litigants present. For instance, although speakers sometimes use the text of a law, especially in *graphē paranomōn* cases, as we might today, as evidence that the act in question does or does not constitute a legal offense, they also use laws in many other ways – as evidence for the views of "the lawgiver" (i.e. Solon) regarding the proper education for a citizen (Aeschines 1), or to emphasize the seriousness of offenses other than those charged in the case (Demosthenes 54), or to illustrate the character of the speaker (Demosthenes 54) or his opponent (Aeschines 1), and more.

---

[12] For a thief, "caught in the act" appears to have meant "caught with the stolen goods" but not necessarily in the actual act of stealing them.

The transparency of the laws allowed litigants (and logographers) to draw on them with ease. Litigants may explain the purpose of a law and draw other sorts of conclusions from it, but only in special cases was there any need to clarify the language of the law. A rare example of this comes in Lysias 10, where the speaker argues that even though the law on slander prohibits the use only of certain designated words, it should be understood as also prohibiting words which mean the same thing.[13] To illustrate this point he quotes several "ancient laws of Solon" containing words that are currently obsolete and explains to the jurors what these words mean (10.15–19). But these words are clearly exceptional, and the speaker implies that their meaning would have been quite clear to people in Solon's day, even though two centuries later they had become obscure. Such exceptions aside, Athenian laws were written with the aim of being easy to read and understand.[14]

It is difficult to know whether the language of legislation at Gortyn and other Greek cities besides Athens was similarly non-technical, since we have very little separate evidence about the ordinary language of Greeks in these other cities. Thus, expressions that seem obscure or technical to us may have been common in ordinary speech. But to judge from the terminology used in the laws about the four different sexual offenses that are punished in the Gortyn Code (forcible intercourse, forcible domination, attempted intercourse, and adultery – 72.2.2–45, cited in Chapter Seven), offenses at Gortyn were not defined any more precisely than at Athens. Thus, the tradition of writing legislation and displaying it publicly that we have documented throughout the Greek world apparently resulted, at Gortyn at least, in the same sort of open texture as we find in Athens.

More difficult to determine is whether the relatively restricted use of written documents in the legal process that is characteristic of Athenian law also characterized law in other Greek cities in the archaic and classical periods. The evidence presented thus far, though limited, suggests that it did. As we have seen, there is no hint in the Gortyn laws that any written texts other than laws were used in litigation, and to the extent that the Gortyn Code provides evidence of judicial procedure, it appears litigation

---

[13] For example, the law prohibits calling someone a "murderer"; the speaker argues (10.6–7) that this should be understood as also prohibiting saying that someone "has killed."

[14] Demosthenes (20.93) notes this aspect of legislation, when he somewhat idealistically comments on the old process for enacting legislation (the Old Legislation Law, discussed in Chapter Eight). One step in this process involved the repeal of conflicting legislation, "so that there is only one law on each subject, and it does not confuse private persons and put them at a disadvantage compared with those who know all the laws. Instead, the same laws, simple and clear, will be available for all to read and understand."

at Gortyn resembled that of Athens, notably in the prominence of direct oral pleadings supported in many cases by the oral testimony of witnesses (Gagarin 2001). As the editors of *IJG* observed more than a century ago, legal procedure at Gortyn was "entièrement orale" (Dareste *et al.* 1891–1904: vol. I, 432).

The evidence from Gortyn is particularly important because Gortyn had an oligarchic form of government headed by a single *kosmos*, and the Gortyn Code regularly speaks of a single judge, the *dikastas*, deciding cases, in contrast to the democratic form of government and the large juries that judged most cases at Athens. And yet not only was the legal process at Gortyn thoroughly oral, it was in some respects even more open to all the city's inhabitants than the legal process at Athens, for the female citizens of Gortyn could themselves bring suits (as well as own property), and even slaves could give testimony and swear oaths. In one notable provision in the Code, a female slave's oath is even given preference over that of a free man in a case of rape (col. 2.13–16).[15] The evidence from Gortyn thus demonstrates that the combination of written legislation and oral judicial procedure was not specifically a consequence of Athens' democratic political system but must have resulted from other, more basic factors in Greek cites that affected their legal systems regardless of their form of government (see further Chapter Eleven). And the accessibility of law that resulted in part from this combination of written and oral elements in the law, was similarly independent of any specific form of government.

The evidence for legal procedure in other Greek cities during this period is more limited and widely scattered, but none of it is inconsistent with the conclusion that the same basic structure of written legislation and oral procedure characterizes all other Greek legal systems. We have already documented the widespread use of written legislation throughout Greece, and have observed that outside Athens there is no sign that writing was used in the archaic period for any legal texts other than laws. In the classical period the use of writing begins to increase in other cities, just as it does in Athens, but the evidence we have indicates that, like Athens, these cities too continued to keep writing out of litigation.

For example, a law from Erythrae from 465–452,[16] restricting the amount of interest that can be charged and providing a penalty and a procedure for punishing violations, directs the prytaneis to introduce

---

[15] The slave is said to be "more oath-worthy" (*horkioteran*), which is generally assumed to mean that her oath prevails against the testimony of her alleged attacker.

[16] *IvEr* 2 (= *Nomima* I.106, *IGT* 75), lines A 27–31.

the cases (*eisagein tas dikas*), write (them?) down (*syngraphein*) and have the name of the debtor written down (*graphesthai*). It is not clear what the prytaneis must first write down (verdicts?), but after this (presumably after a conviction), they must have the debtor's name inscribed, perhaps on a list of public debtors as at Athens. The only other mention of writing in this text is a directive to have this decree inscribed (*anagrapsai*) on a marble stele (lines B 1–7). Similarly a law from Thasos from 470–460[17] provides fines for certain activities that affect a public street, and also fines magistrates who do not collect these fines. The law then provides that "if the fine is not written down (*gegraptai*) for the offender, he shall not pay it (lines 13–14). Both these mid fifth-century laws confirm that writing was now being used for procedural matters, but in both cases, writing is used for the public inscription of the name of a debtor, just as it is in Athens, and not during the trial itself.

Other than these examples, the vast majority of fifth-century laws do not mention any writing other than the texts of laws, and in general inscriptions tend to confirm the picture obtained from Attic oratory, that the proceedings of the trial itself are entirely oral. For example, in connection with the issue of *mnēmones*, a law from Halicarnassus from 465–450[18] prescribes that for eighteen months the word of the *mnēmones* on ownership of property is decisive; after that the possessor can swear an oath and confirm his ownership. There is no mention of writing in this text until the very end, where reference is made to cases being brought according to what is written in the temple of Apollo, which presumably is a reference to a law inscribed there. This kind of reference to writing is typical. Thus, even though the use of writing for other purposes is increasing in the classical period, laws only rarely mention writing that does not refer to a written law.

As a final illustration, let us consider a Delphic law regulating interest rates for loans (the so-called "law of Kadys") from the early fourth century.[19] After a provision specifying the penalties for violations in column 1, columns 2 and 3 contain many provisions directing how one should proceed in case of violations, but nowhere is there any mention of a written loan agreement or any other written document. To be sure, the absence of any mention of writing here and in many other such laws with rules about procedure does not prove that written documents were not used in actual

---

[17] *SEG* 42.785 (translation in Arnaoutoglou 1998: 101–2).

[18] ML 32 (*Nomima* 1.19, *IGT* 84); we examined parts of this law in Chapter Five.

[19] *Fouilles de Delphes* 3(1), no. 294. The Greek text of columns 1–3 can be found in Homolle 1926: 14–16; the remaining columns are too fragmentary to give sense; columns 1 and 3 are also in Bogaert 1976: #41. For an English translation of columns 1–3, see Arnaoutoglou 1998: 46–7.

practice, but the silence strongly suggests that other Greek cities in the classical period resembled Athens in their slowness to use writing for legal texts other than laws, and in the largely oral nature of their legal procedure. In Chapter Ten we will examine other inscriptions from the Hellenistic period that lend additional support to the conclusion that despite the increasing use of writing in many areas of life, the trial remained essentially an oral process. For now, we can be certain about Athens and fairly confident in the case of most other cities, that in the classical period writing was used to record legislation and display it in public, and was also used in the administration of the law. But legal procedure otherwise remained largely oral, and written documents other than laws were of relatively little importance in most situations and were rarely required in court.

The extraordinary nature of this combination of written and oral elements in the law can only fully be appreciated by comparison with other premodern legal systems.[20] Many of these legal systems use both written texts and oral arguments, but nowhere else do we find the same combination of the two as we find in Greece. We have already noted (above, Chapter Seven) that Hammurabi's Code provides evidence of a very different use of writing – that written documents were used throughout the judicial process but legislation was not displayed in order to be accessible to ordinary people. It is also informative to compare Athenian law with the early history of two other premodern systems, early Roman law from the Twelve Tables through the early Republic, and English common law during its formative years. These two periods are especially interesting because both legal systems appear to have developed out of an earlier stage that was rather similar to early Greek law in its use of writing, but both then developed – in rather similar ways to one another[21] – into systems that were very different from Greek law. And as we will see, the differences between these two systems and Greek law can be traced in significant part to their use (and non-use) of written texts.

Roman law[22] undoubtedly existed in some form from the earliest days of the city, but like the Romans themselves, scholars regularly ascribe its

[20] For the term "premodern," see above, Introduction, n. 1.

[21] "The development of the Common Law in the Middle Ages is very similar to the development of Roman Law in many points" (Zweigert and Kötz 1998: 186).

[22] For this brief survey of early Roman law I have relied primarily on Schulz 1946 and Jolowicz and Nicholas 1972, and for the Twelve Tables, Crawford 1996; see also Crook 1995, E. A. Meyer 2004. I might note that Roberto Mangabeira Unger, often considered the father of the critical legal studies movement in the U.S.A., proposes a most interesting (though in my view fundamentally flawed) general analysis of law in society, in which the legal systems of Greece up to 500 and Rome during the Republic are distinguished from those everywhere else in the world (Unger 1976: 120–7).

beginning to a single act of legislation, the Twelve Tables.[23] This large collection of laws, traditionally dated to 450, was written down and publicly displayed. From all indications it, like the inscribed laws of the Greeks, was intended at least in part for practical use,[24] and there are reports during the next few centuries of other scattered pieces of legislation which also were probably put in writing and publicly displayed, though it is not clear how widely knowledge of these texts was disseminated.[25] In addition, the annual praetor's edict was an important source of law, and this must have been delivered in written form at a fairly early time. Another important source of law were the authoritative interpretations of legal issues that were handed down by the *pontifices* around the time of the Twelve Tables. This practice led to the issuing of *responsa* by the early jurists, and these may have been put in writing as early as 300 (cf. E. A. Meyer 2004: 37–8).

As at Athens, the judicial process at the time of the Twelve Tables appears to have been entirely oral.[26] It also seems to have depended on the private initiative of litigants, as in Greece. Thus, it is possible that procedure at Rome in the fifth century resembled early Greek procedure. But it also appears that some degree of formalism established itself in Roman procedure at an early date, perhaps as early as the Twelve Tables (or earlier), and this may have been one of the factors that would soon impel Roman law to take a very different path from Greek law.[27]

In any case, at some fairly early date, in order to bring an action, during the first phase of the suit which took place before the Praetor, a Roman litigant was required to specify the precise procedure or form of action (*legis*

---

[23] Later Roman writers regularly connect the Twelve Tables with Greek legislation, often telling of an embassy sent to study the laws of Solon. Dyck 2004: 402–3 gives a brief summary of differing views on the historicity of this tradition.

[24] "The purpose of inscription in public was no doubt in part practical, in (perhaps larger) part symbolic, to demonstrate that the statute in question was in the public domain" (Crawford 1996: 32). As we have seen, the same dual propose can be ascribed to Greek legal inscriptions.

[25] Crawford 1996: 27–34 argues that "knowledge of the content, wording and characteristic style of Roman statutes was diffused outside the Roman elite" (27), but these laws may not have been as widely known as Greek statutes.

[26] The Twelve Tables may have mentioned a will (*testamentum*, V. 6; cf. V. 3, with Crawford 1996: 639), but if so, this would not have been a written document at this time. In certain cases it is explicitly said that an oral statement is valid; e.g., VI. 1: *Cum faciet nexum mancipiumque, uti lungua nuncupassit, ita ius esto.* ("When he shall perform *nexum* and *mancipium*, as his tongue has pronounced, so is there to be a source of rights.")

[27] "The most immediately noticeable feature of archaic Roman jurisprudence is what we call its actional formalism, by which we mean its tendency to endow every act in law with a definite form" (Schulz 1946: 24–5). "Actional formalism" refers more specifically to the system of *actiones* (see below). Already in the Twelve Tables, VI. 1 (cited in the preceding note) seems to suggest that certain specific words had to be spoken in order to establish *ius*.

actio) to which his case belonged.[28] A litigant had to make his complaint conform strictly to one of the few allowable *actiones*, and a single wrong word could invalidate his case. Such strict formalism could not be enforced without writing, and it appears that the *actiones* were put in writing at an early date. A collection of *actiones* was said to have been published around 300 by Gnaeus Flavius, and they were probably available to the magistrates in writing earlier than this. Later, with the development of the formulary system in the third and second centuries, writing became even more central to the judicial process. At first, the formulary, which was a magistrate's statement of the precise issue to be decided by the judge (*iudex*), may have been simple enough to be issued orally and then remembered during the trial, but as formularies became longer and more complex, they would have had to be written down in addition to being spoken. Verdicts too were issued orally at first but at some point written texts of these began to be collected for use by jurists.

Thus, by Cicero's time, although the amount of written legislation was smaller than in classical Athens (legislation being a less important source of law in Rome) other written texts – *responsa, legis actiones*, and formularies – played a large role in the Roman judicial process. And with the *actiones* and formularies, writing was put at the heart of that process. All these written texts, moreover, were prepared by jurists and magistrates, and most of them were not widely circulated (and were certainly not displayed in public) but were kept for the use of these officials and a few others. Precise cause and effect are difficult to determine, but there was clearly a close connection between the increasing use of writing in the legal process, the growth in size and importance of the legal profession, and the increasingly technical nature of Roman law. Non-professionals, such as the judge and the advocate, retained a role but their importance seems to have diminished as the role of professionals grew larger. Over time legal expertise was increasingly confined to a small group of specialists, and Roman law became more and more a scholar's law.

Equally, if not more illuminating as a comparandum for Greek law is the development of English common law in the period from (roughly) the Norman Conquest in 1066 to the death of Edward I in 1307.[29] Before the Conquest, law in England was almost entirely a matter of local courts deciding cases according to local customs and traditions. Writing played

---

[28] For a good summary of the two-stage legal process in the early Republic, first before the Praetor, then before a judge (*iudex*), see Stein 1984: 27–30. On forms of action see Jolowicz and Nicholas 1972: 175–90.

[29] Baker 1990 provides a good, standard history of this period.

almost no role in these.[30] The king's court did make use of written documents, but its authority was not strong, and although it traveled around the
country hearing cases, its role in legal matters was very limited. After the
Conquest, however, as the Norman kings solidified their power over local
districts and the feudal system gradually disappeared from England, the
king's law began to spread under the guise of "the common law," though in
fact, this law was only common in the sense that the king's law overrode
and eradicated the customs of different communities. The common law
was particularly suited to serving the needs of the landowning class, which
responded by making more and more use of it, and by the death of
Edward I, the common law had almost completely replaced local courts.

The change from local law to common law was in part a change from
oral law to written law. The Norman monarchy's determination to expand
its hold over the whole of England required that it make more use of
writing in the administration of the kingdom. One of the earliest and most
important indications of this is the Domesday Book, a written record of the
state of England in 1086, which William the Conqueror requested for the
purpose of taxation. Based as it was on material gathered in oral inquests
throughout the land, the Domesday Book epitomizes the transition from
local, oral administration to a national, written administration. Fleming's
analysis of the proceedings at an inquest in 1086 reveals that it is not
dissimilar to judicial procedure in Homeric times. But as he makes clear,
recording these proceedings in writing brought about a fundamental transformation in the process.

Oral legal culture, by its very nature, is noisy, heterodox, and confusing; it
contains many points of view. But it is also public spectacle, and as such it
ritualized the whole process of the Norman settlement, and it informed all of
whose who upheld law, whether in villages, boroughs, or shires, about the
permanence of England's tenurial transformation ... When the stories of the
inquest, however, were transformed into text and retold in the Domesday Book,
they were given a single, monolithic voice. The writing of Domesday Book transformed the enterprise of the inquest from a communal event that took place
across the whole of England into a private record. The voice of the Domesday
Book, unlike the voices of the inquest, is that of royal administration: it is
organized, authoritative, and rational.[31]

---

[30] As we noted in Chapter Seven, the collections of written laws issued by Anglo-Saxon kings such as
Alfred played very little role in actual legal affairs.

[31] Fleming 1998: 35. His whole chapter on "The Inquest and the Mechanics of Justice" (11–35) is
important for the use of writing at this time. For a detailed study of the transition from oral to
written procedures, see Clanchy 1993.

Written texts like the Domesday Book were thus essential tools by which the monarchy imposed its rule on the whole of England.

During this period royal control also changed the nature of legal procedure by means of writing. Historically, legislation has been of relatively little importance in common law, in part because common law, at least in theory, was rooted in the customs and traditions of the people of England. Thus, although a few decrees and proclamations issued in writing set out important general rules of law (most famously, of course, the Magna Carta of 1215), during the twelfth and thirteenth centuries the total number of written laws remained quite small. Rules of law were normally determined not by legislation but by the decisions of courts, which at first were simply remembered, but gradually came to be preserved in written court records. Litigation was thus of greater importance in common law than legislation, and it is here that the impact of writing on the procedure had its most dramatic effect.

The transformation came about primarily through the use of writs, which by the end of the thirteenth century had become the basis of all litigation.[32] As the name indicates, a writ is a written document that originally conveyed an order from the king to a local assembly, court, or individual. Before the Conquest writs were used primarily for administrative needs, but under the Norman kings the judicial writ proliferated.[33] The judicial writ was an order from the king commanding a person to appear in his court to answer a complaint, or commanding a royal magistrate, such as a sheriff, to take action on a complaint. In order to initiate, or have a sheriff initiate litigation in the king's court – that is, under common law – an individual had to have the king order the court to act – that is, he had to obtain a writ. Originally, the king had issued an oral directive (through his agents) to the court, but after the Conquest, judicial writs replaced oral

---

[32] "The common law of England is a monument to a brilliant time in western Europe rather than to any single individual ... or to any exclusive national characteristics ... And the law became a monument because it used writing, in the form of Latin writs, as its special instrument" (Clanchy 1998: 112). Cf. Baker 1990: 201, who notes that the author of *Glanville* (1187–9) decided to "concentrate on writs rather than on legislative decrees." The similarity of writs and Roman *actiones* is noted by Zweigert and Kötz 1998: 186, Versteeg 2002: 287.

[33] "Clearly, the [Anglo-Saxon] king interfered in the legal life of local courts from time to time. But our evidence suggests that it was not actually until after the Conquest that writs were *regularly* issued by the king mandating that assemblies remedy particular disputes; and it was not until the Conqueror's reign and after that writs which are wholly judicial come to be preserved in monastic archives. This proliferation of judicial writs marks the Conqueror's and his sons' increasing intrusion into the judicial business of local communities in decades following the Conquest" (Fleming 1998: 30–1, emphasis in the original).

commands,[34] and soon these were being issued by the Chancery in the king's name without his direct involvement. As time went on, the forms of writs were standardized, and the Chancery issued them for a fee upon request, provided the request followed the proper form. The writ then constituted an order to the accused to answer the charge in court. The main difficulty in bringing a suit in common law lay in selecting the writ that was right for the situation the litigant faced; as Baker observes (1990: 66) "the choice of original writ governed the whole course of litigation from beginning to end and the plaintiff selected the most appropriate writ at his peril."[35]

The twelfth century saw the increasing use of judicial writs by ordinary landholders, and by the end of Edward I's reign, the writ had become the heart of the English judicial process. At first, as with the *legis actiones* in Rome, there were only a few kinds of writs, and to be successful a plaintiff had to follow the exact wording of one of the established forms (such as a writ of trespass). Unlike Roman law, however, where the number of *actiones* remained small but the use of each was constantly expanded to cover many different situations, in England the number of different writs increased rapidly. The result, however, was the same: the common law became ever more complex and technical and the legal profession grew rapidly. An ordinary Englishman, even if he could read and write, and even if he knew the language of writs (at first Latin, then often an archaic form of French known as "law French"), could not determine with any assurance which specific writ was most appropriate for the damage or injury he had suffered. He needed the assistance of a professional. As in Rome, therefore, the growth of writing within the judicial process helped make the law increasingly complex and technical, and stimulated the resulting growth of the legal profession.

In Athens, by contrast, even though writing was used to inscribe and publish a very large number of laws and decrees, it never infiltrated the heart of the legal process to the extent that it controlled litigation. An

---

[34] Clanchy (1998: 107–9) describes the effects of the change from the requirement that a person wanting to use the court have "an order from the king" to "have a writ from the king" (both versions are in Glanville). Most notable was an enormous expansion of the royal presence in litigation throughout the country.

[35] Choosing the correct writ is still important in common law in the U.S.A., as can be seen in a recent newspaper article headlined "Wrong writ spurs both sides to action in campaign ad inquiry" (*Austin American-Statesman* for 20 June 2003, p. B7). It seems that in appealing a court's decision, a lawyer had filed the wrong kind of writ on behalf of his clients – a writ of habeas corpus instead of the writ of mandamus that was required – and the appeal was therefore rejected.

ordinary citizen with a complaint was always able to present his own plea orally in whatever words he chose. He never had to prepare a written text, though if he wished, he could make use of written documents, which for the most part were brief and written in non-technical language. But if he did, then these written texts would be read aloud to the jurors, and their significance for the case would be explained by the litigant in his own words. A litigant had to make the initial choice of a charge and a procedure, but the existing categories were extremely flexible, and in many cases any one of several different procedures was acceptable. If he needed to consult a law, he would find that it was written in language that was generally non-technical and relatively easy for ordinary citizens to comprehend. The litigant had no need for legal experts, and so there were none. Any litigant, moreover, with or without the help of a logographer, could give a legal opinion, or could pose as an expert on the meaning of a law or the intentions of the lawgiver, as Demosthenes is especially fond of doing. But a litigant's opinion had no legal authority except to the extent that the jury could be persuaded to agree with it. Thus, to the end of the classical period the legal process remained fundamentally oral – and therefore non-technical, non-professional and rhetorical.

In assessing the use of writing in Athenian law, then, the important factor is not the total quantity of writing in the system, but the fact that it was used primarily for legislation and for the most part remained outside the central legal process. Thus, writing in Athens had both a powerful presence in legislation and a corresponding absence in procedure. Written laws brought order and predictability to the previously existing legal process, and provided a fixed, stable framework within which litigants could negotiate their way in their oral pleadings in court; the absence of writing from the legal process, on the other hand, allowed for a large degree of flexibility within this framework. Written laws made the city's legislation directly available to the people, who could make use of the laws without assistance; and the absence of writing from the legal process similarly worked to ensure that litigants could manage their own litigation and ordinary citizens could judge their cases, without the need for legal professionals, who in most other legal systems form a barrier between the law and ordinary people.

Thus, the presence of writing and the absence of writing worked together to produce a legal system with more structure and order than the dispute-settlement processes of traditional tribal societies that function without writing, yet at the same time allowed ordinary citizens direct access to litigation such as almost never occurs once a society injects writing into the legal process.[36] The discourse of modern legal systems is a private, specialized, technical language, authorized and controlled by a small group of professionals, who effectively prevent access by those outside their profession. The discourse of Athenian law, on the other hand, was largely the language of the people, authorized, controlled and practiced by ordinary citizens, but within the structure provided by a large set of written rules.

These unusual, in fact unique, features of Greek law call into question some of the conclusions scholars have drawn regarding the impact of writing on law.[37] We have already noted (Chapter Four) Goody's conclusion that the process of putting laws in writing was a process of generalization (1986: 166), and have shown that this must be substantially modified in order to accommodate the preserved text of Draco's law. Also requiring modification is the hegemonic view of writing law, that writing was used in many societies, including the non-Greek societies we have used for comparison (Babylonia, Rome, and England), to facilitate the unified administration of large territories and the exercise of authority over large and often diverse populations, in part through the manipulation of law. In these societies writing became a tool for controlling access to the law.[38] As Clanchy (1985, 1993) argues, among the ways in which the use of writing transformed law in medieval Europe, "writing made lawcourts into closed schoolrooms instead of open meeting places."[39]

In many respects the Greeks do not fit this picture. Between the end of the Bronze Age and the conquests of Philip and Alexander, no Greek community ever exercised direct authority over the kind of large, unified territory that characterizes the other nations we have examined, and even in the Hellenistic period traditional Greek cities maintained a considerable degree of autonomy in their legal affairs and did not control or administer significantly larger territories. Thus, Greek law shows that the introduction of writing does not have a single effect but can be used for different effects

---

[36] Nader 2002: 14–16 and *passim* stresses the vital importance of access to the law, noting that many of the societies studied by anthropologists allow easier access than modern legal systems, and lamenting in particular recent trends in the U.S.A. to restrict access to law.

[37] R. Thomas (1992: 15–28) presents a good survey of different views of and approaches to the effects of writing on societies, with references to earlier scholarship.

[38] For this common view, see e.g. W. Harris 1989: 38–40.

[39] Clanchy 1985: 29. Clanchy also notes that writing creates standardization (see above, Chapter 4), but this does not mean that it "level[ed] to some extent the social differences that had dominated considerations of justice since feudal times," as Olsen 1994: 188 credits the use of writs with "Leveling to some extent the social differences that had dominated considerations of justice since feudal times," but access to the law now required professional help, and this cost money.

by different societies. The Greeks were unique, as far as I know, in using writing to make law a popular, communal institution, open to participation by a large segment of the community rather than as a means of imposing autocratic rule on the community. Whether a city's government (*politeia*) was democratic or oligarchic, as in Athens or Gortyn respectively, law remained in the hand's of the people to a degree unparalleled in other literate societies.

CHAPTER 10

Writing Law in Hellenistic Greece

Classical Athenian law is often seen as the high point in Greek legal history, but the story does not end there, and for the sake of completeness, I will briefly look at law in the Hellenistic world.[1] The conquests of Philip and Alexander at the end of the fourth century changed the Greek world in important ways, but in many respects life in Greek cities remained unchanged. Although no longer in control of their relations with other cities or completely free to determine their own leaders (who now needed the support of Macedonian rulers more than of the *dēmos*), these cities continued to regulate their internal affairs, and it appears that private law,[2] at least, continued more or less unchanged in Athens and other Greek cities.

At the same time, Alexander's conquests included many areas that were not previously Greek, in most of which he encouraged Greeks (often his own mercenary soldiers) to settle and even founded new Greek cities. These Greek settlers coexisted with the native inhabitants and often with settlers from other countries, creating new communities which did not have a history of traditional Greek institutions. These new settlers usually came from several different Greek cities, so that except in the most general ways, they lacked a common legal heritage. Given these very different circumstances, it is not surprising that the legal systems in these newly Greek cities and territories differed from those of long established Greek cities. For this reason, for the Hellenistic period I will look separately, first at law in Athens and other traditional Greek cities and then at law in Ptolemaic Egypt, the one newly Greek area about which we are fairly well informed.

---

[1] For a good comprehensive treatment of the Hellenistic world, see Walbank and Astin 1984. The period ends with the conquest of Greece by Rome, which for convenience is often dated to the defeat of Corinth in 146, though in fact it took place over many decades, and not until 30 BCE in Egypt.

[2] I use the terms "public" and "private" here in a non-technical sense. Although the Greeks often distinguished generally between public and private matters, they never created the official categories of Public law and Private law, that we find in Roman law.

Most of our evidence for law in the Hellenistic Greek cities comes from inscriptions, which were written in many different cities over the course of several centuries. No survey, no matter how thorough, can give a complete picture, and the following discussion will be very selective. Few of the sources, moreover, are strictly speaking laws, or even legal documents.[3] But other sorts of documents, such as honorary decrees, provide a fair amount of evidence for law. These texts tend to show not only a continuity from the classical to the Hellenistic period but also a general similarity among Greek cities in these periods, at least with respect to writing law. Much of the evidence pertains to procedure in general, but we will concentrate on texts that refer specifically to the use or non-use of writing.

Athens provides the best evidence for the continuity especially of private law, at least for the first decades of the Hellenistic period.[4] Although certain areas of public law changed significantly, in part because success in public litigation no longer translated into political success, characteristically democratic procedures like *eisangelia* and *graphē paranomōn*, continued to be used, and the large popular courts underwent little change.[5] This allowed a logographer like Dinarchus to continue his lucrative career writing speeches for other litigants until 307, when he left Athens and settled in Corinth, continuing to write speeches until at least 292 (Dionysius of Halicarnassus, *Dinarchus* 2). The preserved titles of Dinarchus' speeches from this period (*ibid.* 10–12) indicate that they are all private cases (damages, assault, inheritance, and other matters). Because no speech from this period survives, we know next to nothing about the use of writing in the legal process in Hellenistic Athens, but the general continuity in private law suggests that the classical combination of written and oral elements persisted, although the use of written documents probably increased.

A similar continuity seems to have characterized law in other Greek cities (Rhodes-Lewis 1997: 473–563). For the most part cities maintained

---

[3] There is no modern collection of Hellenistic legal inscriptions but Dareste, *et al.* 1891–1904 (*IJG*) contains a number of Hellenistic texts; Thür and Taeuber 1994 (*IPArk*) is also useful.

[4] The best historical account of Hellenistic Athens is Habicht 1997. Thür 2001 examines the evidence for private law in new comedy and sees only a subtle change from the classical period; see also Rhodes-Lewis 1997: 9–61, Gagarin 2000b. The few documents from the Hellenistic period in Boegehold 1995 generally reveal features of legal procedure that are familiar from the classical period (e.g., nos. 318, 320, 329, 342a).

[5] When Tarn and Griffith conclude (1952: 88–91) that Hellenistic law was a welcome change from "the old system," which "was about the worst legal system ever invented," they are contrasting classical Athenian juries with later situations in which a small group of visiting judges heard cases, but this practice was exceptional and temporary and is not attested for Athens.

their traditional forms of constitutional government, including a council and an assembly, and most cities which previously had democratic governments seem to have preserved these.[6] Laws and decrees continued to be routinely written down and publicly displayed in virtually all Greek cities. Institutions like the family and citizenship remained largely unchanged, and traditional features of legal procedure, such as the volunteer prosecutor, remained part of the legal systems of many, if not all, poleis in the Hellenistic period (Rubinstein 2003). Another indication of the similarity among Hellenistic legal systems is the frequent importation of judges from other cities. This practice suggests that the legal systems of different Hellenistic cities shared common features, and the judges themselves may have contributed to an increasing homogeneity of Hellenistic law, especially in the Greek cities of the Eastern Aegean and the coast of Asia Minor, where the use of foreign judges is documented from the end of the fourth century.[7]

Other factors, such as the migration of Greeks among cities also worked to make legal systems in different parts of the empire more similar. The expansion of trade would also have increased communication among cities and regions, and this may especially have affected commercial law. Laws affecting maritime commerce in particular became increasingly important, culminating in the Rhodian Sea Law which probably originated in the Hellenistic period and remained the world-wide standard for centuries (Ashburner 1909). One result of increased social and economic intercourse in this period was the development of the common Greek dialect *koinē*, spoken by Greeks and the non-Greek elite throughout the empire. By analogy, scholars sometimes speak of a "legal *koinē*" in the Hellenistic world, though this may imply more unity than actually existed. But a general trend toward such a unity is evident, and just as *koinē* Greek was derived from the Attic dialect with slight modifications, to the extent that there was a legal *koinē*, it may have been derived largely from Athenian law.

One indication of Athenian influence is a partially preserved maritime contract from the second century, probably drawn up in Egypt, which appears to be a direct descendant of the type of maritime contract used in fourth-century Athens.[8] Second, Rubinstein has documented the

---

[6] See Crowther 1992 for arguments against the traditional view that democracy declined through the Hellenistic period; also Rhodes-Lewis 1997: 531–6.

[7] Robert 1973 remains the best comprehensive treatment of this institution; he sees the work of these judges leading to an "adaptation et uniformisation des droits des cités" (1973: 778).

[8] *SB* III 7169, Vélissaropoulos 1980: 356–7, no. 21; on the question of continuity see *ibid.* 308–11. The contract concerns a trading journey to the area of Somalia, but the traders named in it come from different parts of the Greek world. Vélissaropoulos concludes (311) that the contract is a direct descendant of the contract in Demosthenes 35.10–13.

institution of the volunteer prosecutor in dozens of different cities, though this person is not always referred to as *ho boulomenos*, as he is in Athens.[9] Prosecution by whoever wished was first instituted in Athenian law by Solon in the early sixth century (*Ath. Pol.* 9.1, above, Chapter Five), and the practice was a characteristic feature of Athenian law. We cannot be certain that the Athenian practice directly influenced other cities, where the earliest evidence for the practice is from the early fifth century, but this seems likely.

Third, second-century decrees reveal that the *graphē paranomōn* procedure was used in Demetrias (*SEG* 24 395, lines 11–12), and that cases of *paranomōn* and *biaiōn* (violence) were tried in Alexandria Troas (*I Priene* 44, lines 17–18). It can hardly be a coincidence that both these Hellenistic cities, one in Thessaly and one on the coast of Asia Minor, employed a legal procedure, *graphē paranomōn*, that probably originated in Athens in the late fifth century, and which became one of the most prominent features of the Athenian legal and political system in the fourth century. Finally, other procedures similar to those in Athens, are also found in Hellenistic inscriptions (Robert 1973), including *mēnusis* (informing), *euthynai* (the examination of a magistrate's accounts after he finishes his term in office), and *paragraphē* (an objection by the defendant that the case should not have been brought for specific reasons). Even if all these procedures developed independently and not under Athenian influence, the important point is that many of the same procedural features are found in the laws of different cities throughout the Greek world from the fifth to the second centuries and beyond.[10]

What, then, about the use of writing in law? Do we find common features in this regard in the Hellenistic period? Certainly laws and decrees continued to be inscribed and publicly displayed in large numbers in Greek cities, just as in the classical period. For example, the thirty five inscriptions from Arcadia in *IPArk* are evenly distributed over the fifth through first centuries BCE (with one from the first century CE). In Athens, we know that Demetrius Poliorcetes, who controlled the city in the years after Demetrius of Phalerum's downfall in 307, oversaw the revision of laws in Athens, and a decree reveals that at least some of these new laws were published in 304/3,[11] though we do not know if the project was ever

[9] Rubinstein 2003. The number of cities with volunteer prosecutors is said in this article to be forty-six, but Rubinstein now reports (personal communication) that the number is up to eighty-two. It will undoubtedly grow larger.

[10] The issue of unity is more difficult to assess with regard to substantive law; see Gagarin 2005.

[11] In that year Euchares is praised for "attending to the inscription of the laws, so that all those that had been approved by the Nomothetai would be publicly displayed for anyone who wished to see and that no one would not know the laws of the city" (*IG* 11² 487, lines 5–10).

completed. And legal inscriptions are preserved from many other cities throughout this period (Rhodes-Lewis 1997).

With respect to the use (or non-use) of writing in procedure, widely scattered evidence indicates that here too there was a considerable degree of continuity. For example, a treaty between Stymphalos and Demetrias (*IPArk* 17 = *IG* V 2, lines 43–6, dated to 303–300), imposes similar requirements on the use of written documents as in fourth-century Athens: litigants are required to "bring to the court all the witness depositions written down and all the contracts written down and deposit them in the jars (?)[12] until the court meets and decides the case; and if any litigants do not bring witness depositions that they have written down to the Synlytai, they are not to use in court any witness depositions other than those that have been disclosed to the Synlytai." These regulations suggest that at least one of these two cities already had a requirement for the preliminary deposit of written documents that was nearly identical to the Athenian requirement. On the other hand, another provision of this treaty (lines 31–3) requires the judges to write down verdicts, perhaps on a tablet (*deltos*) together with the names of all those who were selected to judge the case, a practice not attested in Athens.

A late-fourth-century law from Thasos[13] prohibits two procedures – denunciation (*endeixis*) and summary arrest (*apagōgē*) – from taking place during certain religious festivals or "on those days on which the arbitrators present the opposing oaths (*antōmosiai*),[14] and receive witness depositions (*martyriai*) and evidentiary documents (*dikaiōmata*), and hold the preliminary hearings of cases." From other inscriptions we know that Thasos had other legal procedures that are found in classical Athenian law, including *phasis* and the use of volunteer prosecutors;[15] here we learn of two other procedures well known from Athenian law, *endeixis* and *apagōgē*,[16] together with public arbitrators, who gather some of the same written documents as in Athenian arbitration hearings.[17] There are differences

---

[12] The editors supply *echinoi* ("jars") to partially fill a gap in the text; even if this is wrong, a container of some sort was specified.

[13] *SEG* 17.415, first published by Salviat (1958). For legal aspects of the text see esp. Salviat 1958: 202–12. For a similar prohibition of legal activity during a festival, cf. *IK Lampsacus* 9 (second century).

[14] The text here suggests that the opposing oaths were put in writing and were detailed enough to serve as the basic statement of each party's case (Salviat 1958: 207). For the citation of written *antōmosiai* in Athenian litigation, see, e.g., Isaeus 3.7.

[15] Salviat 1958: 202–3 with 203 nn. 1–5, and for volunteer prosecutors Rubinstein 2003, esp. 96–8.

[16] The fundamental study of these procedures, which can be considered two phases of the same procedure, is Hansen 1976.

[17] On the arbitrators, see Salviat 1958: 206–9. *Dikaiōmata* ("documents") is not used in this sense at Athens, but the term would certainly include other types of documents in addition to *martyriai* and *antōmosiai* that we know from Athenian cases (Salviat 1958: 208).

from Athenian procedure, such as the greater reliance on officials for the enforcement of law at Thasos; but several of the basic uses of writing in procedure, including the gathering of written documents during the preliminary arbitration hearing, closely resemble Athenian practice.

Similarly, an arbitration decision rendered by a group of 204 citizens from Cnidus in favor of Calymna against Cos in the early third century specifies uses of written documents in ways that closely resemble Athenian procedures.[18] It directs that all the decrees, challenges, and other documents needed for the hearing are to be brought from the two cities under seal and all these written texts (*grammata*) will be given first to the generals, who (after unsealing them) will give them to the two litigants, who will also deposit witness depositions with the court before their pleadings (A 33–9). It next specifies the time allowed to each speaker (39–43), and then addresses the use of these written documents: "The decrees and the challenges and the written indictment in the case (*tan graphan tas dikas*) and anything else that has been brought from the public record are to be read out by whichever clerk (*grammateus*) each side may provide, and also the witness depositions, with the water stopped" (43–5). There follows a provision requiring witnesses to be present in court if they can; otherwise, they are allowed to testify in their own city and their depositions will be sealed and copies (*anagrapha*) given to each litigant (45–65).

Here too, the procedures differ in some respects from Athenian procedure: each party, for instance, appears to have his own clerk read out his documents. But in general the use of written documents is strikingly similar to their use in Athenian procedure. And if we take this text together with those from Arcadia and Thasos discussed above, it becomes clear that the Athenian practice of collecting the written documents before the trial, sealing them up, and then having them read out loud by a clerk was a common feature of the legal systems of Greek cities in the early Hellenistic period. These inscriptions also indicate that writing was being used in other ways than we find at Athens, such as for recording verdicts or the testimony of witnesses who could not be present in court, but in none of these cases does writing intrude into the trial itself except in the form of oral reading, just as in Athens.

Another area of law in which the use of writing expanded considerably in the Hellenistic Greek cities was the public documentation of manumissions. The largest number of these documents record sacred manumissions, which took the form of a legal fiction, in which the owner either sells

---

[18] Magnetto 1997: no. 14 (= *IJG* 1.158–78, Ager 1996: no. 21).

or consecrates his or her slave to a god, leaving the slave free of the master's control, although some of the documents subject this freedom to conditions. The highest concentration of manumission-by-sale inscriptions is at Delphi, where more than 1,000 survive, from about 200 BCE to 100 CE.[19] We also have private manumissions which the owner, or perhaps the freed slave himself, recorded in a public inscription; these include a rather strange group of Athenian inscriptions from the end of the classical period which record the dedication of silver bowls (*phialai*) by former slaves in celebration of their manumission.[20]

One of the reasons for writing and displaying all these manumission texts must have been to protect the freed slave against possible future seizure by publicizing his new status. We know that the practice of manumission was much older than the Hellenistic period, and the forms of manumission seem to have undergone little change. However, these transactions were rarely inscribed and publicly displayed before the Hellenistic period, perhaps because in the classical period cities were more homogenous and a freed slave would more likely be known in the community. But the writing and public display of these texts would be necessary in the more diverse Hellenistic cities, to protect the freed slave from being subject to future claims of ownership. Or this may simply reflect the increased use of writing in general in the Hellenistic period.

In sum, the Hellenistic Greek cities maintained a large degree of continuity in their legal affairs, despite the limits imposed by the new royal authorities. Basic political institutions characteristic of the traditional polis form of government, including law courts still staffed by ordinary jurors in Athens, continued to exist in much the same forms as before. When new laws were enacted, they were publicly displayed, as before, and the substance of private law, at least, appears to have remained fairly stable. The amount of writing steadily increased, both in life in general and in legal matters, but writing continued to be used in legal procedure in much the same way as in the classical period – for administration and for documentation, which was then presented orally in court. New uses of writing are evident, such as the recording of verdicts and the public display of texts confirming private manumissions, but these did not change the trial itself, which remained fundamentally oral. In short, in the traditional Greek

---

[19] See Darmezin 1999; also Hopkins 1978: 133–71 (written in collaboration with P. J. Roscoe). There are also six public manumission inscriptions at Gortyn (*ICret* 4.231–6).

[20] See Lewis 1959, and the brief remarks of Todd 1993: 191–2.

cities, the same combination of written legislation and oral litigation characterized law in the Hellenistic period as in earlier times.

Things were different in those parts of Alexander's empire that were not originally Greek, including Egypt and the newly conquered regions of Asia. Given the scarcity of evidence for other parts of the empire, my discussion will be confined to Egypt, where our primary source for law (and for other aspects of life) is the large body of papyrus documents that have emerged from the sands in modern times, written not only in Greek but in Egyptian demotic and occasionally in other languages.[21] Many of these are private documents – petitions, agreements, contracts, land registers, letters, court documents, and others – which shed light on the legal practices of Greeks and Egyptians during this period. Many public documents also survive, such as royal proclamations, which were also written on papyrus for distribution to the relevant officials.

Egypt had had a strong, centralized government for several millennia before Alexander, and after his death the Ptolemies continued this tradition, ruling Egypt from 323 to 30 BCE. When the Ptolemies came to power, they built an administrative structure for the new province, and established three poleis (Alexandria, Naucratis, and Ptolemais). These poleis were said to be self-governing, and they apparently had their own councils and assemblies, but these bodies had only a small role in governance and were closely controlled by the king and his administration. Perhaps for this reason, they enacted very little legislation (Rhodes-Lewis 1997: 467–9), and in fact, the sort of publicly displayed legislation that survives in such abundance from traditional Greek cities is almost entirely lacking in Egypt.[22]

Outside the main cities, the Greek settlers lived in towns and villages in the *chora* or "countryside." Since these settlers usually came from different home cities, they would have had different legal backgrounds, and thus could not simply draw on a single legal tradition. Moreover, Egypt had its own long-established legal tradition and had long been using writing in legal matters in ways that differed from traditional Greek usage. In

---

[21] Papyri relevant to law can be found in Meyer 1920 and the two-volume Loeb collection of documentary papyri (Hunt and Edgar 1932–4) and elsewhere; there are useful summaries in *SB*. The handbooks and overviews of different areas of law, such as Taubenschlag 1955 or Pringsheim 1950, must be used with care, since in the past half-century our understanding of Ptolemaic law has become less certain, as can be seen by comparing the first edition of the *Cambridge Ancient History* (S. A. Cook *et al.* 1928: 119–20) with the second (Walbank and Astin 1984: 155). Useful overviews of Ptolemaic law can be found in Modrzejewski 1966 and 1995, and Wolff 1966. The survey in Rupprecht 1994: 94–153 is especially useful for its bibliographies.

[22] Most of the Greek decrees from Egypt in Rhodes-Lewis 1997: 461–7 are papyrus texts.

particular, scribes, notaries and written documents played a large role in Egyptian law (Allam 1991: 109–19), and this influenced Greek practice. Greek law in Egypt therefore came to differ substantially with respect to procedure from traditional Greek law, particularly in its use of writing. Substantive law shows somewhat more continuity, and some scholars use the term legal *koinē* or "common law" (Wolff 2002: 35–43) to denote a kind of synthesis of law from many cities, but this expression probably overstates the substantive unity of Ptolemaic law.

Since the Greek settlers generally lived in communities together with the native Egyptian inhabitants, Greek and Egyptian legal practices coexisted. Around 275, Ptolemy II Philadelphus brought order to this situation by issuing rules setting up Egyptian courts (of the *laokritai*) to rule on matters relating to Egyptian laws, often called the "laws of the country" (*nomoi tēs chōras*) and Greek courts (*dikastēria* at first, later courts of the *chrēmatistai*) for the "laws of the cities" (*nomoi politikoi*).[23] In addition to these two systems, the term "royal law" was used for the law that governed the centralized administration of the country and for the laws of the three poleis, but royal law had little effect on the lives of most inhabitants, who used the new Greek or Egyptian courts. The determining factor in deciding which of these two systems would hear a case was normally the language, and therefore the legal system, used in the matter that was in dispute.[24]

It is uncertain whether the *nomoi politikoi* or the *nomoi tēs chōras* were ever formally put in writing or publicly displayed. Despite the fact that writing had been known in Egypt for nearly three millennia, traditional Egyptian law was largely or entirely unwritten. A demotic papyrus reports that in 419, Darius ordered his governor of Egypt "to write down the laws of Egypt," but we do not know whether these actually were written and if so, what form they took or how long they survived (Modrzejewski 1995: 3–6). But this demotic papyrus, a kind of handbook or case-book, shows that some information about demotic laws was available in writing, probably not in the form of actual written laws but as documents intended to help "Egyptian notaries in their professional activity and Egyptian judges in the resolution of difficult cases" (Modrzejewski 1995: 7).

The Greek *nomoi politikoi* may have been written down for a similar purpose. *P. Hal.* 1 from the mid third century is a collection of *dikaiōmata*

---

[23] There is much disagreement about the nature of these *nomoi politikoi*, but the term may designate the laws which were derived from the laws of traditional Greek poleis.

[24] See *P. Tebt.* 1 5 (= *COP* 53), Hunt and Edgar 1932–4: vol. II, no. 210, lines 211–20, as interpreted by Modrzejewski 1978; see also Modrzejewski 1995: 15–16, Pestman 1994: 85–6.

("justificatory documents"),[25] apparently compiled from various sources by a lawyer because of their relevance to a case or cases he was handling.[26] Among these is an excerpt from the *nomos politikos* of Alexandria, which implies that this "civic law" did exist somewhere in writing. Other excerpts (in columns 4 and 5) are laws concerning false witnesses, the liability of slaves, buildings and construction, and different types of assault. It seems that people who wished to bring suit would first consult a lawyer (as we would today), who would consult these *dikaiōmata* to find the relevant law. We do not know the location of the *politikos nomos* of Alexandria from which these *dikaiōmata* were excerpted, but we have no reason to think that it was publicly displayed. Another document (*P. Lille* 1 29)[27] also contains several laws about slavery. The papyrus begins with the text of the first law with no preamble indicating what these laws are, but we probably have here a collection of *nomoi politikoi* like *P. Hal.* 1, assembled and written down for private use, perhaps by a lawyer or notary. Interestingly, one of the laws in this collection contradicts a law on the same subject found in *P. Hal.* 1. This may mean that both documents are private collections of local laws but from different places (Taubenschlag 1955: 95–6).

No text of an actual *nomos politikos* survives, but we do have texts of royal edicts (*diagrammata*) and decrees (*prostagmata*) (Hunt and Edgar 1932–4: vol. II, 54–131). These indicate that in the area of royal law written legislation was the norm. Royal laws were enacted by the king for the governance of both the city of Alexandria and the territory of Egypt. They regulated the administration of a large territory together with the network of officials and commissions required for this task. They were written down because, as other ancient societies including pre-Ptolemaic Egypt had discovered, writing was indispensable for large-scale administration. Edicts and decrees would be circulated among officials, and were sometimes made available to the public by being posted in public places.

These texts show that written legislation had a very different place in Ptolemaic law than in other Greek legal systems. In Egypt only the king and his royal administration truly legislated, in the sense of enacting authoritative legal rules, and most of the royal edicts and decrees he issued

---

[25] See Graeca Halensis 1913: 3–177; parts of the document are included in Hunt and Edgar 1932–4: vol. II, nos. 201 (lines 124–5), 202 (186–213), and 207 (166–85). The *dikaiōmata* were the written documents presented in support of a case, as in *SEG* 17.415 (see above) or *P. Gur.* 2, line 39 (discussed below). They are similar, therefore, to the documents (*atechnoi pisteis*) presented to an Athenian court (Chapter Eight).

[26] See Graeca Halensis 1913: 12–14; Fraser 1972: vol. I, 109–10.

[27] The document is no. 71 in Meyer 1920, and is discussed by Scholl 1995 (esp. 160–3, with the text on 169–71).

were circulated only to those who were charged with implementing or enforcing them or who were otherwise affected by them, but were not displayed for the general public. And the status of other kinds of laws besides royal law seems not to have depended on writing in the way in which legislation in the rest of Greece did. Some of the traditional *politikoi nomoi*, which formed the basis for most decisions of the Greek courts, may have been written down, but if they were, it appears that they were not displayed publicly and thus their authority did not depend on whether or not they were written down somewhere. Notaries and lawyers, who played an important role in Ptolemaic law, may have compiled rules or other sorts of legal advice in writing for their own use, but this sort of writing would have had a different role from anything we know of in Athens, where these professionals were unknown.

Writing also seems to have played a different role – or several different roles – in other aspects of the legal process. Most of the hundreds of legal documents that survive from Ptolemaic Egypt were written by notaries or professional scribes. Some of them, including contracts, wills, and sale or loan agreements, are also known from classical Athens, but the number of such documents seems to be much greater in Egypt than in classical Athens, and even if this impression is due primarily to the greater survival of evidence in Egypt, forensic oratory certainly conveys the impression that Athenians in general did not make nearly as much use of written documents as Greeks in Egypt did. One reason for writing so many documents may have been that transactions in Egypt were often between Greeks from different legal traditions, for whom it would have been necessary to specify arrangements in full detail. Marriage agreements are a good example. The earliest of these, *P. Eleph.* 1 written in 311,[28] is between Greeks whose families came from different cities, Temnos and Cos. After giving the date it reads,

Heracleides takes Demetria to be his lawful wife, both of them being freeborn, from her father and mother (both named) with clothing and jewelry worth 1,000 drachmas. He is to give her all that a freeborn wife should have and they will live wherever he and her father decide. If she is caught doing anything to shame her husband, she will lose the entire dowry, but he must prove his accusation before three men acceptable to both of them. He in turn cannot insult her by bringing home another woman, or having children by another woman, or wronging her in any other way. If he is caught doing any of these and she proves it before three men

---

[28] For the text see Hunt and Edgar 1932–4: vol. 1, no. 1; for discussion see Katzoff 1995; for a thorough account of Egyptian marriage documents see Yiftach-Firanko 2003.

acceptable to both of them, he shall return the dowry and also forfeit 1,000 drachmas, and she and those who help her have the right to exact payment from him or his investments, both in land and in maritime loans, as if it were a court judgment. The contract shall be valid wherever either of them produces it against the other, as if it had been made in that place. Both of them can keep copies of the contract themselves [then come the names of six witnesses]. (translation of Hunt and Edgar, modified)

Some similarities to Athenian marriage agreements are evident, such as the dowry that provides some measure of security for both partners. But there are also significant differences, such as the inclusion of the bride's mother in the agreement together with her father and the relative equality of the terms governing accusations of wrongdoing. We can already see here the greater equality of husband and wife that characterizes Hellenistic marriages.

But the most important difference for our purpose is the simple fact that this is a written contract. Most scholars assume that the contract is modeled on marriage contracts from the classical period (e.g., Katzoff 1995: 38), but no written marriage contract survives from that time, and in fact there is no evidence that marriage agreements were ever put in writing before the Hellenistic period. This argument from silence is not conclusive, and other cities may have been more inclined to use writing than Athens, though there is no evidence that they did or any obvious reason why they should. And there are passages in Attic oratory where a litigant would surely cite, or at least mention, a written marriage contract if one existed. For example, the plaintiff in Demosthenes 41, probably written in the 360s, begins his case with the claim that he had married the daughter of Polyeuctus with a dowry of forty minas but had only received thirty minas at the time with the rest promised on the death of Polyeuctus. To prove this point, he presents witnesses who were present at the betrothal (41.6). Had a written contract been made in this case, surely the speaker would have presented it as evidence in addition to these witnesses, but he says nothing about a contract.

If written marriage contracts were not the norm in the classical period, why do they become standard in the Hellenistic period, apparently right from the beginning? One factor suggested above is that the families of the bride and groom came from different cities, as must have occurred fairly often in third-century Egypt. It was possible for couples to marry in Egypt without a written contract, and many did, but when arrangements were complicated and many details had to be accounted for, then couples used written contracts (Wolff 1939; Yiftach-Firanko 2003: 83–104). In fact, sometimes couples who had long been married without a written contract would later write a detailed marriage contract, either to be certain about all the details previously agreed on or perhaps in order to fix details that they had not worked out at the beginning of the marriage. Some of the conditions prompting the writing of contracts were thus the same (*mutatis mutandis*) as those for writing the earliest laws in archaic Greece – the presence of a diverse population with differing legal traditions and the need for certainty about details – though the ultimate effects of writing contracts were different from the effects of writing laws.

Another reason for the large number of written documents in Egypt was undoubtedly the long Egyptian tradition of scribes and notaries. Under the highly centralized administration of Pharaonic Egypt, legal transactions were commonly recorded by scribes acting essentially as notaries, and the documents were stored in administrative offices. After the Greek conquest, this centralized Egyptian administration ceased to exist, but notaries continued to write contracts, deeds of sale, loan agreements, and the like in demotic for the native inhabitants. In addition, "the scribe played a surprisingly active role in legal proceedings" during the New Kingdom, and scribes continued to play much the same role in the Ptolemaic period, including receiving petitions, making accusations, helping in interrogations, verifying facts, and other activities (Allam 1991: 112–13). Official Greek notaries (*agoranomoi*) are attested at least as early as the beginning of the second century, and probably existed earlier. And another legal professional in Egypt, hitherto unknown in Greece, was the lawyer or advocate. Although advocates may originally have been friends not unlike the co-pleaders (*synēgoroi*) in Athens and elsewhere, by the mid third century a specialized profession developed, and some lawyers even had offices and staffs (Graeca Halensis 1913: 25–31).

Thus, close familiarity with the work of Egyptian notaries and scribes prompted the creation of similar professional groups for the Greeks in Egypt, and the growth of these professions undoubtedly stimulated the increase of writing in legal affairs, and vice versa. In classical Greece, private legal documents were prepared by individuals; there is no sign of scribal involvement. But in Egypt, even in the third century most Greek documents were written by notaries or scribes.[29] Once these professions had arisen, they would soon control the form and language of legal documents just as Egyptian notaries did (and as similar professionals tend to do in all

---

[29] The formulaic complexity of even a short document like *P. Cair. Zen.* 59003, lines 11–22 [= Hunt and Edgar 1932–4: vol. I, no. 31] dated to 259 suggests the involvement of a professional scribe (Modrzejewski 1966: 137–8).

cultures). And this would result in an increase over time in the complexity and amount of detail in legal documents.

Several documents recording sales of land dated to around 100 (Hunt and Edgar 1932–4: vol. I, nos. 27–9) include, among other details, full physical descriptions of all the buyers and sellers, for example, "Taous daughter of Harpos, aged about 48 years, of medium height, fair-skinned, round-faced, straight-nosed, with a scar on her forehead" (*P. Grenf.* II 23 = Hunt and Edgar 1932–4: vol. I, no. 27). One reason for this amount of detail may have been the mobility of the population, which meant that the parties to legal transactions would not necessarily be known to each other or to friends and neighbors who could identify them if necessary.[30] But the formulaic quality of this description suggests that a notarial impulse lies behind the large amount of detail, which often characterizes other elements of the transaction in addition to the identification of the parties. A similar degree of detail is found in some witness depositions, which otherwise resemble those occasionally preserved in Athenian forensic speeches. In one, *P. Zen. Pestm.* 21 (Hunt and Edgar 1932–4: vol. II, no. 253), the witness is described as "about 35 years old, tall, broad, curly-haired, fair-skinned, squarely-set, with a scar on the right of the eyebrows." Here too, it may have been more important in Ptolemaic Egypt than in classical Athens to provide a detailed description of people who were not well known in the community, but notarial practice might also be responsible. And, of course, the more detail, the greater the need for a written document, and for the services of a notary to prepare it.

Along with this increased tendency to record legal transactions in writing came the increasing use of these documents in court. A particularly interesting text in this regard is *P. Gur.* 2 (dated to 226),[31] which is the report of a trial held before a Greek court known as the Court of Ten.[32] The litigants are both Jews but the procedure before the Greek court is Greek. After the date and the names of the judges and other officials, the document informs us that the court is responding to a petition written by Heracleia in response to an accusation (*enklēma*) filed by Dositheus claiming that she had insulted him and asking for damages of 200 drachmas. Dositheus' complete accusation is recorded, detailing the

---

[30] In other documents these physical details are not included, perhaps because the parties are known to one another; e.g., in *P. Oxy.* 1628 (Hunt and Edgar 1932–4: vol. I, no. 40) the parties are said to live on the same street.

[31] Hunt and Edgar 1932–4: vol. II, no. 256; Tcherikover and Fuks 1957–64: vol. I, no. 19.

[32] Only eight judges are named, perhaps because two were challenged or were absent for some other reason. We know nothing about the size of other courts in Alexandria (Fraser 1972: vol. I, 112).

alleged assault and insults (lines 11–35),[33] and the judges then report their decision (lines 35–49):

whereas Dositheus did not appear in court, did not submit a written account (*logon grapton*) of his case, and was unwilling to present his accusation (in person) but Heracleia was present in court with her guardian (*kyrios*), Aristides son of Proteas, an Athenian of the Epigone, and had not only submitted a written account supported by documents (*dikaiōmata*) but was also willing to defend herself (in person) in the case, and whereas the edict which Heracleia submitted among these documents ordered [the judges] to judge . . .[34] [that] when both of the litigants have been summoned to court, if either one of them is unwilling to submit a written account or deliver his accusation (in person) or acknowledge defeat (?) . . . he shall be judged to have done wrong, we have dismissed the case.

The differences between the use of writing in legal procedure here and in classical Athens are striking. First, the document itself is a full written account – perhaps an official record – of what happened in this particular case from the beginning to the end, and even includes the names of the judges and other court officials. This was probably written by a clerk after the verdict, and copies were probably made for the litigants as well as for the court.[35] This has no parallel in Athens. Dositheus' written indictment does have parallels in Athens, though no Athenian indictment we know of presented such a full bill of particulars as we find here. And Athenian indictments were not given to the jury to read at the beginning of the trial but were read out by the clerk at the beginning of the trial. And the written petition, which Heracleia presents to the court and which contains a written account of her case (*logos graptos*), is unparalleled in Athens or anywhere else in archaic and classical Greece, where oral pleading was the rule. Also without parallel is the written petition Heracleia filed earlier, which prompted the court to take action. Virtually every stage of the legal process in this case depends on writing; oral arguments could apparently be heard, but the written account is clearly the heart of this case.

Other documents confirm the greater use of writing in Ptolemaic procedure. For example, in *P. Hib.* 30 (Hunt and Edgar 1932–4: vol. II, no. 247), which is a summons dated before 270, Epimenes summons Perdiccas to court for allegedly failing to pay a debt. The summons gives full details about the debt, adds the names of the witnesses and the date, and then states: "The case will be presented in writing (*anagraphēsetai*)

---

[33] It is unclear why Heracleia petitioned for a trial instead of just presenting a written defense.
[34] The text that fills this gap specifies how the edicts and *politikoi nomoi* are to be used.
[35] Another copy survives (*P. Petrie* 3.21 g), but is less well preserved.

against you in person in the court in Heracleopolis." Writing is also the heart of the case in *P. Tor.* 13, an order to execute judgment, probably from the year 136 (Hunt and Edgar 1932–4: vol. II, no. 264 = *UPZ* 118), to which is appended a record of the trial and the court's decision. This report has the same general form as the report in *P. Gur.* 2, but here the plaintiff, Chonouphis, appeared in court but the defendant did not. Chonouphis presents his petition and then apparently (the text is slightly damaged) adds a fuller oral account of the debt he is seeking to recover. Traditional oral pleading by the litigant is thus allowed in this trial, but here it is a supplement to the written petition, which is the basis of the case.

In sum, Greeks in Ptolemaic Egypt used writing extensively during the whole process of litigation, and a litigant's entire case could be presented to the court in writing; laws, on the other hand, were less often written down and rarely displayed in public. To a large extent this is the reverse of the situation in traditional Greek cities, where all laws were written down and publicly displayed, and written procedural documents had a relatively limited place. Among the reasons for this extensive use of writing in procedure were first, Egypt's traditional use of scribes and notaries, and second, the mixed composition of Ptolemaic communities, as Greeks from different poleis would use writing in order to specify legal arrangements in greater detail. In addition, the increased use of writing in other aspects of life, such as commerce, undoubtedly contributed to the increased use of written legal documents. Similar trends are evident in fourth-century Athens, but the Athenians did not let them affect their legal process, except in the requirements that all evidence be given to the court in writing and that a written contract be provided in the maritime courts.

The relative absence of written legislation in Egypt may have resulted from similar social and political factors. Besides the royal laws, most of which had little effect on the lives of those who lived outside the main cities and were not royal officials, the local laws (*nomoi politikoi*) by which the Greek settlers regulated their daily lives were not necessarily written. Since the Greeks in any particular town or area came from different cities, legislation would have had to be enacted anew, but communities outside the major cities did not have the cohesiveness or authority required for this task, and the central administration had little interest in legislating for local communities. They created courts to decide disputes that arose according to local standards and traditions, that is, according to the local *politikoi nomoi*, but these seem to have been worked out in practice by the appointed magistrates and the notaries and scribes who handled most legal affairs rather than being determined by a formal process of legislation.

Finally, the underlying reason why law in Ptolemaic Egypt differed so greatly from Greek law elsewhere in its use of writing was surely political – the fact that the Ptolemies exercised direct control over the whole country, something most of Greece had not experienced since the Bronze Age. More than two and a half millennia of Pharaonic rule in Egypt had created a large administrative apparatus, which the kings built on in creating their own, Greek administrative institutions. Writing is a regular and probably necessary feature of such large centralized administrations, and Ptolemaic bureaucrats made considerable use of it, as had the Egyptian administrators before them. Thus, to the extent that this administration concerned itself with law, it tended to make use of writing at all levels. Royal edicts and decrees were written and copies were distributed, the courts created by the monarchy relied heavily on written documents, and other legal institutions dependent on writing were created, such as centralized land registries where written documents could be stored. To manage all these documents, a large number of Greek counterparts to the traditional Egyptian notaries and scribes came into being and ultimately formed the first Greek legal profession, whose role in legal matters grew to the point where one could say that "Hellenistic law [sc. in Egypt] is a law of notaries" (Modrzejewski 1966: 138).

The practice of writing down edicts and decrees did not, however, lead to any great concern for legislation at the local level or to any notion that ordinary citizens should have ready access to the laws they were supposed to live by. Quite the opposite. The large royal administrative apparatus, taking its direction from the top, promoted an autocratic view of the place of the common people in the society, namely that they were under the direct authority of the king and his appointed officials at all levels. Notaries and lawyers could help ordinary people make legal arrangements, petition officials, and manage litigation. But the traditional Greek assumption that the people should be able to conduct such business directly on their own, consulting the laws by themselves, pleading their cases without a lawyer, and otherwise managing their affairs without professional help was foreign to the thinking of Greeks in Ptolemaic Egypt. In many respects, law in Ptolemaic Egypt resembled early common law in England (Chapter Nine). In both countries professional notaries seem to have promoted the practice of writing documents, which in turn fostered the growth of their professions. And since notaries in both countries knew the local customs and traditions better than anyone, they had little need for fixed written texts of local laws and no interest in making legislation readily available to those outside their profession.

Conclusion: Writing Greek Law

We have come to the end of the story of writing Greek law, which begins in a period of oral law in which writing played no role, and continues through the earliest use of writing in the seventh century for recording and making public legislation, into the classical and Hellenistic periods when writing was increasingly used in the administration of law and for legal documents other than laws, and ends (for us) in Ptolemaic Egypt, where writing law changes entirely. With the exception of Egypt, we have seen two trends consistently at work: the abundant use of writing for legislation, which was always publicly displayed so as to be read and used by a relatively large segment of the community, and the resistance to using writing during the judicial process. We have also noted some of the consequences of these two trends – that Greek laws have a more open texture, a broader "fringe of vagueness" (Hart 1994: 123) than modern laws, that they are generally written in ordinary, non-technical language, and that the legal professionals so prominent in most other legal systems, including lawyers, notaries, judges, and jurists, are largely absent from Greek law.

All these features worked to make Greek law accessible to a relatively broad segment of the community. From the beginning, those who wrote legislation incorporated physical features, such as dividing marks between words, gaps between topics, and writing in columns, together with stylistic and structural features, such as asyndeton and various logical and hierarchical arrangements of provisions, which would make their texts as easy as possible to read and use. We cannot know how many Greeks could or did actually read these laws, but even the earliest legislation is clearly meant to be read, and to this end it provides assistance to those whose reading skills may be limited. Direct access to this legislation was thus available to people and required no specialized knowledge or professional help.

The relative absence of writing from legal procedure, particularly from the heart of the process, the trial, also contributed to making Greek law accessible to members of the community, who could prosecute others or defend themselves using few if any written texts, and most important, without the help of legal professionals who in most societies control access to law in large part by their control of written texts. Greek litigants could plead their cases in any way they wished, speaking in ordinary, non-technical language, and could also, if they wished, call witnesses and use other kinds of evidence in any way they might want. To this end, Greek legislation regularly includes information about procedure so that those involved in litigation could learn for themselves, without professional help, how they needed to proceed. A number of different procedures were often available to a litigant, at least in Athens,[1] but a litigant could choose whichever one he wished without fearing that his choice was officially or technically wrong. And in classical and Hellenistic Greece, a litigant could use any available written documents he wished, but in court these texts would always be converted into oral speech by being read aloud to the jury, so that the trial retained its fundamentally oral nature even in the Hellenistic period. Thus, both written legislation and oral procedure contributed to the goal of making Greek law as accessible as possible.

This examination of writing and law gives us a new perspective on the old question of the unity of Greek law. As Finley (1966) convincingly argues, differences in the substantive laws of Greek cities are so great that we cannot speak of substantive unity in any meaningful sense. With the exception of Ptolemaic Egypt, however, Greeks everywhere used writing for legal matters in very similar ways, writing legislation in non-technical language and displaying it publicly for practical use, maintaining a system of oral pleading by the litigants themselves without written texts and without professional help, and retaining the non-professional nature of law in general. Thus, we can meaningfully speak of a unity of Greek law which we might call procedural in the broad sense that all Greek cities (except Egypt) share a similar attitude to the purposes and general methods of legislation and litigation.[2]

We have noted, moreover, that these similarities override differences in the specific forms of government of these cities. In particular, features that scholars have often treated as characteristic of Athenian democracy are also

---

[1] It is generally held that procedural law is primary in Athenian law, and Lipsius' still standard handbook of Athenian law (1905–15) is thus arranged according to procedure not substance. But see Carey 1998, who questions some aspects of this conclusion, and also Gagarin 2006a: 273–4, where I discuss Sir Henry Maine's views on substance and procedure in ancient law.

[2] Ironically, the traditional assumption of unity, exemplified in the original target of Finley's criticism, Pringsheim 1950 (*The Greek Law of Sale*), was premised on supposed similarities between law in Ptolemaic Egypt and in Athens.

found in cities like Gortyn, whose government is generally considered oligarchic. Certainly we can see many of these features (and study them) more easily and fully in classical Athens, but we have enough evidence to indicate that at least some other cities shared at least some of these same features. There are differences, to be sure, such as the use of single judges at Gortyn and large juries at Athens, but many of the general features that characterize Athenian law – in particular its non-technical and non-professional character – seem to characterize law in other cities as well. By looking beyond Athens, and by focusing on the place of writing in law, we can understand that features commonly considered characteristically Athenian, are not just Athenian or democratic, but Greek.

We have been able to appreciate more fully these general features of Greek law by comparing its use of writing with that of other premodern legal systems; comparison also allows us to understand the uniqueness of Greek law and to see that the ultimate basis of this uniqueness is cultural and political. As we have noted, Greek society was generally open and non-authoritarian in nature. From the earliest times, Greek communities whatever their form of government give a place to the voices of the non-elite as well as the elite. In Homer, cities are ruled by "kings" but also have larger advisory bodies like assemblies, and the leaders of the Greek army at Troy allow a commoner like Thersites to speak. A tradition of open public discourse is ingrained in Greek thought, poets and other thinkers routinely challenge and criticize their predecessors and rivals, and communities regularly debate issues publicly (Lloyd 1979). Closed, authoritarian groups like the Pythagoreans and other sects do exist, but these groups are always on the fringe of Greek culture and have little effect on the open public discourse of most Greeks everywhere.

Politically, Greece has no tradition of monarchic government. The many "kings" (*basileis*) in Homer and Hesiod are nothing like the absolute monarchs of the Near East and many other early societies.[3] Tyrants may have possessed some of the characteristics of absolute monarchs, but these have probably been exaggerated by Herodotus and other ancient authors, who tended to assimilate the tyrants to Persian monarchs. Even the most "tyrannical" of the Greek tyrants did not establish the same degree of authoritarian control over their cities as the Persian kings did, and their rule was usually limited to two generations at most, Law too appears to have been non-authoritarian from the beginning. In Homer, ordinary

---

[3] S. Morris 2003: 9 argues that even in the Greek Bronze Age, the ruler (*wanax*) was not equivalent to an oriental monarch.

people are significant participants in the legal process, litigants plead their cases by themselves, and in order for settlements of disputes to be effective they must have the approval of the community. As soon as laws are first written, moreover, they impose restrictions on holding office – and this in cities that are far from democratic – and they hold officials responsible for their actions and punish them for violations. None of these features is found in other premodern legal systems.

But perhaps the most important result of the unique use of writing in Greek law was that it kept law accessible. The oral system portrayed in Homer resembles many tribal-law systems, in that all members of the community have direct access to the quasi-formal procedures of dispute-settlement. A person's status in the community may affect his reception in such forums, but it does not restrict his access to them. Modern legal systems and most premodern systems restrict access to the law in various ways,[4] and although many also make available other means of adjudication that partially compensate for this, such as small-claims courts, it is difficult for most people to make use of a modern legal system without professional help.[5]

Greek law began in a period of oral law by providing relatively full access to members of the community in much the same way as in tribal societies. Some of the other legal systems we have examined may have been similarly accessible at their beginning – Anglo-Saxon England (at the local level) and perhaps Rome at the time of the Twelve Tables – but as these other societies began to use writing to provide more formal legal rules and procedures, this writing also created obstacles to access. Only Greek law resisted this tendency. Like these other societies, Greece used writing to formalize and stabilize its rules and procedures, but it not only wrote legislation in ways that would make it available to many, but also kept writing out of the legal process where it could become an obstacle to access. Thus Greece created a formal, rule-based legal system that nonetheless allowed direct access to a broad segment of the community.

In the past, legal historians and many classical scholars have scorned Greek law (or Athenian law, which often stood for Greek law) precisely because of its lack of professional control over the legal process. Typical is the assertion of Tarn and Griffith (1952: 88), cited at the beginning of our discussion of Hellenistic law, that "the old system [i.e. in classical Athens] was about the worst legal system ever invented, for the juries' decisions

---

[4] Restrictions are not necessarily part of the law, but may include such factors as the cost of litigation or the location of judicial forums.

[5] Nader (2002) is not alone in noting a steady decrease in the accessibility of law in the U.S.A.

were habitually influenced by politics, mass passion, and prejudice." Greek law was particularly disparaged by comparison with the rational, systematic, and professional system of Roman law, which has become the basis for so many modern legal systems. Scholars' attitudes are beginning to change as they increasingly recognize that the Athenian system managed to be rule based and adhere in a broad sense to the rule of law, while at the same time remaining open and accessible to its citizens.

This re-evaluation of Greek law has helped stimulate renewed scholarly interest in the field in recent decades (Cohen 2005). But Anglo-American scholars have continued to interest themselves almost entirely in classical Athenian law, leaving other important areas to continental scholars, trained in Roman law, whose perspective is often quite different. One hope of the present study is that it will stimulate more interest in the study of Greek law outside of classical Athens. If the study of Greek law as a whole is to remain healthy, it will require new ideas and new perspectives, which Anglo-American scholars are well positioned to bring to it (see, for example, Rubinstein 2003).

Finally, perhaps the most important reason to study Greek law and to bring it to the attention of legal historians and others outside the field of Classics is that it presents a unique perspective for understanding law in general and U.S. law in particular. As Aristotle perceived, legal argument is not only grounded in reason and objective truth as embodied in "non-artistic proofs," but it also contains a subjective, "artistic" component, which is necessary for "understanding the available means of persuasion concerning any subject whatsoever" (as his famous definition of rhetoric puts it).[6] Most legal systems, beginning with that devised by the Roman jurists, try to reduce this rhetorical element to a minimum, so that every legal issue has a single rational solution. Rhetoric, it is commonly felt, has no place in law.[7] But the assumption that law can or should be completely free of subjective elements is challenged by the postmodern analysis of law, especially the critical legal studies and law and literature approaches. These movements are largely confined to the U.S.A. and Britain, not surprisingly since common law, particularly in the U.S.A., grants a larger role to trial by jury than civil law systems, and this leaves more room for rhetoric and other subjective elements to influence the legal process.

---

[6] δύναμις περὶ ἕκαστον τοῦ θεωρῆσαι τὸ ἐνδεχόμενον πιθανόν, *Rhetoric* 1.2, 1355b25–6.

[7] This feeling became clear in the uproar created by the acquittal of O. J. Simpson on a charge of murder in Los Angeles in 1995, which was widely attributed to the skillful rhetoric of his defense lawyers.

The Athenians did not pretend that subjective elements were irrelevant to decisions about the facts of a legal case, though they did not base their decisions primarily on such elements either. Rather, they saw the need to locate facts within the larger social and political context of a dispute (Lanni 2006). In modern legal systems this larger context is often ruled irrelevant to the legal issues in the case and is excluded as much as possible from the courtroom. But the perceived tension between reason and rhetoric persists, as it must, however much a legal system may try to eliminate one or the other. In seeking a middle ground, the Greeks created a unique system that was rule based and rational but retained a large rhetorical element. Writing and its absence were crucial to the development of this system. The result was not perfect by any means, but it had certain advantages, such as openness and accessibility, that we today would benefit from studying.

Appendices

APPENDIX I: GREEK TEXTS FOR CHAPTER 2

(Arrows indicate the direction of the writing)

1. Dreros 1 (ML 2, *Nomima* 1.81, *IGT* 90). First published in Demargne and van Effenterre 1937b.

> [← θιός ολοιον]

   1. ← ἄδ' ἔϝαδε | πόλι· | ἐπεί κα κοσμήσει, | δέκα ϝετίον | τὸν ἀ-

   2. → ϝτὸν | μὴ κόσμεν· | αἰ δὲ κοσμησίε | ὀπε δικακσίε, | ἀϝτὸν ὀπῆλεν | διπλεῖ | κἀϝτὸν

   3. ← ἄκρηστον | ἦμεν | ἆς δόοι | κὄτι κοσμησίε | μηδὲν | ἤμην. *vacat*

   4. ← ϙόμόται δὲ | κόσμος | κοὶ δάμιοι | κοὶ ἴκατι | οἰ τᾶς πόλιος. *vacat*

2. Gortyn *ICret* 4.14 (*Nomima* 1.82, *IGT* 121).

   1. ←] 'πεντήϙοντα λέβη[τας ϝ]εκάστο καταστᾶσαι. ϙόσμος ὁ ἐπιστάς | αἰ μὴ ἐστείσαιτο, ἀϝτ[ὸν ὀ]πήλεν | καὶ τὸν τίταν | αἰ μὴ 'στείσαιτο τ[ὰν διπλέαν . . .

   2. →] λέβητας κα[τ]αστᾶσαι ϝέκαστον. | τρι[ὅ]ν ϝετίον τὸν ἀϝτὸν μὴ ϙοσμῆν, | δέκα μὲν γνόμονας, | πέντε [δὲ κσ]ενίος | *vacat*

3. Gortyn *ICret* 4.1 (*Nomima* II.22, *IGT* 116).

   1. ←]ονδε | ὄκα πάθηι | μολῆν | [ ]δε | τίνεσθαι [ ]ηι | γιναῖκα ὄιον τ[18–20]αν | πέντε λέβητ[ας

   2. ←] αι θήλεια | τὸι ἀμ[μνὅι (?)]οι | μεκτα[ ]ι | τριάϙον[τα . . . c.12]μεν | πλία δ[ὲ μή

   3. ←] ὄιες κέρσενος | [ ]ια | αἰ ϝίδ[ια

   4. ← ἄνθρ]οπος | ἐνέβαλε | [ ] ἄρϙος | κα[- - ἔμ]βάλοι | ἐκατὸν [λέ]βητας | ϝ[εκαστ

   5. ←]κρηιον τὰς ϝοικιό[νσας (?) - -]νας καὶ το[- - καταστ]ᾶσαι | αἰ δὲ μὴ ἐστείσα[ι | ἄ]τας | ἀϝτὸν [

4. Gortyn *ICret* 4.3 (not in *Nomima* or *IGT).*

   1. ← ἰα]ρὰ | τετελημέ[να . . . c.6]υι | τὅι [ϝ]ελκανί[ὅι]αι | ἐν τᾶι πένπτα[ι . . .

248

2. ←]ν | τέλεον | καὶ αἶγα | ἐν [τᾶι ἔκται] ὄιν θήλε[ι]αν | τõι Ἀπ[έλλονι]εϙ[ ]ς | ταϝῦρος | ἐσ [...

3. ←] τᾶι ῞Ηραι | ὄις | θή[λ]ε[ια | τᾶι Δάμ]ατρι | ὄις | ἐπίτεκ[ς ...

4. ←] αἰ μὲν δύο | θήλει[αι, οἰ δὲ δύ]ο ἔρσενες | καὶ τρ[άγος ...

5. Gortyn *ICret* 4.21 (*Nomima* II.38, *IGT* 123).

   1. ← τὸ]ν | μολ ...

   2. ← ὅστις | μεζατ[ος] ἴοι | ...

   3. ← τõι ἀνπαντõι μ' ἦμεν ἀνκεμο[λίαν ...

4–5. ← ὀμοπάτηρ ἄ κ' ἦι καὶ ὀμομάτηρ ἀ ...
     → ... αἰ δὲ κ' ὀ μ]ὲν πατρōια μολῆι, ὀ δ' ἀλᾶι.

6–8. ← αἴ κ' ἀνποτέρος ἰοντι οἰ μαίτυρε[ς ...
     → ... δικά]ζε[ν] ἀ<ϝ>τὸς ἐπαιρῆι | πέντε λέβ-
     ← ητας | καταστᾶσαι, αἰ δέ κα μολ[ῆι] τ[

6. Chios (*ML* 8, *Nomima* I.62, *IGT* 61).

A]αιης Ἰστίης δήμο
   ῥήτρας: φυλάσσω[ν
   ]ον ⋮ ηρει ⋮ ἦμ μὲν δημαρ-
   χῶν: ἢ βασιλεύων: δεκασ[
   ]ς Ἰστίης ἀποδότω: δημα-   5
   ρχέων ⋮ ἐξπρῆξαι ⋮ τὸν ἐ[
   ]εν δήμο κεκλημένο
   αλοιαι τιμὴ διπλησ[ίη
   ]ν ὅσην παραλοιω[

B]ην δ' ἤκκλητος δί[κη
   ], ἢν δὲ ἀδικῆται: παρὰ
   δημάρχωι: στατῆρ[ας

C ἐκκαλέσθω ἐς
   βολὴν τὴν δημ-
   οσίην· τῆι τρίτηι
   ἐξ Ἑβδομαίων
   βολὴ ἀγερέσθ-   5
   ω ἡ δημοσίη ἐ-
   πιθώϊος λεκτ-
   ἡ πεντήϙοντ' ἀπ-
   ὸ φυλῆς· τά τ' ἄλ[λ-
   α] πρησσέτω τὰ δή-   10
   μο καὶ δίκα[ς ὀ
   ϙό]σαι ἂν ἔκκλ-
   ητοι γένων[τ-

αι] τõ μηνὸς π-
άσας ἐπι[15
]σεερ[

D Ἀ]ρτεμισιῶνος *vacat?*
]ων ὅρκια ἐπι-
ταμνέτω ϙώ[μνύτω
β]ασιλεῦσιν. *vacat*

7. Eretria (*IG* XII 9, 1273/1274, *Nomima* I.91, *IGT* 72–3).

   1. δίκεν : ἐπεὰν : κατομόσει : τίνυ-
     σθα<ι> : τρίτει ἑμέρει : χρέματα
     δόκιμα : κα[ὶ h]υγιᾶ ἰὰν: μὲ τείσ-
     ει [: hέραι]

   2. *vacat* ἐπὶ Γόλο: ἄρχοντος: ἐν πόλει [... 5–6 ...   5

   3. ... 17–25 ...]ιν: τε̃ι hυστέρει: δύϝε
     [στατε̃ρε: τ]ε̃ι [τρίτ]ει: δέκα: στατε̃ρας: ὀφέλεν [:]
     ἰὰν· μὲ τείσει: ἀρχὸς: ἀπὸ ρετõν: ποιε̃σαι
     vacat?] hόστις ἂν: μὲ ποιε̃ι· αὐτòν: ὀφέλεν

   4. τòς πλέοντας: ἀρ[έσ]θαι μισθὸν   10
     hοίτινες ἂν Πεταλάς: ἒ Κέναιον
     ἀμείπσονται: φέ[ρ]εν δὲ πάντας *vacat*
     vacat τος ἐπιδ[έ]μος ἐον[τας
     ]ογνον[. .]ναϲεν *vacat*
     vacat hός [ἂ]ν hέλοι [15
     ] ιαρϕιν [. .] ἀναϕισβετεει *vacat*

8. Naupactus (ML 13, *Nomima* I.44, *IGT* 47).

   Side I

     τεθμὸς ὅδε περὶ τᾶς γᾶς βέβαιος ἔστο κὰτ τòν
     ἀνδαιθμὸν πλακὸς Ὑλίας καὶ Λισκαρίας καὶ τõν ἀ-
     ποτόμον καὶ τõν δαμοσίον. ἐπινομία δ᾽ ἔστο γο-
     νεῦσιν καὶ παιδί· αἰ δὲ μὲ παῖς εἴε, κόραι· αἰ δὲ μὲ κόρα εἴε,
     ἀδελφεõι· αἰ δὲ μὲ ἀδελφεὸς εἴε, ἀνχιστέδαν ἐπινεμέσθο κὰ τὸ   5
     δίκαιον· αἰ δὲ μὲ τοὶ ἐπίνομοι OΙΙ[ΟΝ] hό τι δέ κα φυτεύσεται
     ἄσυλος εἴστο. αἰ μὲ πολέμοι ἀνανκαζομένοις δόξξαι ἀ-
     νδράσιν hενὶ κὲκατὸν ἀριστίνδαν τõι πλέθει ἄνδρας δια-
     κατίος μεῖστον ἀξξιομάχος ἐπιϝοίκος ἐφάγεσθαι, hόστ-
     ις δὲ δαιθμὸν ἐνφέροι ἒ ψᾶφον διαφέροι ἐν πρείγαι ἒ ᾽ν πόλι ἒ   10
     ᾽ν ἀποκλεσίαι ἒ στάσιν ποιέοι περὶ γαδαισίας, αὐτòς μὲ-
     ν ϝερρέτο καὶ γενεὰ ἄματα πάντα, χρέματα δὲ δαμευόσθον
     καὶ ϝοικία κατασκαπτέσθο κὰτ τòν ἀνδρεφονικòν τετμ-
     όν. ὁ δε τετθμὸς ἰαρὸς ἔστο τõ Ἀπόλλονος τõ Πυθίο καὶ
     τõν συνν-

[ἀον· ἔμεν τõι τα]ῦτα παρβαίνοντι ἐξξόλειαν αὐτõι καὶ
   γενεᾶι καὶ πά-   15
ντεσιν, τõι δ' εὐσεβέοντι hίλαος ἔσστο. ἀ δὲ γ[ᾶ τὸ μὲν
   ἔμισον]

Side II
   [κομίζοιεν, ἀξιοδότας ἔστο τὰν αὐτõ õιτινι χρέιζοι.]
vacat
   τον ὑπαπροσθιδίον ἔστο, τὸ δ' ἔμισον τõν ἐπιϝοίκον ἔστο. *vacat*
vacat
   τὸς δὲ κοίλος μόρος διαδόντο: ἀλλαγὰ δὲ βέβαιο-   20
   ς ἔστο, ἀλαζέσθο δὲ ἀντὶ τõ ἀρχõ.

9. Elis (*IvO* 7; *Nomima* I.109; *IGT* 41–3).
   (*A*) κα θεαρὸς εἴε. αἰ δὲ βενέοι ἐν τῖαρõ, βοί κα θοάδοι καὶ
      κοθάρσι τελείαι, καὶ τὸν θεαρὸν ἐν τ-
   αὐτᾶι. (*B*) αἰ δέ τις πὰρ τὸ γράφος δικάδοι, ἀτελές κ' εἴε ἀ
      δίκα, ἀ δέ κα ϝράτρα ἀ δαμοσία τελεία εἴ-
   ε δικάδοσα. (*C*) τõν δέ κα γραφέον, ὃ τι δοκέοι καλιτέρος
      ἔχεν πο(τ) τὸν θεόν, ἐξαγρέον καὶ ἐ-
   νποιõν σὺν βολαῖ πεντακατίο ἀϝλανέος καὶ δάμοι
      πλεθύοντι δινάκοι· <δινά>κοι δέ κα ἐν τρίτ-
   ον, αἴ τι ἐνποιõι αἴτ' ἐξαγρέοι.   5

10. Argos (*IG* IV 506, *Nomima* I.100, *IGT* 29).
   ... τὰ γ]ράθματα ⋮ ⋮ ταδὲν ⋮ ⋮ H<ὲ> ἄγνοι ...
   ... hὲ συγχέοι ⋮ ⋮ τὰς ἀρὰς ⋮ ⋮ τὰς ...
   ... γᾶς ⋮ ⋮ τᾶς Ἀργείας ⋮ ⋮ τὰ δὲ πάμα[τα ...
   ... ⋮ ⋮ αἰ] κα [θ]άνατον ⋮ ⋮ hὲ ἄλλο τι καφὸν ⋮ ⋮ h ...
   ... ἐ]πιτεχνõιο ⋮ ⋮ ε . οι ϝίσζέιε ⋮ ⋮ ιο ...   5
   ... ος ⋮ ⋮ πρό[γ]ρο[φ]ος ⋮ ⋮ ἐξπριιά[σθο ...
   ... α]ἰ δὲ μὲ δαμιιο[ρ]γοῖ τις ⋮ ⋮ hοῖς ...
   ... ς' Ἀργείας ⋮ ⋮ καὶ hοὶ ϝοι ε ...
   ... ο ⋮ ⋮ τοὶ hυλὲς ⋮ ⋮ ἀποδόμ[εν ...
   ... γᾶς ⋮ ⋮ Ἀργείας γα ⋮ ⋮ κατὰ κ ...   10
   ... νέποι]νον ϝοι ἔστο ⋮ ⋮ ποὶ τὰς h[έρας ...

11. Cleonae (*IG* IV 1607, *Nomima* II.79, *IGT* 32).
   a ...]τα τὀλατήριο-
    ν· ἀπόβαμα ξε[...
    ...]ος εἶμεν <αἰ> αἰνητ-
    ον ϝρέξαντα ⋮ ἄ[...
    ...], μὴ μιαρ[ὸ]ν εἶμε-   5

b ν· αἰ ἄ[ν]θ[ρ]οπον hα[ιμάξηι
ποιήσ]αντα χρῆμα μηθ-
έν ⋮ μιαρὸν εἶμεν [αἰ δὲ
κατάρ]ατον, μηθὲν π[αράν-
c ο]μον εἶμεν ⋮ αἰ [. . .   10
ἀνθ]ρόποι μιαρõι· ⋮ κά-
θαρσιν δὲ εἶμεν h[õς αἴ
κά τις ἀ]ποθάνοι, καθαρά-
μενον ⋮ κατὰ νόμ[ον . . .
. . .] hιαρõ δαμο-   15
τε[λέος . . .

12. Tiryns (*SEG* 30.380, *Nomima* 1.78, *IGT* 31. First published in Verdelis, Jameson, and Papachristodoulou 1975; see also Lupu 2005: no. 6).

1–4 . . . ϝετεον ταιδε [. . .] αιϝρε[.]ν τὸνς πλ[ατι]ϝοινάρχονς ἐνς . . . ν δαρ (?) οιϝακτον ταμιον [τὸν]σ πλατιϝοίνον[ς ϝ]εκάστε. αἰ μ᾽ ἐξσθ[ο]άσαιεν ὀφλεν ἐν[ς Δί]ϝα κάθαναίιαν τρ<ιι>αάφοντα μ[ε]δίμμνονς α[. . . διπλ]άσιον [..]ποσταντον πλατιϝοιναρχον ταδ . . . ἀ]ποδόμεν τοι ἰαρομμνάμονι τὸνς πρα[. . .]ς. τὸν δ᾽ ἰιαρομμναμόν[α . . .]εν τὰ δαμόσιια hόπυι κα δοκεῖ τοι δάμοι ἀλλιαιίαν θεν .(?)ια. αιδ . [. . .]απα θαιιεατρα α. *vacat*.

7.2 . . . τ]ὸνς πλατιϝοινάρχονς [τὰ]ν ζαμιίαν παρσχε[ν] τοον φο[ι]νον· αἰ δὲ μὲ hυπερπαρσχ[ο]ιιεν ϝοίφοθεν hο ἐπιγνόμον ἐπελ[ά]στο τον ὀφλον *vacat*?

APPENDIX II: GREEK TEXTS FOR CHAPTER 4

Draco's Homicide Law (*IG* i³ 104, *Nomima* 1.02, *IGT* 11).

1. καὶ ἐὰμ μὴ ’κ προνοίας κτένει τίς τινα, φεύγεν.

2. δικάζεν δὲ τὸς βασιλέας αἴτιον φόνο ἔ[ναι τὸν ἐργασάμενον] ἒ βολεύσαντα· τὸς δὲ ἐφέτας διαγνõναι.

3. αἰδέσασθαι δ’ ἐὰμ μὲν πατὲρ ἔι ἒ ἀδελφὸς ἒ hυε͂ς hάπαντας, ἒ τὸν κολύοντα κρατε͂ν.

4. ἐὰμ δὲ μὲ hοῦτοι ὀσι, μέχρ’ ἀνεφσιότετος καὶ ἀνεφσιõ, ἐὰν hάπαντες αἰδέσασθαι ἐθέλοσι, τὸν κολύοντα κρατε͂ν.

5. ἐὰν δὲ τούτον μεδὲ hε͂ς ἔι, κτένει δὲ ἄκον, γνõσι δὲ hοι πεντέκοντα καὶ hε͂ς hοι ἐφέται ἄκοντα κτε͂ναι, ἐσέσθον δὲ hοι φράτορες ἐὰν ἐθέλοσι δέκα· τούτος δὲ hοι πεντέκοντα καὶ hε͂ς ἀριστίνδεν hαιρέσθον.

6. καὶ hοι δὲ πρότερον κτέναντες ἐν τõιδε τõι θεσμõι ἐνεχέσθον.

7. προειπε̃ν δὲ το̃ι κτέναντι ἐν ἀγορᾶι μέχρ' ἀνεφσιότετος καὶ
   ἀνεφσιο̃.
8. συνδιόκεν δὲ κἀνφσιὸς καὶ ἀνεφσιο̃ν παῖδας καὶ γαμβρὸς καὶ
   πενθερὸς καὶ φράτορας.
9. ...
10. ἐὰν δέ τις τὸν ἀνδροφόνον κτένει ἒ αἴτιος ε̃ι φόνο, ἀπεχόμενον
    ἀγορᾶς ἐφορίας καὶ ἄθλον καὶ hιερὸν Ἀμφικτυονικο̃ν, hόσπερ τὸν
    Ἀθηναῖον κτέναντα ἐν τοῖς αὐτοῖς ἐνέχεσθαι· διαγιγνόσκεν δὲ τὸς
    ἐφέτας.
11. [ἐξ]ε̃[ναι δὲ τὸς ἀνδροφόνος ἀποκτένεν ἒ ἀπάγεν ἐὰν ἐν] τε̃ι
    hεμεδ[απε̃ι ...]
12. ἄρχον]τα χερο̃ν ἀ[δίκον ... χερ]ο̃ν ἀδίκον κτέ[νει ...
    διαγιγνόσκ]εν δὲ τὸς ἐ[φέτ]ας.
13. ...]εις ἒ ἐλεύθερος ε̃ι· κα[ὶ ἐὰν φέροντα ἒ ἄγοντα βίαι ἀδίκος
    εὐθὺς] ἀμυνόμενος κτένει, ν[εποινὲ τεθνάναι.

APPENDIX III: GREEK TEXTS FOR CHAPTER 5

The Agreement with Spensithios (SEG 27.631)

NB The text is written on both sides of the mitra; I give the top part of each
side. The text and interpretation of the lower parts are uncertain; as far as
we can tell, nothing in them relates to writing or remembering.

A 1–13 Θιοί· ἔϝαδε Δαταλεῦσι καὶ ἐσπένσαμες πόλις
Σπενσιθίωι ἀπὸ πυλᾶν πέντε ἀπ' ἑκάστας θροπά-
ν τε καὶ ἀτέλειαν πάντων αὐτῶι καὶ γενιᾶι ὠ-
ς κα πόλι τὰ δαμόσια τά τε θιήια καὶ τἀνθρώπινα
ποινικάζεν τε καὶ μναμονεῦϝεν. ποινικάζεν δὲ   5
πόλι καὶ μναμονεῦϝεν τὰ δαμόσια μήτε τὰ θιήι-
α μήτε τἀνθρώπινα μηδέν' ἄλον αἰ μὴ Σπενσίθι-
ον αὐτόν τε καὶ γενιὰν τõνυ, αἰ μὴ ἐπαίροι τ-
ε καὶ κέλοιτο ἢ αὐτὸς Σπενσίθιος ἢ γενιὰ
τõνυ ὅσοι δρομῆς εἶεν τῶν υἱῶν οἱ πλίες.   10
μισθὸν δὲ δόμεν τõ ἐνιαυτõ τῶι ποινικ-
αστᾶι πεντήϙοντα τε πρόϙοος κλεύκιο-
ς ...

B 1–7 τὸ ϝῖσον λακὲν τὸν ποινικαστὰν καὶ παρῆμε-
ν καὶ συνῆμεν ἐπί τε θηίων καὶ ἐπ' ἀνθρωπί-
νων πάντε ὅπε καὶ ἁ ϙόσμος εἴη καὶ τὸν ποινι-

καστάν, καὶ ὄτιμί κα θιῶι ἱαρεὺς μὴ ἰδιαλο-
... θύεν τε καὶ δαμόσια θύματα τὸν ποινικαστὰ-   5
ν καὶ τὰ τεμένια ἔκεν, μήδ' ἐπάγραν ἦμε-
ν μήδε ῥύτιον αἰλῆν τὸν ποινικαστὰν ...

APPENDIX IV: GREEK TEXTS FOR CHAPTER 6

Texts from ICret 4

1. 4.62 (*Nomima* II.3, *IGT* 144).
   - -]νασ[- -
   - -] οἰ Γο[ρτύνιοι- -
   - - ἐλε]ϝθερο [- -
   - -]ετις δολ[ο - -
   - - κοσ]μίον : ἒ ἄ[λλος- -   5
   - - λ]αγαῖεν ἀ[- -
   - -] τὰ θῖνα : ε [- -
   - -]ι : αἰ δὲ μὲ λε[ιο- -
   - -]οι : πίνεν : τ[- -
2. 4.63 (*Nomima* I.59).
   - -]νανα · · πέρεν εκορμιοκεσλυ[· · ·]α[- -
   - - τᾶ]γ [κρι]θᾶν μεδίμνονς δυόδεκα [- -
   - - ὁ Λεβεναῖος κ]ατὰ τὸ Γορτυνίο κατὰ δὲ τὸ Λεβενα[ίο] ὁ
     Γ[ορτύνιος - -
   - -]ιο[· ·] τῶι Λεβεναίοι καρτερὸς μαῖτ[υς - -
   - - ἄ]ρτον κατ' ἀμέραν πέντε στατῆραν[ς κ]αὶ [- -   5
   - -]γα[·]νο[- -
3. 4.64 (*Nomima* I.8).
   1. θιοί, θυκἀγαθᾶι. δοριὰν ἔδοκαν Διονυσ[ίοι τῶ]ι Κο[- -
   2–3. - - ἀρετᾶς ἐμ π]ολέ[μοι καὶ ἐ]ϝεργεσίας ἔνεκα Γόρτυνς ἐπίπανσα
       ϙ' οἰ ἐν Ἀϝλõνι ϝοικίοντες ἀτέλειαν [πάντον ἀ] ϝτõ[ι καὶ
       ἐσγόνοις - -
   4–5. - - ϝα]στίαν δίκαν καὶ ϝοικίαν ἐν Ἀϝλõνι ἐνδος Πύργο καὶ
       ϝοικόπεδον ἐκσοι γᾶν κ[- -
   6. - -]κον καὶ γ[υν]ασίο. *vac.*
4. 4.41 (*Nomima* II.65, *IGT* 127–8).
   Col. I   - - ἐπὶ τõ]-
   ι ἀδικηθέντι ἤμην,
   αἴ] κα λῆι, τὸ ϝ[ὸν] αὐτ-
   õ δόμην τὸ δὲ κῆνο ἔ-
   κεν. αἴ κά ϝοι μὴ λῆι   5

δέκσαθθαι, τὸ ἀπλό-
<ο>ν τεισῆται. *vac.* αἰ δέ
κα μὴ ἐπιδίηται τὸ π-
αροθὲν ἢ μὴ ἐπελεύ-
σει τὸ τετνακὸς ἢ μὴ   10
δείκσει ἇι ἔγ{ι}ρ<α>τται,
μὲ ἔνδικον ἤμην. *vac.* αἰ
δέ κα σῦς καρταῖπο-
ς παρόσει ἢ κατασκέ-
νηι, τόν τε σῦν ἐπὶ τõι   15
πάσσται ἤμην ὃ κ' ἦι τ-
ὸ καρταῖπος καὶ το

Col. II   - -]ε[- -
ται, τὸ ϝίσϝον κατασ-
τασεῖ. *vac.* ἵππον δὲ κ' [ἠ]μ-
ί[ο]νον κ' ὄνον τὸ μὲν
νυνατὸν ἐπιδίεθαι   5
ἇι ἔγρατται· αἰ δέ κα
τετνάκηι ἢ μὴ νυν-
ατὸν ἦι {η} ἐπιδίεθθαι,
καλῆν ἀντὶ μαιτύρ-
ον δυõν ἐν ταῖς πέν-   10
τε ἇι δείκσει ὀπῆ κ'
ἦι, κ' ὀρκιότερον ἤμη-
ν αὐτὸν καὶ τὸνς μα-
ίτυρανς αἰ ἐπεδίετ-
ο ἢ ἐπήλευσε ἢ ἐκάλη   15
δεικσίον. *vac.* κύνανς
ἀπαμπαιόμενο[·

Col. III   - - αἰ μὲν κ' ἀμπό]-
τεροι ἔπον[ται] οἰ ἀλ-
οῖοι μὴ ἔνδικον ἤμ-
ην, αἰ δέ κα μὴ ἀμπότ-
εροι ὀ [*c.* 4]ενος τὰ-   5
ν ἀπλόον τι[μὰ]ν κατα-
στας[εῖ]. *vac.* αἴ κα τετ-
ράπος ἢ ὄνν[ι]θα παρ-
καταθ[ε]μένοι ἢ κρη-
σάμενος ἢ [ἀλ]λᾶι δε-   10
κσάμενος μὴ νυνατ-

ὃς εἴη αὐτὸν ἀποδόμ-
ην, τὸ ἁπλόον κατασ-
τασεῖ. αἰ δέ κ' ἐπὶ τᾶι
δίκαι [μο]λίον ἐκσαν-
νήσεται, διπλεῖ κατ-   15
αστᾶσαι καὶ θέμεμ πόλι

Col. IV   - - περονσ[- -
δοντι τετραπλεῖ. *vac.*
ὅτι δέ κά τις αὐτὸν
ἀποδδῖ σομελές, τὸ ἁ-
πλόον καταστασεῖ. *vac.*   5
τὸν δὲ Ϝοικέα τὸν ἐπ-
ιδιόμενον μὴ ἀποδό-
θθαι μήτε ναεύοντα
μήτ' ἇ κ' ἀπέλθηι τῶ ἐν-
ιαυτῶ. αἰ δέ κα κοσμί-   10
οντος ἦι ὁ ἐπιδιόμε-
νος, μὴ ἀποδόθαι ἇς κ-
α κοσμῆι μηδ' ἇ κ' ἀπέ-
λθηι τῶ ἐνιαυτῶ. αἰ δ-
έ κα πρὸ τῶ κρόνο ἀπο-   15
δῶται, νικήθθο· ἀμπὶ
δὲ τὸν κρόνον ὀμνύ-

Col. V   [ντα κρίνεν τὸν δικαστὰν]
- -]ι · ισα · [· ·]ν. α[ἰ δέ]
κα μὴ ὀμόσει, τὸ ἁπλ-
όον καταστασεῖ. *vac.*
αἰ δέ κα κελομένο ὀ-
ι κα παρῆι Ϝεργάδδ-   5
ηται ἢ πέρηι, ἄπατον
ἤμην. αἰ δὲ πονίοι μ-
ὴ κελομένο, τὸν δικ-
ασστὰν ὀμνύντα κ-
ρίνεν, αἰ μὲ ἀποπον-   10
ίοι μαίτυρς. *vac.* ἀλλό-
τριον δ' αἴ τί κ' ἀδικ-
έσει ὁ κατακείμεν-
ος, αὐτὸν ἀτῆθαι. αἰ
δέ κα μὲ ἔκηι ὀπῶ κατα-   15
στασεῖ, ὁ νικάσανς
κ' ὁ καταθέμενος

Col. VI   - -]ειο[- -
οδ δὲ μή. *vac.* αἰ δέ τις
τὸν κατακείμεν-
ον ἀδικήσει, ὁ κατ-
αθέμενος μολησε-   5
ῖ καὶ πρακσῆται τ-
ὰς τιμὰνς ἆι ἐλευθέ-
ρο, κ’ ὅτι κ’ ἐσπράκσ-
εται τὰνν ἠμίναν ἔ-
κεν τὸν κατακείμ-   10
ενον, τὰν δὲ τὸν κατ-
αθέμενον. αἰ δέ κ’ ὁ κα-
ταθέμενος μὴ λῆι
μολῆν, ἦ κ’ ἀποδõι τὸ ὀ-
πήλομα αὐτὸς μολή-   15
το. αἰ δέ τί κ’ ὁ κατακεί-

Col. VII   [μενος - -
- -]ν[*c.* 9]ται κ-
ρήματα ἐπὶ ναὸν ἐπι-
διόμεν[ον] ἢ ἐπελεύσ-
αντα ἢ θ[*c.* 6]στα[·
·]λο[*c.* 2–3]α[*c.* 2–3] πεπᾶθαι   5
τουτον [*c.* 5]ια[
[ι]πε[*c.* 3] · αι [τὸ]μ πριάμ-
ενον [τοῖς μεμπ]ο[μέ]-
[νοις τõν] κρημάτον τὰν
ἄταν κατισστάμην ᾶ-   10
ι ϝεκάστο ἔγραται, κ-
αὶ τὸν ἄνδρ’ αὐτὸν ἐπὶ
τοῖς μεμπομένοις τ-
õν κρημάτον ἤμην, αἴ κ-
α μὴ περαιόσει ἦ κα πρία-   15
ται ἐν ταῖς τριάκοντ’ ἀμέ-
ραις. αἰ δέ κα συγνõντι τ-
ᾶν δέκ’ ἀμερᾶν μὴ περαιόσ-
ην, ἀνδοκὰν δὲ καὶ . . .

5. 4.47 (*Nomima* II.26, *IGT* 138)
A?] κατακείμενος. αἰ κ’ ἀδικήσει δõλος ἢ δόλα, ὅτι μέν κ[α κα]-
[τα]θεμένο κελομένο ἀμάρτη-
ι τõι καταθεμένοι τὰν δίκαν

ἤμην, ὅτι δὲ κ’ αὐτὸς πρὸ Ϝιαυτ- 5
ο̃ τõι ἀρκαίοι πάσται τὰν δίκαν ἤμην τõι δὲ καταθεμένοι μ-
ή. αἰ δέ κα νικαθῆι ὁ καθένς, ἀπ-
οδότο τõι καταθεμένοι ὅτι κ’
ὀπήληι. *vac.* αἰ δέ κα τὸν κατακεί- 10
μενον ἀδικήσει ἄλλος, αἰ μὲν
κ’ ἀνπότεροι μολίοντες νικά-
σοντι, τὰν ἡμίναν Ϝεκάτερο-
ς ἐκσίοντι· αἰ δέ κ’ ὁ ἄτερος μ-
ὴ λῆι, ὁ ἄτερος μολίον αἴ κα νι- 15
κάσει αὐτὸς ἐκσεῖ. αἰ δέ κ’ ἀ-
πόληται ὁ κατακείμενος, δικ-
ακσάτο ὀμόσαι τὸν καταθέμε-
νον μήτ’ αὐτὸν αἴτιον ἔμην μήτ-
ε σὺν ἄλλοι, μήτ’ ἐπ’ ἄλλοι Ϝισάμη- 20
ν. αἰ δέ κ’ ἀποθάνηι, δεικσάτο
B   ἀντὶ μαιτύρον δυõν.
αἰ δέ κα μὴ ὀμόσει ἅι ἔ-
γραται ἢ μὴ δείκσει, τ-
ὰν ἀπλόον τιμὰν κατα- 25
στασεῖ. αἰ δὲ κ’ αὐτὸν αἰ-
τιῆται ναὶ ἀποδόθαι ἢ
ἀποκρύψαι, αἴ κα νικ-
αθεῖ, τὰν ἀπλόον τ-
ιμὰν διππλεῖ κατα- 30
στασεῖ. αἰ δέ κα ναεύ-
ηι, ἐμπανία δεικσάτ-
ο.

6. 4.43 (*Nomima* I.47, II.70, *IGT* 130–3)
Aa αἴ κ’ ἄλος ἀδ-
ίκος ἐνεκ[υρ-
άκ]σανς μὴ κ-
αρπόσετ[αι, τ-
ὰς τιμὰνς τõ- 5
ν ἐνεκύρον κ-
αταστασεῖ ἅι
Ϝεκάστο ἔγρ-
ατται.
Ab αἴ κα δõλον ἢ
δόλαν ἀδίκος

ἐνεκυράκσει
ἢ ἐδύσει ἢ ἀπ[ολ-
ύσεται, ἐκς ἠμ-   5
ίνας καταστα-
σεῖ ἒ ἆι τōι ἐλ-
ευθέροι ἔγρα-
τται, τὰ δὲ τρί-
τρα τᾶς ϝήμα-   10
ς καὶ τᾶς ἀνπιδή-
μας ἆιπερ τōι ἐ[λευθέροι.

Ba θιοί· τὰν ἐν Κησκόραι καὶ
τὰν ἐμ Πάλαι πυταλιὰν ἔ-
δοκαν ἁ πόλις πυτεῦσαι. α-
ἴ τις ταύταν πρίαιτο ἢ κα-
ταθεῖτο, μὴ κατέκεθαι τō-   5
ι πριαμένοι τὰν ὀνὰν μηδ-
ὲ [τὰ]ν κα[τά]θεσιν· μηδ' ἐνεκ-
υράδδεν αἰ μὴ ἐπι[μ]ετρ[ῆι] τὰ-
ν ἐπικαρπίαν. *vac.*

Bb θιοί· τō ποταμō αἴ κα κατὰ τὸ
μέττον τὰν ῥοὰν θιθῆι ῥῆν [κ-
ατὰ τὸ ϝὸν αὐτō, θιθεμένοι ἄ-
πατον ἤμην. τὰν δὲ ῥοὰν λείπ-
εν ὄττον κατέκει ἁ ἐπ' ἀγορᾶ-   5
ι δέπυρα ἢ πλίον, μεῖον δὲ μή.

7. 4.78 (*Nomima* 1.16, *IGT* 153).
     θιοί. τάδ' ἔϝαδε τοῖς Γορτυνίοις ψαπίδονσ[ι] *vac.* τὸν ἀπελευ[- -
     - - - - κ]α λῆι καταϝοικίδεθαι Λατόσιον ἐπὶ τᾶι ϝίσϝαι [κ-
     αὶ τ]ᾶι ὁμοίαι, καὶ μέτινα τοῦτον μέτε καταδολό[θαι μέτε συλῆν.
     αἰ καταδολ]οῖτο, τὸν κσένιον κόσμον μὲ λαγαῖεν. αἰ δὲ [συλ-
     ί]οιεν, ἑκατὸν στατῆρανς ϝέκαστον τὸνς τίτανς [ἐσπράδδεθ- 5
     θαι, καὶ τὰν δ]ιπλείαν τōν κρεμάτον ἐστείσαντανς ἀποδόμ[εν
     ]. αἰ δ' οἰ τίται μὲ ϝέρκσιεν ἆι ἔγραται, τὰν διπλείαν ἄ[ταν
         ϝέκαστο-
     ν αὐτōν τōι μ]εμπομένοι ἀποδόμεν καὶ τᾶι πόλι θέμεν.

8. 4.75 (*Nomima* 11.46, *IGT* 147–8, 149, 155). *A* is supplemented from
     4.81.4–14.
A καλ[ῆν δ' ἀντὶ μαιτύρον δυ-
     ōν πρότριτον τὸν] ἐνεκυρ-
     άκσαντα μ[ετρεσιόμενον · α-
     ἰ δέ κα μὲ εἴει] καλίοντι ἄ-

ι ἔγρατται, α[ὐτὸς μετρέθο τ-   5
ε καὶ προπονέ]το προτέταρτ-
ον ἀντὶ μαιτύ[ρον δυῶν παρέ-
μεν ἐνς ἀγορ]άν. ὀμνύμεν δὲ
ἒ μὰν τοῦτο μ[έν ἐστι ἀβλοπί-
αι δικαίος πρὶν] μολέθαι τ-   10
[ὰν δίκαν, ὃ δ᾽ ἐνεκύρακσαν
μὲ ἔμεν]
B ... ὅ]πλα ἀνδρὸς
ἐλευθέρο ὅττ᾽ ἐνς πόλεμον
ἴσκει, πλὰν ϝέμας κ᾽ ἀνπιδέ-
μας, ἰστός, ἔρια κερίθεκν-   5
α, ϝεργαλεῖα σιδάρια, ἄρατ-
ρον, δυγὸν βοῶν, κάπετον, μ-
ύλανς, ὄνον ἀλέταν, ἒ<κ>ς ἀν-
δρείο ὅτ<τ>᾽ ὁ ἀρκὸς παρέκει
κατ᾽ ἀνδρεῖον, εὐνὰ ἀνδρὸς
καὶ γυναικό[ς], ἒ[λε]υθέρο ὀ-   10
C - -]δυ[- -
να ϝέκαστος [
· τι *vac.* αἴ κά τις πρ-
εῖγυς ἒι ἒ ἄλ[ος μ]ὲ νυνατὸ-
ς ἒι ἔρπεν [ἒ κ]α δέει ἐνεκυρ-   5
άδδεν, ἄλλον π[ρὸ] τούτο ἐνεκ-
υ]ράδδοντ[α] ἄπατον ἔμεν. ὀ-
νυμαινέτο δὲ [τ]ὸ ὄνυμα
· ο επατ[· ·] μαίτυρος ὅτι-
μι κενθ[· ·]ι[- -   10
D ·]ατιμ[- -
- - - ἐσπράτται ἒ δικασ-
τᾶι κ᾽ ὅς κα μαίτυραν[ς
- - - κ᾽ ὅττον ἔγρατται ἀ-
μολεὶ πράδεθαι κο ·   5
- -]αστομ[- -
9. 4.81 (*Nomima* II.47, *IGT* 155).
δενδρέον καὶ ϝοικίας ὀ[μόσ-
ον]τι τῶν ὁμόρον ἐννέα οἱ
ἐπάνκιστα πεπαμένοι, μ[ολ-
ἒν· κ]αλἒν δ᾽ ἀντὶ μαιτύρο-
ν δυῶν πρότριτον τὸν ἀπ[· ·   5
· ·]σαντα μετρεσιόμενο-

ν· αἰ δέ κα μὲ εἴει καλίον[τι ἆι
ἔγρ]αται, αὐτὸς μετρέθο τε
καὶ προπονέτο προτέταρ[τον
ἀν]τὶ μαιτύρον δυōν παρέμε-   10
ν ἐνσς ἀγοράν. ὀμνύμε[ν δ-
ὲ ἒ] μὰν τούτο μέν ἐστι ἀβλο-
πίαι δικαίος πρὶν μολέθ[θαι
τὰν] δίκαν, ὂ δ' ἐνεκύρακσαν
μὲ ἔμεν· νικῖν δ' ὄτερά κ' οἰ π[λί-   15
ες ὀ]μόσοντι. *vac.* κ' αἲ κ' ἐς στέγα-
ς ἐνεκυράκσοντι, πονίον[τι μ-
ὲ 'νϝ]οικῖν ὂ ἐνεκύρακσαν συν-
εκσομόσαθθαι τὸν ὁμό[ρον
τō]ν ἐννέα τρίινς, οἶς κα προ-   20
ϝείπει, μὲ ἐνϝοικῖν ὂ ἐνεκύ[ρα-
κσ]α[ν·] αἰ δέ τίς κα τὸν ὁμόρον. *vac.*

Bibliography

(Journal abbreviations as in *L'Année philologique*)

Adam, Sophie, *et al.* (ed.) (2002) *Mélanges en l'honneur Panayotis Dimakis: Droits antiques et société*. Athens.

Ager, Sheila L. (1996) *Interstate Arbitrations in the Greek World, 337–90 B.C.* Berkeley.

Allam, S. (1991) "Egyptian Law Courts in Pharaonic and Hellenistic Times," *JEA* 77: 109–27.

Allen, Danielle S. (2000) *The World of Prometheus: The Politics of Punishing in Democratic Athens*. Princeton.

Anderson, Greg (2003) *The Athenian Experiment: Building an Imagined Political Community in Ancient Attica, 508–490 B.C.* Ann Arbor.

Arnaoutoglou, Ilias (1998) *Ancient Greek Laws: A Sourcebook*. London.

Ashburner, Walter (1909) *The Rhodian Sea-Law*. Oxford.

Asper, Markus (2004) "Law and Logic: Towards an Archaeology of Greek Abstract Reason," *AION. Annali dell'università degli studi di Napoli "l'orientale"* 26: 73–94.

Baker, J. H. (1990) *An Introduction to English Legal History*. 3rd edn. London.

Bauman, Richard (1986) *Story, Performance, and Event: Contextual Studies of Oral Narrative*. Cambridge.

Benveniste, Emile (1973) *Indo-European Language and Society*. Coral Gables, FL. (Originally *Le vocabulaire des institutions Indo-Européennes*. Paris 1969.)

Bers, Victor (1985) "Dikastic *Thorubos*," in *Crux: Essays Presented to G. E. M. de Ste. Croix on his 75th Birthday*, eds. P. Cartledge and F. D. Harvey. Exeter: 1–15.

Bertrand, Jean-Marie (1999) *De l'écriture à l'oralité: Lectures des Lois de Platon*. Paris.

Bile, Monique (2000) "*IC* 4.41 et le sens de ἐπιδίομαι," in Lévy 2000b: 161–74.

Biscardi, Arnaldo (1982) *Diritto greco antico*. Milan.

Blok, Josine H. and André P. Lardinois (eds.) (2006) *Solon of Athens: New Historical and Philological Approaches*. Leiden.

Boardman, John (1998) *Early Greek Vase Painting*. London.

Boegehold, Alan L. (1982) "A Lid with Dipinto," in *Studies in Attic Epigraphy, History and Topology Presented to Eugene Vanderpool* (*Hesperia* Supplement 19): 1–6.

(1995) *The Lawcourts at Athens*. Princeton.

Bogaert, R. (1976) *Texts on Bankers, Banking and Credit in the Greek World* (= *Epigraphica III*). Leiden.

Bohannan, Paul (1957) *Justice and Judgement among the Tiv*. Oxford.

Bonner, Robert J. (1905) *Evidence in Athenian Courts*. Chicago.

Bottéro, Jean (1992) *Mesopotamia: Writing, Reasoning, and the Gods*. Chicago. (Translation of *Mésopotamie. L'écriture, la raison et les dieux*. Paris 1987.)

Brock, Roger and Stephen Hodkinson (eds.) (2000) *Alternatives to Athens: Varieties of Political Organization and Community in Ancient Greece*. Oxford.

Bury, J. B. and Russell Meiggs (1975) *A History of Greece*. 4th edn. London.

Byock, Jesse L. (2001) *Viking Age Iceland*. London.

Cairns, Francis (1984) "ΧΡΕΜΑΤΑ ΔΟΚΙΜΑ: IG XII, 9, 1273 and 1274 and the Early Coinage of Eretria," *ZPE* 54: 145–55.

(1991) "The 'Laws of Eretria' (*IG* XII.9 1273 and 1274): Epigraphic, Legal, Historical, and Political Aspects," *Phoenix* 45: 296–313.

Calhoun, George M. (1919) "Oral and Written Pleading in Athenian Courts," *TAPhA* 50: 177–93.

(1927) *The Growth of Criminal Law in Ancient Greece*. Berkeley and Los Angeles.

Camassa, Giorgio (1988) "Aux origines de la codification écrite en Grèce," in Detienne 1988: 130–55.

Cantarella, Eva (2002) "Dispute Settlement in Homer: Once Again on the Shield of Achilles," in Adam, *et al.* 2002: 147–65.

(2005a) "Violence privée et procès," in *La violence dans les mondes grec et romain. Actes du colloque international (Paris, 2–4 mai 2002)*, ed. Jean-Marie Bernard. Paris: 339–47.

(2005b) "Response to Raymond Westbrook," in Wallace and Gagarin 2005: 25–32.

Cantarella, Eva and Gerhard Thür (eds.) (2001) *Symposion 1997*. Cologne.

Carey, Christopher (1994) "'Artless' Proofs in Aristotle and the Orators," *BICS* 39: 95–106.

(1996) "*Nomos* in Rhetoric and Oratory," *JHS* 116: 33–46.

(1998) "The Shape of Athenian Laws," *CQ* 48: 93–109.

Carlier, Pierre (2000) "Homeric and Macedonian Kingship," in Brock and Hodkinson 2000: 259–68.

Charpin, Dominique (2003) *Hammu-rabi de Babylone*. Paris.

Clanchy, Michael T. (1985) "Literacy, Law, and the Power of the State," in *Culture et idéologie dans la genèse de l'état moderne. Actes de la table ronde organisée par le Centre national de la recherche scientifique et l'Ecole française de Rome. Rome, 15–17 octobre 1984, 25–34*. Rome.

(1993) *From Memory to Written Record: England 1066–1307*. 2nd edn. Oxford.

(1998) *England and its Rulers 1066–1272*. 2nd edn. London.

Cohen, David (1983) *Theft in Athenian Law* (*Münchener Beiträge zur Papyrusforschung und antiken Rechtsgeschichte* 74). Munich.

(1995) *Law, Violence and Community in Classical Athens*. Cambridge.

(2003) "Writing, Law, and Legal Practice in the Athenian Courts," in *Written Texts and the Rise of Literate Culture in Ancient Greece*, ed. Harvey Yunis. Cambridge: 78–96.

(2005) "Introduction," in Gagarin and Cohen 2005: 1–26.

Comaroff, John L. and Simon Roberts (eds.) (1981) *Rules and Processes: The Cultural Logic of Dispute in an African Context.* Chicago.

Comparetti, Domenico (1893) *Le leggi di Gortyna e le altre iscrizioni arcaiche cretesi (= Monumenti antichi* 3). Milan.

Cook, J. M. (1982) "The Eastern Greeks," in *CAH*, 2nd edn. III.1. Cambridge: 196–221.

Cook, S. A., F. E. Adcock, and M. P. Charlesworth (eds.) (1928) *The Hellenistic Monarchies and the Rise of Rome (= CAH,* 1st edn., vol. VII). Cambridge.

Cornell, Tim (1991) "The Tyranny of the Evidence: a Discussion of the Possible Uses of Literacy in Etruria and Latium in the Archaic Age," in *Literacy in the Roman World,* ed. J. H. Humphrey. Ann Arbor: 7–33.

Crawford, Michael H. (1996) *Roman Statutes.* 2 vols. (*BICS,* Supplement 64). London.

Crook, J. A. (1995) *Legal Advocacy in the Roman World.* London.

Crowther, Charles (1992) "The Decline of Greek Democracy?," *JAC* 7: 13–48.

Dareste, R., B. Hassoullier, and Th. Reinach (1891–1904) *Recueil des inscriptions juridiques grecques.* 2 vols. Paris.

Darmezin, Laurence (1999) *Les affranchissements par consécration en Boétie et dans le monde grec hellénistique.* Nancy.

Davies, John K. (1996) "Deconstructing Gortyn: When is a Code a Code?" in Foxhall and Lewis 1996: 33–56.

(2000) "A Wholly Non-Aristotelian Universe: The Molossians as Ethnos, State, and Monarchy," in Brock and Hodkinson 2000: 234–58.

(2004) "The Concept of the 'Citizen'," in *Poleis e Politeiai,* ed. Silvio Cataldi. Alessandria: 19–30.

Davies, Wendy and Paul Fouracre (eds.) (1986) *The Settlement of Disputes in Early Medieval Europe.* Cambridge.

De Brauw, Michael (2001–2) "'Listen to the Laws Themselves': Citations of Laws and Portrayal of Character in Attic Oratory," *CJ* 97: 161–76.

Demargne, P. and H. van Effenterre (1937a) "Recherches à Dréros," *BCH* 61: 5–32.

(1937b) "Recherches à Dréros II. Les inscriptions archaïques," *BCH* 61: 333–48.

Derderian, Katherine (2001) *Leaving Words to Remember: Greek Mourning and the Advent of Literacy (Mnemosyne Supplement* 209). Leiden.

Detienne, Marcel (1981) *L'invention de la mythologie.* Paris: Callimard. (English trans. 1986. *The Creation of Mythology.* Chicago.)

(ed.) (1988) *Les savoirs de l'écriture en Grèce ancienne.* Lille.

Diamant, Steven (1982) "Theseus and the Unification of Attica," in *Studies in Attic Epigraphy, History and Topology Presented to Eugene Vanderpool (Hesperia* Supplement 19): 38–47.

Diamond, A. S. (1971) *Primitive Law Past and Present.* London.

Donlan, Walter (1997) "The Relations of Power in the Pre-state and Early State Polities," in Mitchell and Rhodes 1997: 39–48.

Dow, Sterling (1959) "The Law Codes of Athens," *Proceedings of the Massachusetts Historical Society* 71: 3–36.

Driver, G. R. and John C. Miles (1952) *The Babylonian Laws.* 2 vols. Oxford.

Dyck, Andrew R. (2004) *A Commentary on Cicero, De Legibus.* Ann Arbor.

Eder, Walter (1986) "The Political Significance of the Codification of Law in Archaic Societies: An Unconventional Hypothesis," in *Social Struggles in Archaic Rome: New Perspectives on the Conflict of the Orders,* ed. Kurt A. Raaflaub. Berkeley: 262–300.

Faraguna, Michele (2007) "Tra oralità e scrittura: diritto e forme della comunicazione dai poemi omerici a Teofrasto," *Etica & Politica* 9: 75–111 (electronic publication available at www.units.it/etica).

Fell, Martin (1997) "Konkordanz zu den frühen griechischen Gesetzestexten," *ZPE* 118: 183–96.

Finkelstein, J. J. (1961) "Ammisaduqa's Edict and the Babylonian 'Law Codes'," *Journal of Cuneiform Studies* 15: 91–104.

Finley, Moses I. (1951) "Some Problems of Greek Law (review of Pringsheim 1950). *Seminar* 9: 72–91.

   (1966) "The Problem of the Unity of Greek Law," in *La Storia del diritto nel quadro delle scienze storiche (Atti del primo Congresso Internazionale della Società Italiana di Storia del Diritto).* Florence: 129–42. (Reprinted in *The Use and Abuse of History.* London 1986: 134–52, 236–7.)

   (1978) *The World of Odysseus.* 2nd edn. New York.

Finnegan, Ruth (1992) *Oral Poetry: Its Nature, Significance and Social Context.* 2nd edn. Bloomington, IN.

Fischer, John E. (2003) "*Sanides* and *Sanidia*," in *Gestures: Essays in Ancient History, Literature, and Philosophy Presented to Alan L. Boegehold,* eds. Geoffrey W. Bakewell and James P. Sickinger. Oxford: 237–50.

Fleming, Robin (1998) *Domesday Book and the Law: Society and Legal Custom in Early Medieval England.* Cambridge.

Flensted-Jensen, Pernille, Thomas Heine Nielsen, and Lene Rubinstein (eds.) (2000) *Polis & Politics: Studies in Ancient Greek History Presented to Mogens Hansen on His Sixtieth Birthday, August 20, 2000.* Copenhagen.

Foote, Peter (1977) "Oral and Literary Tradition in Early Scandinavian Law: Aspects of a Problem," in *Oral and Literary Tradition,* eds. Hans Bekker-Nielsen *et al.* Odense: 47–55.

Forrest, W. G. (2000) "The Pre-polis Polis," in Brock and Hodkinson 2000: 280–92.

Forsdyke, Sara (2005) *Exile, Ostracism, and Democracy: The Politics of Expulsion in Ancient Greece.* Princeton.

Fox, Leonard (trans.) (1989) *Kanuni I Lekë Dukagjinit: The Code of Lekë Dukagjinit.* (Translation of the Albanian Text Collected and Arranged by Shtjefën Gjeçov.) New York.

Foxhall, Lin (1996) "The Law and the Lady: Women and Legal Proceedings in Classical Athens," in Foxhall and Lewis 1996: 133–52.

Foxhall, Lin and Andrew D. E. Lewis (eds.) (1996) *Greek Law in its Political Setting: Justifications Not Justice.* Oxford.

Fraser, Peter M. (1972) *Ptolemaic Alexandria.* 3 vols. Oxford.

Gagarin, Michael (1981a) *Drakon and Early Athenian Homicide Law*. New Haven.
(1981b) "The Thesmothetai and the Earliest Athenian Tyranny Law," *TAPhA* 111: 71–7.
(1982) "The Organization of the Gortyn Law Code," *GRBS* 23: 129–46.
(1986) *Early Greek Law*. Berkeley.
(1990) "*Bouleusis* in Athenian Homicide Law," in *Symposion 1988*, eds. Guiseppe Nenci and Gerhard Thür. Cologne: 81–99.
(ed.) (1991) *Symposion 1990*. Cologne.
(1992) "The Poetry of Justice: Hesiod and the Origins of Greek Law," *Ramus* 21: 61–78.
(1994) "The Economic Status of Women at Gortyn: Retroactivity and Change," in *Symposion 1993*, ed. Gerhard Thür. Cologne: 61–71.
(1996) "The Torture of Slaves in Athenian Law," *CPh* 91: 1–18.
(1997) "Oaths and Oath-Challenges in Greek Law," in *Symposion 1995*, eds. Gerhard Thür and Julie Vélissaropoulos-Karakostas. Cologne: 125–34.
(1999) "Rhétorique et anti-rhétorique à Gortyne," in *Des dialectes grecs aux lois de Gortyne*, ed. Catherine Dobias-Lalou. Nancy: 65–74.
(2000a) "The *Basileus* in Athenian Homicide Law," in Flensted-Jensen *et al.* 2000: 569–79.
(2000b) "The Legislation of Demetrius of Phaleron and the Transformation of Athenian Law," in *Demetrius of Phalerum: Text, Translation and Discussion. Rutgers University Studies in Classical Humanities*, eds. William W. Fortenbaugh and Eckart Schütrumpf. New Brunswick, NJ: 347–65.
(2001) "The Gortyn Code and Greek Legal Procedure," in Cantarella and Thür 2001: 41–51.
(2002a) *Antiphon the Athenian: Law and Oratory in the Age of the Sophists*. Austin, TX.
(2002b) "*Logos* as *Ergon* in Isocrates," in *Papers in Rhetoric IV*, ed. Lucia Calboli Montefusco. Rome: 111–19.
(2005) "The Unity of Greek Law," in Gagarin and Cohen 2005: 29–40.
(2006a) "Legal Procedure in Solon's Laws," in Blok and Lardinois 2006: 261–75.
(2006b) "Inscribing Laws in Greece and the Near East," in Rupprecht 2006: 9–20.
(2006c) "The Unwritten Monument: Speaking and Writing Pericles' Funeral Oration," in *III International Symposium on Thucydides: The Speeches*, ed. Marios Scortis. Athens: 176–87.
(2007a) "Litigant's Oaths in Athenian Law," in *Horkos: The Oath in Greek Society*, eds. Alan Sommerstein and Judith Fletcher. Exeter: 39–47.
(2007b) "From Oral Law to Written Laws: Draco's Law and its Homeric Roots," in *Symposion 2005*, eds. Eva Cantarella and Gerhard Thür. Vienna: 3–17
Gagarin, Michael and David Cohen (eds.) (2005) *The Cambridge Companion to Ancient Greek Law*. Cambridge.
Gallia, Andrew B. (2004) "The Republication of Draco's Law on Homicide," *CQ* 54: 451–60.

Gehrke, Hans-Joachim (2000) "Verschriftung und Verschriftlichung sozialer Normen im archaischen und klassischen Griechenland," in Lévy 2000b: 141–59.

Geller, Markham J. and Herwig Maehler (eds.) (1995) *Legal Documents of the Hellenistic World*. London.

Gernet, Louis (1968) *Anthropologie de la Grèce antique*. Paris.

Glotz, Gustave (1904) *La solidarité de la famille dans le droit criminel en Grèce*. Paris.

Goody, Jack (1986) *The Logic of Writing and the Organization of Society*. Cambridge.

(1987) *The Interface Between the Written and the Oral*. Cambridge.

Graeca Halensis (1913) *Dikaiomata: Auszüge aus alexandrinischen Gesetzen und Verordnungen*. Berlin.

Greco, Emanuele and Mario Lombardo (2005) *La Grande Iscrizione di Gortyna: Centoventi anni dopo la scoperta (Atti del Convegno, Atene-Haghii Deka 25–28 maggio 2004)*. Athens.

Green, D. H. (1994) *Medieval Listening and Reading: The Primary Reception of German Literature 800–1300*. Cambridge.

Griffiths, Bill (1995) *An Introduction to Early English Law*. Norfolk, UK.

Guarducci, Margharita (1935–50) *Inscriptiones Creticae*. 4 vols. Rome.

Gwatkin, W. E. (1957) "The Legal Arguments in Aeschines' *Against Ctesiphon* and Demosthenes' *On the Crown*," *Hesperia* 26: 129–41.

Habicht, Christian (1997) *Athens from Alexander to Antony*. Cambridge, MA.

Hagerdorn, Anselm C. (2001) "Gortyn – Utilizing an Archaic Greek Law Code for Biblical Research," *Zeitschrift für Altorientalische und Biblische Rechtsgeschichte* 7: 217–42.

Hall, Jonathan M. (2007) *A History of the Archaic Greek World*. Malden, MA.

Hansen, Mogens Herman (1976) *Apagoge, Endeixis and Ephegesis against Kakourgoi, Atimoi and Pheugontes*. Odense.

(1980) "Athenian *Nomothesia* in the Fourth Century BC and Demosthenes' Speech Against Leptines," *C&M* 32: 87–104.

(1985) "Athenian *Nomothesia*," *GRBS* 26: 345–71.

Harding, Phillip (trans.) (1985) *From the End of the Peloponnesian War to the Battle of Ipsus*. Cambridge.

Harris, Edward M. (1994) "Law and Oratory," in *Persuasion: Greek Rhetoric in Action*, ed. Ian Worthington. London: 130–50.

(2006) "Solon and the Spirit of the Laws in Archaic and Classical Greece," in Blok and Lardinois 2006: 290–318.

Harris, Edward M. and Lene Rubinstein (eds.) (2004) *The Law and the Courts in Ancient Greece*. London.

Harris, William V. (1989) *Ancient Literacy*. Cambridge, MA.

(1996) "Writing and Literacy in the Archaic Greek City," in *ENEPΓEIA: Studies on Ancient History and Epigraphy Presented to H. W. Pleket*, eds. J. H. M. Strubbe, R. A. Tybour, and H. S. Versnel. Amsterdam: 57–77.

Hart, H. L. A. (1994) *The Concept of Law*. 2nd edn. Oxford.

Havelock, Eric A. (1963) *Preface to Plato*. Cambridge, MA.

(1976) *Origins of Western Literacy*. Toronto.

(1982) *The Literate Revolution in Greece and Its Cultural Consequences*. Princeton.

Hedrick, Charles W., Jr. (2000) "For Anyone Who Wishes to See," *AncW* 31: 127–35.

Helm, Peyton R. (1981) "Herodotus' *Mēdikos Logos* and Median History," *Iran* 19: 85–90.

Herrenschmidt, Clarisse (2000) "Writing between Visible and Invisible Worlds in Iran, Israel, and Greece," in *Ancestor of the West: Writing Reasoning and Religion in Mesopotamia, Elam, and Greece*, eds. Jean Bottéro, Clarisse Herrenschmidt, and Jean-Pierre Vernant. Chicago: 67–146.

Hölkeskamp, Karl-Joachim (1992) "Written Law in Archaic Greece," *PCPhS* 38: 87–117.

(1994) "Tempel, Agora und Alphabet: Die Entstehungsbedinungen von Gesetzgebung in der archaischen Polis," in *Rechtskodifizierung und soziale Normen im interkulturellen Vergleich*, ed. Hans-Joachim Gehrke, Tübingen: 135–64.

(1995) "Arbitrators, Lawgivers and the 'Codification of Law' in Archaic Greece: Problems and Perspectives," *Metis* 7: 49–81.

(1999) *Schiedsrichter, Gesetzgeber und Gesetzgebung im archaischen Griechenland. Historia Einzelschrift* 131. Stuttgart.

(2000) "(In-)schrift und Monument. Zum Begriff des Gesetzes im archaischen und klassischen Griechenland," *ZPE* 132: 73–96.

(2005) "What's in a Code? Solon's Laws between Complexity, Compilation and Contingency," *Hermes* 133: 280–93.

Homolle, Théophile (1926) "La loi de Cadys sur le prêt à intérêt. Une crise sociale et politique à Delphes au IVe siècle," *BCH* 50: 3–106, with Plates I–II.

Hopkins, Keith (1978) *Conquerors and Slaves*. Cambridge.

Humphreys, Sally (1991) "A Historical Approach to Drakon's Law on Homicide," in Gagarin 1991: 17–45.

Hunt, A. S. and C. C. Edgar (1932–4) *Select Papyri*. 2 vols. Cambridge, MA.

Isserlin, B. S. J. (1991) "The Transfer of the Alphabet to the Greeks. The State of Documentation," in *Phoinikeia Grammata: Lire et écrire en Méditerranée*, eds. Cl. Baurain, C. Bonnet, and V. Krings. Namur: 283–91.

Jeffery, Lilian H. (1956) "The Courts of Justice in Archaic Chios," *ABSA* 51: 157–67, with Plate 43.

(1982) "Greek Alphabetic Writing," in *CAH*, 2nd edn. III.1: 819–33.

(1990) *The Local Scripts of Archaic Greece*. 2nd edn., with a Supplement by A. W. Johnston. Oxford. (1st edn. 1961.)

Jeffery, L. H. and A. Morpurgo-Davies (1970) "Poinikastas and poinikazein: BM 1969. 4–2.1, A New Archaic Inscription from Crete," *Kadmos* 9: 118–54.

Joannès, Francis (ed.) (2000) *Rendre la justice en Mésopotamie: Archives judiciaires du Proche-Orient ancien (IIIe–Ier millénaires avant J.-C.)*. Vincennnes.

Johnston, A. W. (1990) "Supplement," in Jeffery 1990: 423–80.

Johnstone, Steven (1999) *Disputes and Democracy: The Consequences of Litigation in Athens.* Austin, TX.

Jolowicz, H. F. and Barry Nicholas (1972) *Historical Introduction to the Study of Roman Law.* 3rd edn. Cambridge.

Jones, Gwyn (1984) *A History of the Vikings.* Oxford.

Kapparis, Konstantinos A. (1999) *Apollodorus 'Against Neaira' [D. 59].* Berlin.

Katzoff, Ranon (1995) "Hellenistic Marriage Contracts," in Geller and Maehler 1995: 37–45.

Keynes, Simon (1990) "Royal Government and the Written Word in Late Anglo-Saxon England," in McKitterick 1990: 226–57.

Koerner, Reinhard (1993) *Inschriftliche Gesetzestexte der frühen griechischen Polis.* Cologne.

Kraus, F. R. (1960) "Ein zentrales Problem des altmesopotamischen Rechtes: Was ist der Codex Hammu-rabi?" *Genave* n.s. 8: 283–96.

Kussmaul, Peter (1969) *Synthekai: Beiträge zur Geschichte des attischen Obligationenrechtes.* Basle.

Lafont, Sophie (2000) "Codification et subsidiarité dans les droits du Proche-Orient ancien," in Lévy 2000b: 49–64.

Lambrinudakis, Wassilios and Michael Wörrle (1983) "Ein hellenistisches Reformgesetz über das öffentliche Urkundenwesen von Paros," *Chiron* 13: 283–368.

Langdon, Merle K. (2005) "A New Greek Abecedarium," *Kadmos* 44: 175–82.

Lanni, Adriaan M. (2004) "Arguing from 'Precedent': Modern Perspectives on Athenian Practice," in Harris and Rubinstein 2004: 159–71.

(2006) *Law and Justice in the Courts of Classical Athens.* Cambridge.

Larsen, J. A. O. (1947) "The Origin and Significance of the Counting of Votes," *CPh* 44: 164–81.

Leemans, W. F. (1991) "Quelques considérations à propos d'une étude récente du droit du Proche-Orient ancien," *Bibliotheca Orientalis* 48: 409–37, esp. 414–20.

Lemosse, M. (1957) "Les lois de Gortyne et la notion de codification," *RIDA* 3.4: 131–7.

Lévy, Edmond (1997) "Libre et non-libres dans le code de Gortyne," in *Esclavage, guerre, économie en Grèce ancienne: Hommages à Yvon Garlan,* eds. Pierre Burlé and Jacques Ouhlen. Rennes: 25–41.

(2000a) "La cohérence du code de Gortyne," in Lévy 2000b: 185–214.

(ed.) (2000b) *La codification des lois dans l'antiquité: Actes du Colloque de Strasbourg 27–29 novembre 1997.* Strasburg.

Lewis, David M. (1959) "Attic Manumissions," *Hesperia* 28: 208–38.

(1967) "A Note on *IG* i² 114," *JHS* 87: 132. (Reprinted in *Selected Papers in Greek and Near Eastern History,* ed. P. J. Rhodes. Cambridge 1997: 203–4.)

Link, Stefan (2003) "Kosmoi, Startoi und Iterationsverbote: Zum Kampf um das Amt des Kosmos auf Kreta," *Dike* 6: 139–49.

Lipsius, Justus Herman (1905–15) *Das attische Recht und Rechtsverfahren.* Leipzig.

Lloyd, Geoffrey E. R. (1979) *Magic, Reason and Experience: Studies in the Origins and Development of Greek Science.* Cambridge.

Lombardo, Mario (1988) "Marchands, transactions économiques, écriture," in Detienne 1988: 159–87.

Lönnroth, Lars (1976) *Njáls Saga: A Critical Introduction.* Berkeley.

Lupu, Eran (2005) *Greek Sacred Law: A Collection of New Documents (NGSL).* Leiden.

MacDowell, Douglas M. (1962) *Andokides* On the Mysteries. Oxford.

(ed.). (1971) *Aristophanes* Wasps. Oxford.

(1975) "Law-Making at Athens in the Fourth Century BC," *JHS* 95: 62–74.

(1986) *Spartan Law.* Edinburgh.

(1990) *Demosthenes Against Meidias (Oration 21).* Oxford.

Maffi, Alberto (1991) "Adozione e strategie successorie a Gortina e ad Atene," in Gagarin 1991: 205–31.

Magnetto, Anna (1997) *Gli arbitrati interstatali greci.* Pisa.

Magnusson, Magnus and Heermann Pálsson (trans.) (1960) *Njal's Saga.* Harmondsworth.

Manville, Brook (1990) *The Origins of Citizenship in Ancient Athens.* Princeton.

Mazarakis Ainian, Alexander (1997) *From Rulers' Dwellings to Temples. Architecture, Religion and Society in Early Iron Age Greece (1100–700 B.C.) (Studies in Mediterranean Archaeology* 121). Jonsered.

McKitterick, Rosamond (ed.) (1990) *The Uses of Literacy in Early Medieval Europe.* Cambridge.

Meiggs, Russell and David Lewis (1969) *A Selection of Greek Historical Inscriptions.* Oxford.

Meyer, Elizabeth A. (2004) *Legitimacy and Law in the Roman World*: Tabulae *in Roman Belief and Practice.* Cambridge.

Meyer, Paul M. (1920) *Juristische Papyri: Erklärung von Urkunden zur Einführung in die juristische Papyruskunde.* Berlin.

Meyer-Laurin, Harald (1965) *Gestez und Billigkeit im attischen Prozess.* Weimar.

Millender, Ellen G. (2001) "Spartan Literacy Revisited," *ClAnt* 20: 121–64.

Miller, William Ian (1990) *Bloodtaking and Peacemaking: Feud, Law, and Society in Saga Iceland.* Chicago.

Mitchell, Lynette and Peter Rhodes (eds.) (1997) *The Development of the Polis.* London.

Modrzejewski, Joseph Mélèze (1966) Le règle de droit dans l'Egypte ptolémaïque," in *Essays in Honor of C. Bradford Wells (American Studies in Papyrology* 1). New Haven: 125–73.

(1978) "Chrématistes et laocrites," in *Le monde grec: Hommages à Claire Préaux,* eds. Jean Bingen, Guy Cambier, and Georges Nachtergae. Brussels: 699–708.

(1995) "Law and Justice in the Ptolemaic World," in Geller and Maehler 1995: 1–19.

Morris, Ian (1986) "The Use and Abuse of Homer," *ClAnt* 5: 81–138.

Morris, Sarah P. (1984) *The Black and White Style: Athens and Aigina in the Orientalizing Period.* New Haven.

(2003) "Imaginary Kings: Alternatives to Monarchy in Early Greece," in *Popular Tyranny: Sovereignty and its Discontents in Ancient Greece,* ed. Kathryn A. Morgan. Texas: 1–24.

Muhl, Max (1933) *Untersuchungen zur altorientalischen und althellenischen Gesetzgebung. Klio* Beiheft 29. Berlin.

Murray, Oswyn (1993) *Early Greece.* 2nd edn. Cambridge, MA.

Nader, Laura (2002) *The Life of the Law: Anthropological Projects.* Berkeley.

Naveh, Joseph (1991) "Semitic Epigraphy and the Antiquity of the Greek Alphabet," *Kadmos* 30: 143–52.

Nissen, Hans J. (1993) "The Context of the Emergence of Writing in Mesopotamia and Iran," in *Early Mesopotamia and Iran: Contact and Conflict 3500–1600 BC.* ed. John Curtis. London: 54–71.

Oliver, Lisi (2002) *The Beginnings of English Law.* Toronto.

Olsen, David R. (1994) *The Word on Paper: The Conceptual and the Cognitive Implications of Writing and Reading.* Cambridge.

Osborne, Robin (1985) "Law in Action in Classical Athens," *JHS* 105: 40–58.

(1996) *Greece in the Making 1200–479 BC.* London.

(1997) "Law and Laws. How Do We Join Up the Dots," in Mitchell and Rhodes 1997: 74–82.

(2004) *Greek History.* London.

Ostwald, Martin (1955) "The Athenian Legislation against Tyranny and Subversion," *TAPhA* 86: 103–28.

(1969) *Nomos and the Beginnings of Athenian Democracy.* Oxford.

(1973) "Was There a Concept ἄγραφος νόμος in Classical Greece?" *Phronesis* Suppl. 1: 70–104.

Palaima, Thomas G. (1987) "Comments on Mycenean Literacy," in *Studies in Mycenaean and Classical Greek Presented to John Chadwick. Minos* n.s. 20–2: 499–510.

Palmer, L. R. (1950) "The Indo-European Origins of Greek Justice," *TPhS (Oxford)*, 149–68.

Papakonstantinou, Zinon (2002) "Written Law, Literacy and Social Conflict in Archaic and Classical Crete," *AHB* 16: 135–50.

Parker, Robert (2005) "Law and Religion," in Gagarin and Cohen 2005: 61–81.

Pébarthe, Christophe (2006) *Cité, démocratie et écriture: Histoire de l'alphabétisation d'Athènes à l'époque classique.* Paris.

Perlman, Paula (1996) "Πόλις Ὑπήκοος. The Dependent *Polis* and Crete," in *Introduction to an Inventory of* Poleis (Acts of the Copenhagen Polis Centre, vol. III), ed. Mogens Herman Hansen. Copenhagen: 233–87.

(2000) "Gortyn. The First Seven Hundred Years (Part I)," in Flensted-Jensen *et al.* 2000: 59–89.

(2002) "Gortyn. The First Seven Hundred Years (Part II): The Laws from the Temple of Apollo Pythios," in *Even More Studies in the Ancient Greek* Polis (Papers of the Copenhagen Polis Center, vol. VI), ed. Thomas Heine Nielsen (*Historia* Einzelschriften 162). Stuttgart: 187–227.

(2004) "Writing on the Walls. The Architectural Context of Archaic Cretan Laws," in *Crete beyond the Palaces: Proceedings of the Crete 2000 Conference*, eds. Leslie P. Day, Margaret S. Mook, and James D. Muhly. Philadelphia: 81–97.

Pestman, P. W. (1994) *The New Papyrological Primer*. 2nd edn. Leiden.

Piccirilli, Luigi (1981) "'Nomoi' cantati e 'nomoi' scritti," *CCC* 2: 7–14.

Piérart, Marcel (2003) "Genèse et développement d'une ville à l'ancienne: Argos," in *La naissance de la ville dans l'antiquité*, eds. Michel Reddé *et al.* Paris: 49–70.

Pounder, Robert L. (1984) "The Origin of θέοι as Inscription-Heading," in *Studies Presented to Sterling Dow on his Eightieth Birthday*, ed. W. T. Loomis. Durham, NC: 243–50.

Powell, Barry B. (1989) "Why Was the Greek Alphabet Invented? The Epigraphical Evidence," *ClAnt* 8: 321–50.

(1991) *Homer and the Origin of the Greek Alphabet*. Cambridge.

(2002) *Writing and the Origins of Greek Literature*. Cambridge.

Powell, Marvin A. (1981) "Three Problems in the History of Cuneiform Writing: Origins, Direction of Script, Literacy," *Visible Language* 15: 419–40.

Prent, Mieke (2005) *Cretan Sanctuaries and Cults: Continuity and Change from Late Minoan IIIC to the Archaic Period*. Leiden.

Preisigke, F. continued by Hans-Albert Rupprecht (1913–) *Sammelbuch griechischer Urkunden aus Aegypten*. Wiesbaden *et al.*

Pringsheim, Fritz (1950) *The Greek Law of Sale*. Weimar.

Raaflaub, Kurt A. (1997a) "Homeric Society," in *A New Companion to Homer*, eds. Ian Morris and Barry Powell. Leiden: 624–48.

(1997b) "Soldiers, Citizens and the Evolution of the Early Greek *Polis*," in Mitchell and Rhodes 1997: 49–59.

Raubitschek, A. E. (1972) "A Mitra Inscribed with a Law," in Herbert Hoffman, *Early Cretan Armorers* (with the collaboration of A. E. Raubitschek). Mainz: 47–9.

Rhodes, P. J. (1981) *A Commentary on the Aristotelian* Athenaion Politeia. Oxford.

(1991) "The Athenian Code of Laws, 410–399 BC," *JHS* 111: 87–100.

(2006) "The Reforms and Laws of Solon: an Optimistic View," in Blok and Lardinas 2006: 248–60.

Rhodes, P. J. with David M. Lewis (1997) *The Decrees of the Greek States*. Oxford.

Richardson, M. B. (2000) "The Location of Inscribed Laws in Fourth-Century Athens. IG II² 244, on Rebuilding the Walls of Peiraieus," in Flensted-Jensen *et al.* 2000: 601–15.

Richardson, M. E. J. (2000) *Hammurabi's Laws: Text, Translation and Glossary*. Sheffield.

Robert, Louis (1973) "Les juges étrangers dans la cité grecque," in *XENION: Festschrift für Pan. J. Zepos*, eds. E. von Caemmerer *et al.* Athens: 765–82.

Robertson, Noel (1986) "Solon's Axones and Kyrbeis, and the Sixth-Century Background," *Historia* 35: 147–76.

(1990) "The Laws of Athens, 410–399 BC: The Evidence for Review and Publication," *JHS* 110: 43–75.

Robinson, Eric W. (1997) *The First Democracies: Early Popular Government Outside Athens. Historia* Einzelschrift 107. Stuttgart.

Roebuck, Carl (1986) "Chios in the Sixth Century BC," in *Chios: A Conference at the Homereion in Chios 1984*, eds. John Boardman and C. E. Vaphopoulou-Richardson. Oxford: 81–8.

Roebuck, Derek (2001) *Ancient Greek Arbitration*. Oxford.

Roth, C. P. (1976) "The Kings and the Muses in Hesiod's *Theogony*," *TAPhA* 106: 331–8.

Roth, Martha T. (1995) *Law Collections from Mesopotamia and Asia Minor*. Atlanta.

(2000) "The Law Collection of King Hammurabi: Toward an Understanding of Codification and Text," in Lévy 2000b: 9–31.

Rubinstein, Lene (2000) *Litigation and Cooperation: Supporting Speakers in the Courts of Classical Athens. Historia Einzelschrift* 147. Stuttgart.

(2003) "Volunteer Prosecutors in the Greek World," *Dike* 6: 87–113.

Rupprecht, Hans-Albert (1994) *Kleine Einführung in die Papyruskunde*. Darmstadt.

(ed.) (2006) *Symposion 2003*. Vienna.

Ruschenbusch, Eberhard (1966) *Solonos Nomoi. Historia Einzelschrift* 9. Wiesbaden.

(1968) *Untersuchungen zur Geschichte des athenischen Strafrechts*. Cologne.

Ruzé, Françoise (2001) "La loi et le chant," in *Techniques et sociétés en Méditerranée (Hommage à Marie-Claire Amouretti)*, eds. Jean-Pierre Brun and Philippe Jockey. Paris: 709–17.

Salmon, John (1997) "Lopping off the Heads? Tyrants, Politics and the Polis," in Mitchell and Rhodes 1997: 60–73.

Salviat, François (1958) "Une nouvelle loi thasienne: institutions judiciaires et fêtes religieuses à la fin du IVᵉ siècle av. J.-C," *BCH* 82: 193–267.

Scholl, Rheinhold (1995) "Zum ptolemäischen Sklavenrecht," in Geller and Maehler 1995: 149–72.

Schulz, Fritz (1946) *History of Roman Legal Science*. Oxford.

Sealey, Raphael (1990) *Women and Law in Classical Greece*. Chapel Hill.

(1994) *The Justice of the Greeks*. Ann Arbor.

Sickinger, James P. (1999) *Public Records and Archives in Classical Athens*. Chapel Hill.

(2004) "The Laws of Athens: Publication, Preservation, Consultation," in Harris and Rubinstein 2004: 93–109.

Sigurdsson, Gisli (2004) *The Medieval Icelandic Saga and Oral Tradition: A Discourse on Method*. Cambridge, MA.

Simondon, Michèle (1982) *La mémoire et l'oubli dans la pensée grecque jusqu'à la fin du vᵉ siècle avant J.-C*. Paris.

Sinclair, R. K. (1988) *Democracy and Participation in Athens*. Cambridge.

Snodgrass, Anthony (2000) "The Uses of Writing on Early Greek Painted Pottery," in *Word and Image in Ancient Greece*, eds. N. Keith Rutter and Brian A. Sparkes. Edinburgh: 22–34.

Sokolowski, Franciszek (1969) *Lois sacrées des cités grecques*. Paris.

Stein, Peter (1984) *Legal Institutions: The Development of Dispute Settlement*. London.

Steiner, Deborah Tarn (1994) *The Tyrant's Writ: Myths and Images of Writing in Ancient Greece*. Princeton.

Stoddart, Simon and James Whitley (1988) "The Social Context of Literacy in Archaic Greece and Etruria," *Antiquity* 62: 761–2.

Stratton, Jon (1980) "Writing and the Concept of Law in Ancient Greece," *Visible Language* 14: 99–121.

Stroud, Ronald S. (1968) *Drakon's Law on Homicide.* Berkeley.

(1979) *The Axones and Kyrbeis of Drakon and Solon.* Berkeley.

Szegedy-Maszak, Andrew (1978) "Legends of the Greek Lawgivers," *GRBS* 19: 199–209.

Talamanca, Mario (1979) "Dikazein e krinein nelle testimonanze greche piu antiche," in *Symposion 1974*, ed. A. Biscardi. Cologne: 103–35.

Tarn, William, and G. T. Griffith (1952) *Hellenistic Civilization.* 3rd edn. London.

Taubenschlag, Raphael (1955) *The Law of Greco-Roman Egypt in the Light of the Papyri 332 B.C.– 640 A.D.* 2nd edn. Warsaw.

Tcherikover, Victor A. and Alexander Fuks (1957–64) *Corpus Papyrorum Judaicarum.* 3 vols. Cambridge, MA.

Thomas, Carol G. (1984) "Mycenean Law in its Oral Context," *SMEA* 25: 247–53.

Thomas, Rosalind (1989) *Oral Tradition and Written Record in Classical Athens.* Cambridge.

(1992) *Literacy and Orality in Ancient Greece.* Cambridge.

(1996) "Written in Stone? Liberty, Equality, Orality and the Codification of Law," in Foxhall and Lewis 1996: 9–31. (Also in *BICS* 40 [1995] 59–74.)

(2005) "Writing, Law, and Written Law," in Gagarin and Cohen 2005: 41–60.

Thür, Gerhard (1970) "Zum dikãzein bei Homer," *ZRG* 87: 426–44.

(1977) *Beweisführung vor den Schwurgerichtshöfen Athens: die Proklesis zur Basanos* (Akad. der Wiss., Wien, Sitzungsberichte 310). Vienna.

(1996) "Oaths and Dispute Settlement in Ancient Greek Law," in Foxhall and Lewis 1996: 57–72.

(2000) "Rechtsvorschriften und Rechtsanwendung in Athen (5./4. Jh. v. Chr.)," in *TIMAI J. Triantaphyllopoulos*, eds. Julie Vélissaropoulos-Karakostas *et al.* Athens: 89–100.

(2001) "Recht im hellenistischen Athen," in Cantarella and Thür 2001: 141–64.

(2002) "Gesetzeskodizes im archaischen und classischen Athen," in Adam *et al.* 2002: 397–404.

(2005) "The Role of the Witness in Athenian Law," in Gagarin and Cohen 2005: 146–69.

Thür, Gerhard and Hans Taeuber (eds.) (1994) *Prozessrechtliche Inschriften der griechischen Poleis: Arkadien (IPArk).* Vienna.

Todd, Stephen C. (1993) *The Shape of Athenian Law.* Oxford.

(1996) "Lysias *Against Nikomachos*: The Fate of the Expert in Athenian Law," in Foxhall and Lewis 1996: 101–31.

(2000) "The Language of Law in Classical Athens," in *The Moral World of the Law*, ed. Peter Cross. Cambridge: 17–36.

Todd, Stephen C. and Paul Millett (1990) "Law, Society and Athens," in *Nomos: Essays in Athenian Law, Politics and Society*, eds. Paul Cartledge, P. Millett and Stephen Todd. Cambridge: 1–18.

Unger, Roberto Mangabeira (1976) *Law in Modern Society: Toward a Criticism of Social Theory.* New York.

van Effenterre, Henri (1946a) "Inscriptions archaiques crétoises," *BCH* 70: 588–606.

(1946b) "Une bilingue étéocrétoise?" *RPh* 20: 131–8.

(1961) "Pierres inscrites de Dréros," *BCH* 85: 544–68.

(1973) "Le contrat de travail du scribe Spensithios," *BCH* 97: 31–46.

(1985) "DAMOS, DAMIOI et DAMIORGOI," *ΠΕΠΡΑΓΜΕΝΑ ΤΟΘ Ε´ ΔΙΕΘΝΟΥΣ ΚΡΗΤΟΛΟΓΙΚΟΥ ΣΥΝΕΔΡΙΟΥ*, vol. I: 385–96.

(1989) "Droit et prédroit en Grèce depuis le déchiffrement du Linéaire B," in *Symposion 1985*, ed. Gerhard Thür. Cologne: 3–6.

van Effenterre, Henri and Françoise Ruzé (1994–5) *Nomima: recueil d'inscriptions politiques et juridiques de l'archaïsme grec.* 2 vols. Rome.

van Effenterre, Henri and Micheline van Effenterre (2000) "La codification Gortynienne, mythe ou realité?" in Lévy 2000b: 175–84.

Vanderpool, Eugene and W. P. Wallace (1964) "The Sixth Century Laws from Eretria," *Hesperia* 33: 381–91.

Várhelyi, Zsuzsanna (1996) "The Written Word in Archaic Attica," *Klio* 78.1: 28–52.

Vélissaropoulos, Julie (1980) *Les nauclères grecs.* Geneva.

Verdelis, N., M. Jameson, and I. Papachristodoulou (1975) "Ἀρχαικαὶ ἐπιγραφαὶ ἐκ Τίρυνθος," *AEph* 1975: 150–205.

Versteeg, Russ (2002) *Law in the Ancient World.* Durham, NC.

Walbank, F. W. and A. E. Astin (eds.) (1984) *The Hellenistic World (CAH,* 2nd edn. vol. VII.I). Cambridge.

Wallace, Robert W. (2001) "*Diamarturia* in Late Fourth-Century Athens: Notes on a 'Cheese Pot' (*SEG* XXXVI 296)," in Cantarella and Thür 2001: 89–101.

(2005) "'Listening to' the Archai in Democratic Athens," in Wallace and Gagarin 2005: 147–57.

Wallace, Robert W. and Michael Gagarin (eds.) (2005) *Symposion 2001.* Vienna.

Walker, C. B. F. (1987) *Cuneiform (Reading the Past,* vol. III). Berkeley.

Walker, Keith G. (2004) *Archaic Eretria.* London.

West, M. L. (ed.) (1966) *Hesiod,* Theogony. Oxford.

Westbrook, Raymond (1989) "Cuneiform Law Codes and the Origins of Legislation," *Zeitschrift für Assyriologie und vordasiatische Archäologie* 79: 201–22.

(1993) "The Adoption Laws of Codex Hammurabi," *Journal of the Institute of Archaeology of Tel Aviv University,* Occasional Publications No. 1 (Raphael Kutscher Memorial Volume). Tel Aviv: 195–204.

(2005) Penelope's Dowry and Odysseus' Kingship," in Wallace and Gagarin 2005: 3–23.

(2006) "A Response to Michael Gagarin," in Rupprecht 2006: 21–5.

Whitehead, David (1986) *The Demes of Attica 508/7–ca. 250 B.C.* Princeton.

Whitley, James (1997) "Cretan Laws and Cretan Literacy," *AJA* 101: 635–61.

(2001) *The Archaeology of Ancient Greece.* Cambridge.

Wickham, Chris (2003) *Courts and Conflict in Twelfth-Century Tuscany.* Oxford.

Wilken, Ulrich (1927) *Urkunden der Ptolemäerzeit (Ältere Funde),* vol. I. Berlin.

Willetts, R. W. (1967) *The Law Code of Gortyn. Kadmos* Supplement 1. Berlin.

Wolff, Hans Julius (1939) *Written and Unwritten Marriages in Hellenistic and Postclassical Roman Law.* (*American Philological Association Philological Monographs*, no. 9). Haverford, PA.

(1946) "The Origin of Judicial Litigation among the Greeks," *Traditio* 4: 31–87.

(1966) "Law in Ptolemaic Egypt," in *Essays in Honor of C. Bradford Wells* (*American Studies in Papyrology* 1). New Haven: 67–77.

(1975) "Juristische Gräzistik – Aufgaben, Probleme, Möglichkeiten," in *Symposion 1971*, ed. Hans Julius Wolff. Cologne: 1–22.

(2002) *Das Recht der griechischen Papyri Ägyptens in der Zeit der Ptolemaeer und des Prinzipats*, vol. 1, ed. Hans-Albert Rupprecht. Munich.

Wormald, Patrick (1999) *The Making of English Law: King Alfred to the Twelfth Century*, vol. 1: *Legislation and its Limits*. Oxford.

Yiftach-Firanko, Uri. (2003) *Marriage and Marital Arrangements: A History of the Greek Marriage Document in Egypt. 4th century BCE – 4th century CE.* Munich.

Zweigert, Konrad and Hein Kötz (1998) *An Introduction to Comparative Law.* 3rd edn. Oxford.

Index Locorum

I CLASSICAL AUTHORS

2 INSCRIPTIONS

3 PAPYRI

Subject Index

9 780521 297288